GOD'S WATCHMAN

God's Watchman

John Knox's Faith and Vocation

RICHARD KYLE

☙PICKWICK *Publications* • Eugene, Oregon

GOD'S WATCHMAN
John Knox's Faith and Vocation

Copyright © 2014 Richard Kyle. All rights reserved. Except for brief quotations in critical publications or reviews, no part of this book may be reproduced in any manner without prior written permission from the publisher. Write: Permissions, Wipf and Stock Publishers, 199 W. 8th Ave., Suite 3, Eugene, OR 97401.

Pickwick Publications
An Imprint of Wipf and Stock Publishers
199 W. 8th Ave., Suite 3
Eugene, OR 97401

www.wipfandstock.com

ISBN 13: 978-1-62032-918-4

Cataloguing-in-Publication data:

Kyle, Richard.

God's watchman : John Knox's faith and vocation / Richard Kyle.

xii + 286 pp. ; 23 cm. Includes bibliographical references and index.

ISBN 13: 978-1-62032-918-4

1. Knox, John, approximately 1514–1572. 2. Reformation—Scotland. 3. Theologians—Scotland—Biography. 4. Presbyterians—Scotland—Biography.

BX9223 K95 2014

Manufactured in the U.S.A.

To Donald Sullivan

Contents

Preface   ix

Part One: Historical and Theological Foundations

1. The Reformer in His Context   3
2. The Word of God and Its Interpretation   22
3. God and His Work in the World   55
4. The Path to Salvation   86
5. The Church and Its Many Faces   115
6. The Sacraments and the Crusade against Idolatry   132

Part Two: Vocational Considerations

7. Thunder from the Pulpit   157
8. Son of the Prophets   174
9. The Care of Souls   190

Part Three: Political Considerations

10. The Road to Resistance   207
11. Shocking Politics and Idolatrous Rulers   227
12. Church-State Patterns   243
13. A Few Afterthoughts   259

Bibliography   267

Index   281

Preface

THE YEAR 2014 MARKS the 500th anniversary of the birth of John Knox. The Scottish Reformation and John Knox in particular have been controversial subjects. Was this reformation primarily religious or political or a synthesis of the two? Could it have taken an entirely different direction than it did? Would the Scottish Reformation have occurred without the leadership of Knox? Scholars over the centuries have debated his role in this religious revolution. Despite attempts to minimize Knox's contribution, he is still viewed as the leading figure of the Scottish Reformation.

But what about his various roles—pastor, preacher, prophet, revolutionary, statesman, and more? Knox wore many hats and these vocations impact how people perceive him. The same man who could roar like a lion from the pulpit and advocate regicide could be caring and tender in his pastoral roles. Yes he was both loved and hated by people then and now. How one views John Knox is also influenced by regional differences. Scholars in North America have tended to regard the Scottish reformer in a more positive light than have academics on the other side of the Atlantic.

As a graduate student, I developed an interest in John Knox. This fascination has driven much of my academic career—producing a dissertation, two books, a third co-authored book, and over twenty articles. But for much of the time, I have taken leave from John Knox, moving into other research areas for an additional seven books. Still, I could never get Knox completely out of my system. And for the 500th anniversary of his birth I have returned to the Scottish reformer and have attempted to connect the many strains of his faith with his vocation. Hopefully, this study will demonstrate that Knox was indeed "God's Watchman," a phrase he used to describe himself.

Knox was a man of action, advocating many revolutionary ideas including the slaying of Catholic rulers. Still, these actions and thoughts were shaped by his faith and the events of sixteenth-century Europe, which are described in Part One—"Historical and Theological Foundations." Chapter one, "The Reformer in His Context," introduces the Europe of John

Knox and his life. The next five chapters analyze the major aspects of his faith. Chapter two, "The Word of God and Its Interpretation," examines the reformer's view of Scripture and how it is interpreted.

Chapter three, "God and His Work in the World," describes Knox's perception of God's attributes, especially his sovereignty and immutability. The next chapter, "The Path to Salvation," spells out the reformer's view of salvation, notably predestination and justification by faith. The Christian life for Knox, however, was more than salvation. It involved corporate worship among other activities. Chapter five, "The Church and Its Many Faces," describes the various ways Knox viewed the church. The next chapter, "The Sacraments and the Crusade Against Idolatry," focuses on the driving force of the reformer's career—the fight against the idolatrous Mass. Anything in worship not specifically sanctioned by Scripture was idolatry to Knox.

Part Two, "Vocational Considerations," describes how Knox worked out his faith in concrete terms. The Scottish reformer could preach up a storm—a subject that is captured in Chapter seven, "Thunder from the Pulpit." Knox's animated preaching developed because he regarded himself as a prophet called to pronounce God's judgment, the theme of Chapter eight, "Son of the Prophets." The next chapter, "The Care of Souls," looks at Knox from another perspective, namely his pastoral side.

In Part Three, "Political Considerations," Knox's faith and vocation culminate in his revolutionary political ideas. Chapter ten, "The Road to Resistance," traces the gradual development of Knox's resistance theory. For several years the Scottish reformer had been inching toward resistance against idolatrous rulers. Chapter eleven, "Shocking Politics and Idolatrous Rulers," describes how Knox stepped over the line. He articulated a full blown theory of resistance to Catholic rulers. In four pamphlets published prior to August 1558, he spelled out his ideas regarding government and religion—that is, the rights of subjects against idolatrous and oppressive sovereigns. Knox's political theory entailed more than the overthrow of Catholic rulers. In Chapter twelve, "Church-State Patterns," he articulates a vision of the Christian commonwealth but acknowledges a disestablished alternative if it cannot be established. The last chapter, "A Few Afterthoughts," summarizes the major ideas of this study and looks at Knox's contradictory behavior and influence

As noted earlier, I have published three previous books and numerous articles on John Knox. This current study draws considerable information from these books and articles, which serve as a backdrop for this

Preface

book. To list all of these publications separately in this preface would be cumbersome. Rather, they have been cited in the footnotes and listed in the comprehensive bibliography.

No one writes a book alone. In the time this book has been in gestation, I have accumulated debts to several individuals and institutions. I hope my memory is not short in this regard and that I do not inadvertently omit any thanks that are due. Appreciation must go to Robin Ottoson and the library staff of Tabor College for arranging the acquisition of books and articles. Gratitude is due to the Tabor College administration for providing financial assistance through the Hope Scholars Grant for summer work on this study. Thanks must go Dale Johnson for his ideas regarding John Knox and to Donald Sullivan for directing my earlier study on this subject.

Many debts have been incurred in the production of this book. I thank Ellie Rempel for her work in putting this manuscript in its final form. Appreciation must be offered to Carrol Ediger for editing an early version of the manuscript. Academic publishing presents many challenges. Therefore much thanks must go to the staff of Pickwick Publications for publishing this volume—especially its production editor Robin Parry, assistant managing editor Christian Amondson, copyeditor Dave Belcher, and typesetter Patrick Harrison. Finally, my gratitude goes to an individual who was only involved indirectly with the writing and publishing process—my wife Joyce Kyle. Without her support and patience, my publishing endeavors and professional activities would not have been possible.

Richard Kyle
Hillsboro, Kansas

Part One

Historical and Theological Foundations

1

The Reformer in His Context

REVOLUTIONARY OR SERVANT OF God? Thundering prophet or consummate politician? Nasty old man or spiritual pastor? Ardently loved or passionately despised? Will the real John Knox please stand up? John Knox indeed was a complex and contradictory figure. To be sure, he displayed several faces and wore many hats.

The Scottish reformer, therefore, has been the subject of many interpretations—some wildly different. Knox was a controversial figure in his day. And he continues to be so down to the present. He has been both loved and hated by his contemporaries and historians through the centuries. No sixteenth-century reformer has aroused such a range of emotions and opinions. Few people have taken a neutral stance in regard to John Knox.

These differing opinions largely concern several related questions: What was Knox's role or vocation? How did he perform this role or vocation? What kind of person was John Knox? How important was he to the Scottish Reformation? Historians have expressed different views regarding Knox's role or vocation—prophet, pastor, preacher, reformer, statesman, revolutionary, and more.[1] Actually, most modern scholars have focused

---

1. Different writers have emphasized the roles that Knox played. For some examples, see the following: Ridley, *John Knox*; Reid, *Trumpeter of God*; Russell, "John Knox as a Statesman," 1–29; Johnson, "Prophecy, Rhetoric and Diplomacy;" Macmillan, "John Knox—Preacher of the Word," 5–19; Reid, "John Knox, Pastor of Souls," 1–21; Gill, "He made my tongue a trumpet . . . John Knox, The Preacher," 102–10. See also Kirk, "John Knox and the Historians," 7–26; Kyle, *The Ministry of John Knox*; Kyle, "The Thundering Scot," 135–49; Kyle, "Prophet of God," 85–101; Kyle, "John Knox and the Care of Souls," 133–34.

PART ONE: Historical and Theological Foundations

on two aspects of one general subject: Knox's political ideas, especially his theory of resistance, and his attitudes toward female rulers.[2]

This study attempts to connect these aspects of Knox's life. He functioned as a pastor, preacher, and a reformer of religion on a national level. And such reform often entailed advocating revolutionary ideas—especially the slaying of idolatrous or Catholic rulers. While these roles predominate, they rest on a particular religious faith shaped by his interpretation of Scripture, his view of God, and the events of sixteenth-century Europe. Section one establishes these beliefs. Part two spells out his vocation—namely functioning as a prophet, pastor, and preacher. All of this—his faith and vocation—culminated in his revolutionary political ideas, which are the subjects of section three.

In respect to evaluating Knox, W. Stanford Reid divided the reformer into three camps: his supporters, his opponents, and those in the middle.[3] Knox's advocates have seen him as the "right man for the right time in Scotland." Some of these admirers see little fault in Knox. In their eyes, Knox has no warts and may have even been "St. John."[4]

But the Scottish reformer has had his fierce opponents—both in his day and today. In his time, of course, the leading Catholics denounced him. So did the more secular Protestants who opposed his program. In our day, some biographers and historians have criticized Knox's attitude toward Queen Mary, his outlook regarding female rulers, his advocacy of violence, or minimized his role in the Scottish Reformation.[5] The film

---

2. A partial list would include the following writings: Mason, ed., *John Knox: On Rebellion*; Shepherd, *Gender and Authority in Sixteenth-Century England*; Breslow, ed., *The Political Writings of John Knox*; Mason, "Knox, Resistance and the Moral Imperative," 411–36; Gray, "The Political Theory of John Knox," 132–47; Dawson, "The Two John Knoxes," 555–76; Cassidy, "The Quest for Godly Rule," 1–10; Reid, "John Knox's Theology of Political Government," 529–40; Brown, "In Search of the Godly Magistrate," 553–81; Healey, "Waiting for Deborah," 371–86; Kyle, *Mind of Knox*, 241–305; Burns, "The Political Ideas of the Scottish Reformation," 251–68; Greaves, "Calvinism, Democracy and the Political Thought of John Knox," 81–92; Greaves, "John Knox, The Reformed Tradition, and the Development of Resistance Theory," 1–31.

3. Reid, "John Knox and his Interpreters," 14, 15; Reid, *Trumpeter of God*, 285–86.

4. Views supporting Knox range from near hero worship to a positive attitude. Some examples include the following: Bannatyne, *A Journal of Transactions in Scotland*; Carlyle, *On Heroes, Hero Worship*; M'Crie, *The Life of John Knox*; Spotiswoode, *The History of the Church and State in Scotland*; Reid, *Trumpeter of God*; Froude, *The Reign of Edward VI*.

5. In various degrees, the following writers have taken a critical view of Knox: Lang, *John Knox and the Reformation*; Ridley, *John Knox*; Fraser, *Mary Queen of Scots*; Trevor-Roper, "John Knox," 745ff.; Donaldson, "Knox the Man;" Durkan, "Scottish Reformers," 1–28.

The Reformer in His Context

Mary Queen of Scots portrays Knox as a strange man with a long black beard who jumps out from behind a bush and berates the queen. "The image of John Knox as a cross between Ian Paisley and the Ayatollah Khomeini" seems to be "lodged in the popular mind," says Stewart Lamont.[6]

Fortunately, some observers have taken the middle ground. They do not go overboard in either their praise or condemnation of Knox. Instead, they have sought a measure of objectivity. They regard Knox as a leading figure in the Scottish Reformation, but not the only force. There would have been a reformation without Knox. Still, he helped chart its course. Some observers in this camp have even become somewhat indifferent toward the Scottish reformer.[7]

Whether one views Knox positively or negatively, he certainly pursued his vocation with great vigor. His vocation was to preach the gospel, not to be a writer nor an ecclesiastical organizer or official. His main duty in life was, as he expressed it frequently, "to blow my master's trumpet." He saw himself as a preaching, rather than a writing, prophet proclaiming the gospel of God's grace in Jesus Christ: "For considering myself rather called by God to instruct the ignorant, comfort the sorrowful, confirm the weak, and rebuke the proud by lively voice in these most corrupt days, then to compose books for the age to come. . . ."[8]

Knox expressed his vocation in three overlapping roles—preacher, pastor, and prophet. He served as the pastor or minister of congregations in Scotland, England, and the Continent. Unlike our time, the minister's primary function was to preach God's Word. Thus the roles of pastor and preacher must be regarded as inseparable. As a minister, however, Knox did more than preach. He pastored or shepherded the flock, instructing and comforting them in their trials and tribulations. Still, when Knox preached, he often thundered like an Old Testament prophet—rebuking the proud and corrupt by a lively voice. His vocation focused on individuals, congregations, and entire nations. When attempting to reform religion

---

6. Lamont, *The Swordbearer*. Ian Paisley regards Knox as the model for his career. See MacIver, "Ian Paisley and the Reformed Tradition," 360–61.

7. Some examples of this somewhat vague category include the following: Janton, *John Knox: L'homme et l'oeuvre*; Janton, *Concept et Sentiment*; Dickinson, "Introduction"; MacGregor, *The Thundering Scot*; Whitley, *Plain Mr. Knox*; McEwen, *The Faith of Knox*; Greaves, *Theology and Revolution*; Kyle, *Mind of Knox*; Cowan, "John Knox and the Making of the Scottish Reformation," 22–30; Percy, *John Knox*; Brown, *John Knox*, 2 vols.

8. Knox, *The Works of John Knox*, 6:229. Hereafter this collection will be cited as *Works* followed by the appropriate volume and page number. Also, the quotations from Laing's edition have been modernized to contemporary spelling.

on the national level, Knox often adopted the role and rhetoric of an Old Testament prophet.

In working out his vocation as a prophet, Knox can legitimately be seen as a revolutionary, a political figure, and the reformer of religion on a national level. But he also functioned as a pastor. And in doing so, a softer, more caring John Knox emerged. He could, of course, roar like a lion from the pulpit, denouncing both individual and corporate sins. But when performing his pastoral functions and dealing with individual problems, a gentler John Knox came to the forefront—not the bluebeard that many have portrayed him to be.

THE EUROPE OF JOHN KNOX

Knox did not blow his master's trumpet in a vacuum. He bellowed his sermons against the background and culture of his day. His denunciation of Catholicism must be seen in the context of the larger events—especially the perception of corruption in the Catholic Church and the ongoing Protestant Reformation. Knox wrote his treatises and letters in response to specific situations and problems, often persecution and moral lapses. Such writings were not abstract theological treatises. He offered counseling and spiritual advice to individuals with specific problems—usually issues encountered by first generation Protestants. What's more, his prophetic role must be seen against the backdrop of European events. Protestantism and Catholicism were locked in a cosmic struggle, and Knox saw himself on God's side pitted against the forces of Satan.

Political Factors

As the sixteenth century dawned, Europe stood on the brink of fundamental political change. The medieval, feudal world dominated by the papacy and the Holy Roman Empire came under challenge. To the south and east, Christian Europe faced a hostile Islamic power. But to the west, the discovery of the New World presented many new opportunities—plus a few challenges. All of this was occurring as the Reformation shattered the religious unity of Europe, dividing it into two antagonistic camps.

In such goings on, the major players were Spain, France, England, the papacy, and the Holy Roman Empire. Spain had extensive colonies in the New World and tremendous possibilities for trade and the acquisition of wealth. As yet, England and France possessed no colonies. So they sought

The Reformer in His Context

to finance their wars and expansion elsewhere—usually from the coffers of the mercantile class. Traditionally weak rulers sat as the Holy Roman Emperor. But when Charles I of Spain became Emperor Charles V (1516–56), circumstances changed. Charles created a huge power bloc, which ranged from the Netherlands and the German states to Spain. With the help of the Pope, Charles threatened to corner the French.

Sixteenth-century Europe witnessed constant warfare. To a large extent, these conflicts stemmed from the incessant rivalry between the Hapsburgs—who ruled Spain and the Holy Roman Empire—and the Valois, the ruling family of France. For the most part, England and Scotland stood on the sideline as such conflicts transpired. But when they did enter the fray, they usually did so according to their old alliances. Because of its age-old conflicts with France, England normally sided with Spain. Conversely, fear of England often drove the Scots into the arms of the French—later formalized into the so-called "auld alliance."

Marriage between these royal houses created new alliances and served to complicate these dynastic rivalries. In 1509, Henry VIII of England (1509–47) married Catherine of Aragon—thus cementing a union with Spain, the Emperor, and the pope against France. The French countered with their own blood alliances. Mary of Guise married James V of Scotland (1513–42). The daughter of Henry II of France united with the Spanish royal line; their son Francis I (1559–60) married Mary Queen of Scots, the daughter of James V and Mary of Guise. Scotland stood on the perimeter of European society. Still, such marriage alliances pushed Scotland into the European power game—sometimes as a key player but more often as a pawn.

As the century wore on, religious conflicts compounded these dynastic tensions. By the 1550s, Europe stood on the brink of the period of terrible religious wars. The forces of the Counter Reformation were on the march, threatening to engulf Protestantism. All of this produced an apocalyptic atmosphere. Violence and conflict were in the air and could be detected in the writings of many reformers, including John Knox.

In all of these events, Scotland and John Knox would play a role—a development that was not obvious at the start of the sixteenth century. At this time, Scotland was a poor, primitive, and remote part of Christendom. Political motives drove the developments of the Scottish Reformation. From James I to James V, the Stewart kings and the great nobles constantly struggled for power. Scotland still lived under feudal anarchy. In the 100 years prior to the birth of John Knox, every king of Scotland

PART ONE: Historical and Theological Foundations

had met his death by violence. Only one had been as old as fifteen at accession, and none survived beyond the age of forty-two. Without a doubt, royal power was weak. Both the king and nobility administered such order and discipline as existed. Many vassals considered the lord, not the king, as their sovereign. Both justice and military organization were feudal, contributing to the complexity and instability of society.

By the reign of James V (1513–42), the conflict between crown and nobility began to have religious implications. King James attempted to assert royal authority. In doing so, he alienated many of his temporal lords, thus forcing him to turn to the ecclesiastical lords for support. This alliance produced two results. First, hostilities developed between factions of the nobility and the church leaders who were acquiring power. Second, some of the estranged nobles turned to England for support. For centuries, Scottish nobles had pursued this practice. But now the time appeared more opportune—Henry VIII had turned against the Pope and was reducing the power of the great churchmen in England.

As the secular lords turned to England, the ecclesiastics embraced Scotland's traditional ally, France. France supported Cardinal Beaton, the leader of the Scottish Church, even as England subsidized the "Assured Lords"—Scottish nobles in the pay of England. Beaton became influential in both the Scottish and French courts and was thus in a position to use Scotland as an instrument for France. The church's threefold policy of loyalty to the crown, hostility to England, and friendship with France seemed patriotic to the average Scot. With such an attitude prevalent, a widespread movement toward the "English religion" seemed remote. The church, therefore, sporadically exacted measures from the crown for the suppression of the Protestant heresy. Yet attempts to quell heresy did not succeed. And this failure—added to the disastrous results of Beaton's rash anti-English policy—tarnished the church's French alliance.

It gradually dawned on many Scots that French dominance threatened Scotland's independence more than any menace from England. Revulsion against the church and France produced an inevitable by-product; namely, a rising attitude of favor for Protestantism and England. The Scottish mind hardly distinguished between religious and political alliances. Then, in 1560, following a treaty between England and the Scottish lords, an English expeditionary force ejected the French military from Scotland. Scotland's future now lay with Protestantism and England.

In August 1560, the Scottish Parliament abolished Catholicism and made Protestantism officially the religion of the land. Still, Protestantism was not secure. Parliament ratified the *Scots Confession*, approving the Reformed faith in Scotland. But it failed to take more concrete steps. It rejected the *Book of Discipline*, which would have established Protestantism financially. To complicate matters, during the personal rule of Mary Stewart (1561-67), Protestant Scotland had a Catholic queen. Mary's policies focused primary on diplomatic objectives, but they also presented a threat to Protestantism. These six years witnessed plots, assassinations, and political and religious conflicts. But more important, Mary's personal escapades doomed whatever chances her policies had for success. In July 1567, a coalition of lords forced Mary to abdicate during the same month the infant James VI was crowned king of Scotland. Parliament now established Protestantism on a more substantial basis.

In all of these developments, international politics played an important, if not decisive role. On one hand, foreign events determined the outcome of the Scottish Reformation. Would England continue to aid the Protestant party in Scotland? Would Mary Queen of Scots marry a Protestant or Catholic? Would France and Spain intervene in Scotland to crush the Protestant heresy? Indeed, the Scottish Reformation hinged not only on events in Scotland, but on decisions made in London, Paris, and Madrid.

On the other hand, the survival of Protestantism in England and perhaps even on the Continent depended in part on the success or failure of the Reformation in Scotland. If Protestantism failed in Scotland, would England—ruled by vacillating Elizabeth—retain Protestantism? What's more, if England had returned to Catholicism, Protestantism might have been in jeopardy all over Europe. John Knox understood the importance of such events. He was not just a backward Scot. Rather, he had lived in England and traveled extensively on the Continent. Such experiences helped Knox to think in European terms and to connect political and religious issues.[9]

---

9. This background information regarding the political situation in Europe and Scotland has been drawn from a number of general sources. Ridley, *John Knox*, 1–12; Reid, *Trumpeter of God*, 1–13; Burns, "The Political Background of the Reformation," 1–23; Lamont, *The Swordbearer*, 13–16; McEwen, *Faith of Knox*, 1–13; Buckle, *On Scotland and the Scotch Intellect*, 68–91; Donaldson, *Scotland: James V to James VII*, 3–106; Cowan, *The Scottish Reformation*, 1–26; Lynch, *Edinburgh and the Reformation*, 68–86; Wormald, *Court, Kirk, and Community*, 3–26; Kyle, *Mind of Knox*, 1–3; Bonney, *The European Dynastic States*, 79–187.

Part One: Historical and Theological Foundations

Social and Economic Factors

Like the twentieth century, the sixteenth century witnessed sweeping economic and social changes—transformations that dramatically influenced the reformation of religion in Europe. Old medieval patterns disintegrated. Trade and industry accelerated at a rapid pace. Gold and silver poured in from the New World. New business methods stimulated the economy. The economy experienced its ups and downs with the low point occurring in the late 1550s. Such economic developments dramatically affected the entire fabric of European society. On the whole, the aristocracy came on hard times while the urban bourgeoisie rose in wealth and power. All of this influenced the evolution of the middle class, which in turn impacted the reformation of religion.[10]

On the eve of the Scottish Reformation, the established church did not command extensive loyalty in any of the social classes. The nobility at the top of the social ladder not only desired to evict the church leaders from influential government positions, but also envied the church's wealth. The aristocracy, frequently wealthy in land but short in cash, significantly felt the impact of the century's far-reaching economic changes. No longer indispensable to the national governments as either soldiers or officials, they often had to seek income elsewhere. This transition the upper nobility could make by obtaining positions at court or by acquiring church revenues. The upper echelons of society, therefore, blatantly attempted to control church revenues by any means possible.[11] But the gentry, or lower aristocracy, faced a more difficult situation—one that often led them into competition with the aristocracy for lucrative positions and into conflict with their tenants who resisted their demands for increased rents or services. Frequently, the gentry's main hope was the bourgeoisie, or wealthy element in the towns, who could provide them with loans or lucrative marriage arrangements.[12]

---

10. See Koenigsberger, Mosse, and Bowler, *Europe in the Sixteenth Century*, 28–64; Reid, *Trumpeter of God*, 2–3; Cowie, *Sixteenth-Century Europe*, 79–93; Spitz, *The Protestant Reformation*, 18–34.

11. The aristocracy's desire to retain a sizeable share of the ecclesiastical wealth, among other motives, prompted them to reject the *Book of Discipline*. This document would have used the wealth of the old church to support the new Reformed church, thus depriving the nobility of church revenue. Knox strongly disapproved of the plan to divide up the wealth of the Catholic Church. See *Works*, 2:310; Reid, *Trumpeter of God*, 205–7; Cameron, "The Historical Background," 3–13; Ridley, *John Knox*, 388–401; Donaldson, *Scotland: James V to James VII*, 105, 111, 144.

12. Kyle, *Mind of Knox*, 3.

The Reformer in His Context

The increasing importance of the lesser lords (or lairds) and burgher class provided a major social factor leading to the Scottish Reformation. While the feudal nobility generally experienced a decline, the middle group acquired wealth in trade. Paralleling this expansion of trade came the growth of the Scottish town. The middle class moved in two directions: they formed an alliance with the nobility and became the leaders of the lower classes. Schooled by commercial activity to make shrewd judgments of people and events, the burghers became hardheaded and rationalistic. They also received at least a smattering of education and, in some cases, a good one. To cap it all, the Scottish bourgeoisie were nationalistic.

By the early sixteenth century, therefore, the middle group was prepared for a reformation. With its growing intellectual interests, the burger class increasingly criticized the church. Indeed, the gross maladministration of the church, its notorious immorality and corruption, and strong support for France offended the instincts and nationalism of this class. So when a rival faith came on the scene, the middle class turned its back on the old church. The Reformed Church gave this class a means of fulfilling some of its ambitions. Thus the burghers not only welcomed the Reformation, they took steps to support it. In fact, of all the social groups, the middle class did the most to further the cause of the reformation in Scotland. To a large extent, the Scottish Reformation's success and direction came from the burgher class. From this group emerged John Knox (1514–72).[13]

The poor, at the bottom of the social scale, experienced very hard times. At best, life was difficult. And far from relieving this burden, the church exacted more revenues from them. In countries that experienced better church administration, the monasteries often befriended the poor. Not so in Scotland. Here, maladministration and corruption rendered the monasteries incapable of aiding the poor either spiritually or materially. Merciless absentee abbots and lay leaders appropriated money designed for the poor into their own pockets.

Even Bishop John Leslie, an ardent Catholic whose historical writings sought to support the Catholic cause, painted a bleak picture of monastic life in Scotland. Abbot Quintin Kennedy and Ninian Winzet, two Catholic apologists, criticized clerical corruption more severely than did the Protestants. Indeed, the parish clergy existed in poverty while the

---

13. Reid, "The Middle Class Factor in the Scottish Reformation," 137–53. See also Kyle, *Mind of Knox*, 3–4 ; McEwen, *Faith of Knox*, 13–14; Lynch, *Edinburgh and the Reformation*, 49–55.

ecclesiastical prelates misused the church's wealth. Such a contrast contributed to the decline of the medieval Catholic Church. Thus when the Reformation brought the downfall of the monasteries and the old church, it did not alter the life of the poor for the worse. And unlike the English, the Scots staged no mass uprising in its defense.[14]

Religious Factors

Political, economic, and social developments conditioned Europe for the Reformation. Still, the sixteenth-century Reformation must be seen primarily as a revival of religion. But such a renewal had its roots in the late Middle Ages. In addition to sweeping economic, political, and social changes, the late medieval world witnessed a severe crisis in religious values. The Great Schism, conciliarism, ecclesiastical corruption, anticlericalism, new intellectual movements, and more, all challenged the Catholic Church.

Indeed, to borrow a phrase from Steven Ozment, these "late medieval developments were a threshold as well as a foothold" for the sixteenth-century reformations.[15] And such religious unfoldings reached Scotland. Aside from the corrupt state of the Catholic Church in Scotland, the Scottish Reformation must not be regarded as an "indigenous movement" says Reid. Rather, it was an aspect of the larger religious revival taking place on the Continent.[16]

Religious discontent—often manifesting itself as heresy—appeared in Scotland toward the end of the Great Papal Schism (1378–1415).[17] The years of the Papal Schism were a spiritual disaster for the Scottish church. In impoverished Scotland, the church provided the only path to wealth, and the crown and nobility attempted to capitalize on this situation. By 1550, half of the real estate in Scotland belonged to the church. What's more, sources estimate ecclesiastical revenues about that time to have been approximately £300,000 (Scots) compared to a beggarly £17,000 for

---

14. Laing, ed., *The Miscellany of the Wodrow Society*, 1:89–168, 263–68; Mahoney, "The Scottish Hierarchy," 60; McEwen, *Faith of Knox*, 14, Kyle, *Mind of Knox*, 4; Cowan, *Scottish Reformation*, 68–71.

15. Ozment, *The Reformation in the Cities*, 118.

16. Reid, "Reformation in France and Scotland," 197.

17. The Papal Schism began in 1378 and lasted until 1415. In Scotland, it lasted until 1418 because the Scots were slow in withdrawing allegiance from the last surviving antipope.

The Reformer in His Context

the crown. During the schism years, the proportion could not have been much different.[18]

Therefore, these years saw rival popes bid for Scottish support, granting dispensations for all sorts of irregular appointments to ecclesiastical living. Such dispensations not only violated canonical law, but also made a mockery of common decency and morality. Wealthy benefices went to the crown and nobility as rewards to favorites. As a result, spiritually-degenerate men with little administrative ability rose to high ecclesiastical positions. Such a practice had two results—church discipline tragically declined and the lower clergy fell into miserable poverty. The years following the Papal Schism saw no general improvement. While it should not be exaggerated, ecclesiastical corruption also touched upon other areas of church life—that is, clerical immorality, financial abuse, monastic laxity, and the neglect of religious duties. Despite temporary and local improvements, corruption and laxity continued until the Reformation.[19]

Into this spiritual void came a number of reform movements. The fifteenth century witnessed Lollard activity in Scotland. Bible reading and anticlerical beliefs thrived—to the extent that in 1425, parliament passed legislation against heretics. Lollardy indeed penetrated southwest Scotland, so much so that Knox devoted the opening pages of his *History* to their activities. Yet Lollardy could not reform Scotland. It was largely a negative movement, and reformations need more than negations to succeed. Moreover, Lollardy had no one central positive doctrine—such as Luther's justification by faith—to serve as a focal point.[20]

Popular piety, however, could still exist within the official framework of the church. The Mendicant Orders, the Dominicans, and the observant branch of the Franciscans experienced a revival on the Continent early in the fifteenth century and were well established by mid-century. Austerity and purity of life, a small restoration in learning, and a great emphasis on preaching characterized this revival. In Scotland, this awakening lasted approximately one generation, but even this brief revival helped. Many of the regular ecclesiastics, however, hampered the Observants. Still, James

---

18. Donaldson, *The Scottish Reformation*, 35–37; Reid, *Trumpeter of God*, 6–7; Donaldson, ed., *Accounts of the Collectors of the Thirds of Benefices*, xv.

19. Wormald, *Court, Kirk, and Community*, 79–81; Kyle, *Mind of Knox*, 5; Donaldson, *Scottish Reformation*, 12–17.

20. *Works*, 1:5–12; Reid, "The Lollards in Pre-Reformation Scotland," 269–83; Wormald, *Court, Kirk, and Community*, 79–94.

PART ONE: Historical and Theological Foundations

IV believed that the salvation of Scotland lay in their hands and strongly supported them.[21]

Before the reformation could come, however, Scotland needed a new doctrine of grace and the sacraments. About the time the Observant movement declined, Lutheranism began to enter Scotland, and some of the best friars embraced it. Lutheranism's central tenet, justification by faith, broke from the sacramental concept of salvation. Piety began to move outside the official church. Conditions in Scotland and especially in the church made the country ripe for Lutheranism. The teachings of Luther penetrated eastern Scotland to the extent that in 1525 parliament banned the importation of Lutheran books.[22]

Yet this proscription and other measures proved ineffectual. In 1528, officials convicted Patrick Hamilton of the Lutheran heresy, and Archbishop Beaton ordered him burned at the stake. The archbishop may have silenced one man—but he could not stop the spread of Luther's views. William Tyndale's *New Testament* had arrived in Scotland, allowing people to compare the claims of the old church with the teachings of the Word of God.[23]

We should not underestimate the influence of Lutheranism upon the Scottish Reformation. Though Calvinism ultimately triumphed over the Catholic Church in Scotland, Lutheran ideas continued. The emphasis upon justification by faith—so characteristic of Scottish Reformed teaching—may be partially attributed to the persistence of Lutheran influence. Many of those who afterward became leaders in the Reformation—including Balnaves, Erskine of Dun, and probably Knox himself—received their early nurture from the Lutheran faith.[24]

Despite Lutheranism's importance in Scotland, it failed to bring about a reformation. Why? First, an anti-English attitude prevailed during

---

21. McEwen, *Faith of Knox*, 20–21; Kyle, *Mind of Knox*, 5–6; Wormald, *Court, Kirk, and Community*, 90–93; Ross, "Some Notes on the Religious Orders in Pre-Reformation Scotland," 185–233.

22. Reid, "Lutheranism in the Scottish Reformation," 91–111; McEwen, *Faith of Knox*, 19–20, 55–58; Cowan, *Scottish Reformation*, 89–90; Taylor, "The Conflicting Doctrines of the Scottish Reformation," 245–46.

23. McGoldrick, "Patrick Hamilton: Luther's Scottish Disciple," 81–88; McGoldrick, *Luther's Scottish Connection*, 48–50. See Lorimer, *Patrick Hamilton, the First Preacher of the Scottish Reformation*.

24. See Reid, "Lutheranism in the Scottish Reformation," 91–111; McEwen, *Faith of Knox*, 19–20, 55–58; Kyle, *Mind of Knox*, 6; McGoldrick, *Luther's Scottish Connection*, 55–73; Torrance, "Patrick Hamilton and John Knox," 171–84; Cameron, "Aspects of the Lutheran Contribution to the Scottish Reformation," 12–20.

The Reformer in His Context

the reign of James V. England embraced Protestantism, and any form of it was unacceptable in Scotland at this time. Second, Lutheranism was politically quiescent. Lutheran reformations never succeeded except under the guiding hand of a favorable sovereign, and Scotland had no such prince.[25]

Still, we should not assume that the Scottish Reformation took a leap from Luther to Calvin without the influence of Zurich from the 1530s onward. The effect of Zwinglianism in the years prior to the success of Protestantism needs further research. It must be noted that Lutheranism was a blanket expression covering the views of various continental reformers—including Zwingli and Bullinger, and on occasions, those of John Wycliffe's followers.[26] Knox succeeded in Scotland with a generally Calvinistic theology. Would this triumph have been possible without considerable preparation? Hardly! Evidence indicates that Lutheranism alone could not have paved the way for such a development. Rather, Zwinglianism must have been widespread in Scotland, and along with Calvinism, contributed significantly to the success of the Reformed faith.[27]

But the Catholic Church was not finished. Before the triumph of the Reformed faith, the Scottish Church made one last abortive attempt to reform itself and thus prevent a reformation. Archbishop Hamilton, Beaton's successor, issued a series of statutes designed to reform the church. Published in 1552 as the *Catechism of Archbishop Hamilton*, these statutes represented an attempt by the Scottish Church at a crucial moment in its life to give a complete, though brief, account of what Catholics believed and, in particular, to instruct ignorant priests in the faith. This reform, however, came too late and had little effect. By then, the church could not produce an alternative to reformation.[28]

By 1546, Zwinglian reforming thought had made its way to Scotland, largely through the efforts of George Wishart, a Scottish reformer. Zwingli rejected all forms of worship not expressly commanded by Scripture. Hence, the Swiss version of Protestantism was more uncompromising and separatist than Lutheranism. From such a background, the Reformed Church of Scotland began to emerge as a coherent force.

25. Kyle, *Mind of Knox*, 6–7.

26. Shaw, "Zwinglian Influences on the Scottish Reformation;" Shaw, "Forward, Zwingli Research" ix–xvii.

27. Shaw, "Zwinglian Influences on the Scottish Reformation," 119–39; Shaw, "Foreword, Zwingli Research," ix–xvii.

28. Mahoney, "The Scottish Hierarchy, 1513–1565," 73–75; Donaldson, *Scottish Reformation*, 33–35; Taylor, "Conflicting Doctrines of the Scottish Reformation," 252–53; Cowan, *Scottish Reformation*, 77–78.

PART ONE: Historical and Theological Foundations

Although John Knox began his public ministry in 1547, until 1559, he spent little time in Scotland. But during this time, Protestantism in Scotland progressed politically as well as spiritually. In 1559, Knox returned home at a critical time; plans existed to utilize French military aid to strengthen Catholicism and eradicate Protestantism among the Scots. Thanks to an English alliance and a turn of events, however, Scotland embraced the Reformed faith. Yet the Reformation of 1560 only partially established Protestantism. Mary Queen of Scots nearly undid the work of the Reformation, but in 1567, the Scots deposed her and Protestantism was secure. In these events, John Knox played an important role.[29]

KNOX THE MAN

First impressions carry much weight. How we meet someone often determines our opinion of them. How did the various Protestant reformers make their debut? Jasper Ridley describes their entrance: Calvin can be seen at his desk writing a scholarly work. Cranmer is first seen searching Scripture for texts to justify Henry VIII's divorce and remarriage. Luther is more vigorous—we find him nailing his theses on a door in Wittenberg. But "Knox is the only one who enters carrying a two-handed sword."[30] Whatever else this might say, it tells us that of all the reformers, Knox was a man of action—a characteristic that is evident throughout his life.

His Life

Knox's early life is shrouded in obscurity. Born near Haddington about 1514,[31] he was educated at St. Andrews, probably under the conciliarist and scholastic John Major. In 1536, the Bishop of Dunblane ordained Knox into the priesthood. Due to an oversupply of priests, he may not have obtained a parish and thus served as a notary and a private tutor. Exactly when Knox became a Protestant, we do not know. But Thomas

---

29. Taylor, "Conflicting Doctrines of the Scottish Reformation," 254–55; Reid, *Trumpeter of God*, 1–14; McEwen, *Faith of Knox*, 22; Kyle, *Mind of Knox*, 7–8. For more on the events prior to the Reformation, see Burleigh, *A Church History of Scotland*; Ridley, *John Knox*, 314–34; Cowan, *Scottish Reformation*, 89–138; and Knox's own account in *Works*, 1.

30. Ridley, *John Knox*, 40.

31. Ibid., 529–34; Wilkinson, "The Medical History of John Knox," 83. There is some question as to the date of Knox's birth, but modern research indicates that 1514 is the most probable year. See appendix in Ridley's biography for a discussion.

Guilliame appears to have been instrumental in his conversion, and he subsequently came under the influence of John Rough and George Wishart, a follower of the Swiss reformers. Knox probably acquired his sense of a prophetic vocation from Wishart.[32]

In 1547, after Wishart's martyrdom, Knox went to St. Andrews. Here, he received a call to preach the gospel. When the castle fell, Knox became a prisoner and spent the next 19 months in a French galley ship. During this time, he penned a summary of Henry Balnaves' compendium of Protestant thought based on Luther's commentary on Galatians. In this early work, Knox demonstrated his acceptance of Luther's doctrine of justification.

After his release in 1549, Knox went to England where he stayed until 1554. The English authorities appointed him preacher at Berwick and Newcastle, two frontier towns in northern England. Here, his attack on the Mass as idolatry caused him to be called before the council of the North in 1550 to answer for his views. His sermons in the North drew the attention of the authorities in London. In 1551, they made him a chaplain to Edward VI. As such, Knox assisted in the revision of the *Book of Common Prayer.* He criticized the provision that called for kneeling during Communion. While Thomas Cranmer largely had his way on this issue, Knox appears to have been chiefly responsible for the inclusion of the Black Rubric—a declaration explaining that kneeling at the Lord's Supper does not signify adoration to either the bread or wine. The English authorities also offered Knox the bishopric of Rochester, which he refused for reasons that are not completely clear. Though he criticized the details of English ecclesiastical policy, he generally approved of the religious climate that prevailed in Edwardian England. But things would soon change.

Edward died and the Catholic Mary Tudor came to the throne of England—a move that would turn English religion upside down. By January 1554, events drove Knox into exile. From this time until the deposition of Mary Stewart in Scotland some thirteen years later, he more or less occupied himself with the problem of idolatry—that is, Catholicism. When confronted by idolatry, how should the "the faithful Christian" respond? Should they obey or disobey an "idolatrous" sovereign?

Shortly after arriving at Dieppe, France, Knox completed *An Admonition or Warning,* urging "true Christians" not to participate in idolatrous Catholicism. He then moved to Switzerland. Here, he met with Calvin,

---

32. Biographies of Knox are numerous. I have counted about thirty; the most recent is Marshall, *John Knox.* Among the most noteworthy are those by W. Stanford Reid, Jasper Ridley, Pierre Janton, Lord Eustace Percy, P. Hume Brown, and Thomas M'Crie.

Bullinger, and other Reformed leaders, posing questions on rebellion against idolatrous monarchs and female sovereigns. Knox returned to Dieppe for a short while where he wrote *A Faithful Admonition*—a long publication which attacked Mary Tudor directly, and argued that England was repeating the idolatrous history of Israel.

In 1554, Knox left for Geneva, but at Calvin's urging, he headed for Frankfurt where he became a pastor to the English congregation. A nasty dispute over the *Book of Common Prayer* led to his departure and return to Geneva in 1555. But he did not stay long, returning the same year to Scotland. Here, he openly preached Protestant doctrine with considerable success. Thus the Catholic Church summoned Knox to appear in Edinburgh in May 1556 on a charge of heresy. In an attempt to gain the support of the Protestant nobles, however, Mary of Guise intervened and quashed the summons. Still, the continuing persecution of Protestants in Scotland led Knox to accept a call to the English church at Geneva.

In Geneva, he published several tracts concerning problems in Scotland and England. Though he addressed several subjects, political issues received the most attention. In four pamphlets published in 1558, the reformer clearly set forth his views on the rights of subjects against idolatrous and oppressive rulers. *The First Blast of the Trumpet Against the Monstrous Regiment of Women*—in which Knox argued that female sovereignty contravened natural and divine law—startled Europe. Subsequent tracts—*The Appellation and Letter to the Commonalty*—went even further. Using Old Testament models, Knox urged both the nobles and common people to compel their rulers to make religious reforms.

In these tracts, Knox stated unequivocally some earthshaking propositions: the nobles had the right to remove an unrepentant monarch, while the commonality could set up their own reformed kirk if their rulers failed to act. It was, however, *The First Blast* that gained for Knox a reputation among his contemporaries of being a revolutionary. He primarily targeted *The First Blast* at Mary Tudor. But shortly after its appearance, she died and Elizabeth became Queen of England, making Knox's name odious in her court. During his sojourn in Geneva, Knox also addressed other subjects, especially predestination. In *An Answer*, his longest writing, he defended Calvin's teaching on predestination against an attack by an Anabaptist. In doing so, he focused on the practical necessity of predestination to his view of salvation.

Yet the Protestant Lords of the Congregation sought Knox's return to Scotland and he arrived in May 1559—a critical moment for the

The Reformer in His Context

Reformation's success. After becoming a minister in Edinburgh and a leader of the Reforming party, he devoted himself to preaching and to procuring money and troops from England. The secular lords, nevertheless, did more to acquire aid from England than did Knox. And in respect to political affairs, Knox became somewhat of a liability, so he tended to focus more on religious matters. After the death of Mary of Guise, Knox and other leaders drew up the *Scots Confession*, which Parliament approved in 1560. The confession abolished the authority of the Pope and proscribed the celebration of the Mass. Knox and five others also drafted the *Book of Discipline*, which spelled out the practical and financial aspects of Knox's reform program.

After Mary Stewart's return to Scotland in 1561, Knox came into repeated conflicts with the Queen over her desire to practice the Mass and the worldliness of her court. During 1561–62, he engaged in a controversy over ordination with Ninan Winzet, a Catholic priest and educator. Although he lacked the miracles to prove it, Knox claimed an extraordinary calling—like that of Amos and John the Baptist. Knox also disputed with Quintin Kennedy, Abbot of Crossraguel, regarding the Mass.

Meanwhile, the conflict with Mary reached its conclusion. She had her husband, Lord Darnley, murdered. After this deed, she was captured and Knox demanded her execution. Following her abdication, he preached at the coronation of her son, James VI. Knox now became closely connected with the regent, James Stewart, the Earl of Moray. After Moray's murder in 1570, Knox's political clout diminished, though his fundamental cause triumphed.[33]

His Personality

This brief summary outlines the events that shaped Knox's life and, in turn, his ministry. But what about the inner man? What about his personality? These subjects are more speculative and difficult to document. But they, too, have shaped Knox's ministry and career as a reformer.

Knox has justifiably been described as a "contradictory and complex character"—at once unpredictable and yet so unflinchingly

---

33. I have drawn this brief outline of Knox's life from several sources. Most directly, it came from two of my earlier summaries of Knox's life. See Kyle, "John Knox," in *Dictionary of Scottish Church History and Theology*, 465–66; Kyle, "John Knox," in *Encyclopedia of the Reformed Faith*, 208–9.

PART ONE: Historical and Theological Foundations

single-minded.[34] One side of Knox could be charismatic, hateful, forceful, courageous, and intimidating. To be sure, a cannon at Edinburgh Castle is aptly nicknamed John Knox.[35]

But Knox had another side. On Sunday, this "great voiced, bearded man of God" could beat the pulpit. On Monday, however, he would sit with his parishioners and weep with them over their trials and temptations. While he castigated female rulers (usually Catholics), he could be warm and tender to other women. At times Knox had the courage of a lion. On other occasions, he prudently protected his life, fleeing danger as the need arose. He promoted godly living—but not excessive Puritanism. He was less austere than supposed.[36]

What events forged Knox's personality—contradictions and all? Any answer to this question must be largely speculation. The sources of Knox's anger and hatred are more easily identified. He abhorred Catholicism—which he equated with idolatry—and anyone or anything that promoted it. A short list would include "idolatrous" sovereigns and the French establishment.

Why hate Catholicism? Undoubtedly, the two driving forces include his belief that Scripture condemned idolatry and his calling to be God's mouthpiece. Still, other factors cannot be ignored. Knox's social background pointed him in that direction. He was one of the "middling sort," the social class which tended to be most critical of the church. Knox spent 19 months as a prisoner on a French galley—an experience that intensified his hatred for Catholicism and the French. Moreover, he spent much of his life as a refugee, fleeing three female sovereigns. Without a doubt, such an ordeal fueled his anger toward female rulers. Even the volcanic mood of Europe contributed to Knox's personality. "Knox lived in a world where martyr and apostate were a grim polarity," says E. G. Rupp. In such an uncompromising environment, Knox saw himself as a prophet proclaiming God's judgment.[37]

But what about Knox's gentle and prudent side? This is more difficult to explain. He did have a conversion experience, one that shaped his life. Knox was a deeply spiritual man, one who took seriously the

34. Murison, "Knox the Writer," esp. 33; Kirk, "Knox and the Historians," 16, 22.

35. Rupp, "The Europe of John Knox," 14.

36. Donaldson, "Knox the Man," 18–22; Kirk, "Knox and the Historians," 18, 22–23.

37. Rupp, "The Europe of John Knox," 8–10; Reid, "John Knox and His Interpreters," 15–20; Donaldson, "Knox the Man," 18–24; Edington,"John Knox and the Castilians," 46–48.

New Testament emphasis on love and compassion. This characteristic tempered Knox's harsher tendencies. What's more, the reformer must not be regarded as a backward Scot. He traveled extensively, living in several European countries. He spoke French fluently and understood French society. Of considerable importance, his sojourn in Calvin's Geneva left a deep impression on the reformer. Such factors may have helped forge the "other" John Knox.[38]

How then should we view Knox? He has often been seen in "either . . . or" terms—either as a hero or a villain. To interpret his life in such exclusive categories is a mistake. Rather, a more pluralistic approach to Knox should be adopted. He can be better viewed from a "both . . . and" framework. Depending on the context, he can be regarded as both compassionate and unforgiving, tolerant and uncompromising, etc. And these opposites are not easily reconciled.

---

38. See Reid, *Trumpeter of God*, 1–3, 24–27; Reid, "John Knox, Pastor of Souls," 1–21; Donaldson, "Knox the Man," 26–29.

2

The Word of God and Its Interpretation

As the Renaissance revived the learning of antiquity, the Reformation helped rediscover the Bible. Such a recovery entailed more than the fact that masses of people who had not previously opened Scripture were now reading it. Rediscovery also meant that people now read the Bible in a new light and with a new meaning, that the Word of God, as revealed in Scripture, began challenging the Roman Church for the position of supreme religious authority.

Among other issues, the dispute between Rome and the Reformation focused on the question of authority. Which was supreme—the authority of the church or the authority of the Scriptures? In medieval Catholicism, the church had the last word, but the Reformers demanded scriptural proof on matters of religious belief and practice. Despite differences in their views of the Bible, the continental reformers did not differ in respect to "sola Scriptura." And neither did John Knox and the Scottish Reformation.[1] Indeed, for Knox Scripture became the driving force behind his faith and vocation, especially his crusade to purify religion and overthrow the Catholic faith.

---

1. D'Assonville, *John Knox and the Institutes* 64–66; Oberman, "Preaching and the Word in the Reformation," 16–29; Dickinson, *The Scottish Reformation and Its Influence Upon Scottish Life and Character*, 5–6; Gerrish, "Biblical Authority and the Continental Reformation," 337–40; McEwen, *The Faith of Knox*, 29–33.

THE NATURE OF GOD'S WORD

What was the nature of God's Word to John Knox? He believed it to be the canonical Scriptures, i.e., the books found in the Old and New Testament, excluding the "apocryphal" writings. Phrases such as "the plain Word of God," "the express Word of God," "the plain Scripture," and "the infallible Scripture" constantly confront even the casual reader of Knox's works. Judged from the context in which they occur, he normally understood the Word of God to mean the Bible. Pierre Janton is correct when he says that for Knox the Word was synonymous with Scripture.[2]

Nonetheless, John Knox did not limit the Word of God to the text of Scripture. To him the Word was also a vibrant, living power. Occasionally, he equated the Word with the person of Christ, the power of God—whether it be in the act of creation or in the salvation of a soul—and the gospel message. He also mentioned the spoken Word as the Word of God but apparently only in the context of God's or Christ's words, the words of the prophets and apostles recorded in the Bible, and the message of ministers when they preached God's Word contained in Scripture. Like Calvin and Luther, Knox savagely opposed the Anabaptists who, he believed, substituted an inner light for the written Scripture. Though the Bible needed the work of the Holy Spirit in order to become operative, Knox did not speak of God's Word as some subjective experience divorced from Scripture.

John Knox left no systematic exposition of his views on Scripture, but they are plain from his writings in general. His early works point to the Bible as the Word of God. In the 1548 epistle to the congregation at St. Andrews, Knox seemed to equate the Word with Scripture.[3] In *A Vindication* (1550), which used Scripture to establish the Mass as idolatry, Knox spoke of God's Word as the command of Scripture. Phrases such as the "plain or express Word of God" occur frequently. In one place in *A Vindication* he referred to the "Decalogue" and "Law Moral" as the Word, while in another he called the epistles and gospels "God's Word."[4]

In *A Godly Letter* (1553–54), the reformer bombarded his readers with the phrases "plain and infallible truth of God's Word," and "the plain and evident Scripture." Again in the context of warning believers to flee idolatry, Knox apparently identified the Word with Scripture.[5]

---

2. *Works*, 2:145; 5:420; Janton, *Concept et Sentiment*, 174; D'Assonville, *Knox and the Institutes*, 69.

3. *Works*, 3:9.

4. *Works*, 3:38, 51.

5. *Works*, 3:165–66, 168–71, 173, 175–77, 179, 192, 199, 202.

PART ONE: Historical and Theological Foundations

Knox's *Faithful Admonition* (1554) depicted God's Word as more than the Bible. He declared that God's Word created the heavens and earth. In this context, the Word could not mean the text of Scripture.[6] God's Word was also the power that brought salvation to believers and a lantern to guide the feet of those in darkness. By this statement, Knox probably meant that the Holy Spirit quickened and applied Scripture to the soul of one in darkness. He also referred to the Word spoken by God's messengers, which had the power to draw those chosen by God unto salvation, namely the elect. When considered in the context of Knox's total corpus, it must be concluded that these messengers preached from Scripture.

Knox saw himself in a situation analogous to an Old Testament prophet, but he normally based his message on Scripture, quickened by the Holy Spirit. The canon, he believed, had closed; and the sixteenth-century prophets relied on divine revelation recorded in Scripture—not on any new revelation. For Knox, the Word also had the power to comfort those in duress, to purge sin, to conquer death, to provide wisdom, to suppress tyranny, and to overthrow Satan. Here the Word transcended the text—it seemed to be a spiritual power working in, above, and through the Scripture.[7]

Knox continued to echo similar themes. In a letter to Mrs. Bowes (1553–54), he described the Word of God as no dead text but as a living Word implanting life into the soul. Moreover, the Word received its strength from the Holy Spirit.[8] Knox in *An Exposition Upon Matthew IV* (1556), noted Christ's use of Scripture to repulse Satan. He spoke of the Word as both the written Scripture and the sword of the Holy Spirit. A 1556 letter to the Protestants in Scotland said that God's Word, transmitted through Scripture, was not a dead text but the source of all faith and "the beginning of life spiritual, without which all flesh is dead in God's presence."[9] Again in *The First Blast* and *The Appellation*, both published in 1558, Knox referred to the Word of God and then proceeded to quote Scripture.[10]

In Knox's lengthy tract, *An Answer* (1560), the reformer's most explicit statements on the nature of God's Word can be found. Repeatedly

---

6. *Works*, 3:301.

7. *Works*, 3:263–64; 268, 272, 285, 290, 298, 300–306, 310–12. See Greaves, "The Nature of Authority in the Writings of John Knox, 42.

8. *Works*, 3:338.

9. *Works*, 4:134. For the context indicating that the Word was Scripture, see 136–38.

10. *Works*, 4:397, 469.

he equated the Word of God with written Scripture.[11] Knox apparently emphasized the biblical text as God's Word because he was confronting an Anabaptist whom he regarded as unsound on the matter. To the Anabaptist, the Scottish reformer said that the Word of God amounts to the Holy Spirit speaking plainly in Scripture.[12]

John Knox gave no thought to canonical problems as Luther had done, but rather assumed the full canon. The Scottish reformer would accept only the books of the canon as the Word of God. By canon, Knox followed the Reformation tradition and included all of the New Testament books plus the Old Testament writings found in the Hebrew Bible. In fact, his predestination tract warned the flock against anyone who made the non-canonical writings equal in authority to the books recommended by the Holy Spirit to the church and written by Moses, the prophets, the evangelists, and apostles.[13]

Knox strongly maintained that the canon had closed. Accordingly, and in contradistinction to the medieval canon, he gave no recognition to the apocryphal writings, i.e., the Old Testament books contained in the Septuagint but not in the Hebrew Bible. These books, he believed, were not of the Holy Spirit. The teachings contained therein were acceptable for edification—providing they did not contradict the canonical Scriptures—but Knox would not allow them to establish doctrine: "To your scriptures, which you allege from the book of Wisdom, and from Esdras (his fourth book), I will shortly answer, that although you will ten thousand times deck and decore them with the title of the Holy Ghost, I will not credit them . . . [and] to conformation of any doctrine shall they never serve unto me."[14]

Knox not only refused to add to the canon, but his writings gave no hint of rejecting, or of even criticizing any of the canonical books. In fact, he quoted as Scripture most books of the Old and New Testaments, including James and Revelation—books that some other reformers questioned or ignored.[15]

---

11. *Works*, 5:33, 39, 42, 49, 53, 59, 73, 114, 117, 126, 140, 179, 198, 231, 241, 259, 291, 298, 304, 306, 310, 312, 333, 360, 368, 382, 400, 402, 421. In places Knox uses Scripture and God's Word interchangeably. To cite an example: "[B]y the plain Scriptures of God, I have confirmed the doctrine which we teach, believe, and maintain, and by the same truth of God's Word I have confuted your error" (253).

12. *Works*, 5:310.

13. *Works*, 5: 420.

14. *Works*, 5:102.

15. *Works*, 5:260, 268–69. Henderson, "John Knox and the Bible," 101.

Furthermore, in *An Answer*, Knox again spoke of the Word of God as being more than the text of Scripture. "That God's power, both in one sort and in the other, is contained with his Word, even preached, pronounced, and fore-spoken by his messengers, do all examples in God's Scriptures witness." The Word embodied the power of God that could not only save but punish and destroy. Once more Knox depicted the Word as the eternal power by which God had created all things.[16]

In addition, the reformer believed Jesus Christ to be the living Word. According to Luther, the Bible was the Word of God in the sense that it witnessed to Christ, the incarnate Word. Though Knox seldom spoke of Christ as the Word, Pierre Janton is correct when he claims that for Knox all the Bible was God's Word, but the Word comprised more than the Bible. The Word revealed itself more perfectly in Christ, the incarnate Word.[17] One passage in *An Answer* stated that "the Word of God is of the nature of Christ," while in another Knox called Jesus Christ "the eternal Word."[18] Such statements agree with *The Book of Common Order* (1564), which confessed Christ to be the eternal Word from the beginning by which all things were created and conserved.[19]

Knox echoed similar themes throughout the remainder of his writings. In *An Epistle to New Castle and Berwick* (1558–59), he wrote, as he did in *A Faithful Admonition*, expressing in forceful terms that England must heed the warning of God's messengers. Though the preachers were frail instruments, they spoke with the eternal power of God's Word. The Word here had two functions: to threaten doom to the impenitent and to promise salvation to the repentant.[20] In January 1561, during the discussions resulting from the presentation of the *Book of Discipline* to the nobility, Knox and his colleagues stated that their faith "was grounded upon God's Word, and fully expressed within his holy Scriptures. . . ."[21] In his debates with Quintin Kennedy, the Abbot of Crossraguel (1562), Knox

---

16. *Works*, 5:386–87, 389.
17. Janton, *John Knox: L'homme et l'oeuvre*, 371–72.
18. *Works*, 5:385, 402.
19. *Works*, 6:318. *The Book of Common Order* contained the *Confession of Faith of the Church of Geneva*. Stalker maintains that this book represents Knox's views better than did the *Scots Confession* and the *Book of Discipline*. See Stalker, *John Knox: His Ideas and Ideals*, 203.
20. *Works*, 5:486–87.
21. *Works*, 2:139.

again confirmed that God's Word is expressed verbally through the Old and New Testaments.[22]

John Knox certainly emphasized the Word of God as found in the text of Scripture, but he also had a vital experience with both the written Word in Scripture and the living Word, Jesus Christ. Knox did not reveal a great deal about his innermost spiritual life. In fact, his conversion is known from his deathbed. There he mentioned John, chapter 17, which records Christ's farewell prayer before his betrayal, as the place where first he "first cast anchor."[23] In recalling his conversion, Knox said that the Word of God in Scripture, by the work of the Holy Spirit, enabled him to lay hold on the living Word, Jesus Christ. Knox did not say that the living Word experienced through Scripture, rather than the text of the Bible, is the Word of God.[24]

Knox regarded all manifestations of God's Word, including the text of Scripture, as infallible. In *A Vindication* (1550), the reformer said his position concerning the Mass did not stand upon the opinion of human beings, "but upon the infallible Word of God." Knox in *An Exposition Upon Psalm VI* (1554), confirmed his conscience by the infallible and plain Word of God. To the faithful in London, Newcastle and Berwick (1554), Knox wrote that he "never labored to persuade any man in matters of religion . . . except by the very simplicity and plain infallible truth of God's Word." In the same tract, he declared "the Scriptures of God [to] be infallible." Knox attempted to comfort his mother-in-law, Mrs. Bowes, by appealing to the true and infallible Word of God. In *The Appellation* (1558), he said any church authority must prove their position "by God's infallible Word." *An Answer* (1560) affirmed Augustine's *City of God* because it agreed with "God's infallible Word."[25]

According to Knox, God expresses himself in words and sentences in Scripture. Such a statement, coupled with his literal use of Scripture and belief in biblical infallibility, implies a doctrine of verbal inspiration. Little basis seems to exist, therefore, for the view that Knox did not hold to the infallibility of Scripture.

22. *Works*, 205.

23. *Works*, 6:639, 643, 659.

24. McEwen presents something resembling a neo-orthodox view of Scripture. He claims that Knox meant by the Word of God, not the text of Scripture, but the living Word that comes into the human experience through Scripture. McEwen, *The Faith of Knox*, 38. This study does not embrace such a view because Knox did not stress his experience but the text of Scripture.

25. *Works*, 3:64, 154, 166, 197; 4:519; 5:33.

But what did he mean by infallibility? Did Knox hold the biblical text free from errors? Or did he admit textual error while still believing the Bible to be totally sufficient to convey God's truth? On one hand, he did not attempt—as Calvin had done—to explain the Bible's alleged contradictions and errors. But on the other hand, Knox did not criticize certain elements of Scripture as Luther had done. John Knox's vocation was to proclaim the infallible truth of God's Word, and apparently he gave little thought to the textual problems of Scripture. Though Knox placed tremendous emphasis upon the literal text of Scripture, he never formulated a doctrine of verbal inerrancy.[26]

THE NATURE OF AUTHORITY IN KNOX'S THOUGHT

What source of authority determined individual beliefs, religious practices, church policy, church-state relationships, and even secular developments? Would it be the Church of Rome, church councils, tradition, individual conscience, majority opinion, or even princes and parliaments? At one point or another, all of these entities influenced religious developments and institutions. More specifically, during most of the Middle Ages the Catholic Church exerted immense authority over many areas of life. John Knox would have none of this. He subordinated all other authorities to God's Word.

Scripture

Despite his occasional reliance on other sources of authority, Knox claimed Scripture as his sole authority throughout his public ministry. Knox exalted the authority of Scripture in many situations, but most often, he pushed it in the context of purifying worship. His first sermon at St. Andrews attacked the Mass as idolatry. Shortly thereafter, he found himself in a debate with Sub-prior John Winram and some friars. Among other things, they accused Knox of teaching that "man is bound to observe and

---

26. McEwen, *The Faith of Knox*, 38. McEwen rightly observes that the Reformed assertion of the infallible truth of the gospel through the Scripture is not necessarily connected with the later doctrine of verbal inerrancy. Knox probably equated infallibility with supreme authority and absolute sufficiency. But this biblical authority and sufficiency was dogma to him and not just a matter of experience as McEwen contends. Gerrish, "Biblical Authority and the Continental Reformation," 354–55.

keep the religion that from God is received, without chopping or changing thereof." A debate followed and Knox argued that in regard to religious matters human beings should not add nor subtract anything from what God expressly commanded.[27]

During his stay in England (1549-54), Knox echoed the same themes. Because of his attack on the Mass, the Council of the North summoned him to appear at Newcastle. Here Knox defined idolatry as "all worshipping, honoring, or service invented by the brain of man in the religion of God, without his own express commandment..." This definition underscored the importance Knox placed on the authority of Scripture in religious affairs. Not long thereafter English officials issued the *Second Book of Common Prayer*, which contained a rubric on kneeling at communion. Knox said this rubric did not have biblical sanction, and demanded that it be modified.[28]

Throughout his exile years (1554-59), Knox maintained the supreme authority of Scripture in the religion of God. At the onset of this exile, he wrote back to the faithful in England asserting that in religious questions, he never attempted to persuade anyone except by Scripture.[29] After arriving in Geneva in 1554, he set out for Frankfurt where the Marian exiles—who had fled England in the face of Mary Tudor's persecution—engaged each other in controversy. Richard Cox, the future Bishop of Ely, demanded the continued use of the *Second Book of Common Prayer* on the grounds of tradition, legal precedent, and a desire to retain ties with the English Reformation. Such arguments Knox would not accept, asserting "that as by God's book they (the congregation) must seek our warrant for Religion, without that, we must thrust nothing onto any Christian congregation...."[30]

Although Knox's view did not prevail and the city authorities ran him out of town, he continued to adhere to such a position with utmost vigor. About the same time, the Scottish reformer wrote to an unnamed woman in Edinburgh, condemning vices such as drunkenness and gluttony by the authority of Scripture. Then he turned to the subject of worship and asserted: "honor and service in matters of religion, invented by the brain of man, without the express Word of God ... is service of devils."[31] Knox's

27. *Works*, 1:194, 196-97.
28. Reid, *Trumpeter of God*, 39-93; Ridley, *John Knox*, 113-14; Ridley, *Thomas Cranmer*, 336-38. See chapter 6 for a more detailed account of the episode.
29. *Works*, 3:166.
30. *Works*, 4:44; Vander Molen, "Anglican Against Puritan," 45-57.
31. *Works*, 4:231.

1556 letter to the Queen Regent contended that religion must be measured by the plain Word of God and not by custom and the determination of human beings.[32]

At the close of his 1556 trip to Scotland, Knox wrote a letter counseling the Scottish Protestants to bring both their worship and lifestyle in accord with the commandments of Scripture.[33] His 1558 letter urging the Queen Regent to reform religion also elevated the authority of Scripture over that of any human authority: "for this is our chief proposition, that in the religion of God only ought his own Word be considered; that no authority of man nor angel ought in that case be respected."[34] In *The Appellation* (1558), Knox again defined idolatry as anything done in religion or God's service without the express commandment of Scripture. Moreover, he stressed that "the Scriptures of God are my only foundation and assurance, in all matters of weight and importance."[35]

In *An Answer* (1560), the theme changed, but Knox's emphasis on the authority of Scripture did not. His war on idolatry subsided while he assaulted what he believed to be the Anabaptist heresy. Again and again, he uplifted the Scriptures as the supreme authority in doctrinal matters. Though Knox's debate with the Anabaptist often centers on questions of biblical interpretation, apparently the Anabaptist also challenged Knox's doctrine with extra-biblical sources—i.e., dreams, revelations, and non-canonical books. Therefore, the Scottish reformer frequently declared that "the plain Scripture confutes this your error. . . ." "We affirm nothing which God's Word does not plainly teach us. . . ." Furthermore, Knox now recalled his 1552 answer to a person who disputed with him from a non-canonical book: "You deserve death as a blasphemous person and denier of God, if you prefer any word to which the Holy Ghost has uttered in his plain Scriptures."[36]

Turning to *A Brief Exhortation to England* (1559), the reformer can be found urging the English to once again return to "true religion." One statement summarized Knox's view of authority in this tract and throughout his entire ministry: "Let God's Word alone be the rule and line to measure his religion."[37]

32. *Works*, 4:80.
33. *Works*, 4:431.
34. *Works*, 4:446.
35. *Works*, 4:469–70; 478.
36. *Works*, 5:59, 310, 421.
37. *Works*, 5:516.

The Word of God and Its Interpretation

Knox returned to Scotland in 1559 and no change in his concept of authority can be detected. The *Scots Confession* (1560), which he co-authored, grounded its beliefs in the "infallible truth of God's Word." The authors asked to be notified if anyone found something in the confession contrary to the Bible. Indeed, they confessed that the authority of Scripture came from God and not from any human source.[38]

The *Book of Discipline* (1560), which Knox and his colleagues wrote, based its policy squarely upon the authority of Scripture. In fact, the authors requested that the book be binding only to the extent it harmonized with Scripture.[39] In his debate with Quintin Kennedy, the Abbot of Crossraguel (1562), Knox again placed the authority of Scripture over that of tradition, the church, and even the church fathers.[40] The Scottish reformer maintained this belief in the sole authority of Scripture until the end of his life. Looking back at the end of his career, he defended his attacks on Queen Mary as legitimate obedience to the command of God's Word.[41]

The Church Fathers

John Knox declared Scripture to be his sole authority in religion, but occasionally he turned to other sources. Of these secondary sources, Knox highly respected the church fathers and cited them when they added weight to his argument. Yet, patristic references appear in Knox's writings to be scant when compared to similar citations in the writings of other reformers such as John Calvin. The Scottish reformer cited the church fathers most often during his exile years. A numerical account of these references shows Augustine in front, followed by Chrysostom, Tertullian, and Ambrose. Athanasius, Basil the Great, and Jerome—among others—are also noted.[42]

Knox's tract on the nature of the Lord's Supper rejected the doctrine of real presence because he felt that it contradicts the teaching of Scripture and of such church fathers as Augustine, Jerome, and Origen. Chrysostom

---

38. *Works*, 2:93, 96, 112.
39. *Works*, 2:183–84.
40. *Works*, 2:194, 205, 211, 213, 215.
41. Greaves, "The Nature of Authority in the Writings of John Knox," 32.
42. A sampling would include the following: *Works*, 3:75, 351; 4:310, 314–15, 322, 383–86, 390, 392–93, 492–94, 511–12, 524; 5:32–33, 39, 62, 77, 170–71, 180, 326, 331–32, 344, 419; 6:194, 202, 501, 505. For a listing for each church father, see Greaves, "The Nature of Authority in the Writings of John Knox," 34, 49.

PART ONE: Historical and Theological Foundations

is mentioned in the letter to Mrs. Bowes (1553), and Knox made additions to *An Apology* for Protestants in prison, which selected passages from Tertullian and other early Christian apologists[43]

But not until *The First Blast* (1558) did Knox make wide use of the church fathers along with classical writers and Roman and canon law. Knox liberally cited Tertullian, Augustine, Ambrose, and Chrysostom in defense of his position that God had placed woman in a subordinate status to man, and therefore must not rule over men. Knox's *Appellation* (1558), used the writings of Augustine and Chrysostom to further his contention that the civil power must reform religion. In these references the key to the Scottish reformer's use of secondary sources is evident: a church father had authority so long as he could prove his teaching "by God's infallible Word." Thus the church fathers derived their authority from Scripture.[44]

Knox's lengthy treatise defending predestination contains numerous references to Augustine, but many of these citations came from Calvin's *Institutes*. Nevertheless, in this controversy over predestination, the heart of Knox's view on the authority of the church fathers is encountered: he believed the church fathers—and in this context—Augustine, had authority because they drew their teachings from Scripture.[45]

In the dispute with the Abbot of Crossraguel (1562), Knox struck a familiar note. He agreed with Augustine "that whatsoever the Doctors' purpose, and plainly confirm the same by the evident testimony of the Scriptures, I am heartily content to receive." But whatever they affirm "without the authority of God's Scriptures, I reject."[46] In 1566 or 1567, Knox replied to a letter written by a Jesuit, Tyrie. This response contended that he would not automatically accept the patristic teachings, but only when they agreed with "the written word of the Eternal our God."[47]

Ecclesiastical Authority

A great issue in the sixteenth century concerned the relationship of scriptural authority to that of ecclesiastical authority. Put in simple terms: Which is the authority, the church or the Scriptures? The church,

---

43. *Works*, 3:351; 5:310, 314–15, 322.
44. *Works*, 4:492–94, 511–12, 519.
45. *Works*, 5:331–32. See also 32–33, 39, 62, 77, 170, 180, 326, 344, 419. D'Assonville, *Knox and the Institutes*, 41, 44.
46. *Works*, 6:194.
47. *Works*, 6:501, 505.

according to Catholic theology, precedes the Scripture temporally and logically. The church came before Scripture and therefore does not owe its origin and authority to the Scriptures but exists through Christ and the Holy Spirit, which inhabits the church. The Holy Scriptures, on the other hand, originated from the church and lend their authority to the church. As a consequence, the authority of Scripture becomes secondary to that of the church. John Knox would not accept this reasoning.

Knox can be found contending for the supremacy of Scripture over all forms of ecclesiastical authority in his second letter to the Queen Regent, *The Appellation*, and in his disputes with Quintin Kennedy, Ninian Winzet, and Tyrie. In *A Letter to the Queen Regent* (1558), Knox rejected Catholicism's antiquity and tradition as grounds for authority, because if they were accepted, "the false religion of Mahomet" must be preferred "simply because of its antiquity." Nor would he accept majority opinion (which in this case was Catholic) because in antediluvian times the multitude raged against God, except for Noah and his family. Though Knox did not reject church councils outright, he insisted that the proclamation of one individual founded in biblical truth was of more authority than the "determination of the whole Counsel (*sic*) without the assurance of God's Word."[48]

In the 1558 *Appellation*, Knox expressed himself more precisely in regard to the authority of church councils. The authority of general councils was a much discussed topic in the sixteenth century. In fact, certain continental Protestants even called for a general council to settle various problems of the Reformation. Accordingly, Knox in *The Appellation* called for a general council. Along with Calvin, the Scottish reformer did not reject the authority of general councils, but required their decisions to be in accordance with the Word of God. He held—as did Zwingli and Calvin—that when a church council has authority, it is merely derived from God's Word.[49]

Knox, however, considered the four ancient councils to be in agreement with God's Word and thus of high authority. In a dispute he would accept the authority of church councils providing nothing be admitted against the plain truth of God's Word, nor against the four early councils whose decisions he regarded as co-equal with the authority of the four

---

48. *Works*, 4:446.
49. Davies, *The Problem of Authority in the Continental Reformers*, 76, 130.

gospel writers.[50] In other words, Knox would accept no conciliar decision that ran counter to his beliefs.

The *Scots Confession* also noted the primacy of Scripture over the church and general councils in particular and labeled as blasphemy the notion that Scripture derived its authority from the kirk. Rather, the true church obeyed Scripture. General councils were not infallible but, in fact, made manifest errors in important matters of doctrine. Therefore, the authors of the confession reserved the right to accept or reject conciliar decisions. In fact, the confession described the rightful duties of a council as twofold: first, to confute heresy and publicly confess the faith; second, to promote good policy and order in the church. Councils were not empowered to forge new doctrine, to make binding church law, to give authority to Scripture, nor to develop new biblical interpretations.[51]

The issue of scriptural authority over and against ecclesiastical authority emerged in Knox's debate with Quintin Kennedy, the Abbot of Crossraguel (1562). This disputation centered on the Mass and that argument necessitated an appeal to authority by both parties. According to Knox, Kennedy relied on church tradition, general councils, and church doctors. Against these sources, Knox maintained biblical authority. He would accept the decisions of a general council and the teachings of the church doctors only to the extent that they could be verified by Scripture.[52]

About the same time Ninian Winzet, a Catholic priest, challenged Knox concerning the issue of authority. The questions the priest raised centered on such issues as Knox's lawful ordination to the ministry and his refusal to accept religious ceremony that had no biblical warrant. Since, asked Winzet, Protestants observe Sunday—for which no express scriptural support existed—why could not Catholics also use ecclesiastical authority to support their practices? [53]

In his last major work, *An Answer to Tyrie*, (1572), the question of authority again emerged. Knox affirmed the Scottish kirk as legitimate because it rested on biblical warrant. Conversely, he condemned Catholicism as false because of its reliance on ecclesiastical authority: "We fear not to

---

50. *Works*, 4:518-19. The councils noted were the Council of Nicaea (325), Council of Constantinople (381), Council of Ephesus (431), and the council of Chalcedon (451).

51. *Works*, 2:112-13.

52. *Works*, 6:194.

53. Ridley, *John Knox*, 408-12; Winzet, *Certain Tractates Together with the Book of Four Score Three Questions and a Translation of Vincentius Lirinensis*, 1:32; Greaves, "The Nature of Authority in the Writings of John Knox," 34.

affirm that the Papists, having no better ground for their faith than the consent of men, decrees of councils, an antiquity of time, have no faith, but a fond, yes, a damnable opinion." At the same time, he confirmed the Reformed faith to be "pleasing and acceptable unto God" because it rested on his "own commandment."[54]

Knox vehemently insisted that the church derives its authority from the Scriptures and not the reverse. Although in maintaining this position, he demonstrated a remarkable constancy, a few inconsistencies can be detected. Though he claimed the "plain Scripture" as his sole authority, he obviously interpreted the Bible according to the principles of his own Reformed tradition. For example, in *An Answer* and *An Answer to Tyrie*, Knox apparently invested the principles of the Reformed faith with some authority because he believed them to be biblical. In the predestination tract he wrote, "We build our doctrine upon the evident testimonies of the Scriptures, and upon the chief principals (sic) of our religion and faith."[55]

Also, in the preface to *The Form of Prayers*, two inconsistencies appear. The authors said religious ceremonies invented by the human brain ought to be removed "if they be once abused." At the same time, these writers encouraged singing in the service because it had the approval of Scripture, the witness of antiquity, and the acceptance of the Reformed churches.[56] Supposedly Knox did not write *The Form of Prayers*, though he approved it. Knox did not always get his own way in collective documents, as this example demonstrates.

Other Sources

When enlightened by Scripture, conscience served as a secondary source of authority for Knox. Both Mary Queen of Scots and John Knox made appeals to conscience in their encounters. During their first meeting in September 1561, Mary appealed to conscience in defense of Catholicism. The Scottish reformer replied: conscience required right knowledge that came only from the Word of God, and "I fear that right knowledge you have none." Mary, according to Knox, could have no right conscience because she had a faulty interpretation of Scripture. He also referred to conscience in his fourth meeting with the queen. The reformer stated that his vocation and conscience required him to question her marriage plans.

54. *Works*, 6:488.
55. *Works*, 5:166. See also *Works*, 6:511.
56. *Works*, 4:162, 165.

(A Catholic marriage would threaten the Reformation.) Later in 1563 Knox found himself summoned before the queen and council. When reminded not to sermonize, he said conscience demanded him to speak the truth. Conscience by itself was not enough, but when joined to knowledge derived from biblical teaching, it had validity.[57]

Occasionally Knox made use of secular sources to defend a religious principle. Such references, however, were few and purely supplementary to Scripture and usually in a political context. Knox did not argue a religious issue on purely secular or empirical grounds. Only in *The First Blast* did he use secular arguments with any frequency. In order to reinforce his contention that a woman should not rule a nation, Knox drew support from many sources besides Scripture: the classical writers (particularly Aristotle), Roman canon law, natural law, ancient history, and empirical evidence. For authority in the 1564 debate with William Maitland, Knox cited not only Scripture but also the Magdeburg *Bekenntnis*.[58]

The Word of God and the State

Did John Knox hold the Word of God to be supreme in the affairs of Caesar? For Luther, at least theoretically, the Word of God was supreme in the affairs of state. The state came into existence before the Word of God by a direct act of creation. This act took place as a result of the fall of humanity; for without human sin, government would not be needed. Thus created by sin, the state must be subordinate to the Word of God.[59]

With Zwingli, the state also had independent authorization directly from God, and this jurisdiction carried the state through the execution of its ordinary tasks. In theory, Zwingli did not place the magistrates under direct domination of the Word so long as they refrained from enjoining anything contrary to the Word of God. In the later stages of his thinking, however, the state became increasingly under the authority of the Word, and the Word became the law of political and economic life.[60]

Calvin granted complete independence to the state because it was a direct divine institution, and this autonomy included freedom from

---

57. *Works*, 2:283–84, 388–89, 408–9.
58. *Works*, 4:373–77, 382, 400, 417; 2:353.
59. Davies, *The Problem of Authority*, 50–51.
60. Ibid., 84–85, 89. See also Courvoisier, *Zwingli*, 79–91. This statement is not to say that Zwingli advocated a theocracy where the clergy directed the policies of government. See Walton, *Zwingli's Theocracy*, 225–26; Potter, *Zwingli*, 377.

the church and a distinctiveness of providence. Calvin believed the state derives its authority immediately from God, and the Word has no direct jurisdiction over it. Although the Word describes and confirms the state's authority and function, it creates neither the state, nor its authority and function.[61] Needless to say, events in Germany, Zurich, and Geneva often contradicted the theory set forth by their respective reformers.

In respect to God's Word being dominant in the affairs of the world, Knox—as he so often did—failed to speak systematically. Did he believe the state to be a direct creation of God? While this question cannot be definitively answered, evidence implies he did. First, most Magisterial Reformers believed the state to be a direct divine creation. Second, the importance Knox placed on the magistrate would make such a view a logical step. Third, in *The First Blast* (1558) and *A Sermon on Isaiah XXVI* (1565) he held both the civil power and the boundaries of nations to be established by God's ordinance.[62]

When, if at all, did Knox hold the Word of God to be the supreme authority in secular matters? The Scottish reformer believed Scripture to be the final authority in all religious matters, and that when political or economic concerns invade this realm, God's Word reigns supreme. In the sixteenth century, lines between the sacred and the secular were often indistinct.

For instance, in The First Blast and Sermon on Isaiah, Knox said God committed the sword to the state in order to curb the beastlike qualities of human nature and to punish not only civil crimes—but also "such vices as openly impugn the glory of God, as idolatry, blasphemy, and manifest heresy."[63] In *An Apology* (1557), Knox affirmed that no earthly power is greater than the civil ruler, but such a ruler needs confirmation by the Word of God.[64] According to *The First Blast* the temporal ruler must rule in conformity with the "Law Moral," the unchangeable will of God, known only by God's Word.[65] Knox's sermon on Isaiah even said kings need to know God's will as revealed by Scripture and that the Word of God limits their power in religious matters.[66]

61. Davies, *The Problem of Authority*, 133, 135, 138. See also Niesel, *The Theology of Calvin*, 29–45; Hunter, *The Teaching of Calvin*, 2nd., 191–99; Hunt, "Calvin's Theory of Church and State," 56–71.

62. *Works*, 4:412; 6:235–37.

63. *Works*, 6:236–37; 4:398.

64. *Works*, 1:9; 4:324.

65. *Works*, 4:399.

66. *Works*, 6:239.

Knox never tired of stressing that all persons—regardless of their stations in life—must obey God rather than human beings and God's commandments are found in his Word. The obligation to revolt when a ruler commands something contrary to God's Word demonstrates how serious Knox embraced the authority of Scripture. This emphasis on the authority of the Word of God is not to say Knox believed the Bible to be supreme in nonreligious matters. For example, he did not believe Scripture determines the form of government, nor did he see the Reformation as political ideology.

Conclusion

For John Knox, the Word of God established the criterion for everything sacred, and when the secular invaded the religious realm, it also came under the jurisdiction of the Word. Throughout Knox's writings, Scripture determined his thought and action.[67] God's Word established the foundation for Knox's entire life, for in the Word of God he saw the reflection of his own experience.[68] He visualized himself as Jeremiah or Amos reliving the Old Testament drama. Knox interpreted the Bible very literally—more literally than most of the reformers—and he left us with no political theories or critical remarks that tended to diminish the authority of God's Word. In his stress on the Word of God and on his rejection of all beliefs and practices for which no biblical warrant could be found, Knox may have surpassed the other Magisterial Reformers.[69] At any rate, in defense of the authority of Scripture, John Knox was one of the most fiery exponents of the Reformation.

---

67. It must be noted that Knox was not unique in using Scripture as a basis of argument. In addition to other reformers, both his opponents and supporters made Scripture, to some degree, a basis of argument. Check bibliography for data on Christopher Goodman, Ninian Winzet, Wodrow Miscellany, Thomas Law, and William Tyndale. Also see *Works* for arguments made by Queen Mary, William Maitland, Quintin Kennedy, James Tyrie, and the Anabaptist opponent.

68. Denney, "John Knox: His Religious Life and Theological Position," 285.

69. Warfield insists that on the point of eliminating from the church every doctrine and ceremony that had no scriptural warrant, Knox pressed his doctrine of Scriptural authority even beyond Calvin and the Westminster divines. Warfield, "John Knox, Reformer of a Kingdom," 380. For a strong view of Knox's scriptural authority, see also Johnston, "Scripture in the Scottish Reformation. 1 Historical Statement," 252; Janton, *John Knox: L'homme et l' oeuvre*, 222 ff.

THE INTERPRETATION OF SCRIPTURE

The source of Knox's radical ideas and uniqueness rests not in his views on the nature of God's Word nor in its authority. In these respects the fiery Scottish reformer does not differ greatly from Calvin, Luther, and Zwingli. Perhaps the most radical of Knox's positions concerned the purification of worship and resistance to constituted political authority. For these notions Knox was indebted to many sources: both secular and religious, both ideological and experiential. Nevertheless, an important intellectual fountainhead for the radical and unique components of John Knox's thought can be found in the way he interpreted the Bible—especially in his emphasis on the Old Testament and pronounced literalness.[70]

Knox's Old Testament Emphasis

Scripture exhibits both a large degree of continuity and discontinuity. Continuity is evidenced in the divine plan of salvation—linking the Old and New Testaments inseparably—and in God's moral law, serving as a basis for both the Old and New Testament ethic. Jesus Christ himself illustrated continuity—"Think not I am come to destroy the Law, or the Prophets: I am come not to destroy, but to fulfill." But the fulfillment of such was itself discontinuity, since Jesus also said—"You have heard that it was said by them of old time . . . But I say unto. . . ."—and proceeded to give a deeper, more searching meaning to God's moral law. In respect to overemphasizing continuity at the expense of discontinuity, Knox experienced problems.[71]

Two dangers exist in theology regarding the relationship between the Old and New Testaments: they are either stated to be identical or to differ substantially. Calvin's solution was to recognize the unity and the substance of the two testaments, while pointing to the difference in administration. The testaments harmonize in respect to their basis—God's mercy in Christ; in respect to their promise—eternal life; and in respect to one mediator—Christ Jesus. But the mode of administration of the Old and New Testaments differs. First, the Old Testament was a covenant with Israel, while the New includes all people receiving the gospel. Second, the

---

70. For a discussion on this issue, see Kyle, "The Hermeneutical Patterns in John Knox's Use of Scripture," 19–32; Kyle, "John Knox's Methods of Biblical Interpretation: An Important Source of His Intellectual Radicalness," 57–70.

71. McEwen, *The Faith of Knox*, 39–40; D'Assonville, *Knox and the Institutes*, 73–75.

Old Testament only foreshadowed the truth and grace to come in the New. Third, the Old Testament was a testament of bondage and the New Testament is one of liberty. Though Calvin championed the unity of substance in Scripture, he took account of the epoch, of the times, and of the people in his application of the Old Testament.[72]

Knox not only agreed with Calvin concerning the lack of difference in substance between the Old and New Testaments, but he overemphasized this continuity. His failure to recognize a discontinuity between the testaments led to an over-identification of the Old Testament with the New Testament. Though Knox believed the Old Testament foreshadowed the things revealed in the New, he did not believe the New superseded the Old except—of course—in regard to matters such as the atonement or the new covenant. In fact Knox, like Calvin, employed passages from both the Old and New Testaments to confirm each other. For as the co-authored *Scots Confession* affirms, "the Holy Ghost uniformly speaks within the body of Scriptures."[73]

In accord with the Reformed tradition, Knox's religious thought had the Old Testament as its starting point. The Word of God preached in the sixteenth century was the same Word preached in the Old Testament in the third chapter of Genesis; the true church started in Genesis; election had an Old Testament foundation; and Knox derived his major anti-idolatry theme from the Old Testament.[74]

More specifically, Knox's major premise drawn from Deuteronomy 12:32 dominated not only his view of Scripture but also his concept of reform. At the onset of his public ministry in St. Andrews Castle, he quoted from it: " 'All that the Lord thy God commands thee to do, that do thou to the Lord thy God: add nothing to it; diminish nothing from it.' By this rule, think I, that the Kirk of Christ will measure God's religion, and not by that which seems good in their own eyes."[75] Balnaves' *Treatise on Justification by Faith* (1849), with which Knox agreed, demonstrated a drive for purity

---

72. Mezger, *John Knox et ses rapports avec Calvin*, 76–77; D'Assonville, *Knox and the Institutes*, 71–73.

73. *Works*, 2:111; D'Assonville, *Knox and the Institutes*, 73; McEwen, *The Faith of Knox*, 39–40; Greaves, "The Nature of Authority in the Writings of John Knox," 45–46.

74. *Works*, 2:185; 6:309, 246–47; 5:328–29, 331, 334. These citations are only a few examples.

75. *Works*, 1:197.

of religion.[76] Knox's first theological work, *A Vindication* (1550), quite appropriately brought out this point.[77]

But because Knox made Deuteronomy 12:32 the focal point of his biblical interpretation and a "rule for the Kirk of Christ," his theology acquired its own trademark. This drive evidenced itself particularly in regard to liturgy and ceremony, for here Knox was intolerant of anything not positively approved by Scripture. In this respect Knox demonstrated a radical belief that went beyond even Calvin and Zwingli.[78] The reformer's crusade for purity in worship, drawn largely from the precedents set forth in the Old Testament, ran the course of his career and dominated not only his ministry but much of his religious thought.

In his political thought, Knox relied heavily on the Old Testament.[79] Perhaps it would be unfair to say that he found texts to fit his views, but certainly the Old Testament suited Knox's political beliefs more than did the New Testament. In *A Godly Letter* and *A Faithful Admonition*, the Old Testament references are numerous. Knox alluded to Elisha, Hezekiah, Abraham, Samuel, Phinehas, Jehu, Moses, and Jezebel to name only a few.[80] In *The First Blast*, he referred to Genesis, Deuteronomy, and leaders such as Deborah, Huldah, Josiah, and others.[81] In the context of political thought, Knox fondly cited the prophets for authoritative statements.[82] Most frequently mentioned were Elijah, Amos, and Jeremiah whose cases Knox saw as paralleling his own.[83] But more significant than the number of Old Testament references is the fact that the substance of Knox's political thought originated in the Old Testament.[84]

The obligation to revolt against a ruler who gives a command contrary to God's law is more readily found in the Old Testament than in the

---

76. *Works*, 3:516–17.

77. *Works*, 3:34–35, 37–38, etc.

78. D'Assonville, *Knox and the Institutes*, 70–71; Janton, *Concept et Sentiment*, 174–76.

79. For a complete presentation of the sources of Knox's political thought, see Vesey, "The Sources of the Idea of Active Resistance in the Political Theory of John Knox," 47–227. Vesey contends that the Bible, and particularly the Old Testament, was the source of Knox's political theory.

80. *Works*, 3:165–216, 216, 263–330.

81. *Works*, 4:377–403.

82. *Works*, 2:372–403.

83. *Works*, 1:412; 2:438; 3:170, 234, 245; 4:281, 472–73. This list represents no exact count of references to Jeremiah, but it would seem that Knox cited him the most.

84. Vesey, "The Sources of Knox's Political Theory," 47–227.

New. Related to Knox's political views is his concept of the covenant, and the Hebrew background for this is amply demonstrated.[85] While extracting political theory from the Hebrew prophets can be valid and even commendable, at times Knox's unhistorical and uncritical handling of parts of the Old Testament—such as the sanction of Jehu's bloody deeds—seems rather frightening.

The Old Testament imprint evidenced itself in Knox's application of moral principles. He wanted everyone—particularly Christians—to observe in the literal sense the Mosaic Laws relating to idolatry, adultery, and other crimes disparaging God's glory.[86] For such, the Old Testament punishment of death applies. Though in ways Knox was just a man of his time, it should be noted that in applying God's law, he often lost all perspective of its New Testament modifications. For example, the *Book of Discipline*'s prescription of capital punishment for adultery failed to consider Christ's forgiveness of the adulteress in the eighth chapter of John. But John Knox regarded God as immutable. Therefore, his laws and Word cannot change but must be applied with the same vigor in sixteenth-century Scotland as they had been applied in ancient Israel.[87]

This examination of Knox's view of Scripture has noted his stress on the continuity of the two testaments at the expense of discontinuity. The result of this practice was of no small consequence for Knox's thought. He over-identified the Old Testament with the New, losing sight of the historic process in divine revelation, and thus his theology lacked the Christocentric character found in the religious beliefs of Luther and Calvin.[88]

The New Testament

Despite his overemphasis on the Old Testament, Knox's theology and usage of Scripture contained more balance between the Old and New Testaments than would be expected. New Testament citations in Knox's writings were ample.[89] Knox did not neglect the New Testament. Rather,

---

85. Greaves, "John Knox and the Covenant Tradition," 26–27.
86. *Works*, 4:157; 3:210; 4:500–503; 6:449.
87. *Works*, 6:408; 1:272; 3:247.
88. See also Kyle, "John Knox: A Man of the Old Testament," 65–78.
89. Janton, *John Knox: L' homme et l' oeuvre*, 400. Check this reference for a specific breakdown of the Old and New Testament citations as to men and books. It can be noted that Calvin had a higher ratio of New Testament citations than did Knox. The *Institutes* showed 1,755 citations for the Old Testament and 3,098 for the New. McNeill, *The History and Character of Calvinism*, 213.

he failed to subordinate the Old Testament to the New, as Luther had done. In fact, along with Augustine and Calvin, Knox's thought bore the imprint of the Apostle Paul. Knox's political views were not so biased by the Old Testament that he attempted to establish a theocracy or failed to recognize a civil government in Scotland.[90]

Though he gave a new twist to Romans 13, which commanded all people to be in subjection to the governing authorities, he repeatedly advocated the Pauline concept of obedience to the powers ordained of God. The decree of God established the thrones of all rulers, and thus they must be obeyed in all matters not violating God's law. Knox further used the apostle to condemn female rule and as support for his appeal to civil authorities. In fact, if the Reformation had not been established in Scotland, Knox's model for church-state relationships would have been that of Paul living under Nero—namely, a disestablished church.[91]

Knox paralleled much of the Old Testament with his epoch, but he did not, however, try to apply the institutions regarding salvation, for he recognized the eternal character of the New Testament covenant based on the sacrifice of Christ. Rather, he saw the Old Testament sacrifices as a forerunner of Christ's perfect sacrifice. In *A Vindication*, Knox claimed "the sacrifices of the Old Law were only figures of that very and true sacrifice once offered by Jesus Christ."[92] Moreover, Paul's imprint further evidenced itself in Knox's doctrine of salvation centered in two Pauline concepts: justification by faith but within a predestinarian concept.

Yet in a different way, the mark of the New Testament bore heavily on John Knox. Knox the preacher was also Knox the man and Knox the pastor. In these latter respects the New Testament played a significant role. It is in Knox's letters to Mrs. Bowes that his pastoral side, with its Christological aspects, can be seen. The account of Knox's last days revealed a balanced use of Scripture in his personal life. He read daily some chapters from both the Old and New Testaments. Especially stressed were the Psalms, which he read through every month, and gospel history. When Knox could no longer read, his wife read his favorite passages: John 17, parts of Ephesians, Isaiah 23, 1 Corinthians 15, and Calvin's sermons on Ephesians.[93] Thus it would be accurate to say the Old Testament played a

---

90. *Works*, 2:331–34. See also Kyle, "The Christian Commonwealth: John Knox's Vision for Scotland," 247–59.

91. *Works*, 2:279. See also Kyle, "The Church-State Patterns in the Thought of John Knox," 72–81.

92. *Works*, 3:61; 2:185.

93. *Works*, 6:639, 643, 654. Note the Pauline thrust of the New Testament passages.

dominant role in Knox's thought, but not necessarily a predominant role in his life, nor to the point of relegating the New Testament to a merely peripheral role.

Literal Interpretation

Knox's theological trademark devolved from his interpretation of Scripture. The first feature—as has been noted—is his Old Testament emphasis, and his second trait is a pronounced literalness. Other methods used by Knox included interpretation of unclear passages by the Holy Spirit through clear texts, interpretation by previously established principles, and prophesying and interpretation by the congregation.

But before turning to Knox's hermeneutics, a brief glance at the methods of other Magisterial Reformers would be in order. In general, these reformers emphasized the primacy of the literal sense of Scripture—which related the things done and said in the Bible—as ascertained by a straightforward, natural, and historical approach to the text. This method insisted that interpretation should arise from the text of Scripture itself and not be brought to it from the outside. The goal of this interpretation is to understand what the author of a book meant to say, and he should be comprehended in the straightforward sense unless this method produces manifest nonsense.

The Scottish reformer's hermeneutical principles bore some resemblance to Luther's, but they were closer to those of the Reformed tradition. Luther held to the principles that Scripture interprets itself and that the Bible must be elucidated according to its simple literal sense. Scripture must be interpreted through the perspective of the gospel and is thus Christocentric, that is, centered around Jesus Christ. All of the Bible has a clear meaning in terms of the gospel, and the interpretation of individual passages must be subordinated to the broader meaning of the gospel. Luther always began with the hermeneutical principle that Scripture could not be in conflict with Christ, that is, with the gospel.[94] Knox shared Luther's literalness but not the German reformer's Christocentrism.

---

94. Goldingay, "Luther and the Bible," 35–40; Spitz, "Luther's Sola Scriptura," 740–45; Gerrish, "Biblical Authority and the Continental Reformation," 342–43, 346–47; Althaus, *The Theology of Martin Luther,* 76–80. Luther regarded the Book of Romans as containing the key to the whole Word of God. By the gospel, Luther did not mean the Four Gospels—Matthew, Mark, Luke, and John. Rather, he meant the message of the gospel.

The Word of God and Its Interpretation

Knox and Zwingli interpreted Scripture in a very similar manner. Both believed the Bible to be clear in itself and that difficult passages can be cleared up by reference to other texts. The idea that the church or any person should become the interpreter of the Bible was intolerable to Zwingli, for the Word of God is clear and lucid in and of itself. One only needs to approach the text in the proper frame of mind because Scripture expounds Scripture, and the clearer passages elucidate the meaning of obscure passages. More specifically, in respect to worship—particularly over the use of images—the Zwinglian Reformation used the Bible as a book of precedents interpreted in a spiritualistic way. Though many of Zwingli's doctrines were Christocentric, he was inclined to approach the question of reformation as one of reforming abuses, and so his reading of the Bible tended to have that orientation.[95]

Calvin also asserted a literal interpretation of Scripture and that various parts are mutually explanatory. Self contradictions in the Bible are out of the question and obscure passages resolve themselves by references to clear passages. But Calvin placed more emphasis on the interior witness of the Holy Spirit as the supreme criterion upon which the authority of Scripture is founded than did the other reformers. Not only did the Holy Spirit inspire the authors of Scripture, but he also illuminates the readers of the Bible. The witness of the Spirit adds nothing to Scripture, but it gives the believer certainty as to the meaning of the Bible.[96]

Biblical interpretation can emphasize the substantive content of Scripture or the literal form of the Bible. Luther can be found accentuating the substance of the Bible over the literal form of Scripture. For example, Luther regarded the Bible as God's Word, but because the message of James (with its emphasis on good works) ran counter to what he believed the substance of Scripture to be (gospel and grace), he depreciated that epistle's place in the canon. Calvin, however, maintained a healthy balance between the substance and the letter of the Scriptures. On one hand, Calvin was too conservative to tamper with the letter (e.g., canonicity) of Scripture, but, on the other hand, he assigned primary authority to the substantive content.

Knox in contrast to Luther and Calvin, placed the literal forms of Scripture above the substantive content, particularly in regard to purifying

---

95. Yule, "Continental Patterns and the Reformation in England and Scotland, 308, 311, 317; Locher, *Zwingli's Thought: New Perspectives*, 190; Courvoisier, *Zwingli*, 34; Davies, *The Problem of Authority*, 76–77, 79–80.

96. Gerrish, "Biblical Authority," 355–56; Wendel, *Calvin*, 86, 89–90; Davies, *The Problem of Authority*, 118. For additional information, see Forstman, *Word and Spirit*.

PART ONE: Historical and Theological Foundations

worship. In this respect, Knox largely regarded the Bible as a book of precedents—that is, as containing preceding instances which served as authoritative examples or patterns for future cases that were similar or analogous. Along with Zwingli, Knox's concept of reformation often focused on the problem of reforming abuses in worship. And, as a consequence, he tended to interpret Scripture as if it were a book of literal models.

In this respect, Knox could be called a "radical" reformer who knew no middle way even in what Calvin called "indifferentia."[97] Knox told some women in Edinburgh that in religion there is no middle way. Either it is the religion of God or that of Satan. Everything in religion must have the sanction of Scripture or it is of the devil.[98] Calvin would have agreed with this statement so long as the Scriptures did not become a set of regulations. This danger was ever present in Knox's writings, though in actual deed he often demonstrated flexibility.

Because Knox believed that the plain Scripture—with the aid of the Holy Spirit—was understandable to the average person, he primarily used the literal method for ascertaining the meaning of a particular passage. His 1560 answer to the Anabaptist illustrated this hermeneutical method: "But I delight in nothing so much as the simple and native meaning of the Scriptures, as they be alleged in their own places by the Holy Ghost."[99] Furthermore, Knox expressed his literalness by bombarding readers with phrases such as "the plain Word of God," "the express Word of God," or "the strict Word of God."[100]

Besides, Knox's stress on the literal interpretation lent additional support to the view that he held to the infallibility of Scripture, for often the reformer decided an entire issue by the meaning of a word. Even opponents of this position, such as James McEwen, admit Knox could "hang a whole volume of divinity on the turn of a Biblical phrase."[101] In 1564 William Maitland of Lethington and Knox debated the question of whether a subject could slay a ruler. The debate centered on the story of Jehu as recorded in 2 Kings. Maitland contended that Jehu was a king when he executed judgment on the house of Ahab. Conversely, Knox said Jehu was

---

97. D'Assonville, *Knox and the Institutes*, 69–70.
98. *Works*, 4:232.
99. *Works* 5:261–62.
100. *Works*, 3:35–36, 37–38; 4:437, 468; 5:516.
101. McEwen, *The Faith of Knox*, 39.

a mere servant when he received the command to execute.[102] Thus the reformer used the turn of a passage to support one of his major doctrines.

Interpretation by the Holy Spirit

Inseparably related to the literal interpretation of Scripture was Knox's third major hermeneutical principle—the Holy Spirit's interpretation of ambiguous passages by the use of clear texts. In meeting with Knox, Mary Queen of Scots struck at the Achilles heel of Protestantism by raising the question of whose explanation of the Bible to accept. "You interpret the Scriptures (said she) in one manner, and they interpret in one other; Whom shall I believe? And who shall be the judge."[103]

Knox's answer to the Queen demonstrated that he believed the Bible to be intelligible to all people, and thus the native meaning of the Bible with the aid of the Holy Spirit sufficed. The Holy Ghost had inspired every verse, and as God, he can never be self-contradictory. Therefore, the meaning of vague texts must be in agreement with the interpretation of distinct passages. Given the plain meaning of Scripture and the work of the Holy Spirit in explaining difficult passages, Knox believed only the obstinately ignorant would fail to understand the meaning of biblical passages.[104]

Knox certainly explicated the inner workings of the Holy Spirit, but emphasized the Spirit's work in salvation, sanctification, and the hatred of sin rather than in the work of interpreting Scripture. While he underscored the Spirit's external work—namely, the inspiring of Scripture and speaking through God's messengers, he did not stress the inner witness as Calvin and Bucer did.[105]

Interpretation by Established Principles

Related to Knox's major hermeneutical rules are his methods of interpreting Scripture by his own previously established principles and by the tenets of the Reformed tradition. Knox illustrated the former in his debate

---

102. *Works*, 2:446. For a discussion regarding Knox's relationship with Maitland, see Blake, "Knox and Lethington, 9–20.

103. *Works*, 2:284.

104. Ibid.

105. *Works*, 2:18; 5:102–3; Wendel, *Calvin*, 156–57; Stephens, *The Holy Spirit in the Theology of Martin Bucer* 101ff. On the contrary, McEwen stresses the interior witness of the Spirit in Knox's view of Scripture. See McEwen, *The Faith of Knox*, 38.

with Lethington and in *The First Blast*. In these instances Knox set forth a principle that he skillfully used to his advantage: Was one extraordinary example from Scripture sufficient to establish a law that people should follow? If that example runs contrary to God's law, then it is not a commandment. But if one example agrees with the law, it stands as a commandment. For example, Knox argued that Deborah's extraordinary example did not establish female rule because it contradicted God's law. On the other hand, Jehu's slaying of the king's household agreed with God's general law of putting an idolater to death and was thus an example to follow.[106]

In a dispute, Knox rested his whole case on the belief that true religion can be manifestly known. On the great majority of occasions, he accepted Scripture literally as he demanded others to do. But Knox's literalism fell normally within the framework of Reformed tenets, and when a literal reading of a passage ran counter to this position, he usually opted for his established principles. For instance, the Anabaptist opponent—in the predestination debate—confronted Knox with a verse that presents a problem for many predestinarians: "For he wills the death of no creature, but wills all men to be saved, and to come to a knowledge of the truth."[107] After some verbal quibbling, Knox fell back on his great principle of God's immutability: All people are not saved in fact, and for God to will them to be, would make him a failure or mutable.[108]

Prophesying and Interpretation by the Congregation

Prophesying did not involve predicting the future but rather pertained to interpreting Scripture. And as such had a twofold meaning—namely, meetings in which Scripture was interpreted, and a method or technique that involved exegesis and application, with a particular emphasis on the latter. During the sixteenth century, prophesying was primarily identified with meetings or corporate exercises. Still, the exegetical and application aspects loomed large with Knox, and has been termed as his "prophetic hermeneutic." Prophesying, as practiced in many Reformed churches, was derived from the Pauline text of 1 Corinthians 14: "Let the prophets speak

---

106. *Works*, 2:447, 4:403–4. Other negative examples used by Knox were the cases of the Israelites stealing and having a plurality of wives.

107. *Works*, 5:406.

108. *Works*, 5:406–9. Knox went on for seven pages resorting to basic Calvinistic presuppositions. The crux of the argument was his statement "God wills the death of no creature" was a particular statement referring to a sinner, not to all sinners as the Anabaptist claimed.

two or three, and let the other judge.... For you may all prophesy one by one, that all may learn, and all may be comforted." [109]

It is not clear where the prophesying exercises were first established, but in Zurich—where the term was first encountered—this practice involved academic exercises designed for the systematic exegesis of Scripture. In John a' Lasco's orders for his London church, prophesying took the form of weekly meetings of the congregation with its pastor. At this time, the discussion of doctrine was open to all church members. The English exiles encountered something of the same sort at Geneva, where such meetings were variously called "interpretation of the Scriptures" and "prophecy."[110]

The group or congregation played an important role in Knox's scheme of biblical interpretation. Knox went to great pains to prevent anarchy and subjectivity in scriptural interpretation. The alleged Anabaptist idea that the Holy Spirit might reveal one truth to one person for a certain text and something entirely different to another particularly concerned Knox. He felt that the explanation of the individual must agree with that of the congregation. In fact, the Genevan *Form of Prayers*, *A Letter of Wholesome Counsel*, and the *Book of Discipline* set down similar criteria for group procedures.[111]

Believers were encouraged to have private Bible study daily, but no member was sufficient to read and study Scripture without the help of others.[112] Therefore, a conference or assembly must be held once a week. In the *Book of Discipline* version, believers gathered for prophesying, that is, they employed exercises which elucidated Scripture for the edification of the entire church.[113] Such sessions rigidly applied the Pauline standards of 1 Corinthians 14 directing the interpretation of prophecy plus some of their own regulations. All doctrine and interpretation that came out of

---

109. Collinson, *Elizabethan Puritan Movement*, 168–76.

110. Ibid., 168–77; New, *Anglican and Puritan*, 106–7; Knappen, *Tudor Puritanism*, 253–56.

111. *Works*, 2:242–43; 4:137–39, 179. In Spotiswoode's history similar and identical rules for interpretation can be found. Spotiswoode, *The History of the Church and State in Scotland*, 170–71.

112. *Works*, 4:134–35; 2:240–42.

113. *Works*, 2:242–45, 296–97. Some contemporary theologians interpret 1 Corinthians 14 as referring to prophecy in the sense of a "charismatic utterance" and predicting the future rather than as model for the interpretation of written Scripture. Along with Calvin and others, the sixteenth-century Scots regarded 1 Corinthians 14 as a format for interpreting written Scripture.

these meetings were subject to the authority of the assembly, but within the local church, the ministers and elders made the judgment.[114]

Despite Knox's belaboring that Scripture was plain in itself, he never suggested that the services of the trained exegete and theologian are unimportant. He knew that the ordinary believer may not have either the time or ability to achieve a proper interpretation of the Bible. A major purpose of Knox's educational system was, therefore, to train men for exegeting Scripture. A requirement for the office of minister was that a man be knowledgeable in doctrine and the Bible. Since the Scots regarded the Scripture as a unity of revelation and not as isolated proof texts, a trained theologian was essential in order to interpret individual passages according to the larger principles of Scripture.

Closely related to both Knox's Old Testament emphasis and his pronounced literalness are the exegetical and analogous aspects of prophesying, that is, his "prophetic hermeneutic." This method—employed by the Marian exiles and early Puritans—applied scriptural examples to contemporary affairs and often led to tenuous historical analogies, largely designed to promote current ideas and policies.[115]

Knox's failure to adequately recognize the Bible's discontinuity, not only between the Old and New Testaments—but between biblical history and his day—is related to this peculiar method of interpreting Scripture, called either "prophesying" or the "prophetic hermeneutic." He often transferred people and events from the Old and New Testaments to his own time so literally that historical repetition occurred.[116]

Knox constantly drew parallels between Israel and Scotland and Israel and England—parallels that often go beyond analogies or lessons and seem to become historical equations. For example, in *A Faithful Admonition,* Knox recalled his last sermon preached before King Edward VI

---

114. *Works*, 2:242–45; 4:137–39, 179. Without elaborating on the details of the procedure, several points should be noted. First, the Holy Spirit was called upon to guide the whole process in order to utilize the various gifts of the congregation. Knox did not want any unresolved problems over a biblical text, and if a passage could not be resolved, it must be written down pending its true explanation through God's inspiration. He also stressed a willingness to communicate with anyone who had differences over a text, and thus the interpretation appeared to be a result of communication and cooperation. But when the group reached an explanation it must be accepted by all. In fact, no interpretation could be admitted that disagreed with the principles of the Reformed faith.

115. Vander Molen, "Providence as Mystery, Providence as Revelation," 40; Vander Molen, "Anglican Against Puritan," 47.

116. D'Assonville, *Knox and the Institutes*, 74–75.

in 1553. This sermon, which condemned Edward VI's ungodly ministers, paralleled the wicked ministers of David and Hezekiah with the hidden papists in Edward's ministry. In the story, Old Testament Israel equaled England; Edward VI compared to David; Achitophel became Dudley, Edward's minister; and Shobna corresponded with the Marquess of Winchester, Edward's treasurer.[117] Also in *A Faithful Admonition*, Knox paralleled the English Reformation with the story of the disciples at sea: the calm part of the voyage compared to the rule of Edward VI while the storm corresponded with Mary Tudor's rule and the return of Catholicism.

Knox's 1555 sermon at Frankfurt—when he compared the sin of Noah's son, Canaan, to the difficulties between himself and the advocates of the *Book of Common Prayer*—is another example of this exegetical method. Knox compared situations, and then decided that although Canaan should have been punished for revealing his father's shame, the reformer should speak out against shameful practices within the English church. The analogy between Knox and Noah's son is hardly convincing.[118] Nevertheless, John Knox saw the drama of biblical times, particularly the story of corporate Israel, being reenacted in sixteenth-century England and Scotland.

THE INFLUENCES

Knox's firm views on Scripture and authority emerged at the onset of his ministry and showed little development through the years. However, as his theological thought matured by the late 1550s, and as he got into situations calling for biblical authority, a heightened emphasis can be detected. Among the various influences on Knox's view of Scripture, two stand out—the church fathers and the Swiss reformers. Knox's general view of the Bible resembled those of the fourth and fifth century churchmen.[119] Moreover, his position on the authority of Scripture and the method of its interpretation stood closer to the Swiss reformers—Zwingli and Calvin—than it did to Luther. Certainly, Knox received an introduction to the church fathers in the course of his theological training. Most likely, the early Reformed influence came by way of two sources: Zwingli and Bullinger via George Wishart and Calvin's *Institutes*.

---

117. *Works*, 3:280ff.

118. *Works*, 3:272-90; 4:32. See also *A Brief Discourse of the Troubles Begun at Frankfurt in Germany Anno Domini*, 38-39.

119. Henderson, "John Knox and the Bible," 100.

Part One: Historical and Theological Foundations

Many similarities can be noted between Knox's view of Scripture and that of the church fathers. Knox accepted the biblical narrative as historical, precisely as did Ambrose and Augustine. The doctrines of authority, inspiration, and infallibility of Scripture—which emerged in Knox's thought very early can be found in the writings of Justin, Tertullian, Clement, Irenaeus, and Athanasius. Knox's principle of accepting nothing in religion without biblical warrant can be found in Tertullian's writings. The doctrine of the sufficiency of Scripture, to which Knox adhered, also had precedent with the fathers. Athanasius insisted upon it; Cyril of Jerusalem held to it. The affinities of Knox's view of Scripture with early Christian thought did not stop with authority and inspiration. Knox followed Origen, Irenaeus, and Augustine in his stress upon the plainness and perspicuity of Scripture. And like Augustine, Knox assumed the literal meaning of Scripture, but when obscure passages did arise, he interpreted them in the light of clear passages.[120]

Zwingli tended to view Scripture as a guide for the reform of ecclesiastical abuses to the extent that at times he even looked at the New Testament as a book of precedents for patterns of worship. Luther, in contrast, saw the Bible as containing the gospel and not as a book prescribing standards of worship, and he normally allowed in worship the things not expressly prohibited in Scripture. Knox followed Zwingli on this account, and such a view probably came to Knox via George Wishart. Wishart returned to Scotland from Switzerland in 1543 or 1544 and Knox, in his *History*, identified himself with Wishart by late 1545. Wishart's influence on Knox at this time is generally acknowledged.[121]

In respect to Scripture, such influence is plausible for several reasons. First, Knox's general admiration for Wishart and his teachings is beyond dispute. Second, Wishart, like Knox, greatly emphasized the fundamental authority of Scripture. He defined heresy as false opinion clearly against the Word of God, and since heresy stems from ignorance of the Bible, only God's Word can remedy it. Wishart, in fact, tended to meet accusations leveled against him with confident appeals to the authority of Scripture. Furthermore, Wishart stressed his impotence to teach without the express witness of the Bible. Like Knox, he would accept the authority of general

---

120. Henderson, "Knox and the Bible," 102–9; Greaves, "The Nature of Authority in the Writings of Knox," 37–38.

121. *Works*, 1:137; Reid, *Trumpeter of God*, 27–34; Glick, "Non-Calvinist Influences on the Scottish Reformation," 173–77; Yule, "Continental Patterns and the Reformation in England and Scotland," 308–9, 311, 313–14.

councils only if their decisions accorded with the Bible.[122] Lastly, Wishart translated the *Helvetic Confession* prepared by Bullinger and others. This confession tolerated more in worship that did not have specific biblical sanction than Knox would. Still, this document generally agreed with his views on Scripture. For example, the confession asserted the central authority of Scripture and affirmed the Bible as its own interpreter.

It cannot be certain, but John Hooper—the English reformer—may have been another avenue for Zwingli's views to reach Knox. Hooper had been influenced by many Zwinglian views, and he insisted that nothing should be tolerated in religion without the express warrant of Scripture. Knox certainly came into contact with Hooper's views during his stay in Edwardian England.[123]

Calvin also believed all religious ceremony must have the express warrant of Scripture, but in practice he tended to tolerate matters of indifference more than Zwingli and Knox would.[124] Nevertheless, despite certain differences, the imprint of John Calvin appears on Knox's doctrine of Scripture. Knox did not go to Geneva until 1554, but most certainly Calvin influenced Knox before this date. With five editions of the *Institutes* (1536, 1539, 1541, 1543, and 1545) in print before the start of Knox's public ministry in 1547, it is improbable that he failed to acquaint himself with the contents.

In fact, Knox's first ministry at St. Andrews bore the mark of Reformed theology generally—and perhaps Calvin specifically—regarding the administration of communion, idolatry, and the authority of Scripture.[125] More directly, in his first sermon, Knox said the mark of the true church is to be "the voice of its own pastor, Jesus Christ"—meaning the Word.[126] In the first edition of the *Institutes*, Calvin also stated a mark of the true church to be the Word—the voice of the "Good Shepherd," Jesus Christ.[127] Pierre Janton parallels some of Knox's early works with the

---

122. *Works*, 1:150-65.

123. Laing, ed., *The Miscellany of the Wodrow Society*, 1:11-12; Greaves, "The Nature of Authority in the Writings of John Knox," 39-40; Locher, *Zwingli's Thought*, 364-65.

124. An example of Knox's tolerating matters of indifference is found in his "Epistle to the Congregation of Berwick, 1552," 261-64. Here Knox permitted kneeling at the Lord's Supper providing it did not signify adoration of the elements. See chapter 6 for more details.

125. *Works* 1:189-203.

126. *Works*, 1:190.

127. Calvin, *The Institutes of Christian Religion*, 4.11.4. The notation used here and

Institutes and concludes that Calvin influenced Knox in regard Scripture, authority, and the canon prior to his first trip to Geneva.[128]

Of more importance are the affinities between Knox and Calvin in regard to the Word. To be sure, they had differences already mentioned but a list of their agreements is impressive. Not only did they both uphold so unconditionally the supreme authority of Scripture, but they also believed the words of the Bible to be inspired. They interpreted the Bible literally, and while normally the plain Scripture sufficed—in the case of problem passages—they held that the Bible interpreted itself by means of a clear text. Knox and Calvin placed the Word before the church and not the reverse: the church did not interpret the Word, but rather the Word established the church and was one of its marks. Both reformers based their entire theology on Scripture.

---

in further references to the *Institutes* refers to book 4, chapter 11, section 4. See also D'Assonville, *Knox and the Institutes*, 2–3, 68.

128. *Works*, 3:201; Janton, *Concept et Sentiment*, 174; Reid, *Trumpeter of God*, 75.

3

God and His Work in the World

As A MAN OF action, John Knox did not write about abstract theological doctrine. Therefore, he had little to say about the Godhead or the relationship of the three persons to each other. In fact, as a man of the Old Testament, he focused on the nature of God and his activity in the world. Knox's perception of God's work in the world, especially his sovereign control over all activities, rested on his view of God's nature—namely, his omnipotence and immutability. While the Scots reformer was thoroughly orthodox, his Old Testament orientation led him to write far less about Jesus Christ and the Holy Spirit. Moreover, the Trinity was not a major issue in Scotland or in the Reformation generally. On this account, the Church of Rome was orthodox and Knox concerned himself with fighting Catholic doctrine at variance with Protestant theology. Even more so, he tended to focus on Catholic practices which he regarded as abomination to God. So except for castigating Radical reformers and some sectaries, condemned by Catholics and Protestants alike, Knox did not address Trinitarian issues.[1]

However, Knox's view of God—like his interpretation of Scripture—became a driving force in his vocation as a prophet and reformer of religion. His belief that an omnipotent and immutable God could not change fueled his condemnation of Catholicism as idolatry. His providential view of history saw God as determining all human events from the largest to the

---

1. Knox made few references to the Trinity and Trinitarian doctrine. One such reference was his summary of Servetus' position on the subject. See *Works*, 5:226. In addition, Knox in his summary of *Balnaves on Justification by Faith* omitted all the references to the Trinity. Cf. *Works*, 3:13 with 3:40.

smallest. Such thinking drove his desire to purify religion and overthrow the Catholic faith in Scotland and elsewhere.

THE TRINITY

Knox's views on the Trinity must be derived mainly from the confessional statements he approved. The *Scots Confession* described God as "eternally infinite, immeasurable, incomprehensible, omnipotent, invisible: one in substance, and yet distinct in three persons, the Father, the Son, and the Holy Ghost."[2] The confession characterized Christ as "very God and very man," having "two perfect natures."[3] The document also stressed that the wonderful conjunction between the Godhead and manhood in Jesus Christ does proceed from the eternal and immutable decree of God. Moreover, the confession repudiated the heresies of Arias, Marcion, Eutyches, Nestorius, and others that either denied or confounded the eternity of Christ's Godhead or the validity of his human nature.[4] In addition to confirming the eternal Godhead in familiar terms, the *Book of Common Order* spoke of Christ as being conceived by the Holy Ghost and born of a virgin. The *Book of Common Order* also confirmed the Holy Spirit as God equal to the Father and Son and as proceeding from the Father and Son.[5]

The orthodoxy of Knox's Trinitarian doctrine is obvious. He played a major role in the formation of the eminently authoritative *Scots Confession* and the *Book of Common Order*, which contained Trinitarian doctrine. Earlier he had listed the 14 points against Servetus and acknowledged them as heresy. In support of Calvin, Knox declared Servetus' denial of the Trinity to be blasphemy. In his tract on predestination, Knox said that Servetus was not persecuted but suffered a lawful death for blasphemy as set down in Deuteronomy 13.[6] Finally, in *The Appellation* Knox fully accepted the doctrine of the four early councils as being in complete harmony with the Scripture and thus of equal authority with the Four Evangelists.[7] These

---

2. *Works*, 2:97.

3. *Works*, 2:99

4. *Works*, 2:99–100.

5. *Works*, 6:318–19, 322. The *Book of Common Order* confessed the Holy Spirit as springing from the Father and the Son. So did the *Westminster Confession* of 1647, but the *Scots Confession* of 1560 did not. *Works*, 2:103–4; Cowan, *John Knox*, 233.

6. *Works*, 5:226–29. Knox said Servetus was executed simply because God commanded death for blasphemy. In this statement, Knox's emphasis on the letter of the law, rather than on any theological substance, is evident.

7. *Works*, 4:518–19. See also 6:362–63.

councils formulated the doctrines of the Trinity and Christ's nature as accepted by both Catholics and Protestants alike.

THE NATURE OF GOD

Knox's concept of God did not differ significantly from Luther's, Calvin's, and Zwingli's ideas of God. In this regard, the reformers agreed more than they disagreed, and their differences were more a matter of emphasis than direct discord. All—to some degree—held God to be the infinite, omnipotent, sovereign creator, and presently active sustainer of the universe. They attributed such qualities to God as love, anger, mercy, justice, holiness, immutability, and omnipotence. Knox, to no surprise, closely resembled especially Calvin and Zwingli in his concept of God.

Divine Immutability

A focal point of Knox's thought, particularly his political thought, was his concept of God. In his *History*, Knox clearly rejected the concept that limited God to heaven or had him quiescent.[8] Rather, the God of John Knox intervened in human affairs; nothing transpires in history that God has not ordained because his providence encompasses all events. As the sovereignty of God dominated Calvin's thought, the immutability of God reigned supreme in Knox's thinking. Though immutability is but an aspect of divine sovereignty, such a modification can be seen as a shift in emphasis between Knox and Calvin. As one reads Knox's writings, the immutability of God pervades nearly every aspect of his thought. In fact, Knox regarded any attempt to make God mutable as tantamount to denying God.[9]

Without divine immutability, Knox's thought on history, predestination, providence, idolatry, the punishment of sin, political matters, and virtually everything else has little basis. Indeed, as Knox noted often, the law of God never changes. Therefore, God must respond to sin in the same manner in Scotland as he did at Sodom and Gomorrah, or anywhere. The justice of God is infinite and immutable, and what he damned in one place

---

8. *Works*, 1:12. See also Kyle, "The Divine Attributes in John Knox's Concept of God," 161–72.

9. *Works*, 3:191, 247, 358; 4:399, 478; 5:26–27, 33, 287, 315; 6:408. Knox, "Epistle to the Congregation of Berwick, 1552," 254–55. It would be difficult to exaggerate the emphasis Knox placed on the doctrine of immutability.

cannot be excused in another.[10] For example, in 1554 Knox comforted his brethren in England by declaring that because God is immutable, he would stir up another Jehu against their idolatrous rulers.[11]

On occasions, Knox saw God as responding to a situation in the same way at all times, and consequently somewhat of a prisoner of his own nature. Thus the stress on God's immutability led the Scots reformer to demand that God's law be upheld in the Commonwealth of Scotland as if it were Old Testament Israel. Next, it inclined Knox to parallel events and people from the Old and New Testaments with events and his people of his time so literally that history seemed to be reenacted. Finally, God's immutability played a central role in the reformer's scheme of salvation. In his tract concerning predestination, Knox said God's love toward his elect—those predestined to eternal salvation—is immutable. Consequently, those elected can never fall out of divine love nor be eternally lost. Election had taken place in God's eternal council and therefore could not change.[12]

Notwithstanding Knox's all-prevailing affirmation of divine immutability, exceptions and even apparent contradictions to this doctrine could be found in his writings. In the heat of controversy, the reformer admitted that God cannot be bound by his own laws. For instance, in *The First Blast* (1558), such an exemption appeared in the reformer's attempt to explain exceptions to God's general prohibition against the role of women in government: "For God being free, may, for such causes as be approved by his inscrutable wisdom, dispense with the rigor of his law, and may use his creatures at his pleasure."[13] What this statement does to the concept of immutability is uncertain. In some passages dealing with practical problems, Knox did not always make clear which laws are moral and thus immutable and which laws are a matter of administration.

Divine Omnipotence and Sovereignty

Though Knox emphasized divine immutability, he did not neglect the other attributes of God. As expected, these distinctions were those most

---

10. *Works*, 3:171, 191; 4:399; 6:408.
11. *Works*, 3:247.
12. *Works*, 5:44–51.
13. *Works*, 4:404. For a similar statement see *Works*, 4:375. The Bible speaks of God repenting toward Saul. In his letters to Mrs. Bowes, Knox noted that such a statement does not represent divine mutability, but rather God simply subjecting himself to human languages in order to help human understanding.

readily found in the Old Testament. In the reformer's mind, the omnipotence and sovereignty of God ranked second only to his immutability.[14] These attributes emerge most often in the context of Knox's predestination tract, where the reformer declared God demonstrated his omnipotence in the battle with Satan—whose purpose God constantly frustrates. What seems at times as a victory for Satan is only an appearance, "for God is omnipotent, and is compelled to suffer nothing which he has not appointed in his eternal counsel...."[15] In 1548, Knox wrote to the congregation at St. Andrews that God uses the forces and circumstances destroying the just for his glorification and for the profit of his congregation. For example, when Joseph's brothers sold him into slavery, God thwarted the evil purpose of Satan by making Joseph second only to Pharaoh.[16]

Knox believed that all events are ordained by an omnipotent, immutable God whose eternal will and purpose cannot be frustrated by any creature, whether human or angelic. Knox apparently did not use the word *sovereign* in reference to God, but in the political arena this attribute was certainly what the reformer implied. In his 1561 confrontation with Queen Mary, he said, "My travail is that both princes and subjects obey God."[17] The Scots reformer desired God's sovereignty to be established in a real sense in Scotland, but he did not present God as a capricious tyrant. In *An Answer*, Knox condemned theologians of the Nominalist school for such a view of God: "So do they teach us a certain end why he does this or that...." Rather, for this imagination of the absolute power of God, "which the Schoolman [sic] have invented, is in execrable blasphemy...." They are saying God was "a tyrant that appointed things [not] to equity, according to his inordinate appetite."[18]

Other Divine Attributes

Closely related to the distinctions of immutability and omnipotence is the feature of divine prescience. Knox saw divine prescience as far more than

---

14. *Works*, 1:23; 3:5–8, 84; 5:33, 133, 390; 6:415.

15. *Works*, 5:103. In the same context Knox said that the Godhead is free from passions. God is omnipotent and when the Holy Ghost used phrases such as "God suffers" or "sorrows," God was simply subjecting himself to human languages in order to help human understanding.

16. *Works*, 3:5–8.

17. *Works*, 2:283.

18. *Works*, 5:39.

mere foreknowledge. Rather, he believed that in God's eyes, all things that have been or ever will be are perpetually present. To God's eternal knowledge, nothing is past or future; all things are present—not in the sense of Platonic imaginations, but present in actuality. In *An Answer*, Knox wrote, "But we say that all things be so present before God, that he does contemplate and behold them in their verity and perfection."[19]

In addition, the God of John Knox evidenced the human characteristics of wrath, jealousy, mercy, justice, goodness, and love. Knox in the role of an Old Testament prophet, continually pronounced the threats and wrathful judgments of God against realms and nations to whom God's Word had been offered and rejected.[20] For instance, in *A Godly Letter* (1554), he saw plagues as a result of divine vengeance because God's law is universal and his judgments come upon all nations rebelling against this law. God's reprisals come both in this life, usually in the form of plagues, and in the world to come.[21]

Surprisingly, Knox's thought contained many of the softer attributes of God usually identified with the New Testament, but certainly found in the Old as well. In 1554, he described God as a merciful God who promises to show mercy on the nation and individual that repents. Knox, however, usually mentioned mercy as something bestowed on the elect—for as his predestination tract pointed out, the elect are the object of God's goodness and love.[22] God is good to Abraham's seed, and he demonstrates this goodness in his loving providence. But if God's love is both immutable and directed toward the elect, Knox made no mention of God's loving the entire world or lavishing mercy upon the reprobate.[23]

Furthermore, God's will, as Knox saw it, is ultimately inscrutable to human reason and free of restraints. Whether Knox was influenced in this regard by Nominalism via Calvin is uncertain. But when the Anabaptist adversary pressed him on matters of providence, election, and particularly reprobation—the Scottish reformer described divine will as hidden and incomprehensible to human understanding.[24] Besides, Knox's God is free—free not only from his own laws but also from the laws of nature. In

---

19. *Works*, 3:35.

20. *Works*, 3: 165–66. See also Kyle, "John Knox: A Man of the Old Testament," 65–78; Kyle, "Prophet of God: John Knox's Self-Awareness," 85–101.

21. *Works*, 3:170–71.

22. *Works*, 3:140, 168, 320.

23. *Works*, 5:504, 47–48, 51.

24. *Works*, 4:374; 5:41, 310.

debating the Anabaptist opponent on reprobation, Knox declared God to be free in the sense that he is not subject to the laws of nature, nor to any human will.[25]

Knox's notion of God was not primarily philosophical. For example, in *An Answer*, he vehemently refused to compare divine providence with Stoical necessity or divine prescience with Platonic forms.[26] He derived his concept of God from the Bible interpreted according to the principles of the Reformed tradition, that is, the rules of belief generally derived from the Zwinglian and Calvinist reformations.

Though Knox constantly related Scripture to divine immutability, omnipotence, and prescience, he seldom defended those attributes with Scripture: he assumed them. He moved from these suppositions to Scripture, building belief and practice on the assumption plus Scripture. For example, when the 1558 *Appellation* advocated an appeal to the civil magistrates for the correction of religious abuses—Knox based two biblical examples upon the principle of immutability: "lawful it is to the servants of God, opposed by tyranny, to seek remedy . . . by imploring the help of Civil Magistrates." Indeed, "what God has approved in Jeremiah and Paul, he can [not] condemn" when others make such a request.[27]

PROVIDENCE

The notion of providence concerns God's permanent and universal activity in the world. God not only created the world, but having once created it, he remains its absolute master, takes an interest in it, intervenes in it at any moment, and abandons none of his power to the play of natural laws or chance. This definition describes the idea—common to Luther, Calvin, Zwingli, Bucer, and Knox—of the continuous action of God in the midst of his creation. In contrast other reformers—such as Luther's successor, Philip Melanchthon—allowed for a large element of contingency in life.[28]

Knox spoke most directly to the issue of divine providence in his 1560 treatise concerning predestination. In fact, he viewed predestination as an aspect of divine providence. In this treatise, in which Calvin

---

25. *Works*, 5:80–84.
26. *Works*, 5:33–35.
27. *Works*, 4:478.
28. Wendel, *Calvin*, 177–78; Hunter, *The Teaching of Calvin*, 142; Niesel, *The Theology of Calvin*, 61–79. Knox did not separate providence and predestination, but for the sake of organization this study will do so.

emerged as the dominant influence, Knox defined God's providence as "that sovereign empire and supreme dominion, which God always keeps in the government of all things in heaven and earth contained."[29] Knox along with Calvin eliminated all chance from the universe and rejected the notion that God's predestination and providence resembles the fatal necessity of pagan Stocism. The Scottish reformer affirmed God as Lord, Moderator, and Governor of all things—concluding that God's providence not only governs the heaven and earth and all insensible creatures but all the wills and counsels of human beings, "so that they tend and are led to the scope and end which he has proposed."[30]

Knox labeled as blasphemy any attempt to ascribe to stoical necessity the work of God's providence. Necessity did not make the plagues against Pharaoh nor transform Nebuchadnezzar into a beast nor compel Cyrus to destroy Babylon and proclaim liberty for God's people. These and other events proceeded from God's eternal counsel and immutable decree.[31] Furthermore, Knox said God's providence does not fail in its purpose: all the universe—including the sun, moon, and stars—obeys God and all creatures execute his commandments, and nothing transpires contrary to the will of God.[32]

In the eyes of Knox, divine providence works three ways. First, God governs all creatures according to the condition and properties with which he created them. This governance, which Knox called nature, receives little interference from God once it is set in motion. The second and broader manner of God's providence concerns humanity and the elements of nature in general. Here more divine intervention, both direct and indirect, is evident. This category includes the governance and chastisement of his faithful servants and general good gifts to all people—namely, as rain, heat, wind, fair weather, and the fruits of the earth. Prosperity, adversity, abundance, hunger, war and peace are all the works of God. The creatures producing these results are but inferior causes and agents to execute God's will, and God uses as instruments not only insensible creatures and human beings but even devils and Satan himself. For example, God used the Egyptians and Assyrians to punish his people and Satan to punish Saul.

---

29. *Works*, 5:35. See Kyle, "John Knox's Concept of Providence and Its Influence on His Thought," 395–410.

30. *Works*, 5:32.

31. *Works*, 5:35. Knox's Anabaptist opponent called divine providence and predestination "Stoical Neccessity." But even Melanchthon objected to determinism as "Stoic fatalism." See Manschreck, *Melanchthon*, 293.

32 *Works*, 5:172.

God and His Work in the World

The third type of divine operation consists of God's governance to the elect, in whom his Holy Spirit dwells. Knox believed that God works in the elect directing them to perform his will and purpose. God illumines them, draws them closer to himself, regenerates them, gives them the desire to pray, and helps them to resist Satan.[33]

The Scots reformer categorically denied that God can have two wills—both a decretal or absolute will and a permissive or contingent will. God absolutely decrees everything, and there can be no distinction between this absolute will and those things that do not externally appear to be God's will. God wills mercy, injustice, temperance, chastity, and all other things he desires his elect to manifest. On the other hand, God wills cruelty, injustice, excess, filthy life, and blindness for sin. This last category especially applies to the reprobate, not only for punishment, but also for God's own wise ends.[34]

Knox accepted Augustine's notion regarding God's active role in evil and rejected Julian's position that God passively suffers evil against his will but causes none himself. The wicked are not merely given over to their own sins. Rather, the power of God compels them to sin.[35] God did more than passively allow Job to be plagued and Israel and Judah to suffer destruction. Accordingly, the Scots reformer underlined the point that God does not speak of permission, but about his active tearing down. Thus, in the mind of John Knox no room existed for the permissive will of God. To support this contention he quoted Isaiah 5: "I will plainly declare unto you what I will do in my vineyard; I shall take away the hedge of it, I shall break down the wall, that it may be trodden upon: I shall make it waste: and shall also so forbid the clouds that they shall neither send down rain nor moisture upon it."[36]

Yet in a different sense God does have two wills: the first for communication with himself to constantly manifest his glory; and the second for communication with his instruments in charge of his glory. These wills, the revealed and unrevealed, might seem to be contradictory, but Knox used the example of Abraham and Isaac to illustrate that they are not. Outwardly the revealed will of God seemed to instruct Abraham to slay Isaac, but as is known, God stayed Abraham's hand and prevented this deed.

---

33. *Works*, 5:169–77. See also *Works*, 5:21, 86; 4:112; 6:362. God even preserved the angels.

34. *Works*, 5:367–68.

35. *Works*, 5:332.

36. *Works*, 5:334.

Did God change his mind or is there a discrepancy between the revealed and unrevealed will of God? Knox emphatically said no to both possibilities. Because God is immutable, his eternal counsel cannot change. In *An Answer*, Knox asks if "God in his eternal counsel determined that Abraham should kill his son" as Abraham so understood? Whoever dare affirms so "makes God subject to mutability, and denies him to be God, whose wisdom, knowledge, purpose, and counsels be stable, and appointed for all eternity."[37]

God's providence encompasses all creatures and includes both punishment and general good. Yet Knox underscored God's providence to the kirk and the elect. According to the *Scots Confession* of 1560—God preserves, instructs, and honors the church in all ages from Adam to the second coming of Christ.[38] In both an exhortation to England (1559) and in a sermon on Isaiah, Knox claimed God has sustained, fed and clothed the seed of Abraham—which includes the Church of Scotland—throughout history. God made a covenant with Abraham, and because God is good and immutable, his care remains constant. When God makes a covenant with any realm or nation, he becomes to them a conductor, teacher, protector, and father. Moreover, this preservation of Abraham's seed has not always been by natural means because—as Knox points out—God prepared a whale for Jonah, fed Israel in the wilderness, and protected the three Jews in the furnace.[39]

CONCEPT OF HISTORY

The Protestant Reformation restored a sense of dynamism and divine purpose to history at a time in European development when this meaning was in danger of being lost. The immediate result of this renewal was to instill several generations of Protestants with a fresh interpretation of the past and a vivid sense of historical destiny. The unanticipated and perhaps undesired result was the modern idea of progress—the secular shell of the Augustinian-Protestant concept of history with the religious core removed.[40]

---

37. *Works*, 5:314–15.
38. *Works*, 2:98–99.
39. *Works*, 4:112; 5:504; 6:251.
40. Harbinson, "History and Destiny," 395; Harbinson, *Christianity and History*, 271. See Kyle, "John Knox's Concept of History, 5–19.

God and His Work in the World

John Knox, though certainly not the pivotal figure in this development, nevertheless contributed to this process—particularly in the restoration of dynamism and divine purpose to history. This contribution, notwithstanding, the primary value in examining Knox's concept of history is that it pervaded most aspects of his thought and served as an important source of motivation in his drive to establish Protestantism in Scotland.

Knox did not organize his ideas in most areas of his thought. Consequently, despite authoring a major work of history, he did not formulate a precise philosophy of history. His notion of history, therefore, must be reconstructed from not only his *History* but also from his other writings. Along with most Protestant figures, the Scots reformer believed history to be providential, dynamic, linear, apocalyptic, and containing a sense of mystery. Nevertheless, God's providential role in history, and a sense of an apocalyptic struggle throughout the ages clearly dominated Knox's historical thought. Because the apocalyptic has a predestinarian twist—a sense of God's determining a cosmic conflict between good and evil—the providential element logically took precedence over the apocalyptic in Knox's concept of history.

These two components—the providential and apocalyptic—were largely an outgrowth of Knox's personal experiences and religious faith. In fact, David Murison contends that Knox's *History* is a volume of selective and frequently impressionistic memoirs, a trait not unknown among Scottish historians of the sixteenth century.[41]

Personal experiences, to a considerable extent, shaped Knox's apocalyptic worldview. His powerful sense of vocation (e.g. his identification with the prophetic tradition) and persecution at the hands of Catholic powers (e.g., Wishart's death, the stay in a French galley, and Mary Tudor's oppression) all combined to produce in Knox's historical thought some marks of the apocalyptic tradition—namely a polarized view of the universe with a sense of struggle and a recurring pattern of history.

To even a greater degree, Knox's notion of history was derived from and largely dependent on his religious faith—that is, his concepts of God, providence, predestination, the covenant, Scripture, and the Christian commonwealth—and on his hermeneutical principles. This relationship of faith and history, however, does not imply that other sources (e.g. Martin Luther, John Calvin, and the English Protestant apocalyptic tradition) did not influence—directly or indirectly—Knox's notion of history.

---

41. Shaw, *Reformation and Revolution*, 42–43.

Part One: Historical and Theological Foundations

Providential Component

Knox's concept of history virtually depended upon his understanding of God's nature and work in the universe because a providential view of history was the centerpiece of his historical thought. Utterly convinced of the sovereignty of God over all history, the reformer thus believed all events—from the largest to the smallest—to be decreed by God for reasons known only to himself. Along with the vast majority of the religious figures of his time, Knox knew nothing of a "watchmaker" God—a God who set the universe into motion and then merely let it run. The Scottish reformer's doctrine of absolute providence demanded that he maintain a philosophy of history in which the hand of God intervened in all events.

Still, Knox was no fool in this regard for he also recognized that events had secondary causes (i.e., human beings), and he knew the importance of worldly considerations to these weak instruments of the Lord. For example, in a note to England written in 1550 requesting money for the Congregation, he said that dire poverty had weakened the Scottish Protestants to the extent of making them susceptible to French overtures. "France seeks all means to make them friends, and to diminish our number."[42]

Yet the victory was always God's. Knox had a single tract-philosophy of history—the hearts of human beings, their thoughts, and their actions were in the hands of God. Thus—along with Calvin, Zwingli, Bucer, and Luther—Knox strongly perceived a divine ordering to history. Nevertheless, this statement is not to imply that the Scottish reformer saw history as a manifestly clear process. The reader of Knox's *History* can detect the sense of mystery that he held in the relationship of God to history, for after all, the reformer believed the ways of God to be inscrutable to human beings.[43]

Knox's providential view of history raises several related questions. He tended to compare rather rigidly the contemporary churches in England and Scotland to biblical Israel and to certain periods in church history.

42. *Works*, 6:80; Lee, "John Knox and His History," 78–88.

43. Such a providential view of history was not automatic for the sixteenth century. Melanchthon placed much less stress on the providential element in history. Several Scottish contemporaries, George Buchanan (1506–82), John Leslie (1526), and Robert Lindsay (1532?–78) made an attempt at historical writing. Though the purpose for their histories differed from that of John Knox's *History*, none of these writers said much about the hand of God intervening in the events of history. See Buchanan, *The History of Scotland*, 1:310–11; Leslie, *The History of Scotland*, 1:xvii; 2:223; Lindsay, *The Historic and Chronicles of Scotland*, 1:cxlviii, cxliv.

Did history, therefore, become another source of revelation for Knox, as it appears to have become for some later Puritans such as Thomas Beard, author of *Theatre of God's Judgments* (1597)? In other words, because all events are the result of divine activity, does history reveal the "counsels of God?"[44]

Though Calvin emphasized that all events are derived from God's actions, only God knows the ultimate meanings of these occurrences. Human beings cannot interpret God's "end" and "method" by observing events because divine providence is essentially a mystery. Moreover, Calvin limited "true" knowledge of God to special revelation based on faith and Scripture.[45]

The Anglican leaders, among the Marian exiles, unintentionally took the first steps toward transmuting Calvin's "mysterious providence" into a form of divine revelation. These Anglicans took much of the mystery out of providence by identifying English history, including the development of their religious establishment, as God's action in history. Beard went much further toward explaining God's particular actions by developing a view of providence and history as special revelation.[46]

The roots of this development can be found in the Puritans' habit of turning to historical analogy as a means to promote their policies—that is, the exegetical technique of "prophesying," which applied scriptural examples to contemporary affairs.[47] Though Knox employed rigid historical analogies, to argue his point—as did many of the early Puritan leaders—this usage did not lead him to conclude that because history revealed God's actions, it was special revelation.

First, Knox regarded God's work, as recorded in the Bible, as special revelation but not necessarily his subsequent actions in non-biblical history. The reformer's unshakeable belief in divine immutability led him to predict a reenactment of portions of Old Testament history in contemporary England and Scotland, but such perceived repetition did not mean that Knox regarded this history as special revelation. Next, Knox, perhaps more than any major reformer, demanded that all areas of religion conform to God's Word, which was primarily found in Scripture. The Frankfurt Anglicans contended that what Scripture did not ordain in

---

44. *Works*, 3:273-89; Vander Molen, "Providence as Mystery, Providence as Revelation," 27-47.

45. Calvin, *The Institutes of Christian Religion*, 1.16; 2.4; 6.1-3.

46. Beard, *The Theatre of God's Judgments*.

47. Vander Molen, "Providence as Mystery," 40.

their religious institutions was shaped by God over the course of English history. Knox fiercely opposed this adiaphoristic doctrine that permitted "things indifferent" so long as no biblical mandate was violated. Rather, the reformer demanded that religious practice have the express command of Scripture before it could be employed.[48]

Third, Beard's approach to history helped insert the Weber-Tawney thesis, also called the prudential view of providence, into Calvinist thought. According to this view, while the poor can be held in distain because they are out of favor with God, the successful can be perceived as obtaining God's favor.[49] This issue will be encountered later, but Knox did not uphold a concept of history that would support the Weber-Tawney thesis.[50] Fourth, though Knox believed God to be at work in England and Scotland, the reformer was too much of an internationalist (he lived and traveled in several European countries) and too much of an ecumenist (he fellowshipped with most Christians except Catholics and Anabaptists) to view any national history as a primary repository of divine providence.[51] Lastly, though Knox drew rigid historical analogies from Scripture—it would be anachronistic to impose a later development upon him, for he still maintained a sense of mystery in respect to the divine providence in history.

Apocalyptic Component

The second major motif in Knox's concept of history was his apocalyptic thought. Knox's historical thought never separated the providential and apocalyptic elements—they were intertwined throughout his writings with the former as the logical cause of the latter. Nevertheless, a strong providential view of history does not demand an equally significant interest in the apocalyptic tradition. For example, despite Calvin's emphasis on a sovereign God dynamically working his will in history, the reformer

---

48. *Works*, 1:192, 194; 3:34–35, 38, 44, 46, 48–52, 54–61, 119–60, 339, 345, 357, 371, 384–85, 389; 4:373–420, 433–59, 467–523, 528. This theme pervades Knox's writings and there are many more examples.

49. Tawney, *Religion and the Rise of Capitalism*, 219–26; Weber, *The Protestant Ethic and the Spirit of Capitalism*, 11.

50. *Works*, 2:211; 3:13,366, 374; 4:433; 5:425; 6:252; Maccuum, *John Knox*, 33; Janton, *Concept et Sentiment*, 69–86.

51. Reid, *Trumpeter of God*, 1–3; Greaves, "The Knoxian Paradox," 85–98.

God and His Work in the World

generally maintained an anti-apocalyptic bias—i.e., his eschatology remained moderate and non-speculative.[52]

English apocalyptic thought generally contained three characteristics: a polarized view of the universe, a catastrophic explanation of events, and a firm concern with prophecy as its fulfillment.[53] The first two traits loomed the largest in Knox's thought, though the third was not absent. He wrote no commentaries on Daniel and Revelation, nor on any books of the Bible for that matter, nor a history that dealt with periods of church history from the ascension of Christ. Yet he cast the present into the apocalyptic context of the final battle between two armies. These two armies had battled through history, but in Knox's time they were embodied in the Protestant and Catholic churches, that is, the "true" and "malignant" churches.[54]

As a man of the present, Knox focused his attention on the contemporary manifestation of this "evil" army—namely the Roman papacy—which he denounced as the Antichrist.[55] The Scots reformer also saw the return of Christ and judgment as impending, but he was not obsessed with this line of thought for there remained the task of establishing Protestantism in Scotland. Nevertheless, in speaking of the last days, Knox demonstrated the clear linear movement of history toward its divinely appointed end.[56]

Other Components

Though not as prominent as his notions of divine providence and the apocalyptic, Knox's concepts of the church, the covenant, and the purification of religion also affected his historical thinking. The church of John Knox often changed in response to historical situations, but his themes of the continuous church and the small flock related to his historical thought. Actually, these themes also can be regarded as an aspect of his apocalyptic thought. In an attempt to legitimatize the Reformed kirk to a Jesuit in

52. Quistorp, *Calvin's Doctrine of the Last Things*, 158–62; Holwerda, ed., *Exploring the Heritage of John Calvin*, 110, 127–28, 131.

53. Christianson, *Reformers and Babylon*, 8–9; Firth, *The Apocalyptic Tradition in Reformation Britain*, 42–47. See also Ball, *A Great Expectation*, 1–14.

54. *Works*, 1:33, 398–99, 413; Bale, "The Image of Both Churches," preface.

55 *Works*, 3:3, 81, 190–91; 2:543; 3:24; 4:446, 470, 511, 513; 6:12, 192, 400–402; Watt, *John Knox in Controversy*, 13; Froom, *The Prophetic Faith of Our Fathers*, 2:450–55.

56. *Works*, 3:231, 241–44, 288; 4:262, 303–5; 6:494–95. See Kyle, "John Knox and Apocalyptic Thought," 449–69.

1568, Knox argued that all aspects of the faithful, "true" church of his day formed a continuous line with the faithful in Israel. On the other hand, Israel had its unfaithful, false prophets, and idolaters—and such people formed a direct, continuous line with the Church of Rome in Knox's day.[57]

Knox's favorite expression of the visible church was the suffering small flock consisting primarily of the elect. Throughout history this church manifested several outward forms, but it was God's instrument in the cosmic struggle with Satan throughout the ages, and as such, played a key role in Knox's apocalyptic view of history.[58] The reformer's concept of the covenant also related to his historical thought. The "Deuteronomic view of history" is used in Old Testament studies to refer to an interpretation of events as being either favorable or unfavorable to Israel in direct relationship to its faithfulness to the covenant with God. The translators of the Geneva Bible, in a similar manner, read into their annotations their own view of history: the English nation—in covenant with God—would be blessed or cursed just as Israel, that is, in direct correspondence with the nation's faithfulness and obedience to the laws of God.[59]

John Knox was one of these translators and thus maintained a view of history similar to his colleagues. In drawing analogies between Israel and either England or Scotland, the Scottish reformer believed these nations would be judged in accordance to their faithfulness to the covenant. He did not, however, regard either England or Scotland as "chosen" nations, and again, he was too much of an internationalist to limit the covenant obligations to these nations. In fact, Knox did not push the idea of the covenanted nation extensively.[60]

The Scots reformer viewed history largely as a perpetual conflict between two churches and two armies. The "true" church fought to exterminate idolatry and to purify religion. As a consequence, Knox—portraying himself as a Hebrew prophet—depicted the Scottish Reformation as a reenactment of Israel's struggle against idolatry. Not surprisingly, this theme of a vigorous conflict against idolatry (i.e., Catholicism)—whether implicit or overt—permeated nearly page of his *History* in many different and unrelated contexts. Knox did not define idolatry in the strict literal sense of substituting a false god for a true god. Rather, the reformer

---

57. *Works*, 3:231, 239; 4:481, 487, 513; 6:309, 311, 315.

58. *Works*, 3:5; 4:263; 6:272, 569–70; Janton, *Concept et Sentiment*, 69–70, 94.

59. Danner, "The Theology of the Geneva Bible: A Study in English Protestantism," 85–96, 184–94.

60. Greaves, "The Knoxian Paradox, 85–98.

portrayed idolatry in a most comprehensive manner, that is, to trust and honor anything besides God.[61] Thus, Knox's definition broadly encompassed most activities of the "malignant" church throughout history.

HISTORY AT WORK

It now remains to illustrate Knox's philosophy at work in his writings. His historical thought was not highly developmental. Rather, most components, especially his providential and apocalyptic views of history, were in place early. At times certain motifs became ascendant, but these shifts portrayed little actual development. In one of his earliest writings, *A Vindication* (1550), most elements of Knox's historical thought were evident in embryonic form. He revealed his apocalyptic thought by paralleling the Roman Mass with the idolatry in ancient Israel and Egypt, which he described as the kingdom of the Antichrist. In addition, shades of the pattern of the history that Knox would develop more fully at a later date emerged in this tract. Utilizing an ecclesiastical history as his source, he referred to the Greater Litany of the Church of Rome under Gregory I (540–604), and decided this ceremony to be the time when the Antichrist sprang up and established his authority.[62]

Early Writings

Other motifs in Knox's historical thought—especially his emphasis on divine providence—were manifest in *A Godly Letter* (1554), written to the English Protestants. While in exile, Knox declared that England's suffering under Mary Tudor, especially the plagues and natural disasters, was a result of God's immutable justice being called down on that disobedient nation. What God has condemned through his prophets in ancient Israel, he now proscribed by his modern day prophets—including John Knox.[63] In this tract, the reformer drew extensive parallels. Judea, ruled by the good king Josiah, was destroyed after his death because of a resurgence of idolatry; England blessed by God during the reign of Protestant Edward

---

61. *Works*, 1:192, 194.
62. *Works*, 3:36, 39.
63. *Works*, 3:165, 167–70, 173.

VI, now faced the threat of ruin because the people had submitted to idolatry under the Catholic Queen, Mary Tudor.[64]

While Knox came close to predicting God's future action based on his past performance, he still maintained a sense of mystery in history. God, Knox noted, is omnipotent and is not bound by our contemplations, and may choose to suffer disobedience.[65] *Two Comfortable Epistles* (1554), also penned to the afflicted church in England, continued Knox's theme of a suffering small flock. Utilizing both the Bible and Josephus as sources, the reformer compared the embattled English congregation to the church from the death of Christ to the destruction of Jerusalem.[66]

A Faithful Admonition—written to the same audience—contained much of importance in respect to Knox's historical thought: it illustrated clearly his use of analogies that came close to being historical equations and his pattern of church history. The rigid historical parallels, between Old Testament characters and the hidden papists in the government of Edward VI, were associated with Knox's prophetic hermeneutic and have been noted previously.[67] Also in *A Faithful Admonition*, Knox for the first time clearly described his perspective of church history. The church's history had a definite pattern of development: the church started out well and then encountered serious difficulties and persecutions. God delivered Israel out of Egypt, but then the false believers faltered in the wilderness. Knox illustrated this pattern by the disciples in a storm at sea. When the disciples passed to sea in obedience to Christ's commandment, the weather was fair, but suddenly a storm arose. If the storm had existed from the beginning, few would have ventured out. But then the seas were moved by a vehement and contrary wind that blew against the disciples' boat. Knox compared the wind to Satan for neither the wind nor Satan can be seen, but their results can be observed and felt.

The reformer applied this analogy to the entire scope of the church's history. With only a boat for transportation in this unstable world the early church began well, but about 800 CE—which was at mid-sea—the doctrine of transubstantiation developed. Knox saw this storm as brought by Satan. Furthermore, he transposed the sea analogy specifically to the Church of England where the Reformation through Edward VI was seen as the calm phase of the voyage—followed by the storm under Mary Tudor

---

64. *Works*, 3:187–91.
65. *Works*, 3:209.
66. *Works*, 3:237, 241.
67. *Works*, 3:280ff. See chapter 2 for the details of this historical analogy.

and the return of the infamous transubstantiation doctrine. Satan's instruments again perverted the gospel and persecuted the saints. Yet, as in the original parable, the true disciples of Christ will not perish because God shall continue to protect his elected and afflicted church until the final victory at the end of the world.[68]

In *An Exposition Upon Matthew IV* (1556), Knox continued to draw analogies between Israel and England, repeating the theme of an omnipotent and immutable God acting in the present as he did in the past. Knox's apocalyptic view of history also emerged quite clearly. He referred to Satan's kingdom warring against Elijah, but the victory went to God when Jehu destroyed the house of Ahab. In fact, Knox stated that Jesus Christ has provoked Satan to do battle because of his persecution against God's elect, and then the reformer proceeded to assure his readers that God still does battle for his followers.[69]

The *Familiar Epistles* (1556–58) said little new, but again Knox stressed God's control over all events, including the activity of Satan.[70] In a letter to the Scottish Protestants (1557), the reformer encouraged them to continue in the faith for the days of this corrupt world are short, and Christ will return shortly to rescue his oppressed flock.[71] Knox's additions to *An Apology* (1557) sharply drew the battle lines for the two armies throughout history. Protestants have been chosen out of this world to fight for Christ, their sovereign captain, against Satan, the prince of this realm.[72] *The First Blast* (1558), for which Knox is well known, contributed little to his historical thought, except to demonstrate the reformer's use of nonbiblical historical sources (e.g., the church fathers, classical philosophy) to buttress his arguments from Scripture[73]

A Letter to the Queen Regent (1558) distinctly illustrated Knox's providential and apocalyptic view of history. He said God's eternal providence not only appointed his elect to do battle, but also determined their final victory in these last days, not by resisting but by suffering.[74] In *The Appellation* (1558), Knox continued the apocalyptic theme in the context of developing his theory of resistance to rulers. Here he brings the cosmic

---

68. *Works*, 3:273–89, 332.
69. *Works*, 4:95, 102–3, 106, 112.
70. *Works*, 4:241, 249.
71. *Works*, 4:262.
72. *Works*, 4:322, 342.
73. *Works*, 4:366, 373–74, 382.
74. *Works*, 4:433, 435.

battle up to date and labels the Roman Church, including the bishops, as the present generation of the Antichrist. This current battle, in Knox's mind, was but a continuation of the struggle—between light and darkness, good and evil, and the "true and "malignant" churches—that has gone on since the dawn of history.[75]

Knox's 1560 treatise concerning predestination inter-mixed his providential and apocalyptic views as distinctly as did any of his writings. Nowhere does the reformer articulate the militant dichotomy between the Catholic and "true" Christian church as he does here. Knox took Augustine's division of the two cities and transmuted them first into two churches and then into two armies. In God's counsel a difference existed between human beings, but all were in one lump or mass. From this mass God appointed two seeds to come forth, and these two seeds represented the two churches. From the seed of Eve came the individual elect, which composed the church of Christ, and from the seed of the serpent sprang the reprobate and the church of Satan.[76]

Knox extended Augustine's doctrine of two cities—God appointed two companies of people from the beginning to do battle. One army was the elect spouse of Christ, the church of God; the other, the malignant synagogue of Satan. This battle would not end until Christ's second coming, which would usher in the judgment.[77] Thus Knox's historical thought evidenced a dynamic linear movement toward an appointed end. At the close of his work on predestination, Knox utilized and recommended the history of John Sleidan, entitled *Commentaries*—a work which the Scottish reformer would also utilize in his *History*.[78]

History of the Reformation

Upon returning to Scotland in 1559, Knox began writing his *History of the Reformation in Scotland*, a task that would last until 1571. The reformer's convictions regarding God's sovereign control of history and the division of the world into two armed camps remained with him and became the dominant motifs in his *History*. Although Knox emphasized the themes of persecution and martyrdom in his description of the early years of the Reformation in Scotland, he did not model his *History* solely upon the

75. *Works*, 4:478–79, 512.
76. *Works*, 5:61–62.
77. *Works*, 5:62, 407, 413.
78. *Works*, 5:423ff.

God and His Work in the World

martyrologies of Jean Crespin and John Foxe. Rather, because of his interest in contemporary religion and politics, Knox had more in common with the approach of John Sleidan. When Knox wrote the preface to his *History*, he echoed the purpose declared by Sleidan in his preface to the *Commentaries:* Each man wrote a history of religion demonstrating the conflict between Protestantism and Catholicism and touched upon political and military activities only to the extent they engaged the subject of religion.[79]

Despite this same approach, Knox's *History* reads very different from Sleidan's. In part, this variance developed because of differing versions of the apocalyptic tradition. Sleidan hoped the Reformation would be accomplished by a great emperor whose reign was prophesied for the last age of the world.[80] Following Bale and Foxe, Knox put his faith not in princes but in the small congregation of the elect. Emphasizing his prophetic role, Knox told a story of two armies locked in an apocalyptic struggle.[81]

Knox wrote his *History* in the framework of the pattern of the church's history that he previously established in *a Faithful Admonition*. The church throughout history has started out well and then encountered serious difficulties and persecutions. Along this line, the Scottish church began well, but after its victory many apostates within the church sank it into depression and idolatry. Knox's *History* established this theme: *Books* 1 to 3 describe the victory of the godly, while *Book* 4 tells of their decline from the purity of God's Word.[82] Within this pattern, Knox told a story of the Scottish Reformation that focused on his providential and apocalyptic philosophy of history.

Knox's providential and apocalyptic concept of history emerged in his description of detailed events, personal affairs, political developments, and military battles. In his *History*, the reformer did not portray the struggles (Protestantism versus Catholicism, church versus state, revolution versus reaction, future versus past) in a political sense. Rather, Knox's *History* depicted a holy war "between the saints of God and these bloody wolves who claim to themselves the title of clergy."[83] Knox subordinated every issue to the conflict between the Roman Church and the gospel of

79. *Works,* 1:3–5; Sleidan, *A Famous Chronicle of oure time,* Preface. The English edition published in 1560 is too late to have used by Knox.

80. Sleidan, *A Famous Chronicle of oure time,* Preface; Firth, *The Apocalyptic Tradition,* 128.

81. *Works,* 2:281; Firth, *The Apocalyptic Tradition,* 128.

82. *Works,* 2:266. Lee, "John Knox and His History," 86–87.

83. *Works,* 1:4; Dickinson, *The Scottish Reformation,* 19–20.

Christ. This struggle became a grim, merciless battle between the forces of light and the forces of darkness. Knox first opposed the Queen Regent, and later he combated her daughter Mary Queen of Scots. In this dramatic struggle—which Knox's *History* described in epic fashion—Satan's attack on the gospel aroused God himself: "Thus ceased not Satan, by all means, to maintain his kingdom of darkness, and to suppress the light of Christ's Evangel. But potent is he against whom they fought; for when they waged war in greatest security, then began God to show his anger."[84]

In this war God's hand manifested itself in all events: in one place a journey may be postponed to the disappointment of those waiting in ambush, while in another, the heart of a bitter opponent may be moved.[85] During the confrontation at Cupar Muir (1559), "God did so multiply our number, that it appeared as men rained from the clouds."[86] Knox also attributed the episode of the ordinance at Haddington (1548) to a similar miracle: here God conducted the fires so that more than a hundred of the French bullets fell only as two shots.[87]

Knox understood this development well because he believed that the same God who had razed the walls of Jericho and had divided the waters of the Red Sea was still at work. The God who punished sin by the flood could still display anger at the wickedness in Scotland. In every natural disaster, Knox saw a wrathful God punishing sin: "God from heaven, and upon the face of the earth, gave declaration that he is offended at the iniquity that was committed even within this Realm; for upon the 20th day of January there fell wet in great abundance, which in falling froze so vehemently, that the earth was but one sheet of ice."[88]

Famines and plagues were no accident. Rather, they represented God's visitation upon Scotland for sin. Knox saw plagues as God's favorite means of punishment.[89] He attributed defeat in battle not to the enemy's superiority, but to God's direct intervention. The English victory at Solway Moss (1542) was due to "the hand of God fighting against [the] pride ... of his own little flock."[90] Furthermore, Knox reacted in anger when the Scots attributed victory to their own strength. The Defenders of the Castle

---

84. *Works*, 1:119.
85. *Works*, 1:131–32.
86. *Works*, 1:351.
87. *Works*, 1:223.
88. *Works*, 2:417.
89. *Works*, 1:270–72.
90. *Works*, 1:351.

of St. Andrews (1547) bragged of the thickness of their walls, and Knox responded by prophesying that the walls "should be but egg shells" and "you shall be delivered into your enemy's hands."[91] Likewise, he did not see the Queen Regent's death in terms of natural causes, but rather in the sense of divine punishment.[92]

Later Writings

Knox's letters and tracts written during the 1560s, though not focusing on history, did reflect the reformer's providential and apocalyptic worldview. He mentioned familiar themes: Christ, the captain, led his people in a great battle with Satan; and God raised some leaders up in Knox's time to discover the iniquity of the Babylonian harlot, the Church of Rome.[93]

In his *Answer to Tyrie* (1572), Knox continued his previous pattern of history, but gave it a new wrinkle. Following the ideas of Augustine, the reformer argued that the last days had begun with Christ's Incarnation and would continue until his return in judgment. The last days ran the course of church history—including the first preaching of the gospel, the defection from it during the Middle Ages (approximately 800 CE), and its restoration in the world. Knox believed he was living in the recovery stage, which had begun during the Reformation but was not yet complete.[94] This model of church history, introduced in Knox's earlier writings, continued to reflect a linear pattern that accorded roughly with the past millennial schemes of some Protestant writers.[95]

In the debate with Tyrie, Knox utilized other historical sources—especially Aventinus's (Johan Thurmair) history of Bavaria—which recounted the vices and crimes of the popes during the Middle Ages and the prophecies of Antichrist found in the commentary of Joachim of Fiore. Knox used these writings and others to support his contention that the Apocalypse of John applied to the Roman Church alone and not the Roman Empire. The reformer quoted Joachim as identifying the whore of Revelation with the false church in Rome, which contrasted so completely with the poor pilgrims who made up the "true" church.[96] Herein can be

91. *Works*, 1:205.
92. *Works*, 1:220.
93. *Works*, 6:12, 21, 192, 251.
94. *Works*, 6:494-95.
95. *Works*, 6:508.
96. *Works*, 6:505-7; Reeves, *Joachim of Fiore and the Prophetic Future*, 136-37.

found the basis for Knox's uncompromising condemnation of Rome and his supremely partisan approach to the writing of history.

John Knox was not a historian by profession. Rather, he vigorously pursued his vocation of preaching God's Word—an undertaking that clearly works its way into his historical thought. A sixteenth-century writer can be excused for not employing the methods of modern historians. Nevertheless, Knox's interpretation of the past, in many ways, must be regarded as theology rather than history. Though Knox saw the present in the light of the past, particularly from the vantage point of the Old Testament, he was primarily a man of the present.

Consequently, he used past events—whether in his polemical writings or *History*—for the purpose of promoting "true" religion as he perceived it. Past events to Knox were worth transcribing only to glorify God and to show his handiwork and the futility of opposing him. As a result, Knox's concept of history not only reflected his religious faith and personal experiences, but also became a powerful force in his thinking—prompting him to contend for the Reformed faith in an exceedingly vigorous manner. The importance, therefore, in examining John Knox's concept of history is that such an investigation opens another window to the thought world of this prominent Scottish reformer.

THE PROBLEM OF EVIL

Closely related to the doctrine of providence is the question disputed by theologians for centuries: Who causes evil in the world—God, Satan, or humans themselves? Given Knox's rigid concept of predestination, the problem of evil inevitably arose for him also. For the most part, he dealt with the problem in his 1560 predestination tract. If God's sovereign will accomplishes all things, then God must be the author of evil. Knox vehemently rejected such a conclusion. He affirmed that God's eternal counsel no less determined humanity's fall than it determined human creation, yet this does not make God the author of sin. God is the mover of all things, but in Knox's mind this action does not make him the cause of human wickedness.[97]

In *An Answer*, Knox asserted two seemingly contradictory propositions with the utmost fervor: He vigorously avowed God to be the perpetual mover of all things—but in an attempt to avoid attributing evil to God, he argued with equal vigor that humans freely choose evil. God

97. *Works*, 5:170, 174–75, 182, 339.

created humankind good, but it willingly makes itself evil and the slave of Satan. Granted a particular perspective of Scripture, the Bible teaches such a paradox. At least John Knox thought so because he went to great lengths to establish both God's absolute providence and human responsibility.[98]

God's work in and by his creatures does not impede the wicked deeds done by human beings; indeed, God's work differs from the deeds of the wicked even when they are the instruments of God. Avarice, ambition, envy, or cruelty provokes the wicked to iniquity—and they do not look to either the end or purpose of what they are doing. Because of this impulse, the evil work takes its character from the root of its origin: the wicked affection and purpose in the mind of the transgressor. Thus, if God compels a person to slay another wicked individual, this action cannot be sin for God because the purpose is not evil. But the wicked slayer unquestionably sinned because the purpose was his own, and evil. A wicked human being has two compelling purposes: the righteous purpose of God—which he fails to comprehend, and his own wicked purpose. Human beings freely exercise this last purpose and for this action they are responsible.

To add force to his argument, Knox took Beza's *Propositions against Castellio*, and included them in his presentations.[99] These propositions described an evil work as any task that does not have the will of God for an express commandment. The workers of iniquity are causes—insofar, as they operate by their own motion—and instruments, insofar as they are moved by another. For example, when the hangman, by the commandment of the magistrate, kills a person; when humans hurt others by the instigation of Satan—two perform the work. Such workers are instruments, "not simply as the hammer or axe is in the hand of the smith or hewer, but they are such instruments as also moved by their own inward motion."[100]

Furthermore, when someone commands evil, God designs the broad purpose for a righteous end, but human beings purpose the specific sin.[101] Wicked persons in performing acts of iniquity do not obey God's will, either secret or revealed, but follow their own lusts. Reprobates cannot obey because obedience requires a knowledge of God's will that they neither have nor desire. Whoever does anything ignorant of God's revealed will, commits a sin against God regardless of how they serve the divine pur-

---

98. *Works*, 5:90, 110, 113, 188. See Romans 9:19ff. for a passage in which Paul seems to argue such a paradox.

99. Sebastian Castellio or Castalio (1515–63). He was a native of Savoy, a French minister, and a humanist who opposed Calvin's views on election and predestination.

100. *Works*, 5:186.

101. *Works*, 5:170, 174–75, 182, 339.

pose. Sin occurs because the wicked do not look to God's end and purpose when performing the act. In this regard, Knox demonstrated his biblical base. Quoting Calvin, he referred to Acts 2:23—"That by the determinate counsel and prescience of God was Jesus betrayed and crucified by the hands of wicked men."[102] Knox cited the Assyrian and Chaldean attacks on Israel and Judah as other biblical illustrations.

In Knox's thought, Satan certainly causes evil, but the Scottish reformer did not make him a general scapegoat who lessens human responsibility. God has created human beings as free agents capable of resisting Satan, but they voluntarily choose to obey the devil.[103] Yet Satan blinds the senses of many so that they violate and corrupt God's most holy laws and ordinances. Knox saw Satan's role as primarily one of instigating and corrupting. In the case of Adam and the first sin, the reformer noted a dual responsibility: Adam sinned because of Satan's temptation and the intent of his heart. This dual role of Adam's acting in response to the devil's prompting set the pattern for all future sin.[104] Because Satan leads the wicked and almost personifies human evil, Knox saw his hand in every form of moral wickedness. Though the devil's hand emerges in all moral evil, the reformer did not use Satan to explain natural evil. For earthquakes, famines, plagues, and other natural disasters, he saw only the hand of God. In particular, Knox referred to the plagues sent by God to punish sin, especially the sin of corporate idolatry.[105]

JESUS CHRIST

Turning to Knox's ideas on Christ, it can readily be seen that he was less Christocentric in his theology than Luther, Calvin, or Zwingli. Since Knox overemphasized the Old Testament and saw himself in the role of an Old Testament prophet calling Scotland to repentance, his thought was naturally theocentric. Although Knox did not doctrinally subordinate Christ to God the Father—his Trinitarian thought was orthodox—he nonetheless placed the role of God the Father in the forefront.

Knox, writing more as a preacher and a pastor, said little about Christ in the technical theological sense. The reformer particularly avoided areas of theological controversy such as Christ's deity and manhood; rather he

---

102. *Works*, 5:182, 339.
103. *Works*, 5:143.
104. *Works*, 5:441, 170, 343.
105. *Works*, 3:234; 5:503–7; McEwen, *The Faith of Knox*, 87.

God and His Work in the World

assumed them as a preacher would. But judged from the *Scots Confession*—which he, in large measure, influenced—his position on Christ's incarnation, deity, manhood, death, passion, resurrection, ascension, and offices left no hint of heterodoxy.[106]

To say Knox lacked Luther's or even Calvin's Christocentricism—or that he was more theocentric than Christocentric—is a relative statement. Knox did not ignore Christ. Rather, certain Old Testament themes, such as divine immutability and anti-idolatry dominated his perspective of the Bible. In fact, Knox the man and Knox the pastor could be quite Christ-centered. The Scottish reformer recounted little of his spiritual life, but it is known that he had an encounter with Christ via John 17. Because of this meeting, Knox had a living faith in Christ as Savior and Intercessor.[107] He did not, however, interject this experience into his teaching on Christ as Luther had done. Knox, in his pastoral role, clearly emerged in his letters to Mrs. Bowes (1553–54). These letters, in which Christ came to the forefront, emphasized Christ the Savior and Christ the Intercessor to the distraught Mrs. Bowes.[108]

Yet Knox did underscore several aspects of Christology—namely Christ's combative characteristics and his offices as savior, head of the church, and mediator. For Knox—as well as for Calvin, Luther, and Zwingli—Jesus Christ was not the emasculated figure sometimes found in the history of the medieval church. Knox viewed Christ as a "son of thunder" similar to the ancient prophets and a God who did not appear meek and lowly nor turn the other cheek.[109]

In Knox's view, Jesus Christ did not come to abolish the bloody deeds of such Old Testament figures as Jehu.[110] In a 1559 sermon to the kirk, Knox used the text of Christ purifying the temple of buyers and sellers to condemn the papists and idolaters. These texts vividly illustrated Christ's combativeness, and no sooner did Knox finish the sermon than the people set to work purging the church and breaking idols.[111] In his *Exposition Upon Matthew IV* (1556), relating to the temptation of Christ in the

---

106. *Works*, 2:99–103; 6:318–21, 363–64.

107. *Works*, 6:643, 660.

108. *Works*, 3:336–402. See Reid, "John Knox, Pastor of Souls," 1–21; Kyle, "John Knox and the Care of Souls," 133–44.

109. Brown, *John Knox*, 2:121.

110. Lang, *History of Scotland*, 2:60. Lang's view, however, might be tempered somewhat by the fact that he was strongly anti-Knox.

111. Laing, ed., *The Miscellany of the Wodrow Society*, 1:60. It would seem that Knox did not intend such destruction.

PART ONE: Historical and Theological Foundations

wilderness, Knox again demonstrated Christ's warlike qualities. He called Christ Prince of Peace, Master and Champion, and showed him provoking and challenging Satan to do combat. Reflecting his apocalyptic worldview, Knox regarded Jesus Christ as a war leader, who fought for Christians in battle. And because he possessed all power in heaven and earth, he could have repulsed Satan with a word.[112]

To be sure, Knox overemphasized certain aspects of the Old Testament, but not in regard to the offices of savior and head of the church. In the Letters to Mrs. Bowes, Knox confessed "Christ Jesus to be the only Savior of the world" and that redemption came through the death and shed blood of Jesus Christ.[113] From his *Summary of Balnaves on Justification by Faith*, which clearly enunciated Luther's great theme of justification by faith, it can be certain that Knox was squarely in the mainstream of the Reformation's purpose of restoring the gospel of Jesus Christ to its rightful place.[114]

Next, the Scottish reformer distinctly perceived Christ's relationship to the church. To Mrs. Bowes, Knox described the elect as "members of Christ's body" and the "flock of Jesus Christ;" and said that Jesus was their "only pastor" and "great Bishop, of their souls."[115] Knox held Christ to be the Head and King of the church, and he stressed Christ's execution of this office. Christ not only guided, ruled, and defended his subjects, but he also made statue laws his subjects must obey in preference to laws of a prince.[116]

In addition, Knox strongly emphasized Christ's role as intercessor or mediator. In his 1553 *Declaration of the True Nature and Object of Prayer*, Knox related Christ's role as mediator to his concept of God and humanity. The reformer believed God to be holy and humankind to be sinful. Therefore, no one could stand alone in God's presence. Without Christ as mediator, any attempt by a human to enter God's presence by prayer was odious to God. Knox ruled out the intercession of saints and angels because intercession depended on a perfect mediator. Because mediation involved two parties—the offender and offended—the mediator must have the trust of both parties. And only Jesus Christ could fulfill this role

---

112. *Works*, 4:101, 103–4, 112.

113. *Works*, 3:342, 359.

114. *Works*, 3:3–27; Denney, "John Knox: His Religious Life and Theological Position," 283ff. See chapter 4 for a fuller elaboration of justification.

115. *Works*, 3:371, 389–90.

116. Lorimer, *John Knox and the Church of England*, 60.

because he was perfect and without sin. To make anyone else a mediator was to usurp Christ's honor.[117]

Lord Percy contends Knox saw Christ as, above all else, the mediator between God and humankind. Knox was supremely concerned with denying the priest's share of this office of intercession rather than with what Luther so strongly accented—the priesthood of the believer. The Scottish reformer rejected priestly intercession because it intruded into Christ's office as the only mediator between God and the elect, and not because such intercession impeded Christian prayer.[118]

From Knox's account of George Wishart's teaching, it is known that Wishart taught the priesthood of the believer, rejection of the priest's role of intercession, and Christ's office as the only mediator. Thus it can be conjectured that Wishart helped influence Knox's rejection of all mediators between God and humanity except for Christ.[119] Yet, Calvin's influence may have dominated in this regard. Some similarities exist between Knox's *Declaration of the True Nature and Object of Prayer*—written before his trip to Geneva—with the treatment of prayer found in the 1539 and 1543 editions of Calvin's *Institutes*. Besides a general mastery over Knox's notion of prayer, the *Institutes* seemed to influence him in respect to Christ's role as mediator.[120]

THE HOLY SPIRIT

Except for degrees of emphasis, little in Knox's thought on the Holy Spirit differed from that of the other Magisterial Reformers. He accorded the Holy Spirit the full status of deity, co-equal with God the Father and God the Son. The major role of the Holy Spirit in the inspiration, interpretation, and illumination of Scripture has been noted. In this work, the function of the Holy Spirit was indispensable. Knox, however, did not stress the role of the Holy Spirit in illuminating Scripture as Calvin did. Nevertheless, for Knox and the continental reformers—Luther, Calvin, and Zwingli—the Word and the Spirit became almost inseparable. Luther said the Spirit does not work alone without the Word but rather in and through

---

117. *Works*, 3:94–95, 97–98.
118. Percy, *John Knox* 56–57.
119. *Works*, 1:161, 163.
120. D' Assonville, *John Knox and the Institutes*, 29–30. For a study on the general spread of Calvin's ideas see Reid, ed. *John Calvin and His Influence in the Western World*, 33–52.

the Word. The activity of the Holy Spirit, therefore, depends on a person's previous hearing of the external Word.[121] As indicated in his 1558 letter to the Queen Regent, Knox also believed that the internal working of the Spirit corresponds to and depends on the hearing of the external Word of God.[122] In fact, the sectarians who envisioned the Spirit as speaking directly concerned all the Magisterial Reformers including Knox.

Equally indispensable is the Holy Spirit's work in salvation, sanctification, and prayer. The *Scots Confession* and the *Book of Common Order* confess that faith comes from no inherent powers in human beings, but from the Holy Ghost who performs the act of regeneration, irrespective of our merits. Good works do not proceed from human merit or free choice, for human nature cannot even think a good thought. The only source of good works in humankind is the Spirit's work of regeneration and continuing sanctification.[123] Finally, in his declaration on prayer, Knox upheld the bond between the Holy Spirit and prayer. Arguing from Romans 8:26, he said the wellspring of prayer is the Holy Ghost who "stirred up our minds, giving unto us a desire or boldness to pray."[124]

Besides the above functions and characteristics of the Holy Spirit, Knox set forth some unrelated ideas that deserve notation. First, in his tract concerning predestination, he showed a Calvinistic characteristic by insisting that the Holy Spirit works for God's majesty.[125] Next, in his accord with the view that saw the Holy Ghost as God but yet a personal being, Knox attributed personal characteristics to him. For example, a denial of election's biblical base "will corrupt the mind of the Holy Ghost."[126]

But most pronounced was the Holy Ghost's function of promoting hatred for sin. The Holy Spirit hates sin and he encourages believers to do likewise. In a 1554 epistle to the English Protestants, Knox declared carnal hatred to be sinful, but at the same time, he noted a spiritual abhorrence—which David called a perfect hatred. And the Holy Ghost engenders this hatred in the hearts of the elect against contaminators of holy statues. Jeremiah demonstrated such a hatred when he asked for vengeance upon God's enemies, and Knox contended that prayers for this spiritual hatred

---

121. Althaus, *The Theology of Martin Luther*, 37.
122. *Works*, 4:449.
123. *Works*, 2:103–4; 6:322.
124. *Works*, 3:84–85.
125. *Works*, 5:103.
126. *Works*, 5:126.

were acceptable to God.[127] Even as Knox presented Jesus Christ as combative and somewhat lacking in gentler virtues, so he characterized the Holy Spirit less as a source of comfort than as actively simulating hatred for sin.

Finally, though Knox acknowledged the Holy Spirit's activities in most areas, he stated in his predestination work "that miracles, and the visible gifts of the Holy Ghost, given in the days of the Apostles are now ceased." He regarded prophecy largely as the interpretation of Scripture and not primarily a miraculous gift of the Holy Spirit—and "tongues" as known languages such as Latin, Greek, and Hebrew rather than a supernatural work of the Holy Spirit.[128]

---

127. *Works*, 4:341; 3:245.
128. *Works*, 5:295; Spottiswoode, *The History of the Church of Scotland*, 170–71.

4

The Path to Salvation

THE QUESTION, WHAT MUST I do to be saved? has evoked a variety of responses throughout history. On this question, the Magisterial tradition stood apart from both Catholicism in particular and to a lesser extent from Anabaptism. For the Magisterial Reformers, the twin pillars of salvation were justification by faith and predestination. In these acts, God initiated grace, and human beings could do nothing but receive it. The reformers' rejection of synergism (human beings cooperating with God in the spiritual renewal of the soul), their notion of justification as the forensic act of God imputing the righteousness of Jesus Christ to sinners, and their teaching of predestination in unmistakable terms made reconciliation with the Roman Church impossible.

Catholic doctrine taught the following: one must prepare for grace, one must cooperate with God in his prevenient grace, and faith was an intellectual acknowledgment that could not stand alone. At the heart of Catholic soteriology were the sacraments; without the sacraments there was no infusion of grace and consequently no salvation. The sacraments—particularly baptism, the Eucharist, and penance—had saving powers, not merely strengthening powers as in Protestantism.

To be sure, any church adopting a theory of synergism could not adhere to rigid predestination, and Catholicism did not. The Roman Church harbored two tendencies, semi-Augustinianism and semi-Pelagianism, of which the latter gradually gained the upper hand. While semi-Pelagianism allowed human nature an element of freedom and thus based predestination on foreseen faith and obedience, semi-Augustinianism retained—in a modified form—Augustine's emphasis on the enslavement of the human will and thus the absolute need of divine grace for spiritual renewal.

Still, another response came from the Anabaptists who gave justification a new interpretation and either abandoned or revised the doctrine of predestination in a universalist direction. The whole of Anabaptist soteriology presupposed the forensic atonement of all humankind through the work of Calvary—something different from the forensic justification of the individual believer, as in Lutheranism. Thus justification was far more than a legal transaction in a heavenly court. It meant, for the one freely responding to God, a new life—a life of discipleship in obedience to the risen Lord. Anabaptism did not repudiate the Lutheran doctrine of justification, but rather attempted to read a stronger ethical content into it.[1]

JUSTIFICATION

For Luther the doctrine of justification by faith was central—not simply one doctrine among others, but the basic and chief article of faith on which the entire doctrine of the church stands. The Reformed theologians, Zwingli and Calvin, firmly held to the doctrine of justification by faith, but to them it did not occupy the central position that it had with Luther. Though all three said, or implied, that election must precede justification, Zwingli and Calvin laid stress on predestination as opposed to Luther's emphasis on justification.

There is no question that John Knox's view of justification harmonized with the mainstream of sixteenth-century Protestant thought on the subject. His confession of faith coincided with that of Luther, Zwingli, and Calvin on the great articles of justification and good works.[2] Rather, the difficulty is the quandary of who influenced Knox and to what extent. In the context of soteriology, the question centers on a possible shift from a Lutheran emphasis on justification by faith to a Calvinistic one on predestination.

Was such a shift made, and if so, when and to what extent? Scholars are by no means in agreement regarding these questions, and some of them identify with either of two trends. One view contends that Knox continued in the general Lutheran, rather than Calvinistic tradition of Scottish Protestants until approximately his 1554 trip to Geneva—and followers of this view insist Knox was not devoid of Lutheran tendencies in

---

1. Berkhof, *The History of Christian Doctrines*, 137, 144–45, 147–49; Tillich, *A History of Christian Thought*, 213–18; Williams, *The Radical Reformation*, 839; Estep, *The Anabaptist Story*, 145–47.
2. *Works*, 3:13–28; Lorimer, *John Knox and the Church of England*, 19.

the concept of salvation even after 1554.[3] The opposing opinion says Knox was a Calvinist earlier and he formulated his views on predestination before meeting Calvin.[4]

Before any conclusions can be attempted on the above issues, Knox's thought on justification must be examined. Though the doctrine underwent only slight, if any change, it was more pronounced in his earlier ministry. Knox's first sermon in 1547 concerned itself primarily with identifying the papacy as the Antichrist, but he did mention that the Scriptures taught that humankind could be "justified by faith only" and "the blood of Jesus Christ purges us from all sins."[5] Then the reformer proceeded to condemn papal doctrine attributing salvation to works of the law and human inventions such as pilgrimages, pardons, abstaining from meat, and other practices.[6]

But the substance of Knox's views on justification by faith emerged more in his 1548 *Summary of Balnaves on Justification by Faith*. Because Knox summarized and recommended another man's work, some historians question whether this tract can be representative of his thought at this time.[7] However, there are indications that Knox's summary, apart from Balnaves's own treatise, can be regarded as representative of Knoxian thought. For example, the Scots reformer explicitly said he purposed not to illustrate, commend, nor advance Balnaves's work since it was godly and perfect—but rather to give his own confession to the doctrine of justification. Furthermore, Knox, claimed to accept fully everything contained in the article.[8]

---

3. McRoberts, ed., *Essays on the Scottish Reformation*, 249; Reid, "Lutheranism in the Scottish Reformation, 109–11; McEwen, *The Faith of John Knox*, 70. Knox briefly visited Geneva in 1554, but it was during his lengthy stay (1555–59) that his theology developed and matured.

4. Macmillan, *John Knox*, 44–47. For similar implications see Hastie, *The Theology of the Reformed Church*, 48–51; Whitley, *Plain Mr. Knox*, 29. This view rests on the wider range of theology and not just salvation. Also W. Stanford Reid, while he does not mention predestination in particular, seems to have moved this way in a later work. See Reid, *Trumpeter of God*.

5. *Works*, 1:191.

6. *Works*, 1:191.

7. Macmillian, *John Knox*, 44; Ridley, *John Knox*, 75. Both contend this summary was not representative of Knox's thought in 1548.

8. *Works*, 3:9. Those agreeing that the summary represented Knoxian thought would be Stalker, *John Knox*, 144–45; Brown, *John Knox*, 2 vols., 2:376.

Balnaves's treatise appeared to be Lutheran in content, but how directly Luther influenced this document is disputed.[9] Nevertheless, Knox—in his summary of it—concurred with Luther's doctrine of justification by faith. He stated the substance of justification is "to cleave fast unto God, by Jesus Christ, and not by ourselves, nor yet by our own works."[10] Here a typically strong Lutheran rejection of works as a means of salvation is encountered. The Scottish reformer asserted that the wicked believe works to be a part of salvation, but a true preacher must exclude them from justification as did Christ and the prophets. Yet Knox did not condemn good works—for as shall be seen—he held them to be a fruit of justification, but not the cause of it.

Very similar to rejecting justification by works was the repudiation of the law as an instrument of salvation. Since neither good works nor obeying the law suffices, one must seek justice from Christ whom the law could not accuse.[11] Further, according to Knox, Scripture clearly teaches that faith in Christ is the only acceptable vehicle for apprehending justification and the mercy of God.[12] Finally, he contended that the faith of the Old Testament and that of the New Testament, which he possessed, were one and the same. The patriarchs stood in God's favor in the future promised Seed. And Knox stood in God's grace by faith in the Seed that had already been revealed.[13] Such a position of exact continuity in the promise of the gospel and in the content and object of the faith bore resemblance to

---

9. For those contending Balnaves's treatise was Lutheran, see McEwen, *The Faith of Knox*, 54. McEwen claims Professor Watt conclusively proved Balnaves's work to rest on Luther's *Commentary on Galatians*. For those saying Balnaves's treatise was not specifically a product of Luther's thought, see especially Reid, *Trumpeter of God*, 61, and more generally D'Assonville, *Knox and the Institutes*, chapter 1. The case here rests on the similarity of Balnaves's treatise with Calvin's *Institutes*. Calvin, *The Institutes of Christian Religion*, 3, 11–16. It must be remembered that Luther influenced even Calvin in regards to justification and that their views on the subject were similar. See Wendel, *Calvin*, 133. Though the substance of Balnaves's work bore some similarity with both Luther's commentary and Calvin's *Institutes*, the tone and degree of resemblance would seem to lean in favor of Luther's *Commentary on Galatians*. However, to say the issue is conclusively proven would be an exaggeration. Rupp even notes the similarity of Balnaves's work to Luther's *Preface to the Romans* and suggests that perhaps Balnaves did not read Luther firsthand but knew him through Tyndale's writings. See Shaw, ed., *A Quatercentenary Reappraisal*, 7.

10. *Works*, 3:15.
11. *Works*, 3:18–19.
12. *Works*, 3:20.
13. *Works*, 3:20.

the "Federal Theology" or the covenant theological system that developed more formally at a later date.[14]

Furthermore, Knox expounded the doctrine of justification by faith in other early writings. In *A Vindication* (1550), justification by faith is evident, though he subordinated and linked it to his anti-idolatry theme.[15] Even more revealing was Knox's *Epistle to the Congregation of Berwick*, written in 1552, in which the reformer explained what he considered the five points of the gospel to be. First, he said, God by his providence has placed life and salvation in Christ—who through the Father becomes the source of earthly justice, sanctification, wisdom, and redemption.

Second, Christ—together with such gifts as remission of sins, resurrection of the body, and everlasting life—has been given to the elect church of God. Next, Knox developed the gospel theme of true faith justifying people before God without respect to their past or future works. Hence, God's children were adopted and chosen in Jesus Christ before the foundation of the world and are to walk in the good works God has prepared. Fourth, the gospel injunction regarding a holy and godly conversation meant obeying God in all the days of one's life and praising him for appointing the elect to be heirs.

Finally, by the gospel, Knox understood invocation to God only by Christ and thanksgiving to God for his great benefits. These invocations were sometimes private, but Knox commanded that they be done openly in participation of Christ's sacraments.[16] At this early stage, Knox associated many things with the gospel and thereby understood it as something far more than simply a salvation message. The gospel included not only justification, but also sanctification, good works, and proper prayer and worship. Justification was by faith—but within a predestinarian context—and as Knox's theology acquired depth, it obviously moved toward a Reformed position.

After the mid-1550s, justification by faith still remained a vital doctrine with Knox, but he mentioned it less than previously, perhaps because he tended to subordinate it to predestination and other concerns. In *The Appellation* (1558), Knox stressed Christ as the only name under heaven

---

14. Covenant theology was taught in the sixteenth century by Bullinger, Olevianus, one of the authors of the Heidelberg Catechism, and others; but its largest development came in the seventeenth century under Cocceius. McGiffert, *Protestant Thought Before Kant*, 153. See also McEwen, *The Faith of Knox*, 78–79; and Janton, *Concept et Sentiment*, 177–79; Baker, *Heinrich Bullinger and the Covenant*, 1–25.

15. *Works*, 3:33–70.

16. Knox, "Epistle to the Congregation of Berwick, 1552," 258.

The Path to Salvation

whereby a human being can be saved.[17] Here the doctrine remained intact, but again it evidenced a close link with sanctification, the sacraments, and predestination. In the *Familiar Epistles* of 1555-58, Knox can be found saying the elect are clothed with the righteousness of Christ because of their faith and the Holy Spirit's sanctification.[18] Again the reformer noted that the elect have faith and the Holy Spirit is the agent of sanctification, but this statement seemed to be the first reference to God's crediting of Christ's righteousness to the sinner. Thus Knox asserted a cardinal notion of justification, namely, the imputation of Christ's righteousness.

The *Additional Prayer, Etc.*, not written by Knox but sanctioned by him, inseparably linked justification and sanctification and said justifying faith proceeds from the Holy Spirit as a special gift.[19] In his 1560 work on predestination, Knox continued to tie the gospel and justification in with the doctrine of election. Justification comes by faith, but faith itself is a gift from God and nothing in a human being produces it: Faith is altogether the work of God and the result of election rather than the cause of it. The proper order for Knox was election, faith, and then good works.[20]

Before proceeding to the doctrine of predestination, it would be beneficial to survey the Lutheran influences in Scotland as they related to the doctrine of justification. Lutheranism was the dominant heresy in Catholic Scotland until at least 1540 and perhaps even a little later than 1545.[21] Justification by faith was central to Lutheranism, so it comes as no surprise to find it spreading in Scotland from approximately 1526 to 1546. The prologue of Murdock Nisbet's *The New Testament in Scots* consisted of the translation made about 1525 of Luther's own preface to the New Testament. This prologue accentuated the necessity of a trusting faith in Christ as the only means for salvation.[22]

Patrick Hamilton, who in 1548 became the first Scottish Lutheran to be tried and executed, wrote *Patrick's Place*—a work clearly Lutheran in emphasis and concerned with explaining how humankind could be justified. This work reiterated many times the absolute necessity of faith and

---

17. *Works*, 4:467.
18. *Works*, 4:229.
19. *Works*, 6:364.
20. *Works*, 5:279-83. This major work on predestination was written in 1559 but not published until 1560.
21. McRoberts, *Scottish Reformation*, 252; Reid, "Lutheranism in the Scottish Reformation," 102; Gilck, "Non- Calvinist Influences," Locher, *Zwingli's Thought*, 367-73. Locher argues that much of this Lutheran influence was in fact Zwinglian thought.
22. Law, ed., *The New Testament in Scots*, 1:4.

PART ONE: Historical and Theological Foundations

the relative unimportance of human actions for "no work neither saves us nor condemns."[23] The explicitly Lutheran doctrine of faith in Christ also occurred frequently: "That faith of Christ is, to believe in him; that is, to believe his word, and to believe that he will help you in all your need."[24] At Hamilton's trial, the Catholics accused and condemned him for his Lutheran views: "We have found also, that he has . . . taught diverse opinions of Luther . . . No man is justified by works, but by faith only."[25]

The teaching of justification continued to be prominent. About 1535, the learned Dominican, Alexander Seton, taught that "to satisfy for sin lies not in man's power, but the remission thereof comes by unfeigned repentance, and by faith apprehending God the Father merciful in Jesus Christ."[26] Throughout this period, from 1525 to 1546, Lutheran books were imported. The contents of most are unknown, but John Gau's work, *The Richt Vay to the Kingdom of Heuine*, does serve as an example. Gau, a Scot exiled in Malmo, practically translated his work from a Danish treatise of Christiern Pedersen. Gau's writing was typically Lutheran in that it emphasized the doctrine of justification by faith and the priesthood of believers.[27] Wedderburn's "Gude and Godlie Ballaties," whose inspiration was largely Lutheran, had a great influence in Scotland during the 1540s. The Lutheran heresy, already spreading, now circulated by means of songs and ballads. The doctrinal content of these poems belonged theologically to the earlier era of German influence, and evidence indicates that Knox came into direct contact with them.[28]

This treatment of the doctrine of justification is not to suggest that Lutheranism failed to attack Catholicism in other areas, and Reformed influences were not already coming into Scotland. It is simply to say that Lutheran influence was strong and probably predominant in Knox's doctrine of justification by faith. Most certainly the Lutherans attacked other Catholic doctrines. This assault can be seen in the plans of the provincial council of 1549 for dealing with heresy.[29] Equally certain, Luther's doc-

23. *Works*, 2:33.
24. *Works*, 1:27.
25. *Works*, 1:511.
26. *Works*, 1:45, 56. The preceding references to Lutheran influence in Scotland came from Knox's own *History*. These citations are an indication that Lutheran thought and activities impressed Knox.
27. Gau, *The Richt Vay to the Kingdom of Heuine*, xiv–lxxi.
28. Mitchell, ed., *A Compendious Book of Godly and Spiritual Songs*, xiv–lxxi.
29. Patrick, Introduction to *Statues of the Scottish Church 1225–1559*, 123–24, 126–27.

trine of justification influenced the Reformed brand of Protestantism in this regard.

Nevertheless, it is difficult to evaluate Reformed influence on Knox in respect to justification. Wishart, though evidencing a Lutheran strain in his theology, said little, if anything about justification by faith.[30] Wishart's influence on Knox in the areas of Scripture and prayer has been encountered, and his ideas shall be met again when dealing with the sacraments, idolatry, and the papacy—but in the area of justification, Wishart apparently had little influence. If so, Knox made no note of it.[31] Furthermore, according to Pierre Janton and V. E. D'Assonville, Knox had read Calvin's *Institutes* by 1550, and the *Institutes* speak to the subject of justification. Nevertheless, though Knox was Reformed in most aspects by 1552, Calvin's influence regarding justification cannot be measured.[32]

Several conclusions emerge from this examination of Knox's thought on justification. First, while Knox emphasized the doctrine more in his pre-Geneva days, he retained it in a living sense throughout his life. Second, the Bible teaches justification by faith, and since Scripture was Knox's primary authority, his ultimate source for this doctrine was the Bible.[33] Third, the strong Lutheran influence in Scotland must have helped point John Knox to the doctrine of justification as found in the Bible. And lastly, as time progressed he closely identified justification with a more complete doctrine of salvation including predestination and sanctification.

---

30. Some see Wishart as a "Lutheran" while others say he started out as a Lutheran but, as a result of a trip to Switzerland, changed to more of a Reformed position. Nevertheless, his theology contained Lutheran ideas. See Reid, "Lutheranism in the Scottish Reformation," 107; Gilck, "Non-Calvinist Influences on the Scottish Reformation," 176–83.

31. See *Works*, 1:149–71; Laing, ed., "The Confession of Faith of the Churches of Switzerland," in vol. 1 of *The Miscellany of the Wodrow Society*, 1:1, 11–22. Only by implication could it be said that Wishart influenced Knox in the doctrine of justification. The Catholics did not accuse Wishart of teaching the doctrine as they accused others. But Wishart evidenced other Lutheran influences (e.g., priesthood of the believer) and did teach the Epistle of Romans, a key book for the doctrine of justification by faith. See *Works*, 1:153–54.

32. *Works*, 3:201; Reid, *Trumpeter of God*, 75–76; D'Assonville, *Knox and the Institutes*, 2–4, 23, 29; Janton, *Concept et Sentiment*, 95. D'Assonville notes the *Institutes* general influence on Knox by 1547 and more specific influence by 1550.

33. The best scriptural illustrations for justification by faith are Romans 3, 4, and 5 and Ephesians 2:8, 9. For evidence that Knox retained this doctrine throughout his life, see *Works*, 3:16–17, 20, 22; 4:467.

Part One: Historical and Theological Foundations

PREDESTINATION

Though all Magisterial Reformers held to the doctrine of predestination, it is normally associated with John Calvin. It is also generally accepted that John Knox adhered to the doctrine of predestination in some form. Nevertheless, the specifics of Knox's predestinarian faith are not common knowledge, and the scholars who have written on this subject have often registered points of disagreement.[34]

Therefore, the primary objective of this section is to focus on the details, the historical development, and the context of the Scottish reformer's concept of predestination, and secondarily to analyze the points of scholarly difference on this subject. These variances pertain to Knox's lengthy treatise on predestination, to Calvin's influence on Knox's predestination thought, and to specific points of predestinarian doctrine. Did Knox's large predestination tract really represent his views on that doctrine? For his predestinarian thought, was Knox largely indebted to John Calvin or to a wider range of Reformed influences including George Wishart, John Hooper, Huldrych Zwingli, and Heinrich Bullinger? Some scholarly disagreements also pertain to Knox's positions regarding supralapsarianism or infralaprianism and on single or double predestination.[35]

Knox's Approach

John Knox's writings concerning predestination primarily span from 1552 to 1559. In all probability, Knox read Calvin's *Institutes* by 1550 and incorporated the doctrine into his thinking some time after this date, particularly during the years 1553 and 1554. In his works before 1552 and after 1559, allusions to predestination are insufficient to constitute a sound base for judgment.[36] The best sources are Knox's writings to Mrs. Bowes (1553–54), *An Answer* (1560), and to a lesser extent, *A Faithful Admo-*

---

34. McEwen, D'Assonville, Janton, and Greaves have written chapters or parts of chapters on Knox's predestination thought. Most of these writings have been on Knox's predestinarian beliefs as they pertain to a specific subject such as ecclesiology, the matter of Calvin's influence, or the questions pertaining to Knox's predestinarian treatise. Greaves chapter is the most descriptive in the general sense, but even this focuses on the matter of Knox's treatise concerning predestination. See McEwen, *The Faith of Knox*, 61–79; D'Assonville, *Knox and the Institutes*, 33–63; Janton, *Concept et Sentiment*, 91–109; Greaves, *Theology and Revolution*, 25–43.

35. See Kyle, "The Concept of Predestination in the Thought of John Knox," 53–77.

36. Janton, *Concept et Sentiment*, 92–93, 95. Some references to predestination before the 1550s include *Works*, 3:17; 4:123, 135, 270; 6:187, 252, 410.

nition (1554), and *Letters to His Brethren* in Scotland (1557). Otherwise, the reformer made few references to the subject, and even those citations occurred in the sense of practical application rather than in setting forth doctrine. *An Answer*, however, was by no means insignificant, for it encompassed nearly an entire volume of about 170,000 words—excluding the lengthy quotations from the work he was refuting.[37]

Knox's approach to predestination during the 1550s was practical in orientation and shaped by historical circumstances. He tended to emphasize predestination, as did the small flock concept of the church, during troubled times and prior to the establishment of the Reformation in Scotland. For John Knox, the 1550s were troubled times—characterized by the return of Catholicism to England under Mary Tudor, subsequent exile, disputes in the English refugee church at Frankfurt, and a failure to establish the Reformation securely in Scotland. Consequently, Knox's predestination thought probably had a powerful psychological basis as well as a theological and historical background.[38]

More specifically, in writing to Mrs. Bowes, Knox's predestinarian approach was pastoral. Mrs. Bowes, his mother-in-law, was a spiritually disturbed woman who needed assurance of salvation and Knox used predestination toward this end. In *A Faithful Admonition*, Knox frequently alluded to the elect as a persecuted remnant. His large treatise, *An Answer*—written at the request of the English refugees in Geneva—replied to the challenge of an anonymous English Anabaptist, and it assaulted all those opinions and sects loosely referred to as Anabaptist.[39]

When Knox wrote *An Answer* in 1558 or 1559, he was far more mature in his ecclesiastical experience and theological conscious than at any other time before, and this tract represented his greatest dogmatic work. Though largely influenced by Calvin in the treatise, Knox followed the method of Zwingli and Bullinger who first turned the doctrine of

---

37. The full title was *An Answer to the Cavillations of an Adversary Respecting the Doctrine of Predestination*. This study will use the short title, *An Answer*. This volume is 468 pages (Laing's edition) and probably was written in late 1558 and early 1559. See *Works*, vol. 5, and Ridley, *John Knox*, 290.

38. Janton, *Concept et Sentiment*, 97, 105–6. Janton probes the psychological motivation to Knox's thought not only in regard to predestination but over a wider range of his ideas and specifically in respect to the reformer's ecclesiology.

39. The book to which Knox responded was *The Confutation of the Errors of the Careless by Necessity* (ca. 1557). This adversary was one of unusual acuteness and ability, and it is suggested that he was the English Anabaptist, Robert Cooche. *Works*, 5:17; Williams, *The Radical Reformation*, 781; Ridley, *John Knox*, 291. See Kyle, "John Knox Confronts the Anabaptists, 493–515; Kyle and Johnson, *John Knox*, 111–34.

predestination into a weapon against the Anabaptists. By so doing they cut the ground from under the feet of the radical argument by shifting the basis—from appeal to experience, from justification and saving faith, and even from the argument about baptism—to God's design for salvation in Christ before the foundation of the world.[40] In the perceived free handling of Scripture by these sectaries, the Magisterial Reformers saw released a spirit of unrestrained inquiry, which in their view would have imperiled the existence of every church that had broken from Rome and dissolved church and state alike.[41]

Richard Greaves agreed that Knox's orientation to the subject of predestination was practical, but he disputes the notion that *An Answer* was written to refute the challenge of an anonymous Anabaptist. Knox's treatise concerning predestination was written shortly after the *First Blast of the Trumpet Against the Monstrous Regiment of Women*, which not only displeased Calvin, but also upset some English Protestants. Greaves contended that Knox wrote *An Answer* largely as a pedantic exercise to maintain his working relationship with Calvin and his disciples, and as a message to the English Protestants to remain loyal to Reformed doctrine.[42] This interesting theory has merit. The *First Blast*, indeed, upset Calvin, and Knox may have desired to please the Swiss reformer. Nevertheless, there is no solid evidence on which to reject Knox's stated purpose for writing his treatise—i.e., to reply to an Anabaptist.

Knox's practical and pastoral approach to predestination corresponded with the manner in which he expressed himself in other areas of dogmatics. The reformer made no attempt to systematize his theology nor to construct political theory. His thought came in response to real situations—and this nonsystematic, pragmatic style was even evident in Knox's only serious attempt at an organized theological presentation.

Though *An Answer* is a lengthy treatise, it is far from being a systematic one. He replied to an Anabaptist who had attacked Calvin's teaching regarding predestination. And instead of developing an orderly argument, Knox assailed the Anabaptist's book, chapter by chapter. The result was repetition, and repetition that was by no means consistent with itself. So Knox, bound by his opponent's argument, approached predestination in

---

40. Shaw, *John Knox: A Quatercentenary Reappraisal*, 10.

41. Brown, *John Knox*, 1:257.

42. Greaves, *Theology and Revolution*, 28–29; Greaves, "The Knoxian Paradox," 91–92.

The Path to Salvation

a haphazard way—and one is left with the impression that the reformer never felt truly at home in the subject[43]

Not only was Knox's approach to predestination practical and pastoral, but it was also personal. He had no doubt whatever that he was numbered among God's elect. John 17—a predestinarian chapter, which recounts Christ's prayer for the elect—was the source of his confidence.[44] Knox saw himself as among those God had given to Christ and whom Christ would preserve, sanctify, intercede for, and take unto himself. His personal confession would include: "I JOHN KNOX . . . most certainly believe, that in the same Christ Jesus; of free grace he did elect and choose me to the life everlasting before the foundation of the world was laid."[45] The Scottish reformer not only saw himself elected to eternal salvation but also chosen on the side of God in the great battle with the forces of Satan. This conviction became a source of both Knox's strength and weakness. Being called as a servant of God and absolutely convinced of the ultimate triumph of the divine cause, the reformer's prevailing mood became one of confidence, conviction, and also intolerance.[46]

Knox's writings on the subject of predestination, particularly his large treatise, also must be viewed in the context of several theological trends. First Knox, as a Marian exile, reflected the views of the English Protestant apocalyptic tradition, which regarded Rome as the whore of Babylon described in the Book of Revelation. This theme ran through Knox's career, but it was quite pronounced in his treatise concerning predestination. Here Knox likened the "true" Christian church and the Catholic Church to two armies, which God so divided and ordained to a cosmic struggle until the return of Christ.[47]

Second, and more significant for the subject of predestination, was the contemporary theological controversy taking place on the Continent. Predestination was a generally accepted doctrine from the very beginning

---

43. McEwen, *The Faith of Knox*, 64; Greaves, *Theology and Revolution*, 29–30. Knox's method of argumentation, though awkward by modern standards, was a well recognized form in the sixteenth century. See Hargrave, "The Predestinarian Offensive of the Marian Exiles at Geneva," 118. For information on Knox's pastoral and practical side, see Reid, "John Knox, Pastor of Souls," 1–21; Kyle, "John Knox and the Care of Souls," 133–44.

44. *Works*, 6:639, 643, 659.

45. *Works*, 5:130.

46. *Works*, 5:412–13; 6: 271, 641; Cowan, *John Knox*, 373; Mackie, *John Knox*, 22–23.

47. *Works*, 5:413; Firth, *The Apocalyptic Tradition in Reformation Britain*, 111–34; Christianson, *Reformers and Babylon*, 3–46.

Part One: Historical and Theological Foundations

of the Reformation, although it was not a source of contention in the early years. The importance of the teaching grew, however, until after mid-century, when a rigorous position on double predestination increasingly became a test of orthodoxy in Reformed circles. But this development did not happen without a struggle. Calvin was at the center of the controversy—particularly in his argument with Jerome Bolsec, an ex-Carmelite who was arrested in 1551 for attacking Calvin's doctrine of double predestination. Other battles over predestination followed, such as the quarrel between Theodore Bibliander and Peter Martyr in Zurich, and Jerome Zanchi's problem in Strassburg.[48]

As Calvin's concern over the spread of anti-predestination views grew, the issue increasingly came to the forefront in Geneva. Theodore Beza, who would become the leader of the Genevan church after Calvin's death, published a summation of Calvin's doctrine of predestination in 1555. The next year, William Whittingham, one of Knox's advocates in Frankfurt, translated it into English with the title—*A Brief Declaration of the Chiefe Points of the Christian Religion set Forth in an Index of Predestination*. The year 1556 saw another work pertaining to predestination published at Geneva. Anthony Gilby, who also supported Knox in the controversy at Frankfurt, wrote *A Briefe Treatise of Election and Reprobation*. Knox certainly knew about these works regarding predestination. In fact, the Geneva Bible, which he helped to translate, included the doctrine of predestination in the marginal notes. Thus Knox formulated his views concerning predestination, particularly those found in his large treatise, at a time when predestination was of concern to many religious leaders.[49]

Knox's Writings Prior to 1559

Knox's earliest writings spoke to the subjects of justification, the purification of religion, and the Lord's Supper; and in these first treatises the issue of predestination did not arise.[50] The Scottish reformer first made a serious reference to the doctrine of election in his 1552 *Epistle to the Congregation of Berwick*. Not only did Knox frequently use the word *elect*

---

48. Baker, *Heinrich Bullinger and the Covenant*, 27–28; Parker, *John Calvin*, 111–15.

49. Danner, "Anthony Gilby: Puritan in Exile," 415–16; Hargrave, "The Marian Exiles," 112–18; *The Geneva Bible*. A facsimile of the 1560 edition, Eph 1; Rom 8; Greaves, *Theology and Revolution* 27, 40–41; Danner, "The Theology of the Geneva Bible, 164–67.

50. *Works*, 3:13–75; Knox, "The Practice of the Lord's Supper Used in Berwick by John Knox, 1550," 29–92.

in this tract, but also in his summary of the gospel he related the doctrine of predestination to other aspects of salvation: Divine providence is the source of election, the church is established by election, and God chooses his children in Jesus Christ before the foundation of the world. Knox asserted that there is no "other cause moving God to elect and choose us than his own infinite goodness and mere mercy."[51]

As Knox's theology acquired depth, his soteriology obviously moved toward a Reformed position. In many ways, his thinking at this point on election resembled that of Zwingli and Bullinger—namely, a moderate form of predestination accentuating election and relating it to other aspects of the gospel. Nevertheless, there is no evidence as to the exact source of Knox's doctrine at this time.[52]

Knox's *Epistles to Mrs. Bowes* written over the years 1553 and 1554 reveal several aspects of Knox's early predestination thought. First, they indicate Knox had some awareness of the doctrine of double predestination even before meeting Calvin. Knox asserted that the reprobate flee God and cannot love him.[53] Second, in these epistles, Knox related election to the doctrines of assurance and sanctification. Knox's later treatise, *An Answer*, dealt primarily with the objective side of salvation. Salvation comes from belief in Christ, but the elect believe because they have been ordained to do so, and thus election assures salvation.[54]

Still, Knox's unstable mother-in-law, Mrs. Bowes, doubted her election. Her problems first focused Knox's attention on the subjective and interior side of assurance. After first pointing out to Mrs. Bowes that assurance rests on something outside of her—the unchanging promise of God—Knox then advocated the dangerous course of self inspection. According to Knox, election must produce certain fruits and signs or something is wrong. Absence of sin is not such a sign because the elect could sin grievously, and at times even resemble the reprobate. Despite the elect's sin, however, God does not abandon them to perdition but hears their petitions and enables them to resist sin. Mrs. Bowes was not, therefore, to despair of her election because of isolated lapses into sin. In fact, Knox pointed out that her worries concerning her sin indicated she was of the elect. Though the elect need not lose hope if they fall into sin, they cannot

---

51. Knox, "Epistle to the Congregation of Berwick," 258.

52. Locher, *Zwingli's Thought*, 124–32; Baker, *Bullinger*, 27–54; Greaves, *Theology and Revolution*, 38.

53. *Works*, 3:349.

54. *Works*, 5:26–82.

be devoid of all positive signs. The elect cannot delight in persistent evil-doing and have a deep aversion to godliness and still claim the assurance of election. Rather, they must evidence a positive godliness and a genuine desire to live a pure, holy life.[55]

Third, Knox related predestination to an aspect of his ecclesiology. He regarded the invisible church, known only to God, as synonymous with the elect. Conversely, the visible church contained both the elect and reprobate. Nevertheless, Knox believed the visible church most likely to contain the elect was the small, persecuted flock. In these epistles written to Mrs. Bowes and during the reign of Mary Tudor's reign in England, Knox said, "There are few that are chosen . . . and therefore ought you greatly rejoice, knowing yourself to be one of the small and contemptible flock to whom it has pleased God . . . to give the kingdom."[56] For the small flock, election was no abstract doctrine but a support in the moment of trial. Knox used election to comfort and exhort the menaced flock. Such a theme also came through in *An Exposition Upon Psalm VI* (1554), *A Faithful Admonition* (1554), and *A Letter of Wholesome Counsel* (1556).[57]

Knox's 1554 *Exposition Upon Psalm VI*, also written to Mrs. Bowes, contained frequent mention of the elect. Knox, however, developed no systematic doctrine of predestination at this time. But rather, he continued the themes found in the *Epistles to Mrs. Bowes*—namely, references to the reprobate that indicate some movement toward a doctrine of double predestination, mention of the Holy Spirit's work in creating in the elect signs of their election, and further use of election to comfort the persecuted small flock. Still, he seemed to make a fresh statement in his condemnation of Pelagianism as a heresy and its emphasis on free will, natural human power, and good works as a means of salvation.[58]

During the remainder of 1554, Knox's pen continued to be active. His *Godly Letter of Warning* made no mention of predestination. But it did contain the first reference to Calvin, and demonstrated that prior to meeting the Genevan, Knox already had been reading the Swiss reformer's works and had a high opinion of him.[59] Though Knox barely alluded to election in his *Two Comfortable Epistles* of May 10 and 31, the subject

---

55. *Works*, 3:338–39, 341–42, 345, 349–50, 353, 358, 360, 362–63, 371, 374, 377, 384, 393.

56. *Works*, 3:351.

57. Some examples are *Works* 3:293, 349, 351, 377; 4:123–24, 135.

58. *Works*, 3:121–24, 131,142–43.

59. *Works*, 3:201.

The Path to Salvation

arose frequently in *A Faithful Admonition*. Nevertheless, he still did not make any systematic statements concerning predestination, but continued his previous themes—comfort and encouragement for the elect who could be found in the small flock, insistence that the professors of faith demonstrate signs of their election, and scattered references to the reprobate.[60]

By 1556 Knox had been to Geneva, where predestination was increasingly becoming an important issue. Knox's writings, however, did not evidence any immediate surge of interest in the subject. In fact, his earliest 1556 works—a letter to Mary of Guise and an exposition on Matthew 4—scarcely pertained to predestination. Thus only scattered references to Satan persecuting the elect can be found.[61] His *Answers to Some Questions Concerning Baptism* noted election in the context of the covenant. Though in other writings, Knox alluded to a general and conditional covenant to all the inhabitants of a realm, and even said that the covenant and election do not coincide; this baptismal tract spoke of a permanent covenant in the context of election to individual salvation. Even iniquity could not break this covenant because this promise of God made to the elect cannot be changed nor frustrated.[62]

In *A Letter of Wholesome Counsel*, Knox again indicated that election made godly living possible for the elect. Temptation cannot overcome the elect because they have been called from ignorance to taste God's mercy, which encourages them to build up their faith by the study of Scripture.[63] *The Form of Prayers* (1556), which included Calvin's *Catechism* and was used by the English Congregation at Geneva, made several references to predestination. *The Form's* Confession of Faith mentioned the elect and the reprobate in connection with several subjects: baptism, the last judgment, and the invisible church which "is not seen to man's eye, but only known to God, who . . . has ordained some, as vessels of wrath, to damnation, and has chosen others, as vessels of mercy to be saved."[64] Although Knox did not write this confession, he approved of it.[65]

Though the interest in predestination in Geneva continued to be strong, only one of Knox's 1557 writings made significant references to

---

60. *Works*, 3: 266, 276, 285–86, 304, 313–14, 316, 318, 323–24, 326.
61. *Works*, 4:75–76, 102, 105, 108.
62. *Works*, 4:123. For illustrations of Knox's ideas on the general and contractual covenant, see *Works*, 5:177, 484.
63. *Works*, 4:135.
64. *Works*, 4:171–72.
65. Greaves, *Theology and Revolution*, 39; Hargrave, "The Marian Exiles," 113.

the doctrine. Neither the *Familiar Epistles,* penned from 1555 to 1558, nor Knox's notes to *An Apology* do more than vaguely allude to the subject.[66] *The Letters to His Brethren* in Scotland, however, recorded some important statements concerning predestination. Knox not only reiterated some of his previous themes on the relationship of election to good works, but he also made statements that he later developed in his large predestination treatise. Knox condemned the Scottish Protestants who believed that human free will is free and therefore denied election and reprobation. He insisted that under no circumstances can good works or human choice bring about election. Knox not only said these advocates of free will denied the Godhead, but he associated them with the heresies of Arianism and Pelagianism. At this point, Knox clearly related predestination to its source—the omnipotent providence of God. Knox, therefore, regarded it as blasphemy to deny predestination.[67]

Knox's 1558 writings reveal his preoccupation at this time, namely the overthrow of idolatrous rulers and the establishment of "true religion" in England and Scotland. Consequently, Knox's political pamphlets (e.g., *The First Blast, The Appellation, A Letter to the Commonalty*) and other tracts contain only a few references to the elect and reprobate.[68] Therefore, as Knox embarked on his major predestination treatise, two points should be observed. First, Knox had not given any extensive treatment to the subject of predestination in his pre-1559 writings. He did not, as Calvin had done, develop the doctrine gradually over a period of years. Rather, Knox moved suddenly into a lengthy treatment of the subject. Second, what Knox had written concerning predestination in these earlier works harmonized with his forthcoming expanded treatise on that subject, partly because the reformer's earlier writings on this doctrine were quite general and pastoral.

Knox's Predestination Treatise

Knox probably wrote *An Answer* in late 1558 and early 1559, and it was published in 1560. At the onset of this lengthy treatise, Knox stated his agreement with the judgment of John Calvin on the subject of predestination.[69]

66. *Works,* 4:223, 297, 327.
67. *Works,* 4:262, 269–70, 272–73, 276.
68. *Works,* 4:366, 401, 436, 527.
69. *Works,* 5:30. See also Kirk, "The Influence of Calvinism on the Scottish Reformation," 158, and D'Assonville, *Knox and the Institutes,* 33–34, 43.

From Knox's frequent references to Calvin and the content of his work, such a statement seems essentially correct. The predestinarian thought of the two reformers, however, exhibited secondary differences due to methodology and circumstances, and possibly even one variance on a substantial issue. Richard Greaves does not necessarily contest Calvin's influence in the treatise, but he questions Knox's motive in underscoring his agreement with Calvin. Knox, Greaves insists, had to soothe Calvin because *The First Blast* had upset the Swiss reformer.[70]

Predestination was not the very center of Calvin's teaching, nor was it for Knox. Yet at the same time, in *An Answer* the doctrine was not just a theoretical matter for Knox, but had practical importance—revealing a mainspring of his thinking and action.[71] Calvin's predestinarian thought ranged over a broader field than did Luther's and Knox's largely because his dogmatic formulations were also wider. James McEwen, therefore, contends Knox followed Luther's method rather than Calvin's in taking a more narrow approach to predestination. Knox began with the doctrine as it related to personal salvation and then made excursions into the broader field of Christian theology.[72] His nonsystematic and even haphazard approach to predestination makes it difficult to conform or deny McEwen's judgment. It is certain, however, that Knox related predestination to other areas of his theology.

In *An Answer*, Knox went to great lengths to emphasize the practical necessity of predestination to his view of salvation. Without the doctrine of predestination, faith could not be taught nor established.[73] True faith springs from election and not the reverse for "if you understand that Election has no promise without faith, I answer, That God's free election in Jesus Christ needs neither promise nor faith . . . but (only) his own good pleasure in Christ."[74] Redemption, from start to finish, depended on God's free election and without it no salvation is possible.[75] In fact, Knox implied that predestination and the gospel were nearly synonymous.[76]

Though in his treatise Knox accentuated predestination more in the context of soteriology, he certainly integrated it into other areas of

---

70. Greaves, *Theology and Reformation*, 152.
71. Reid, *Trumpeter of God*, 152.
72. McEwen, *The Faith of Knox*, 70.
73. *Works*, 5:25.
74. *Works*, 5:279–80.
75. *Works*, 5:26–28, 63, 278–81.
76. *Works*, 5:38.

dogmatics—namely, God and providence, the church, human nature, and good works. Salvation depends on election, but Knox grounded predestination itself in his concept of God. For Knox God is, of course, immutable and absolutely sovereign. Consequently, predestination is an immutable and sovereign decree.[77] God can never repent of election, neither can the elect refuse election nor finally perish despite their sin. Conversely, the reformer regarded reprobation as equally immutable and divinely determined.[78] Knox—just as Calvin had done in the 1539 edition of the *Institutes* and as Zwingli had done earlier—connected divine predestination and providence: predestination was but a decree within the larger context of providence.[79]

In a nonsystematic sense, Knox's ecclesiology rested squarely on predestination. The church consists of the elect of God: and if there is no election, there is no church. Actually, only the small flock and invisible church experiences predestination, for the notion of an elected church opposes the national concept of the church.[80] In fact, Knox dedicated his predestination treatise to the church for its instruction: "But yet I say that the doctrine of God's eternal Predestination is so necessary to the Church of God, that without the same can Faith neither be truly taught, neither surely established. . . ."[81] Predestination not only establishes and multiplies the church but also preserves it. Thus Knox largely related predestination to his ecclesiology in times of stress (e.g., while exiled from 1553 to 1559, when fearful of the Counter-Reformation in 1565). This preservation theme confirmed predestination more as a doctrine for the elect than for the damned.[82]

Yet Knox—writing in apocalyptic language—insisted that the church of Satan, i.e., the reprobate, also came about because of divine predestination. Therefore Knox apparently regarded predestination as more corporate than individual because the church is the society of the elect preserved by God.[83] But, along with Calvin, Knox never elevated election to a mark

---

77. *Works*, 5:27, 63–67, 70, 73, 280–81. See also Janton, *Concept et Sentiment*, 10.

78. *Works*, 5:405–6.

79. *Works*, 5:31–32; D'Assonville, *Knox and the Institutes*, 43–44; Locher, *Zwingli's Thought*, 124.

80. Janton, *Concept et Sentiment*, 94–95.

81. *Works*, 5:25.

82. *Works*, 2:293, 299; 6:249–51; Janton, *Concept et Sentiment*, 97, 102.

83. Janton, *Concept et Sentiment*, 97, 102.

of the visible church for the elect and reprobate cannot be conclusively determined.[84]

Knox also rested his notions of sanctification and good works on his doctrine of predestination. The reformer's sequence was election, true faith and salvation, and then good works. Without the doctrine of predestination human beings could not have a humble knowledge of themselves. True humility comes when the elect become aware that God has illumined their eyes and elected them to salvation, while leaving others in darkness and perdition. The humility that comes through the knowledge of election is the mother of all virtue and the root of all goodness. Thus, in *An Answer*, Knox contended that the doctrine of predestination established good works. No other doctrine could make one thankful to God and obedient according to his commandments.[85]

In the treatise, Knox defined predestination as the eternal and immutable decree of God, by which he once determined within himself what he will have done with every individual. God did not create all people to be of the same condition.[86] Predestination for Knox included both election and reprobation, which numbered all of humanity in God's decree. Along with most sixteenth-century reformers, Knox certainly rejected the modern revulsion toward predestination as something cruel, harsh, and unjust. The Scottish reformer proceeded to give a larger definition of predestination: "It is the most wise and most just purpose of God, by which, before all time, he constantly has decreed to call those whom he has loved in Christ . . . that they may be assured of their adoption by the justification of faith. . . ."[87]

Knox firmly adhered to both the positive and negative sides of predestination—election and reprobation.[88] This double-edged predestination evidenced itself in several ways. In the eternal counsel of God there existed a difference in humankind even before creation.[89] Knox did not speculate about the number elected to life or reprobated to death. Rather, he simply stood on what he believed to be clearly revealed—the fact of

84. D'Assonville, *Knox and the Institutes*, 102.
85. *Works*, 25–30.
86. *Works*, 5:36.
87. *Works*, 5:36.

88. There is no question that Knox held to both election and reprobation. The question pertains to what type of reprobation Knox maintained? Was it Calvinistic active reprobation or Augustinian passive reprobation? This issue will be encountered later.

89. *Works*, 5:73.

individual election and reprobation.⁹⁰ The Anabaptist opponent accused Knox of using logic more than Scripture to support the doctrine of double predestination. But Knox insisted the position was biblical and logical arguments were only handmaidens of Scripture.⁹¹

Consequently, he defended predestination by the use of the third chapter of Genesis and Paul's epistles. Reflecting the spirit of the English apocalyptic tradition, Knox said that in God's counsel a difference existed between human beings, but all were in one lump or mass. From this mass God appointed two seeds to come forth, and these two seeds represented the two churches. From the seed of Eve came the individual elect, which composed the church of Christ, and from the seed of the serpent sprang the reprobate and the church of Satan. While God promised the elect victory, his irrevocable sentence condemned the reprobate to destruction.⁹² Yet it must be noted that Knox placed much more emphasis on the positive election of sinners to salvation, than on the reprobative aspect of predestination.⁹³

Freedom—both human and divine—played a major role in Knox's concept of predestination. In *An Answer*, he insisted that no activity, regardless of its apparent unimportance, took place without God's ordaining it to come to pass. Yet this absolute providence does not destroy human responsibility nor make God the author of sin. Predestination being so closely related with providence must be associated with the same conclusions. On one hand, Knox insisted on outright predestination. But on the other, he placed great stress on human responsibility and the fact that God did not predestinate humans to sin: "Although, I say that so he has ordained the fall of man, that I utterly deny him to be the author of sin."⁹⁴

God's freedom, more than human freedom, was important to Knox, and he never tired of emphasizing the fact of God's free election. God freely chose whom he would to salvation or perdition without any consideration of any foreknown works or faith on the part of human beings. Prescience, which based divine election on God's foreknowledge of events, endeavored to achieve a synergism—a kind of cooperation between God

---

90. *Works*, 5:394.

91. *Works*, 5:61. According to D'Assonville, Knox emphasized philosophic determinism as the cause of reprobation. This issue will be encountered later. D'Assonville, *Knox and the Institutes*, 59–60.

92. *Works*, 5:61–62.

93. *Works*, 5:44. Janton notes that, except for *An Answer*, reprobation received little development in Knox's thought from 1554–56. See Janton, *Concept et Sentiment*, 95.

94. *Works*, 5:169.

and humankind in election. God knew in advance who would believe and who would not, and he elected or rejected accordingly. In *An Answer*, Knox faithfully followed Calvin on this matter and bitterly opposed this traditional doctrine of foreknowledge.[95]

Knox acknowledged the existence of prescience but he gave it a different definition: "But we saw that all things be so present before God, that he does not contemplate and behold them in their verity and perfection."[96] The Scottish reformer adamantly refused to separate divine foreknowledge and divine will. When God foresees something, it comes to pass because his power is omnipotent.[97] To the Anabaptist's claim that election rested on foreseen works and faith, Knox belabored the theme that God's free election had no restraints whatever. To quote one passage: "[W]e constantly affirm that neither faith, neither works, neither yet any quality that is, or that God foresaw to be in us, is the cause of our Predestination or Election to life everlasting."[98]

The Word of God plays a major role in the predestination process. In *An Answer*, Knox attributed the differences between the elect and reprobate to the contrary work of Scripture. The Word of God, by the power of the Holy Spirit, illuminates the eyes and softens the hearts of the elect. On the contrary, the reprobate, though hard anyway, are further hardened after contact with God's Word. To support this position, Knox cited the martyrdom of Stephen as one example: before being martyred, Stephen preached the Scriptures with the result that the reprobate became more hardened than before. Thus Knox saw Scripture in a dual role: "The Word falling into the heart of the Elect, does mollify and illuminate, as before is said, but falling into the heart of the Reprobate, it does harden and excecate [to blind] the same, by reason of the quality and incurable corruption of the person."[99]

God manifests his goodness, mercy, and justice in predestination. Knox insisted that to measure divine mercy by numbers was blasphemy for God's mercy cannot be gauged by whether he ordained more or less

---

95. D'Assonville, *Knox and the Institutes*, 48–49.

96. *Works*, 5:36. According to D'Assonville, Knox took his definition almost literally from the *Institutes*. See D'Assonville, *Knox and the Institutes*, 49.

97. *Works*, 5:133–34.

98. *Works*, 5:230. Other passages denying that predestination depended on foreknowledge are *Works*, 5:73, 147–48, 150, 281–82. A favorite passage used by Knox to support God's free election and to reject restraints such as foreseen faith and works is Romans 9. Here and elsewhere, Knox simply belabored the issue of God's free election.

99. *Works*, 5:387.

to salvation than to perdition. The reformer maintained that God's mercy and goodness have been manifested in two ways. All humankind—the elect and reprobate alike—participate in God's general goodness and temporal blessings; in fact the wicked seem to prosper more than the chosen ones. Second, the elect have nothing that they did not receive by mercy, for they too deserve judgment and not election. Even reprobation demonstrates God's justice. Whereas all people merit judgment, God is not unjust in giving the reprobate their due punishment.[100]

While Knox repeatedly confessed that election took place before the foundation of the world, his Anabaptist antagonist contended for a general election of all humanity, rather than for the election of individuals. Furthermore, he argued that individuals could fall from election. Knox responded to these contentions by reasoning for only one election—that of individuals to eternal life.[101] The reformer did, however, admit to a general vocation, by which all people are called to some knowledge of God that falls short of election. To quote Knox: "That there is a General vocation, by which the world by some manner of means is called to a knowledge of ... But that there is an Election of life everlasting, except that which is and was in Christ Jesus ... I am assured that neither Scripture affirms."[102]

Not only did the reformer speak of a limited election, but he also believed God's love to be limited. In *An Answer*, Knox categorically rejected the Anabaptist's contention that God loved all human beings. God, not being bound by the natural law to love all his offspring, loved whom he chose to love and condemned whom he wished. In Knox's words: "You (the Anabaptist) make the love of God common to all men; and that do we constantly deny...."[103] But this limited love did not mean God's love was less than perfect.[104] God loved his elect with an immutable love, and though they sinned and apparently fell, his love remained constant. He hated their sin but not them.[105]

---

100. *Works*, 5:86–88.

101. *Works*, 5:96. In Ephesians 1, Paul stated that election took place before the foundation of the world. See *Works*, 5:72–73, 97.

102. *Works*, 5:117.

103. *Works*, 5:56–60, 235.

104. *Works*, 5:59.

105. In *An Answer*, Knox took verses, particularly from Romans 5, referring to Christ's death and implied that they pertained only to the elect. For example, the reformer hinted that the "we" in the following verse referred only to the elect: "when we were sinners Christ died for us...." Nevertheless, Knox did not expressly say that Christ died only for the elect. See *Works*, 5: 236–37.

In his predestination treatise, as in his letters to Mrs. Bowes, Knox also related election to the doctrine of assurance. The belief that those who are truly redeemed may have the certainty of salvation is often described as *assurance*. The assurance of salvation has, of course, two sides—the objective and subjective. In *An Answer*, Knox did not focus on the subjective aspect of this article of faith, as he had done in his correspondence with Mrs. Bowes. Rather, he insisted that true faith had as its foundation the immutable election of God. Salvation comes from belief in Christ, but the elect believe because they have been ordained to do so, and thus election assures salvation.[106]

Ultimately, Knox grounded assurance in his concept of God. God is immutable and constant, and once he chose one to salvation, this election cannot change. Nevertheless, in his predestination treatise, Knox did not entirely ignore the subjective element in assurance. He insisted that since the Holy Spirit seals and sanctifies the elect, there must be some evidence of the Spirit's operation in the heart or election is doubtful: "that if we find not the Spirit of Christ working in us, that then we can never be assured of our election."[107] Even when the elect backslide, their faith can never be totally destroyed. Unlike the reprobate, there must always remain some root and spark of faith in the elect.[108] When the elect sin, as did Adam and David, they still retain faith and do not reject God's grace as do the reprobate. So faith, repentance, and the working of God's grace are definite signs of election.[109]

The chief difficulty with the doctrine of predestination arises in regard to its negative side—reprobation. Therefore, Knox's Anabaptist opponent centered his attack on reprobation, which he called "this horrible doctrine."[110] So Knox, in *An Answer*, found himself defending a subject not developed elsewhere in his writings, and one with which he was uncomfortable.[111] Here Knox openly attempted to expound Calvin's view in regard to double predestination. Even though he had some success, he apparently deviated from Calvin at two points: confusion between double and single predestination and a different emphasis on the cause of reprobation. These variations arose partly because Knox, being bound by

---

106. *Works*, 5:26–28.
107. *Works*, 5:210.
108. *Works*, 3:243, 341, 393; 5:243, 401.
109. *Works*, 5:243, 401.
110. *Works*, 5:89.
111. Janton, *Concept et Sentiment*, 95; Greaves, *Theology and Revolution*, 37.

PART ONE: Historical and Theological Foundations

his opponent's argumentation and terminology, constantly gave the appearance of escaping from a tight corner. This situation, of course, led to confusion, shifts of thought—and even outright contradictions.

That Knox held to double predestination is not a matter of debate, for he clearly referred to both election and reprobation.[112] But whether his concept of reprobation contained both the elements of preterition (passing by) and condemnation (dishonor and wrath) or just that of preterition (which resembles only single predestination) is a difficult matter. Both elements were present in Knox's thought. But for the most part, he spoke of reprobation either so generally the components were not discernable—or as if this decree was primarily an act of preterition with condemnation coming as a natural result of God's bypassing some individuals.

The aspect of condemnation can be found in Knox's predestination treatise. He specifically placed reprobation and punishment in a cause and effect relationship as Calvin had done: "And from that same eternity has reprobated others, whom . . . he shall adjudge to torments and fire inextinguishable."[113] Still, more numerous and explicit were the passages presenting reprobation as a decree of preterition as Augustine had represented it. Knox spoke of the reprobate as those whom God "leaves to themselves to languish in their corruption . . . till that they come to perdition."[114] Representative of Knox's teaching on passive reprobation was the following: "that God in his eternal counsel . . . has of one mass chosen vessels of honor . . . and of the same mass has left others in that corruption in which they were to fall, and so were they prepared to destruction."[115]

Why did Knox apparently accent the element of preterition and give the impression of maintaining only single predestination? Any answers to this question must be a matter of conjecture. First, in a treatise acknowledging Calvin's influence, it is doubtful that Knox would have openly rejected the Swiss reformer's position. Instead, it might be that Knox was simply inconsistent on this issue. Second, the Scottish reformer relied heavily on the 1539 and 1550 editions of the *Institutes* for the content of his predestination treatise. In these editions, Calvin did not develop a pronounced doctrine of reprobation. Third, Knox was uncomfortable with the subject of reprobation and an emphasis on preterition presented fewer difficulties in his debate with the Anabaptist. Next, the Scottish reformer might

---

112. *Works*, 5:73, 171, 394, 61–62, 407–8, 51, 65, 41, and others.
113 *Works*, 5:61.
114. *Works*, 5:125–26.
115. *Works*, 5:112–13. See also Danner, "The Theology of the Geneva Bible," 166.

The Path to Salvation

have been influenced by either Zwingli or Bullinger on this matter, but this hypothesis is uncertain. Fifth, Knox was first and foremost a preacher and thus did not emphasize nor develop any aspect of reprobation, especially not its harsher element.

What caused reprobation? The Scottish reformer insisted on two causes—the hidden will of God and the sin of humanity. The hidden will of God was the primary source of all things and thus caused reprobation. To substantiate this claim Knox quoted Augustine via Calvin's *Institutes*: "Why did God so? It is answered, because so he would. But if you proceed asking, Why he would? You seek a thing greater and more high than God's will, which can not be found." Continuing on the same subject Knox said, "that he (God) has just causes (but hid from us) in rejecting part of men."[116]

However, at this point Knox apparently ran counter to Calvin and created difficulties for himself in his debate with the Anabaptist. Calvin emphatically stated that people should concern themselves with the secondary cause of reprobation—sin, rather than with the primary source, God's hidden will. The Geneva reformer guarded against meaningless speculation about the hidden cause while stressing the reason indicated by Scripture—human sin. But now Knox did just the opposite. To him, any cause outside the will of God led to confusion. Thus he made God's will not only the primary source of reprobation but nearly the exclusive cause: "But because that in his Word there is no cause assigned (God's good will only excepted) why he has chosen some and rejected others."[117]

Nevertheless, due to the difficulties caused by his opponent, Knox at times shifted emphasis to the point of near contradiction. He grudgingly acknowledged a second but subordinate cause of reprobation, human sin: "as I neither excuse their manifest rebellion, neither yet deny it to be a most just cause of their condemnation, so utterly deny I that their present sins were the only or chief cause of their reprobation."[118] But this concession did not satisfy his opponent, who insisted that if God's ordinance caused reprobation it also must be the cause of sin.[119] This contention Knox would not allow. God's absolute providence notwithstanding, reprobation did

---

116. *Works*, 5:39. The brackets are mine.

117. *Works*, 5:391. See also *Works*, 5:408. "If you say, that death and damnation cometh not from God's will, but by sin and unbelief of man, you have relieved yourself nothing" (D'Assonville, *Knox and the Institutes*, 60–61).

118. *Works*, 5:71.

119. *Works*, 5:112.

not cause sin. "Man therefore falls (God's providence is ordaining), but yet he falls by his own fault."[120]

Knox's Later Writings

In Knox's predestination treatise the mark of John Calvin is discernable. To an extent, Knox and the other leading figures of the English church in Geneva came under the influence of John Calvin in this regard, especially during the years of 1556 to 1559. Nevertheless, Knox's writings after his major treatise on predestination mentioned that subject even less than his pre-1559 works. In all probability several circumstances contributed to this situation. One, Knox tended to mention this subject during times of persecution; and with the establishment of Protestantism in Scotland, this oppression abated. Two, he was preoccupied with the writing of the *History of the Reformation in Scotland* and thus wrote less on other subjects. Next, predestination was not always pertinent to the topics he addressed in the post-1560 years. Finally, in his major predestination tract, he probably said all that he had to say on the subject.

In 1560, the year following the writing of *An Answer*, Knox and his colleagues drafted the *Scots Confession*. Chapter 8 addressed the subject of election, otherwise the *Confession* contained only scattered references to election and even less to reprobation. This chapter referring to Ephesians 1:4, affirmed the election of believers in Christ before creation, and mentioned the reprobate only once. The chapter on sin spoke of the Holy Spirit's work in the heart of the elect. Chapter 16 described the church as a company of the elect, both past and future. The next chapter, which addressed the immortality of the soul, mentioned both the elect and reprobate. Chapter 21 noted the role of the sacraments in assuring the elect of their union with Christ. The last chapter of the *Confession* declared that both the elect and reprobate may be members of the visible church.[121] Though Knox certainly approved of the *Confession*—including its treatment of predestination—Duncan Shaw might be correct in his assertion that John Willock, who was influenced by Bullinger and John 'a Lasco, wrote the chapter on election.[122]

References to predestination can scarcely be detected in a series of letters written by Knox from 1559 to 1562 or in his tract debating the Mass

---

120. *Works*, 5:168.
121. *Works*, 2:100–101, 98, 108, 113–14, 119–20.
122. Shaw, *Reformation and Revolution*, 59–60.

with the Abbott of Crossraguel (1562). John Knox wrote his *History* from 1559 to 1571. In this lengthy work, Knox obviously developed no doctrine of predestination, but his concept of history—which reflected both his notion of God's absolute sovereignty over all events and his attachment to the apocalyptic tradition—naturally alluded to the subject. Not only did the God of John Knox control history; but history itself—particularly the Scottish Reformation—was a battle between the forces of God and the forces of Satan, i.e., the elect and the reprobate. Though Satan persecuted the elect, God had ordained that they would triumph for his glory.[123]

Knox's *Sermon on Isaiah XXVI*, preached before Lord Darnley in 1565, did contain frequent references to the elect and reprobate. From 1562 on, troubles mounted for the Reformed kirk. Protestantism had been established legally but not financially, and the threat of the revival of Catholicism hung like a foreboding shadow over Knox. Under such conditions, Knox returned to the theme of a predestinated church, only this time it was not the small flock of the exile years, but the invisible church within the visible kirk. The visible church contained both the elect and reprobate.[124] Knox's last writing, *An Answer to Tyrie*, penned in 1568, concentrated on the visible church and contained nothing of note in respect to predestination.

SANCTIFICATION AND GOOD WORKS

Knox had something to say about sanctification and good works, particularly in his letters to Mrs. Bowes, but the reformer made both so dependent on other areas of dogmatics (e.g. election, assurance, the Holy Spirit, humanity) that any detailed treatment here would result in needless repetition. To sanctify means to set apart for a divine purpose, and as such it is closely related to election. In theological terminology, justification, election, and sanctification are separate—but Knox tended to blur such distinctions. He believed that sanctification performed by God's free grace through the Holy Spirit depends entirely on election.

The *Scots Confession* defines good works as only those deeds done in faith and at God's commandment. Conversely, evil works are those done against his injunction and without the express commandment of his Word.[125] A sampling of Knox's writings clearly points toward a divine source for good works. To Mrs. Bowes Knox would say, "The Justice of

---

123. *Works*, 1:119, 131–32, 351, 223; 2:417; 4:298, 303–4; 6:271.
124. *Works*, 6:243, 252, 256, 266–68, 270, 272.
125. *Works*, 2:107.

Jesus Christ must quench and extinguish your sins; . . . the power of Christ must overcome your weakness and infirmity."[126] In other writings during the mid-1550s, Knox indicated that only the Holy Spirit, dwelling in the elect, can be the source of good works. The Holy Spirit causes faith, and faith is the fountainhead of good works. The elect do good works because they remain as branches in Jesus Christ.[127] In his 1560 predestination treatise, Knox stated, "that as God . . . has called us to the dignity of his children, so has he sanctified us, and appointed us to walk in pureness and holiness all the days of our life; that we continually fight against the lusts and inordinate affections that remain in this our corrupt nature. . . ."[128] Conversely, in the same treatise the reformer insisted that the reprobate do not have the spirit of regeneration and thus cannot perform works acceptable to God.[129]

A charge often leveled at predestination is that it produces moral laxity. But in spite of the importance of election to Knox, he was no libertine. He recognized that the sinful nature continues after regeneration. Though the elect occasionally and even disastrously fall into sin, the pattern of their life has to be one of godliness and resistance to sin. If not, they probably are not among the elect, for sanctification is a sign of election. In fact, in *An Answer*, Knox used the example of Calvin's Geneva to refute the charges of libertinism. For here (as he contended) purity of life prevailed, vice was punished, and the poor received care.

In fact, Knox's emphasis on the holiness of the visible church is some indication of the importance he placed on godly living. The Scottish reformer went beyond the other major reformers in demanding the purification of worship in the church. Church discipline is an external device to promote sanctification. And the fact that Knox and the Scottish Reformation went beyond Calvin—in making this restraint a mark of the church—indicates not only the turbulent situation that existed in Scotland but also the significance the Scottish reformer placed on godly living. When Knox contested the arguments of James Tyrie in 1566–67, he placed considerable emphasis on holiness as a true mark of the church. Because Catholicism lacked the holiness that springs from genuine faith, Knox argued that it was not the true church—in spite of its claim to universality.[130]

126. *Works*, 3: 384.
127. *Works*, 3:21; 4:47.
128. *Works*, 5:210.
129. *Works*, 5:394, 174–76.
130. *Works*, 6:498.

5

The Church and Its Many Faces

THE LEADERS OF THE Protestant Reformation not only intended a revival of personal piety; they aimed as well to reshape the corporate forms of religion. They did not convert individuals to the Protestant faith only to abandon them to a state of religious detachment. Rather, the Protestant Reformers labored to rebuild the church and felt themselves called to be agents of its restoration. They steadfastly believed that the Holy Catholic Church had been instituted by God for the nurture and fellowship of souls and that outside of this body exists "no ordinary possibility of salvation." Accordingly, the founders of Protestantism laid great emphasis upon the nature and function of the church. Ecclesiology was a notable and principal part of their theology.[1]

CONCEPT OF THE CHURCH

Though John Knox did not write a treatise on ecclesiology per se, church considerations occupied an important, if not dominant place in his writings. The primary objective of Knox's career was the establishment of "true" religion (the Reformed faith) in Scotland, and this endeavor could be achieved to a large extent through the vehicle of the church. As a consequence, passages on the nature and functions of the church can be found in Knox's writings from his first sermon in 1547 to his last tract, published in 1572. Despite the importance he placed on the church, these writings do not reveal any strikingly new ideas in respect to sixteenth-century ecclesiology. For the most part, his position harmonized with that of the

---

1. See Kyle, "The Nature of the Church in the Thought of John Knox," 485–501; McNeill, "The Church in Sixteenth-Century Reformed Theology," 251.

Part One: Historical and Theological Foundations

other Magisterial Reformers. Knox's originality rests not in the invention of new concepts but in the degree and manner in which he applied common ideas (e.g. purification of the church).[2]

As in Knox's view of Scripture and God, his doctrine of the church evidenced no drastic development. But this situation does not mean that his ecclesiology was static. Rather the totality of his church doctrine remained constant, but his emphasis fluctuated with the circumstances. For example, he emphasized the small flock during the exile years, a national church to establish the Reformation, and the invisible church when problems arose in the Scottish kirk.[3] With the exception of certain specific tracts on idolatry, baptism, and the Lord's Supper, Knox's ideas on the church have to be gathered piecemeal from his writings. Much of the reformer's thought on the nature of the church came after 1558. In fact, his fullest expression on the subject came in *An Answer to Tyrie*, a tract published in 1572 but completed by 1568.[4] However, Knox's ecclesiastical thought before 1558, or for that matter prior to his 1554 trip to Geneva, generally harmonized with his later doctrine.

In any attempt to diagnose Knox's concept of the church, certain difficulties arise—namely those of ambiguities and even contradictions. The church of John Knox displayed many faces. Alternately and even simultaneously—as historical circumstances dictated—Knox's church was invisible and visible, universal and local, a small flock and a national organization, suffering and triumphant, elected and covenanting, a true church and an antichurch. Furthermore, he tended to confound church and nation. Nevertheless, some categorization facilitates an understanding of Knox's ecclesiastical tendencies.

The Predestinated Church

The span of Knox's writings, particularly those from 1553 to 1565, clearly indicated that the Scottish reformer grounded his concept of the church in election: God's act of predestination established the church, his providence sustains it, and the members of the church consist of the elect from all ages

---

2. Janton, *Concept et Sentiment*, 111.
3. Ibid., 44, 47, 157.
4. *Works*, 6:473. This work was sent abroad at the time as a farewell address. (Thus the delay in publication). Its purpose was to arm the church against adverse propaganda.

and all nations.[5] Because Knox's church consisted of the elect of God, he could conceive of no church apart from election. His 1560 tract concerning predestination, which reflected the views of the English apocalyptic tradition begun by John Bale, noted that from the very beginning God appointed two seeds—the seed of the woman and the serpent's seed—to spring from one mass. From the woman's seed sprang the church of the elect while from the seed of the serpent came the malignant or reprobate church.[6]

Knox's doctrine of the church was related to his concept of history. With the early writers of the Protestant apocalyptic tradition, Knox regarded the Catholic Church as the whore of Babylon described in the Book of Revelation, and made such an identification in his first sermon. This theme became more explicit in Knox's predestination treatise where he continued to develop the militant dichotomy between the Protestant and Catholic churches. Here Knox insisted that God has ordained two societies of people from the onset of time to do battle. One army is the church of God, the elect bride of Christ, while the other is the malevolent synagogue of Satan. This battle would not end until Christ's second coming.[7] Thus Knox regarded himself as a prophet in this cosmic struggle which God has decreed between the "true" church (Protestant faith) and the antichurch (Catholic Church). In such an apocalyptic contest, Knox developed his concepts of the church—including its ministry, the sacraments, and his own prophetic calling.

Knox related predestination primarily to the small flock and invisible church. While he spoke frequently of the former prior to the establishment of the Reformation in 1560, he stressed the latter when problems arose in the Reformed kirk of the 1560s. The invisible church, known only to God, was synonymous with the elect. Nonetheless, Knox did not make election a criterion for the visible church, for only God could separate the elect and reprobate. But the visible church most likely to contain the elect is the small, persecuted flock. Knox's letter to Marjory Bowes, the daughter of Mrs. Elizabeth Bowes, during Mary's reign in England said: "There are few that are chosen . . . and therefore ought you greatly rejoice,

---

5. *Works*, 5:25; 2:108–9.

6. *Works*, 5:62.

7. *Works*, 5:413. In chapter 3 of his book, Janton deals at length with the antichurch. See Janton, *Concept et Sentiment*, 53–66. While this present work sets aside no section on the antichurch (the Roman Church), it relates to Knox's views of history, apocalyptic thought, and the continuous church.

knowing yourself to be one of the small and contemptible flock to whom it has pleased God ... to give the kingdom."[8]

For the small flock, election is no abstract doctrine but a support in the moment of trial. Knox used election to comfort and exhort the menaced flock. Such a theme came through in *An Exposition Upon Psalm VI* (1554), *A Faithful Admonition* (1554), *Epistles to Mrs. Bowes* (1553–54), *A Letter of Wholesome Counsel* (1556), and in some of Knox's other pre-1560 writings.[9] In his predestination treatise (1560), Knox related election more to establishing and preserving faith in the church. Because of the preservation theme, Knox confirmed predestination more as a doctrine for the elect than for the damned. Yet he regarded the church of Satan, as coming about because of divine predestination.[10]

The Continuous Church

John Knox believed the church in both its invisible and visible forms, continued back to Adam. The theme of a continuous church was not absent from Knox's earlier writings, but its major thrust came in *An Answer to Tyrie* (1572). Here Knox countered his opponents' claim to antiquity and apostolic succession by a different construction of antiquity and succession. The reformer stressed that the Scottish kirk was not new, but part of the universal church of God that went back to Adam, Abel, and Abraham in particular. Thus Knox presented his form of antiquity and succession as extending to Abraham who believed the same Word of God and the same promises that were currently believed in Scotland.[11]

In Knox's tracing the church back to Abraham, several interesting parallels are evident. The gospel could also be traced back to the third chapter of Genesis, where God promised that Eve's seed would crush the serpent's seed. Also, circumcision compared to baptism and the Lord's Supper related to the Passover celebration. But most important was the parallel between Israel's faithful with the "true" Protestant church and the unfaithful of Israel with Catholicism.

Knox constantly compared Israel and the church—Israel contained both the faithful and unfaithful as did the Scottish kirk, or for that matter the realm of Scotland. Because of his view of the covenant, Knox did not

---

8. *Works*, 3:351.
9. Some examples are *Works*, 3:351, 349, 377, 293; 4:123–24, 135.
10. *Works*, 5:25.
11. *Works*, 6:491–92.

carefully distinguish between the nations of Scotland and England and churches found therein. The faithful in Israel belonged to the invisible, universal church and were the object of God's blessing. The faithful Jews formed a continuous line with the faithful, true church in Scotland. On the other hand, Israel had its unfaithful, false prophets, and idolaters. Such people—members of the antichurch—formed a direct, continuous line with the Church of Rome in Knox's day. Moreover, the reformer equated the Jewish synagogue and the high priest of Christ's day with the Roman Church and their priests of his time. Though Knox did not directly say so, he implied that the Reformed Church came from Eve's seed while the Catholic Church—which was the antichurch—sprang from the serpent's seed.[12]

Knox even allowed for some legitimate continuity in the Roman Church. He stoutly denied Roman succession to the Church of Jerusalem and insisted that it had fallen from the true catholic faith. Yet, along with Calvin and Luther, Knox did not believe that God had completely abandoned the Church of Rome, as evidenced by his acceptance of their baptism. What Knox did reject was what he regarded as Catholicism's false faith, idolatry, and superstition.

The Invisible Church

In conformity with the Reformed tradition, Knox accorded an important place to the invisible church. His writings spoke most often to some form of the visible church because, after all, this entity is what he attempted to establish. Nevertheless, the very essence of Knox's church was its invisible form—for this church, known only to God, contains the elect of all ages. Knox wrote most often of the invisible church in confessional statements, in the context of the predestinated and continuous church, and in certain historical circumstances the theme emerged, e.g., when the holiness of the visible church came under question.

As historical situations changed, Knox emphasized different aspects of the church. During the exile of the 1550s, he stressed the concept of an elected, suffering, small flock. The *Scots Confession* of 1560 registers Knox's most definitive statement on the invisible church. Chapter 15 stated that from the beginning of history this church has existed and is composed of

---

12. *Works*, 3:231, 239; 4:481, 513; 4:309, 311, 315. Janton says Knox's form of apostolic succession and confounding of church and state perpetuated Catholic views to some degree. See Janton, *Concept et Sentiment*, 47, 123, 139, 160.

the elect of God, who correctly worship and embrace him. The sole head of this church is Jesus Christ, and it is catholic or universal, containing all of God's elect throughout the ages past as well as the future. As so defined, this church is known only to God.[13]

From 1562 on, troubles mounted for the Reformed kirk of Scotland. Protestantism had been established legally but not financially. The threat of Romanism's revival hung like an ominous cloud over Knox. Mary Stewart had married the Catholic, Lord Darnley. First David Ricco, Mary's secretary, next Darnley, and then Moray, the regent for James VI were murdered. The Scottish kirk was rife with tensions and struggles. Under such conditions Knox spoke of the invisible church—a church pure and indestructible. At this point Knox probably returned to a theme analogous to that emphasized during his exile—that is, the church in both situations (small flock and invisible church) contained the elect, maintained purity, and faced danger.[14] But in *A Sermon on Isaiah XXVI* (1565), Knox did not repudiate the visible church, nor did he disassociate it from the visible church. Rather he said the visible kirk contained the invisible church. The visible church contained "a great number that were hypocrites . . . that had turned their back to God . . . and yet were some godly, as a few wheat . . . among the multitude of such chaff."[15]

An Answer to Tyrie, also written under pressing circumstances and emphasizing the visible church, did contain the invisible church theme. Here Knox noted the importance of the spiritual nature of the church, arguing that it is composed of the godly elect, and therefore, its visible form has to be holy. Though observers cannot tell precisely who is a member of the visible church, perceptive people can determine which visible churches generally embrace the members of the invisible church and which do not.[16] Therefore, in situations after 1560, Knox returned to his concept of the small flock but now in the form of the invisible church within a national church. Moreover, the national kirk did not attain the purity Knox desired. Consequently, he never quite reconciled certain personal and inner tensions he had between the visible and invisible churches. Furthermore, one must suspect that as the visible church failed to meet Knox's expectations, he took refuge in the notion of the invisible church and the small flock.[17]

13. *Works*, 2:108–9; Cheyne, "The Scots Confession of 1560," 334.
14. Janton, *Concept et Sentiment*, 164.
15. *Works*, 6:243.
16. *Works*, 6:486–87, 502, 508; Greaves, *Theology and Revolution*, 50.
17. Janton, *Concept et Sentiment*, 158, 196.

General Characteristics of the Visible Church

Knox's doctrine of the invisible church notwithstanding, he did not neglect the visible church. In fact, the visible church in some form can be found in Knox's writings from the beginning to end. Knox, however, set forth his most explicit statement of the visible church in response to Tyrie's taunts that the Scottish kirk was invisible. Knox contended "that the Kirk of God, within Scotland this day, is as visible . . . within the Realm of Scotland, as ever she was in Corinth, Galatia, Philippi (yea, or yet in Rome itself)."[18]

For Knox, the visible church came in various forms. At times it was a small flock elected of God but persecuted by Catholicism. When Protestantism became established in 1560, it was a national church. On other occasions Knox spoke of a particular congregation within the national kirk. Finally, the church was universal, containing all the elect of all ages and not bound to one place nor one time. And Knox never quite harmonized these variations within his ecclesiastical thought.

Knox did not see the invisible church as beginning in Christ's time, nor did he limit the visible church to the New Testament age. Reflecting both his concept of the covenant and the apocalyptic tradition, in *The Appellation* (1558), Knox noted that the visible church appeared in both its true and false senses in the Old Testament. The Scots reformer not only traced a continuous line from spiritual Israel to the invisible church of his day, but he also paralleled visible Jewish religion with the church in Scotland. When the Israelites were faithful to God, Knox tended to liken them to the true, visible church. Conversely, when the visible church of the Jews was wicked, Knox identified them with the Roman Church.[19] Thus Knox suggested that the visible forms of both Protestantism and Catholicism can be found in the Old Testament.

The Magisterial Reformers believed Satan had confounded the minds of people by designating Catholicism as the true church. Therefore, definite criteria were needed to discern a true visible church from a false one. On this point, Bucer differed from Luther, Calvin, and Zwingli. All four agreed that the pure preaching of God's Word and the correct administration of the sacraments were signs of the true church. Bucer, however, added a third criterion—ecclesiastical discipline. In this respect, Knox apparently, and the Scottish Reformation more definitely, leaned toward Bucer.

---

18. *Works*, 6:494.
19. *Works*, 4:479–80.

PART ONE: Historical and Theological Foundations

Knox and the Scottish Reformation made discipline a third mark for several possible reasons. One, Peter Martyr and Martin Bucer influenced the English reformers, who, in turn, may have influenced Knox. Two, discipline was especially appropriate for the turbulent Scots. Next, the practice of the Genevan Consistory, which had the power of excommunication, might have influenced Knox in regard to ecclesiastical discipline. In addition, Knox's emphasis on the church's righteousness may also have been a strong motivation for the Scottish church's adoption of discipline as a mark of the church. His general principle—that nothing must be included in the church unless it has the express scriptural sanction—prevented him from verbalizing the significance of discipline as a mark of the church. Still, his emphasis on holiness would point in that direction.

In his debates with James Tyrie (1566-72), Knox repudiated Catholicism's claim to be a true church on the basis of its universality. Rather, he insisted on the righteousness of the church as a criterion: A church that does not have holiness is not a true church.[20] On the other hand, Gordon Donaldson says that if discipline was a mark of the church for the Scottish kirk, it was subordinate to the Word and the sacraments.[21] Nevertheless, though Knox said little about discipline as a criterion personally, the confessions he played a major role in writing set three criteria for recognizing the true visible church. Both the *Geneva Confession* of 1556 and the *Scots Confession* of 1560 listed the three marks of the pure preaching of God's Word, the right administration of the sacraments, and ecclesiastical discipline: "The Notes, therefore, of the true Kirk of God we believe, confess, and avow to be, first, The true preaching of the word of God. . . Secondly, the right administration of the sacraments [and] . . . Last(ly), Ecclesiastical discipline uprightly ministered."[22]

Yet Knox believed the church to be more than correct preaching, more than a common intellectual belief, more than correct worship, and more than the administration of ecclesiastical discipline. From an early epistle to believers at Berwick (1552) to his last tract (1572) Knox insisted

---

20. Janton, *Concept et Sentiment*, 13, 158; Monter, *Calvin's Geneva*, 138-39; *Works*, 6:489; Greaves, *Theology and Revolution*, 51-52. Davis argues the Anabaptists influenced the Reformed concept of discipline, particularly that of Bucer. See Davis, "No Discipline, No Church: An Anabaptist Contribution to the Reformed Tradition," 49ff.

21. On this question sources differ, although the following contend Knox included discipline in the criteria: Reid, *Trumpeter of God*, 134; Macmillan, *John Knox*, 191-92; Mackie, *John Knox*, 16; Janton, *Concept et Sentiment*, 118, 123-24, 144, 158.

22. *Works*, 2:110. See *Works*, 4:172-73, for a similar statement in the *Geneva Confession*. In *An Answer to Tyrie*, Knox mentioned only the Word and the sacraments. *Works*, 6:492, 494. See also *Works*, 4:285.

the church is, first and foremost, the body and spouse of Christ and consists of those who embrace him in genuine faith.[23] The essential character of the church, therefore, lies in its relationship to Jesus Christ. The church must constantly remain in the covenant made with Christ Jesus by his apostles. In such a relationship Christ is king and head of the church. Therefore Christ not only guides, rules and defends, but he also made laws the faithful must obey rather than the laws of secular princes.[24]

Knox saw the church both as a small flock running counter to the prevailing religion and as a national church determining the faith of a commonwealth. In a 1564 discussion with Maitland, Knox set forth these two aspects of the church, each with its own responsibility. When but a small remnant, the church only has to maintain the integrity of its faith. But when Protestantism had been established and in sufficient numbers, Knox insisted that it must suppress idolatry (i.e., Catholicism).[25] This reasoning may be illustrated by contemporizing Knox's principles. The twenty-first century evangelical church in China is correct in being countercultural and primarily concerned with truth and survival; but in the United States, this church—consisting of sufficient numbers—must also create a moral climate favorable to the faith.

The Small Flock

The aspect of the visible church most constant with Knox was the small flock. Such a concept permeated Knox's writings from beginning to end. At the onset of his career, the visible church in a 1548 epistle was "the small flock of Jesus Christ." While at the end of his ministry, he noted the "little flock" in a response to Tyrie (1572), his last major work.[26] But before the establishment of Protestantism in 1560 and especially in 1553 and 1554, the small flock came to the forefront most often.[27]

Because the context of the small flock fluctuated, it is difficult to give it a precise name. In *An Epistle to the Congregation of St. Andrews* (1548),

---

23. Knox, "Epistle to the Congregation of Berwick," 1552, 253; *Works*, 6:322–23, 194, 433, 489; 2:108–9; 3:358–59, 377.

24. Lorimer, *Knox and the Church of England*, 60.

25. *Works*, 2:442; Blake, "Knox and Lethington: A Lesson in Religious and Political Alienation," 16–17.

26. *Works*, 3:5; 6:507.

27. *Works*, 3:5, 178, 241, 245, 264, 266, 273–80, 351, 388–90; 4:263, 459; 6:272, 507, 569, 591, are but a few citations.

PART ONE: Historical and Theological Foundations

the small flock was the historic church persecuted in every age.[28] However, in *A Faithful Admonition* (1554), Knox noted that God had miraculously nourished the small flock in England.[29] In *Letters to His Brethren* (1557), he referred to the Protestant community in Scotland as the small flock.[30] Even in his sermon on Isaiah (1565), after the establishment of Protestantism, Knox indicated that the small flock existed in an abused condition under Mary Stewart.[31] Moreover, in a prayer after Moray's death, Knox placed the small flock in a cosmic struggle with Satan.[32] At times the small flock was part of the English and Scottish churches, while on other occasions the universal church itself was a small flock.

Election and suffering played a major role in Knox's concept of the small flock. According to the reformer, God did not elect all of Israel, nor did he elect the national church that contained both wheat and chaff; rather he elected only a small flock. This remnant, chosen by God to life eternal, experiences hardship in this world. Suffering and constant struggle characterize its life; indeed Knox believed suffering to be a sign of election. Though the church will triumph, God permits persecution to reduce its pride; for there is to be no saintly living in this life without persecution.[33]

The small flock occupied a special place in Knox's affections. His vocation was to preach the gospel and minister to the small flock. But needless to say, many differences existed between Knox's small flock and the Scottish national kirk. Because the *Book of Discipline*, which contained the blueprint for the activities of the church, intended to encompass not only the small flock but the entire nation in the kirk as well—certain contradictions inevitably arose. Actually, the *Book of Discipline* focused more on the national kirk and contained few references to the concept of a small flock. Though Knox alluded to two aspects of the visible church in his 1564 debate with Maitland, he preferred the small flock model—that is, an exclusive, pure, and primitive Protestant church. This form of Protestantism, which Knox conceived to be "true religion," was if Knox had his way, to permeate every aspect of national life. It would seem that Knox's sentiment lay with the small flock and not the national kirk, but the small flock could not establish Protestantism in Scotland. Thus Knox used the

28. *Works*, 3:5.
29. *Works*, 3:266.
30. *Works*, 4:263.
31. *Works*, 6:272.
32. *Works*, 6:569–70.
33. Janton, *Concept et Sentiment*, 69–70, 94–95.

national kirk as a means to unite people. And when this task was partially accomplished, that is, when Protestantism was at least the legal religion, he seemed to look back with nostalgia to the small flock.[34] If any established church fulfilled his ideal of the small flock, it was Calvin's church at Geneva rather than the national kirk at Edinburgh.[35]

The National Church

In Knox's discussion with Maitland, a second type of visible church emerged—a national kirk. In August 1560, parliamentary action abolished Catholicism and made Scotland a Protestant country. Yet this enactment did not make Scotland Protestant in fact, nor did it really establish a Reformed Church. The majority of the people still adhered to the old faith— or were as before—indifferent and only trying to ascertain when religious change would bring some social, economic, or political gain. Accordingly, the apparent victory of Protestantism did not lead to religious unity but to further division between those who were Reformed by conviction and those who primarily sought gain.

The *Scots Confession*, enacted by Parliament, set the ideological tone for the Reformed Church, but the *Book of Discipline*, designed to establish the church financially, failed to pass. In fact, Protestantism was not even legalized in the opinion of the future rulers, Francis and Mary. Though 1560 to 1562 saw progress in the establishment of Protestantism, the years 1562–67 witnessed a struggle with Mary Stewart and the threat of revived Catholicism.[36] It is no wonder that in 1563 Knox heard some say "That we have nothing of our Religion established, neither by Law or Parliament."[37]

Under such conditions Knox wrote about the national church. He spoke most often of this kirk in such post-1560 writings as his *History* and in a response to Tyrie. But the shadows of this concept—namely that the church was a mixed body containing both the godly and ungodly came early in his writings, particularly in the context of predestination. The reformer did not declare the small flock to be pure, i.e., it comprises only the elect and the godly. Rather, Knox regarded the persecuted small flock as the visible church most likely to contain the elect and maintain a standard

---

34. Blake, "Knox and Lethington," 16–18; Janton, *Concept et Sentiment*, 137, 157, 197.

35. *Works*, 2:16.

36. Reid, *Trumpeter of God*, 191–92, 195, 220, 222.

37. *Works*, 2:385.

of holiness. In 1552 he told his congregation at Berwick that the church also included the wicked.[38] In 1557 problems arose because some devout people separated from the young church, even before its establishment by law, because not all adherents of the Reformed faith lived exemplary lives. Knox insisted that doctrine and the correct administration of the sacraments, not morality, distinguished the "true" church from the "malignant" church—and in doing so indicated that the church is a variegated organization containing both the godly and ungodly.[39]

In sixteenth-century Scotland, church and nation were coterminous—each was coextensive with the whole population, and church and state were but different aspects of one and the same society. In such a context Knox easily confounded church and society, drawing analogies between Israel and the church and between Israel and Scotland.[40] Knox related the covenant to the national church. He believed the covenant points both church and society toward a common obligation, and as Israel covenanted with God to destroy idolatry, so must Scotland. Since the reformation of religion is not the business of the church but also of the people, the national kirk had to purify religion within Scotland—that is, preach correct doctrine, properly administer the sacraments, and punish sin in order to fulfill the covenant obligation. Nevertheless, Knox did not emphasize the idea of a covenanted nation as did the Scottish Covenanters. He was inclined toward nationalism only in a nominal way.[41]

In *A Brief Exhortation to England* (1559) and the *Book of Discipline* (1560) Knox's plans for a Christian commonwealth are evident. The reformer saw the state supporting the church in maintaining the Christian commonwealth in tangible ways, e.g., sustaining Reformed schools and ministers. He believed that church and state should be twin pillars of God's house on earth, twin aspects of the government of God's people. In such a way, Knox and the authors of the *Scots Confession* understood a Protestant country. It was a nation that agreed to live in compliance with the gospel, one that consented to organize both its civil and religious life in accordance with the same beliefs.[42] Parliament's endorsement of the *Scots Confession* inferred the acceptance of a similar perception of a Protestant

---

38. Knox, "Epistle to the Congregation of Berwick," 225.

39. *Works*, 4:262–67; Greaves, *Theology and Revolution*, 49–50.

40. *Works*, 2:286, 442–43; Donaldson, *The Scottish Reformation*, 131.

41. *Works*, 6:492, 496–99. But if Greaves is correct, Knox did not emphasize the idea of a covenanted nation as did the Scottish Covenanters. Greaves, "The Knoxian Paradox," 96–97.

42. *Works*, 2:118–19.

country, but by refusing the *Book of Discipline,* the worldly wise rejected Knox's godly policy as "devout imagination."[43]

Universal and Local Church

Another way to look at the church in a twofold light is from the position of the universal and local church. According to Calvin, the universal church is the multitude collected out of all nations, though dispersed, but agreeing in doctrine and bound together by the tie of common religion. Included in the universal church are single churches existing in different towns and places, and even single individuals within these churches. Calvin insisted that the universal and local churches are not two separate churches but one. The single church is the universal church existing in a particular place, and being autonomous, it exercises and obtains the name and authority of the church.[44]

The *Scots Confession* noted both of these aspects of the church.[45] It is, however, in *An Answer to Tyrie* that Knox spoke most directly to the dual aspect of the "universal Kirk" and "particular Kirk." The Scottish reformer, in fact, placed more emphasis on the local congregation than on either the national kirk or the universal church.[46] Underscoring the Scriptures that recognized local churches ("Jerusalem, Samaria, Antioch, Corinth, Galatia, Philippi, Rome") as full-fledged, autonomous churches—Knox stated that the kirk is not confined to one particular place: "our Kirk, which is not bound to any one place, but is dispersed upon the face of the whole earth; having one God, one faith, one baptism, and one Lord Jesus, Saviour of all that unfeignly believe."[47]

In his frequent references to the "Kirks," "particular Kirk," "congregations," the Scots reformer made it clear that he recognized the local church as being autonomous and possessing full authority so long as it maintained Reformed principles.[48] Correspondingly, he supported the principle that one church could not dominate another. He stated, "We usurp no authority above (our) brethren, but remit all men to do their own judge(ment),

---

43. Dickinson, *The Scottish Reformation*, 8.

44. D'Assonville, *Knox and the Institutes*, 86–87; Calvin, *The Institutes of Christian Religion*, 4.1.104.

45. *Works*, 2:110–11.

46. Greaves, *Theology and Revolution*, 52.

47. *Works*, 6:497. See also page 494.

48. *Works*, 6:492, 494, 496, 499, 503, 510–11.

and do reverence all congregations, who do agree with us in the principals (sic) of our faith, as the particular Kirks of Jesus Christ."[49] Furthermore, Knox saw the Church of Scotland as part of the "Kirk universal," and thus in its relationship with the universal church, he called the national church a "particular Kirk." But in it relationship to the local church, he apparently regarded the Church of Scotland as the "general Kirk," or simply the "kirk," to distinguish it from the "particular Kirks" or local congregations.[50]

EXTERNAL ORGANIZATION OF THE CHURCH

Scholars have hotly contested Knox's views on the external organization of the church. One group, represented by Stanford Reid, insists Knox did not want the episcopacy established. But while he taught no full-blown Presbyterianism, the Scots reformer actually laid the foundation for such a system.[51] Another school led by Gordon Donaldson contends Knox only desired to correct the episcopacy, not abolish it. Rather, Knox favored a reformed episcopacy and Presbyterianism was the work of Andrew Melville.[52]

The issue is complicated and evidence could be mustered in support of both positions or variations of these possibilities. Several facts, however, seem reasonably certain. First, Knox actually said very little about any form of church organization, nor was he concerned about the details of church polity—whether episcopalian or protopresbyterian. Second, Knox did not view the episcopacy in a favorable light. He certainly rejected the Catholic understanding of the episcopacy, and he seemed to hold little love for even the Anglican episcopacy. When offered a bishopric in 1552 in England by Northumberland, Knox refused it, possibly for a variety of reasons other than the fact that the office was a bishopric.[53] In a sermon at Frankfurt (March 1555) Knox denounced abuses in the episcopal system

---

49. *Works*, 6:511.

50. *Works*, 6:492, 494, 496, 499, 503, 510–11.

51. Reid, "Knox's Attitude to the English Reformation." Other members of this school, starting in the sixteenth century down to the twentieth, would include: Andrew Melville, David Calderwood, Hume of Godscroft, Thomas M'Crie, Peter Lorimer, P. Hume Brown, A. M. Renwick. They taught that Knox wanted a Calvinistic and Presbyterian church that went far beyond the English Reformation.

52. Donaldson, *The Scottish Reformation*, chs. 5 and 7. See also Greaves, "The Knoxian Paradox," 94; Smout, *A History of the Scottish People*, 64–65. In his work on *The Presbyterian Tradition*, Warr said Knox accepted the idea of the episcopacy.

53. Lorimer, *Knox and the Church of England*, 149ff.

which had been tolerated under Edward VI.[54] In a more general sense, a reading of his *History* and some of his polemical pamphlets leaves one with the impression that Knox did not prefer the episcopacy.[55]

Nevertheless, some critical questions must be raised in respect to the reformer's attitude toward the episcopacy. Did Knox oppose the episcopacy per se or did he merely object to the abuses associated with that form of church government? Did Knox reject all forms of the episcopacy, even a reformed episcopacy? Closely related to Knox's attitude toward the episcopacy is the question of the office of the superintendent, established by the *Book of Discipline*. Was the office of the superintendent intended to be a version of the episcopacy? Were the superintendents "reformed bishops," that is, bishops as the Scottish reformers believed them to be in the primitive church? What was Knox's attitude toward the office of the superintendent? A third established fact is that presbyterianism did not develop until a decade after Knox's time, but the roots of such a system could be detected earlier—certainly in the writings of Beza, perhaps sooner. As James Kirk points out, the polity which emerged in the years between 1586 and 1592 was unmistakably Presbyterian in character—and the parliamentary ratification of the polity received in 1592 was simply an acknowledgment of the progress made by the presbyterians in transforming a somewhat indeterminate polity into one that was thoroughly Presbyterian.[56]

John Knox established no definite ecclesiastical polity—neither protopresbyterian nor episcopalian. Still, the total thrust of his writings would seem to point to a preference for a protopresbyterian system or at least a distaste for the episcopalian arrangement. This statement, however, is not to say Knox categorically rejected any form of the episcopacy. If the episcopal system could fulfill the major functions of the ministry—that is, preach the Word and purify religion—Knox would accept such a system, though it would not be his ideal choice.

Knox's writings contain anti-episcopalian attitudes. He desired to establish Protestantism and thereby purify worship in the Scottish kirk. In Knox's opinion, the great obstacle to the implementation of these objectives was the Roman Church, and the bishops obviously played a major role in this obstruction. Moreover, the Scottish reformer's concept of the

---

54. *Works*, 4:33; Ridley, *John Knox*, 204.

55. Knox contrasted the "lord-like bishop" with the "painful preacher" of the Word. *Works*, 6:559.

56. Kirk, ed., *The Second Book of Discipline*, 151. See also Beza's letter warning Knox of the episcopacy. *Works*, 6:613–15.

ministry conflicted with the traditional job description of a bishop. His views on the issue were thoroughly Reformed—that is, the minister's task was first and foremost to preach the Word, and secondarily, to administer the sacraments. Ecclesiastical administration was not a primary function of the minister.[57]

Two factors concomitant to the episcopacy turned Knox away from such a polity: he adamantly rejected the doctrine of apostolic succession; and he would not approve any system that did not recognize the underlying equality of all ministers—including bishops, whose only superiority was the exercising of delegated supervisory powers. The offices of the superintendent and bishop have certain affinities: both performed administrative, disciplinary, and judicial functions. Conversely, the two offices had many dissimilarities. The basic function of the superintendent—in contrast to the existing practice of the bishops—was to preach, to found churches, and to appoint ministers. Unlike the Catholic bishops, the superintendents did not possess the sacramental powers of confirmation and ordination.[58]

Richard Greaves argues that Knox and the other authors of the *Book of Discipline* conceived of superintendents as "reformed bishops"—that is, a preaching and administrative office—which embodied the characteristics of the primitive bishop of the early church. This reasoning, of course, changes the prevailing concept of the bishop. One might ask: When then is a bishop a bishop?[59] It is certainly conceivable that Knox would have accepted this type of bishop, but such a notion of the bishop did not predominate in the sixteenth century.

UNITY IN THE CHURCH

Though Knox gave room for some local autonomy among the local kirks and staked out no clear position in respect to church polity, he opposed disunity in no uncertain terms. Prior to the establishment of Protestantism, he pressed for unification. In a *Letter of Wholesome Counsel* (1556), Knox encouraged the Scottish Protestants to meet in assemblies because

---

57. See a discussion under the sacraments in chapter 6. See also *Works*, 3:26; 6:620–21.

58. *Works*, 2:205–9; Greaves, *Theology and Revolution*, 80–81; Reid, "Knox's Attitude To the English Reformation," 12–13; Donaldson, "The Scottish Episcopate at the Reformation," 349.

59. Greaves, *Theology and Revolution*, 80–82; Reid, "Knox's Attitude To the English Reformation," 12–13.

"no member is of sufficiency to sustain and feed itself without the help and support of another."[60]

By 1557 a different problem arose. Some people had separated from the young kirk because of dissatisfaction with the morality of various members. In a letter to Scotland, he soundly condemned those who "have separated themselves, from society and communion of their brethren, in sects damnable; being bold to affirm, that among us there is no true Kirk. . . ."[61] Elsewhere, in his predestination treatise, he castigated the Anabaptists for seceding from the church.[62] When a movement in England advocating separation from Anglicanism arose in the late 1560s, Knox would not support it.

By now Protestantism had been established in Scotland and Mary Stewart had abdicated her throne. Knox, therefore, would risk no schism in Scotland nor a break with England by supporting English separatism. These conditions notwithstanding, Knox's concept of the church probably would have led him to condemn the separatists. Despite his heavy emphasis on the holiness of the church, Knox would not risk disunity in the body except for matters of substance—i.e., fundamental doctrine and corrupt worship.[63]

Furthermore, Knox stressed unity on another level, that is, he had a sense of ecumenicity. Notwithstanding Knox's emphasis on the national kirk and his sharp confrontations with those of different beliefs, he participated in the universal fellowship of Christians. He directed his intolerance toward Catholics and Anabaptists (who were not included in the fellowship) and not toward Lutherans nor those of other Reformed beliefs.[64] Yet, in no sense did Knox sacrifice what he believed to be truth for unity. Rather, he sought a unity of truth.

---

60. *Works*, 4:137.
61. *Works*, 5:137.
62. *Works*, 5:301. See Kyle, "John Knox Confronts the Anabaptists," 493–515.
63. Lorimer, *Knox and the Church of England*, 298–300; Greaves, *Theology and Revolution*, 52–53; Knappen, *Tudor Puritanism*, 212–15.
64. Greaves, "The Knoxian Paradox," 85–98. Calvin, Cranmer, and others also advocated unity among the churches breaking from Rome.

6

The Sacraments and the Crusade against Idolatry

While the church of John Knox came in both invisible and visible forms, he had to concern himself with its visible forms—the small flock and the national church established by law and encompassing the entire nation. The invisible church, of course, was known only to God. How could a "true" visible church be known? The Scottish Reformation identified the visible church by three marks: the true preaching of God's Word, the right administration of the sacraments, and the enforcement of ecclesiastical discipline. During the Middle Ages, in Knox's eyes, the Catholic Church had compromised and corrupted both the preaching of Scripture and the sacraments. While preaching was Knox's priority, he had definite ideas regarding the sacraments and he launched a crusade to see that they were administered according to the dictates of God's Word. Anything less, he regarded as idolatry.

THE SACRAMENTS

A sacrament is a religious rite regarded as either a channel or a sign of divine grace. In the sixteenth century, sacramental doctrine became a flashpoint for dispute. Rome and the reformers quarreled incessantly over this issue. So did the Lutherans, Zwinglians, Calvinists, and Anabaptists. Such a conflict developed because implicit in sacramental dogma are beliefs concerning salvation, the church, and Christ's nature. And it was in regard to the sacraments that these dogmatic differences materialized in the life and practice of the church.

The Sacraments and the Crusade against Idolatry

Regarding justification and grace, medieval sacramental doctrine rested on two principles. The medieval church regarded justification as a gradual process in the soul of human beings by which they became holy or just. Grace was the supernatural power that directed an individual in the way of holiness or justification. But for grace to be effective—it had to be received initially, infused periodically, and it required the full cooperation of the human will. In Catholic doctrine, the sacraments were the channels by which God infused supernatural grace into human nature. Seven sacraments—not two—were needed to transmit all the grace humanity needed. Baptism canceled the guilt of original sin and left the soul innocent, provided no other sin was committed. Other sins, however, were always perpetrated. The soul then needed penance to give renewed infusions of grace and to restore the condition of baptismal innocence.

During the Middle Ages—even after the Fourth Lateran Counsel of 1215—the Roman Church did not maintain a consistent Eucharistic doctrine. Among theologians, three positions in regard to the Eucharistic change could be detected. One group contended that the bread and wine remained present along with the body and blood of Christ. Other theologians argued that the bread and wine were annihilated with only the substance of the Lord's body and blood remaining. A third group contended that at the words of consecration, the essence of the bread and wine was changed into the substance of Christ's body and blood. This position became known as transubstantiation and carried the day after the Reformation. Despite these different meanings regarding the Mass, the average person knew that it meant Calvary's sacrifice was insufficient to satisfy God for humankind's sin. There could be no salvation unless the priest constantly offered the body and blood of Christ. Under these meanings of the Eucharist, the priest's power reached its apex and the Word of God became peripheral. The study of Scripture and the preaching of the gospel were secondary when they existed at all.[1]

Against this Catholic sacramental system, the Protestant reformers revolted. Christ had died once, and faith in his sacrifice sufficed for salvation. Grace was God's free gift and need not be infused by the sacraments.

---

1. This general information regarding the medieval sacramental system has come from several general sources plus two more specific references. See McGiffert, *A History of Christian Thought*, 2:313–31; Berkhof, *The History of Christian Doctrines*, 227–69; Gonzalez, *A History of Christian Thought*, 2:49–51, 147–54, 277–78; Pelikan, *The Christian Tradition: Reformation of Church and Dogma (1300–1700)* 50–59; Burkill, *The Evolution of Christian Thought*; Macy, "The Dogma of Transubstantiation in the Middle Ages," 11–41; McCue, "The Doctrine of Transubstantiation from Berengar through the Council of Trent," 385–430.

PART ONE: Historical and Theological Foundations

While the reformers did not totally eliminate the sacraments, they reduced them to two and gave them a different significance. But as to their exact meaning they disagreed—sometimes quite intensely.

John Calvin defined the sacraments as a testimony of God's grace toward the elect, confirmed by an external sign (e.g., baptism and the Lord's Supper), in which the faithful give a mutual declaration of honor toward God. The Swiss reformer regarded the sacraments as an aid in confirming the faith—similar to preaching the gospel. Calvin stressed the special blessing of the spirit in the sacraments. Yet he insisted on their secondary and supplementary character, whereas the gospel and the Word suffice in themselves. Since the sacraments only confirm the divine promise, they can add nothing to the pledge, but are a means of making one believe in it. Thus the sacraments consist of the Word, an external sign, and the work of the Spirit. Calvin opposed both the Zwinglians, who said the sacraments give no evidence of God's grace, and the Catholics, who attributed great virtues to the rites. Calvin retained only two sacraments—baptism and the Eucharist—which represent Christ's work in the remission of sins and redemption.[2]

The Zwinglian view of the sacraments differed from that held by the Catholics, Lutherans, and Calvinists. To Zwingli, the sacraments held no intrinsic power, nor was Christ's body present in either form of real presence—transubstantiation or consubstantiation. However, Zwingli would not go to the Anabaptist extreme and make the sacraments a bare sign or symbol. Thus he considered a sacrament as a kind of induction or pledge into the covenant. To receive a sacrament is to enlist in Christ's forces and to obtain, in return, a reminder that one must remain faithful. Sacraments are signs or ceremonies by which individuals offer themselves before the church as disciples of Christ. In stressing the ecclesiastical significance of the sacraments, Zwingli said that the church needed the sacraments more than the believer does. Though baptism and the Eucharist were important to Zwingli, he felt that they do not equal the Word, nor did he esteem them as did Calvin or Luther.[3]

Luther also contended for only two sacraments: baptism and the Lord's Supper. He believed the sacrament to be a combination of the Word

---

2. See Wendel, *Calvin*, 312–18; Niesel, *The Theology of Calvin*, 211–28; Hunter, *The Teaching of Calvin*, 166–90; Parker, *The Oracles of God*, 60–61; Wallace, *Calvin's Doctrine of the Word and Sacrament*, 133–74.

3. Locher, *Zwingli's Thought*, 14–217; Courvoisier, *Zwingli*, 63–64; Richardson, *Zwingli and Cranmer on the Eucharist*, 5–19; Walton, *Zwingli's Theocracy*, 212–13; Stephens, *The Theology of Huldrych Zwingli*, 180–83; Stephens, *Zwingli*, 76–84.

of promise with a sign. A sign in itself is not a sacrament, for a symbolic act must be instituted by God and combined with a promise to be a sacrament. The decisive element in the sacrament is the Word. He saw the sacrament as nothing without the Word because it has no other content than the promise of the Word. Yet since the sacrament is a form in which the Word comes, it has a unique significance. The sacrament gives human beings a pledge and seal of God's promise that should strengthen faith. Its physical character adds to its uniqueness because the pledge can be grasped by our senses and made valid for the body also.[4]

Knox and the Sacraments

One of the three marks of the church in Scotland was the sacraments. Knox said little about the sacraments as a whole. Rather, he spoke of them separately. It is, therefore, necessary to apply some specific statements generally and to utilize the confessional documents. The reformer did not define a sacrament, but his general ideas can be reconstructed from several sources. In his brief 1556 work on baptism, Knox said the sacraments "are ordained to be seals of justice and faith, so are they also a declaration of our profession before the world."[5] The sacraments are signs and seals of God's promise, and along with Calvin and Bucer, Knox contended they are more than this confirmation. He regarded baptism as primarily a sign, but the Lord's Supper is a continuous process by which the benefits of Christ's death sustain the soul of the elect. The sacraments have no magical power, nor are they merely signs. Rather, they spiritually feed the believer's faith.[6]

In Knox's concept of the church, continuity existed between the church in the Old and New Testaments and between the Hebrew church and the Scottish kirk. Therefore, he also saw continuity in the sacraments. Baptism parallels the Jewish rite of circumcision. As circumcision symbolizes one's entrance into the covenanted nation of Israel (the Old Testament church), baptism signifies one's entrance into the body of Christ (the church). Similarly, the Lord's Supper extends the Jewish Passover. As the Passover represents God's deliverance of the Israelites, the Lord's Supper signifies the church's salvation.[7]

---

4. Althaus, *The Theology of Martin Luther*, 345–48; Bornkamm, *Luther's World of Thought*, 93–114; Watson, *Let God Be God*, 160–65.

5. *Works*, 5:120, 125.

6. *Works*, 5:172; 2:114–15; Wendel, *Calvin*, 315.

7. *Works*, 3:13; Knox, "Memorial or Confession to the Privy Council of Edward VI, 1552," 272.

Which is more important: preaching the Word or administering the sacraments? Catholic thought subordinated the Bible to the sacraments while the Reformed tradition and even to a greater extent with the Anabaptists—the opposite held true. But Luther balanced the Word with the sacrament and gave it more of a central place than did the Reformed theologians and Anabaptists.

Scholars have debated whether Knox subordinated the sacrament to the Word or made them more co-central as Luther did. One school, led by W. Stanford Reid, says Knox regarded the sacrament as necessary but not as central as the exposition of the Word. James McEwen represents a different line of thought. He maintains that in Knox's mind, Christ established the church by the Lord's Supper: "None in the Reformed world made the Sacrament basic for the church itself, as Knox did."[8] In Knox's writings, evidence exists for either interpretation, but the weight of the proof more readily supports the former. This statement is not to make Knox an echo of Calvin in this regard. But it is to maintain that Knox placed the Word first and the sacraments, though necessary, second.

This position can be argued from several vantage points. First is the total context of the Reformed tradition. These reformers recognized the preaching of God's Word as the primary task of the ministry. They dethroned the Mass, and the pulpit—not the altar became the focal point.[9] From this trend, John Knox did not deviate. A second support—notwithstanding Knox's contradictions and ambiguities—is the total thrust of his writings. A theme running through John Knox's life was his sense of calling. He believed his vocation to be the preaching of God's Word as found in the Scriptures—not the dispensing of the sacraments, though this also was important.[10]

A third argument can be deduced from the totality of Knox's thinking. In his mind, the Word obviously took precedence over the sacraments. Nowhere did Knox designate the sacraments as the first mark of the church. Rather, the true preaching of God's Word came first with

---

8. For arguments that place the sacrament second to the Word, see Reid, *Trumpeter of God*, 51; D'Assonville, *John Knox and the Institutes*, 18–19, 81–103. See also MacRae, "The Scottish Reformers and Their Order of Public Worship," 5:3, 26. For arguments contending Knox held the sacraments to be co-central with the Word, see McEwen, *The Faith of Knox*, 45, 57; Percy, *John Knox*, 189–90. See also Donaldson, *The Scottish Reformation*, 82; Greaves, "John Knox, The Reformed Tradition and the Sacrament of the Lord's Supper," 248–49; Dunlop, "Baptism in Scotland After the Reformation," 85–86.

9. Parker, *Oracles of God*, 21.

10. *Works*, 1:187–88. See Lamont, *The Swordbearer*, 38.

the sacraments as a second sign. Not only were the sacraments a second note, but both the *Form of Prayers* and *Scots Confession* described them as annexed to the promise of God in order to confirm the Word.[11] Knox thought of the Word as establishing the criteria for the proper administration of the sacraments and thus becoming the criterion for all worship, including the Lord's Supper. Preaching the Word and administering the sacraments were considered to be necessarily connected. But while the Word can be preached without the administration of the sacraments, they cannot be dispensed unless preceded by preaching and instruction.[12]

All of this is not to say that Knox considered the sacraments to be peripheral. Rather, he regarded the Word as central and the sacraments as vital and necessary, but second to preaching the gospel. In fact, in his 1556 tract on baptism, he evidenced a strong ecclesiastical character by firmly uniting Word and sacrament: "That no man is so regenerate, but that continually he has need of the means which Christ Jesus . . . has appointed to be used in his Kirk . . . The Word and the sacraments has Jesus Christ ordained and . . . ought not the bold presumption of man to separate the same."[13]

The Scottish Church administered the sacraments according to the Geneva Order. The *Book of Discipline*, which adopted the Geneva format, never had legal authority. Still, the Fourth General Assembly of Scotland did confirm the section on church administration in 1562 and 1564.[14] Thus some broad points in the *Book of Discipline* concerning the dispensing of sacraments should be noted along with Knox's other ideas on sacramental administration. Most important was the often repeated condition that the true preaching of the Word must accompany the dispensing of the sacraments. They must be administered by legitimate ministers—that is, Protestants preaching the Word of God. Along the same line, Knox stressed ecclesiastical separation as a criterion for a lawful sacrament. One had to completely leave the papal society before he or she could participate in a legal sacrament—and no Catholic could share in the Reformed sacrament.[15] The sacrament only applied to the faithful and to their seed. The Scots administered baptism to both the believers who were of age and

11. *Works*, 2:115–17; 4:186; Kirk, "The Religion of Early Scottish Protestants," 403–4; McMillan, *The Worship of the Scottish Reformed Church*, 169.

12. *Works*, 2:186–88. See Cameron, ed., *The First Book of Discipline*, 16.

13. *Works*, 4:121.

14. Barkley, *The Worship of the Reformed Church*, 24; Maxwell, *John Knox's Genevan Service Book, 1556*, 6–9.

15. *Works*, 2:115–16; 4:191.

to their children, but they limited the Lord's Supper to believers living a godly life.[16]

Several other issues are related to the public administration of the sacraments. God ordained the sacraments for the church and not for use as charms. Even though the Lord's Supper played a role in the early gathering of the Scottish Church, it must always be celebrated by at least two or three gathered in Christ's name. Moreover, the Scots disallowed private baptism.[17] Lastly, a woman could not administer the sacraments. The Scottish reformers reasoned that if the Holy Spirit forbade a woman to teach a congregation, then she could not administer the sacraments.[18] Still, observing all of the preceding conditions could not make the sacrament effectual in each believer. Only the work of the Holy Spirit could do this. In addition, the proper dispensing of the sacraments demanded knowledge and understanding on the part of both the administrator and the recipient. This conviction was a major motive behind Knox's philosophy of education.[19]

Baptism

Although they differed widely concerning the Lord's Supper, the Protestant reformers agreed far more than they disagreed on the question of baptism. The major disagreements on baptismal doctrine were not among the reformers themselves, but between them and their Catholic and Anabaptist opponents. All of the reformers rejected Catholicism's belief that baptism removes original sin. Conversely, they rejected the Anabaptist position of adult baptism based on conscious faith and rebaptism.[20]

Luther, Zwingli, and Calvin all adhered to the concept of infant baptism and saw this rite as placing individuals in a covenant relationship with God. First, baptism—which God gave primarily to strengthen the believer's faith in him—indicates the promise of the gospel and the sign by which the faithful enter the church. Second, baptism is the public confession of the faithful. Luther emphasized the first category while Zwingli stressed the second. Calvin and Bucer combined both of these notions. The Reformed theologians defended infant baptism as a continuation of

---

16. *Works*, 2:117–18.
17. *Works*, 4:187; 6:316.
18. *Works*, 2:116; 6:316.
19. *Works*, 2:116, 212.
20. See Kyle, "The Major Concepts in John Knox's Baptismal Thought," 21–30.

circumcision by Scriptural inferences, whereas Luther defended it primarily by church tradition.[21]

Knox set forth no direct baptismal theology. But his thought on this matter emerged as he dealt with problems related to the Catholic and Anabaptist procedures. Most of Knox's thought on baptism came in his 1556 treatise, *Answers to Some Questions Concerning Baptism*. He probably wrote this work on his trip to Scotland. It answered questions about the validity of Catholic baptism, the question of rebaptism, and the purpose of baptism.

In both the Catholic and Anabaptist doctrines of baptism, Knox found real threats to the fledgling kirks he desired to establish. Essentially, he rejected Catholic baptism as an idolatrous practice. However, since Knox also rejected Anabaptist rebaptism as a disintegrating threat to both church and society, he said that those baptized in infancy under the Catholic rite need not be baptized again. In dealing with these practical issues, Knox contributed little new to baptismal theology.

Knox believed, as did Bucer and Calvin, that the sacraments are both a sign and a means of spiritual nourishment. He did, however, regard baptism as primarily a sign—a manifestation of the believer's first entrance into the household of God and league with him. If baptism signifies the first entrance, the Lord's Supper declares the covenant and continual league with God by which Christ nourishes the believer. As Knox put it: "For the one, namely, baptism is the sign of our entrance, but the other is the declaration of our covenant, that by Christ Jesus we would be nourished, maintained, and continued in league with God our Father."[22]

In no sense did Knox regard baptism as regenerative. According to the *Form of Prayers*, this sacrament is administered in water primarily to teach the faithful that as water cleans outward filth, so the blood of Christ purges the soul from inward corruption. The visible water or outward action has no power. Rather Christ—by the power of the Holy Spirit—works in the heart of the elect, the expurgation that baptism outwardly signifies.[23]

For Knox, the lack of baptism does not prejudice one's salvation. But short of death, he would accept few excuses for not being baptized. Christ

---

21. Wendel, *Calvin*, 318; Althaus, *The Theology of Luther*, 65–7; Bromiley, ed., *Zwingli and Bullinger*, 119–28. See Lotz, "The Sacrament of Salvation," 645–57; Raitt, "Three Interrelated Principles in Calvin's Unique Doctrine of Infant Baptism," 51–61; Grislis, "Calvin's Doctrine of Baptism," 46–64.

22. *Works*, 4:124–25. See Dunlop, "Baptism in Scotland After the Reformation," 85–87.

23. *Works*, 4:188; Kyle, "Knox's Baptismal Thought," 23.

commanded baptism, and anyone choosing to ignore this command could not enter the fellowship of the faithful. According to the *Form of Prayers*: "But we having respect to that obedience which Christians owe to . . . the . . . ordinance of Christ . . . do judge them only unworthy of any fellowship with him, who contemptuously refuse such ordinary means . . . appointed to the instruction of our dull senses. . . ."[24]

Undoubtedly, Knox also had secular motives for rejecting the papal and Anabaptist notions of baptism, but his baptismal tract only mentions religious reasons. He saw the Catholic doctrine of baptism as an adulteration and profanation of the baptism that Christ had initiated, and something God's children should avoid. Besides rejecting Catholicism's regenerative theology, Knox saw "spatter, salt, candle, guide . . . lards, oil, and rest" as further corrupting papal baptism—for he regarded all human additions in religion as idolatry.[25] In addition, Catholic baptism did not contain the promises of salvation in Christ nor was it accompanied by the open preaching of God's Word.[26] Believers could not participate in such a baptism nor could they offer their children to it, because in doing so, they would "have fellowship with devils," and offer their children "not to Christ Jesus his son, but to the Devil."[27]

However, Knox attempted to straddle the fence between what he saw as the papal corruption of baptism and Anabaptism's total rejection of paedobaptism. In doing so, he adopted a moderate position that did not entirely reject the Catholic view. With the Reformation restoring the sacrament of baptism to its original purity, the elect could not participate in the papal rite. But if they had previously received the Roman baptism, they need not be rebaptized.[28] So long as Knox saw the Anabaptist sectaries as presenting a disruptive threat to both church and society, he would not consent to rebaptism under any circumstances. Thus in agreement with Calvin and Luther, he asserted that God had not completely abandoned the Church of Rome, despite its corruption. Christ instituted baptism. Its validity, therefore, could not be utterly abolished by Satan's attacks and humankind's abuses. Besides, the elect did not need rebaptism because the Holy Spirit purged from their heart all corruption that might be received from the papal rite.[29]

24. *Works*, 4:188; Kyle, "Knox's Baptismal Thought," 23.
25. *Works*, 1:197 (quote); 4:119; Kyle, "Knox's Baptismal Thought," 23.
26. *Works*, 4:119.
27. *Works*, 4:119–20.
28. *Works*, 4:122.
29. *Works*, 4:122.

The Sacraments and the Crusade against Idolatry

Knox also rejected rebaptism because of the nature of the baptismal rite itself. He considered it as an external sign and not the cause of regeneration or virtue. So that regardless of its corruption, there could be no effect on the work of the Holy Spirit. Since Christ's justice is inviolable and the faithful's league and covenant with God constant and certain, there is no need to repeat this sign of a believer's entrance into the household of God. One baptism in this life sufficed. But the other sign, the Lord's Supper, must be repeated.[30]

Knox wrote his baptismal tract in a soteriological context and related the issue of rebaptism to his doctrines of God, election, the covenant, and the church. In Knox's mind, rebaptism negates God's immutability and sovereign election. It denies a covenant to eternal salvation and runs counter to his concept of the church. In Knox's words, God's "majesty changes not as man does, but that his gifts and vocation are such, as of... which he cannot repent him [self] towards his elect. And therefore need they not to return to the external sign of baptism."[31]

Knox opposed private baptism, so much so that Jasper Ridley sees the rigidity of the reformer's resistance to private baptism as perhaps an original contribution to sixteenth-century theology. While Ridley may be stretching a point, some of Knox's contemporaries disagreed with him. Men such as Calvin and Valerand Poullain allowed for private baptism in extreme cases, but Knox would not.[32] Knox's English contemporary, Bishop Ridley, commented about the Scottish reformer's opposition to private baptism in a letter to Bishop Grindal: "As for private Baptism ... he (Knox) will say, 'It is better than to let them die without Baptism.' For this his better, what word has he in Scripture? And if he has none, why will he not follow the sentences of the old ancient writers do more allow?"[33]

In harmony with the Protestant reformers, Knox adhered to paedobaptism while rejecting the Anabaptist interpretation of adult, believer's baptism. The *Form of Prayers* defended infant baptism by making it a continuation of circumcision. An infant entered into the family of Israel and the Old Covenant by circumcision, and into the church and New Covenant by baptism. Both baptism and circumcision confirm how God

---

30. *Works*, 4:124–25.

31. *Works*, 4:124.

32. Ridley, *John Knox*, 195. Valerand Poullain was the leader of the French Protestants at Frankfurt and a disciple of Calvin. See Kyle, "Knox's Baptismal Thought," 27.

33. *Works*, 4:61.

adopted his children and brought them into his household, whether it be the church or Israel.[34]

The basic point of the entire dispute over infant baptism concerned the doctrine of the church. Acceptance of the Anabaptist view of baptism inevitably carried with it an adoption of their doctrine of the church. The Anabaptists aimed at a gathered church with baptism as a testimony of faith; whereas the Protestant reformers defended infant baptism because they viewed the church as a community in league with God containing those making an external profession.

The Lord's Supper

Great controversy centered around the Eucharist. To one degree or another, sixteenth-century religious thought witnessed at least five positions. Essentially, the issue revolved around the nature of Christ's presence in the sacrament. How should Christ's words, "This is my body" and "This is my blood," be interpreted? Literally, symbolically, or spiritually? The traditional, medieval Catholic interpretation was literal in the strictest sense. To the senses, the bread and wine remain the same. But actually in the miracle of the Mass—through the priest's words at consecration—the substance of the bread and wine are transformed into the literal body and blood of Christ. This doctrine of transubstantiation—given definite formulation in the early thirteenth century—carried with it many consequences. The Eucharist not only provided grace and spiritual nourishment, but it also made a sacrifice for sin—one that could be offered for the benefit of those present or absent, living or dead. More and more as time passed, Catholicism emphasized the sacrificial aspect of the Eucharist.[35]

The sixteenth-century reformers reacted most vehemently to this doctrine of transubstantiation and its naturally related act, the sacrificial Mass. Though they unanimously opposed the Catholic Eucharist, they differed in formulating positive alternatives to it. Luther's view—often characterized somewhat inaccurately as consubstantiation—contended that the actual body and blood of Christ exist in, with, or under the elements of bread and wine. Unlike transubstantiation, this view postulated no

---

34. *Works*, 4:187; Knox, "Memorial or Confession to the Privy Council of Edward VI," 272.

35. McGiffert, *Christian Thought*, 2:319–20; Gonzalez, *Christian Thought*, 2:329–30; Tillich, *A History of Christian Thought*, 154–58; Pelikan, *Reformation of Church and Dogma*, *(1300–1700)*, 55–59; Burkill, *Christian Thought*, 216–17.

permanent association between the elements and Christ's body and blood. Rather, God's Word affects the relationship and not priestly action.[36]

Zwingli, however, saw it differently. The words "This is my body" and "This is my blood" are plainly figurative or symbolic. He regarded the Lord's Supper as a memorial (thankful recollection), a pledge (the reassurance of faith), and a public confession (union with the church). This position did not mean that Zwingli denied the spiritual presence of Christ in the Lord's Supper. Rather, what Christ did in the past is spiritually present to the believer by faith. This action, nevertheless, was past and in no way could the signs serve as a vehicle to communicate Christ's body.[37] The radical reformers presented no unified position regarding the Lord's Supper. But regarding the Eucharist, the Swiss Anabaptists generally carried Zwingli's symbolism further and made the Lord's Supper largely a commemorative service. They emphasized the believer's communion, one with another, more than with God.[38]

Calvin and Bullinger, whose views were very similar, stood between Luther and Zwingli on the issue of Christ's presence in the Lord's Supper. Calvin rejected any physical presence such as Luther postulated. On the other hand, his attempt to give the Lord's Supper an objective content turned him away from Zwingli's purely spiritual union with what Christ had done in the past. According to Calvin, the spiritual reality of the body and blood of Christ is present in the Eucharist in truth and substance by the intermediation of the Holy Spirit. But they are not identified with the elements. Though Calvin rejected the transfusion of the substance of Christ's body, he affirmed that the benefits of the Lord's Supper are not just signified, but given. The believer spiritually receives the body of Christ without the body being localized in the elements.[39]

36. Althaus, *The Theology of Luther*, 375–403; Watson, *Let God Be God*, 160–65; Gritsch, *Martin Luther—God's Court Jester*, 63–64.

37. Bromiley, *Zwingli and Bullinger*, 178–79; Courvoisier, *Zwingli*, 67–70; Gerrish, "The Lord's Supper in Reformed Confessions," 224–29. Gerrish has called Zwingli's view "symbolic memorialism." Zwingli's symbolism was more than a "bare sign" to the believing recipient. See also Locher, *Zwingli's Thought*, 220–28; Stephens, *Theology of Zwingli*, 218–59.

38. Williams, *The Radical Reformation*, 86, 89, 222; Neuman, "The Anabaptist Position on Baptism and the Lord's Supper," 140–48.

39. Wendel, *Calvin*, 334, 342; Hunter, *Teaching of Calvin*, 178–90; Gerrish, "The Lord's Supper in Reformed Confessions," 229–31; Parker, *John Calvin*, 42–48. See also McDonell, *John Calvin, the Church, and the Eucharist*, 156ff.; Wallace, *Calvin's Doctrine of the Word and Sacrament*, 196–216; Ellis, "The Genesis of Martin Bucer's Doctrine of the Lord's Supper," 225–51; Gerrish, "John Calvin and the Reformed Doctrine of the Lord's Supper," 85–98; Kibble, "The Reformation and the Eucharist," 43–56.

Part One: Historical and Theological Foundations

John Knox and the Lord's Supper

John Knox regarded the theoretical aspects of the real presence controversy as secondary to the practical aspects. He saw himself called—not to debate the alternatives to transubstantiation—but to destroy it and the Roman Mass. At the outset, his mission was primarily, though not entirely, destructive. Before the Reformed Church could be established in Scotland, the Church of Rome had to be torn down and this meant eliminating the idolatrous Mass from the liturgy.

Despite Knox's negative emphasis, he had a positive Eucharistic doctrine, however difficult it is to categorize. Yet two definite statements can be made. First, Knox's view of the Lord's Supper was basically set during the earliest stages of his ministry. Second, he clearly adhered to the Reformed concept in this regard. Still, scholars debate which specific Reformed label to hang on Knox. In Eucharistic doctrine, did Knox follow Calvin, Bucer or Bullinger—or was he no more specific than the Reformed tradition? [40] Nevertheless, there can be no debate concerning his Reformed stance in this regard. This position was illustrated by Knox's natural acceptance of the *Consensus Tigurinus*, the agreement of Zurich concerning the Lord's Supper that Calvin and Bullinger reached in 1549.[41]

For the account of Knox's Communion service in 1547, the major source must be his history, written years later. If his memory is reliable, he was not Lutheran in this service because he administered it "in the same purity that now it is ministered in the churches of Scotland, with the same doctrine, that he taught unto them."[42] Knox's assertion here and elsewhere opposed real presence and indicated that he was no Lutheran. In fact, this statement said Knox celebrated the first Communion at St.

---

40. Greaves says that Knox's debt in regard to the Lord's Supper is primarily to Bucer with Bullinger and the *First Helvetic Confession* also playing a major role. Calvin influenced Knox in this regard, but less than has traditionally been supposed. See Greaves, "John Knox and the Lord's Supper," 238–54. In relating Knox to the *Institutes*, D'Assonville naturally points out Calvin's early influence on Knox's view of the Lord's Supper. See D'Assonville, *Knox and the Institutes*, 6–22. Reid indicates the Calvinistic tenor of Knox's sacramental thought before he left England. See Reid, *Trumpeter of God*, 51, 76, 93. See also Kirk, "The Influence of Calvinism on the Scottish Reformation," 157–79. McEwen and Percy minimize Calvin's influence on eucharistic thought. McEwen insists that Knox went well beyond Calvin in uplifting the sacrament. See McEwen, *Faith of Knox*, 45–60; Percy, *John Knox*, 189–90. Sources such as Lorimer and Ridley find it difficult to be more specific than the general Reformed label. See Lorimer, *Knox and the Church of England*, 130–31; Ridley, *John Knox*, 92.

41. Ridley, *John Knox*, 92.

42. *Works*, 1:201–2.

The Sacraments and the Crusade against Idolatry

Andrews exactly as he now celebrated it in the 1560s. Traditionally, this statement has meant that Knox's first Communion was Calvinistic. But more recently, it has been argued that it might reflect a broader range of Reformed influences.[43]

After spending more than a year on a French galley, Knox landed in England in early 1549. The years 1549 and 1550 saw Knox writing several tracts related to the Lord's Supper. However, *A Vindication that the Sacrifice of the Mass is Idolatry* tells us what Knox opposed in the Mass, but little on what he believed the Lord's Supper should be.[44] And *Practices of the Lord's Supper* says little more than Knox celebrated the Lord's Supper in the spirit of the Reformation.[45]

But *A Summary of the Lord's Supper* tells us more. The Lord's Supper, being ordained of God, uses the visible symbols to lift the faithful into invisible and spiritual things. By the elements God not only confirms his promises to the believer's senses, but Christ is present and spiritually eaten by faith. *A Summary* also evidences a horizontal dimension to the Lord's Supper. Christ gathers the church by means of the sacrament. Not only does the Lord's Supper confess a doctrine, but it also joins believers together in "a bond of mutual love among us."[46] In fact, none but believers are to participate—for the sacrament is not a work of salvation—but rather a seal and confirmation of faith. In regard to the meaning of "This is my body," Knox rejected any form of real presence. Conversely, he also repudiated any notion that the bread and wine are bare signs. Instead, he interpreted the words sacramentally and not literally, "for in the Sacrament we receive Jesus Christ spiritually, as did the Fathers of the Old Testament."[47]

Knox's practice on his 1555-56 trip to Scotland from Geneva informs us about the relationship of the Lord's Supper to the established church. James McEwen contends that on this trip, Knox founded the

---

43. Greaves, "John Knox and the Lord's Supper," 250–52.

44. *Works*, 30–70; Ridley, *John Knox*, 96–97; Reid, *Trumpeter of God*, 78.

45. Knox, "The Practice of the Lord's Supper Used in Berwick by John Knox, 1550," 290–92.

46. *Works*, 3:73. In the horizontal dimension of *A Summary*, Greaves draws a parallel with Bucer. Bucer emphasized a strong element of fellowship among believers in the Lord's Supper. Greaves, "John Knox and the Lord's Supper," 245. On the other hand, D'Assonville sees Calvin's unmistakable influence in *A Summary*. He parallels Knox's emphasis on the promise of God with a similar principle in the *Institutes*. See D'Assonville, *Knox and the Institutes*, 16–17.

47. *Works*, 3:74–75.

PART ONE: Historical and Theological Foundations

visible church by the sacrament. But in each case, Knox followed the liturgical practice common to both primitive Christianity and many of the Reformed churches of his time: he preached the Word first and administered the sacrament second.[48] What existed here was not so much an extraordinary elevation of the sacrament, but an administration of the Lord's Supper before the establishment of a publicly organized kirk. Instead of an exceptional uplifting of the sacrament as McEwen contends, Knox demonstrated an absence of ecclesiasticism. Rather than waiting for "the face of a public kirk" to be established, Knox administered the sacrament to the small flock or "privy kirk."[49]

The visible church came in two forms: the small flock and the national kirk established by law. The former was an organized church because the church existed where two or three were gathered in Christ's name. Moreover, these "privy kirks" elected preachers, appointed elders and deacons, and conducted worship according to a Reformed pattern. Yet these "privy" kirks usually met secretly in homes and lacked the elements of ecclesiasticism the established kirk had. Two marks of the church—preaching the Word and administering the sacraments—were found in the small flock. But the third mark, discipline, waited for an established church. Knox did not differ from Calvin in that he made the sacrament co-central with preaching. Both men elevated the Word over the sacrament. Rather he differed from Calvin in administering the Lord's Supper before the small flock had attained an orderly state. On the other hand, Calvin discouraged similar churches in France from celebrating Communion until they had organized their church in an orderly manner, as so defined by the standards of the sixteenth century.[50]

In 1556, Knox became a minister of the English congregation at Geneva. This church based its worship on the *Form of Prayers,* drafted by Knox and others at Frankfurt, but influenced and approved by Calvin. Calvin's view (Bucer's, too), which had the believer spiritually eating of Christ's body and blood, was evident: "For . . . if with a truly penitent heart

---

48. *Works,* 1:250. See footnote 8. See also Kirk, "The Religion of Early Scottish Protestants," 403.

49. *Works,* 1:245–51; 2:151; Greaves, "John Knox and the Last Supper," 248–50. See also Kirk, *Patterns of Reform,* 15.

50. *Works,* 1:245–5; 2:151; Greaves, "John Knox and the Lord's Supper," 248–50. Both Greaves and McEwen note that Calvin advised the Huguenots to delay administering the Lord's Supper until their churches had been organized in an orderly fashion. See McEwen, *Faith of Knox,* 53, 55; Walker, *John Calvin,* 384; Kirk, *Patterns of Reform,* 15.

The Sacraments and the Crusade against Idolatry

and lively faith we received that holy sacrament, (for then we spiritually eat the flesh of Christ and drink his blood, then we dwell in Christ and Christ in us)."[51]

The *Scots Confession*—drawn up by Knox and five fellow ministers in 1560—portrayed the Lord's Supper as continuous from the Old Testament Passover. Moreover, God instituted it to demarcate those within the covenant, to exercise the faith of believers, and to seal in their hearts the assurance of his promise and union with Christ. The *Confession* utterly rejected the "bare sign" view of the sacred meal because when rightly used, the soul receives nourishment. It equally denied transubstantiation, but accepted a spiritual operation. The Holy Spirit makes the faithful to feed upon the body and blood of Christ in a spiritual manner. Though Christ's body remains in heaven, believers by the proper use of the Lord's Table spiritually eat the body and drink the blood of Christ.[52]

In this declaration, the Scottish reformers demonstrated Calvin's and Bucer's idea of Communion with the body and blood. On one hand, the reformers denied the sacraments to be bare signs. But on the other, they carefully distinguished between Christ in his natural substance and the elements in the sacramental signs: "Whosoever slanders us, as that we affirmed . . . (the) Sacraments to be only naked signs, do injury unto us . . . we must confess, that we make one distinction between Christ Jesus, in his natural substance, and between the elements in the Sacramental signs. . . ." As a result, they adopted a mediating position: We "will neither worship the signs in place of that which is signified by them; neither, yet do we despise and interpret them as unprofitable and vain."[53]

The sacramental doctrine expressed in the *Scots Confession* presents two problems: Does this doctrine represent Knox's views on the subject? To what extent did Calvin influence this doctrine? The first dilemma is not difficult. As Duncan Shaw points out, the *Confession* was not solely Knoxian. Others, such as John Willock, played a role in writing the *Confession* that is often overlooked.[54] Still, the views set forth in the *Confession* harmonized with Knox's previous sacramental statements. The reformer, therefore, had no major disagreement with the *Confession's* sacramental position.

---

51. *Works*, 4:192.
52. *Works*, 2:115–17; Cheyne, "The Scots Confession of 1560," 337–38.
53. *Works*, 2:115–17.
54. Shaw, "John Willock," 59–60; Cheyne, "The Scots Confession," 323.

But the second question—the extent of Calvin's influence—arouses the disagreement of scholars. Whose ideas are reflected in the *Confession's* view of the Lord's Supper? Calvin's? Or the Bucer–Bullinger compromise worked out in the *First Helvetic Confession?* Though the *Scots Confession* itself came directly out of the continental Reformed milieu with its varied sacramental views, its language reflected Calvin's influence. Was this because both Calvin and Knox followed Bucer in this regard?[55]

THE CRUSADE AGAINST IDOLATRY

Knox's primary concern in the sacramental area, and probably his greatest anxiety in general, was idolatry. In his campaign against idolatry, a fundamental distinction between the Lutheran and Reformed presentations of Protestantism can be seen. While Luther protested the doctrine of works or the Judaic element in the Roman Church, Zwingli and Calvin raised their voices against the doctrine of image worship or the pagan element in that church. Whereas all the reformers accepted the two Protestant positions thus stated, the Lutherans emphasized the former distinction while the Reformed theologians stressed the latter.[56]

The fight against the idolatrous Mass, along with its counterpart of establishing "true worship," can be seen as the great motive of Knox's career.[57] In the pursuit of this objective Knox exceeded the vigor of his Reformed colleagues, and perhaps in this excess displayed his most unique trait. The consequences of his literal Old Testament hermeneutic, with its starting point in Deuteronomy 12:32, manifested itself clearly in the fight against idolatry. From the very onset of his public career, to his death in 1572, Knox maintained great hostility to the Mass. Under certain circumstances this theme intensified, but it can hardly be considered developmental.

Though the crusade against idolatry pervaded most of Knox's writings, its logic is largely repetitious and can be illustrated by selected passages. Knox's *History* vigorously portrayed the struggle against the idolatrous Mass. After all, Knox depicted the Scottish Reformation as a

---

55. Gerrish, "The Lord's Supper in the Reformed Tradition," 238–39; Kirk, "The Influence of Calvinism," 159–61; Reid, *Trumpeter of God*, 192; Greaves, "John Knox and the Lord's Supper," 251. See also Hazlett, "The Scots Confession 1560," Reid, "French Influence on the First Scots Confession and Book of Discipline," 1–14.

56. See Kyle, "John Knox and the Purification of Religion, 265–80; Macmillian, *John Knox*, 45.

57. Percy, *John Knox*, 116.

The Sacraments and the Crusade against Idolatry

reenactment of Israel's fight against idolatry. Not surprisingly this theme of idolatry, whether implicit or overtly stated, permeated nearly every page of his *History* in many different and unrelated contexts.

Starting with his first sermon in 1547, Knox made his attack on the Mass synonymous with his fight against idolatry. Here he presented his basic proposition: the task of human beings is not to devise a religion acceptable to God, but rather to simply observe without alteration religion received from God. In particular, the Scots reformer insisted that the sacraments could not be mutilated, and that the Mass is an "abominable idolatry, blasphemous to the death of Christ, and a profanation of the Lord's Supper."[58] Accordingly, the contrast between the Mass and the Lord's Supper drove Knox to extremes in his denunciation of the Mass. Wishart had previously attacked idolatry and the Roman Church, but as Knox recorded in his *History*: 'Master George spoke never so plainly.'"[59]

A Vindication of the Doctrine that the Sacrifice of the Mass Is Idolatry

After Knox returned from a duration on a French galley in 1549, he denounced the Mass in northern England. From his defense of this denunciation came *A Vindication*, Knox's most direct attack on idolatry. Knox's approach combined scriptural citations with scholastic logic and history. In medieval fashion, he based his argument on two syllogisms. In these syllogisms the key to Knox's crusade against idolatry and perhaps his thinking in general clearly emerges.

He did not define idolatry in the strict literal sense of substituting a false God for a true God. Given such a definition, ceremonies without number might be introduced into the "religion of God" without any one of them involving worship of another God (e.g., use of the cross, or of oil and salt in baptism, or of kneeling and wafer-bread in the Lord's Supper). Rather, Knox defined idolatry in the widest sense possible; for idolatry, as he said, entails not only the worship of that which is not God—but also to trust in anything besides God. To honor anything in religion contrary to God's Word is to lean on something other than God, and therefore idolatry.

The first syllogism stated, "All worshipping, honoring, or service invented by the brain of man in the religion of God, without his own express

58. *Works*, 1:194.
59. *Works*, 1:192.

149

commandment is idolatry. The Mass is invented by the brain of man, without any commandment of God. Therefore it is idolatry."[60] In this tract, Knox went to considerable lengths to anchor his major premise in biblical proof texts. For example, he cited the episode in which Saul offered a sacrifice to appease God's wrath when Samuel, the priest, was absent. Saul sinned in that he usurped the function of the Levitical priest, and thus honored God without an express commandment.[61]

But Knox attempted to prove the minor premise, that the Mass is the invention of human beings and thus idolatry, primarily by negations. For example, he asserted that the Latin word *Missa* has no Hebrew equivalent signifying an oblation or sacrifice, and that it could not be proved by Scripture that Peter and James celebrated the first Mass in Jerusalem. Thus Knox defended his minor premise by placing the burden upon the Catholics to prove from Scripture that the New Testament church celebrated the Mass.[62]

Knox then proceeded to his second syllogism: "All honoring or service of God, where unto is added a wicked opinion, is abomination. Unto the Mass is added a wicked opinion. Therefore it is abomination."[63] Again, Knox defended the major premise by citing Old Testament examples where the Jews distorted the sacrifice by adding a wicked opinion thus making it an abomination. One illustration from Micah—in which the prophet said no external work can atone for sin—specifically attacked the Mass and extended Knox's definition of idolatry: "For idolatry is not only to worship the thing which is not God, but also to trust or lean unto that thing which is not God, and has not itself all sufficiency." Thus Knox not only condemned the Mass as idolatrous worship, but also as a false atonement. The idea that the Mass could reenact Christ's sacrifice or in any way atone for sin was an abomination to Knox. He defined an idolater as one "whose heart believed remission of sins by a vain work, done by himself or by any other in his name"[64]

Knox sustained his minor premise, that the Mass is a wicked opinion joined to the honoring of God, by insisting the papists plainly taught the Mass sacrificed and made an oblation for sin. According to Knox, the apostles and prophets proved this teaching to be an abomination. Christ

60. *Works*, 3:34.
61. *Works*, 3:35, 38, 44, 46. Knox illustrated this major premise frequently.
62. *Works*, 3:48–49, 51.
63. *Works*, 3:52.
64. *Works*, 3:54.

offered his life once, and this sacrifice needs no repetition. The New Testament covenant, made once and confirmed in Christ's blood, can never be dissolved. If the Mass were a sacrifice, then Christ must be slain again and again and to believe this logic would be blasphemy. Furthermore, Knox would not permit anyone to defend the Mass as a pretext for the Lord's Supper. The Communion had been instituted, he said, in perpetual memory of the benefit received by Christ's death—whereas Romanism intended the Mass as a sacrifice.[65]

Some evidence indicates that Knox's tract, *A Vindication*, depended on Calvin's *Institutes*.[66] Whether this judgment is correct or not, differences between Knox and Calvin in regard to idolatry can be detected. *A Vindication* consisted mainly of two sections: a first rejected the Mass purely on the basis that God's Word did not command it; and a second rejected the substance of the Mass in principle. In the first section the dominance of Knox's literal Old Testament hermeneutic based on Deuteronomy 12:32 can be seen. In the second section, where Knox rejected the substance of the Mass, he seemed to follow Calvin. Calvin tolerated the so-called indifferentia in regard to the external forms of the sacrament. But Knox was less tolerant in this regard, for he regarded the Bible as the codified Word of God and religion as a somewhat external institution that could be maintained by the whole nation.[67]

Later Writings

Knox's crusade against idolatry certainly did not diminish after his major work on the subject. Though he did not again attack idolatry so logically or so directly as he did in *A Vindication*, the theme continued to dominate his thought. During his exile (1554-59), the crusade intensified but took different paths. In one place, Knox comforted believers who were being persecuted by the papists and warned them to separate from idolatry. In another he denounced nations for their breaking of the covenant and corporate idolatry. But increasingly the Scots reformer developed his anti-idolatry theme in a political context and as a springboard to resistance. Nevertheless, because the logic behind this development is repetitive, no detailed treatment will occur here.

65. *Works*, 3:54-61.
66. D'Assonville, *Knox and the Institutes*, 9-15.
67. See Calvin, *The Institutes of Christian Religion*, 4.17:1-50, particularly 43; D'Assonville, *Knox and the Institutes*, 14-15.

PART ONE: Historical and Theological Foundations

Trying times came when Edward VI passed away and Mary Tudor became queen. During this time of transition (1553–54) Knox's writings reflected mounting concern over idolatry. His correspondence with Mrs. Bowes (*Psalm VI* and *Epistles*) urged her to continue in the faith and issued a warning never to submit to the idolatrous Mass.[68] *A Godly Letter* (1554) warned believers remaining in England not to succumb to idolatry. Envisioning himself as Jeremiah, Knox developed the theme that England transgressed worse than Judah and would be punished accordingly. Because England—once in league with God under Edward VI—broke the covenant and fell into idolatry (Catholicism), God's judgment would come in the form of plagues and natural disasters. At this point, Knox did not invite revolt, nor did he attack Mary; he only condemned popery and demanded that individual believers separate from idolatry.[69]

Though Knox warned against idolatry in most writings during his exile, in four letters published before 1558, he politicized the anti-idolatry theme. In fact, as shall be seen later, the fight against idolatry became the springboard for his political theory. In these four letters (*The First Blast, A Letter to the Queen Regent, The Appellation,* and *A Letter to the Commonalty*), Knox set forth his views on the rights of citizens against idolatrous (Catholic) rulers. First he requested the Queen Regent to suppress idolatry and reform the church. Then he followed with pleas to the nobles to force such reforms and a summons to the commonalty to pressure the ruler for the same end.[70]

Mary Tudor died November 1558, and Elizabeth became queen. Though she was to make England Protestant once again, the refugees abroad did not immediately appreciate the situation. Under these conditions, Knox wrote *A Brief Exhortation to England*. Essentially this tract said the whole population of England had sinned by submitting to idolatry during Mary's rule or at least in not resisting her. Accordingly the collective guilt of England could only be purged by reintroducing Protestantism and eliminating all "dregs of papistry." Once this task was done, Knox hoped discipline would prevent any regression into idolatry. Knox advocated many methods, including revolt, to overthrow idolatry. But once this mission was achieved and the true church established, then ecclesiastical

---

68. *Work*, 3:119–60, 337–402. Specifically see 339, 345, 357, 371, 384, 389.

69. *Works*, 3:165–215. Specifically see 166, 168–70, 172, 175, 178, 181, 187–97, 212, 214.

70. *Works*, 4:373–420, 433–59, 467–520, 523–38.

discipline and the civil sword must work together to prevent any recurrence of idolatry.[71]

After the establishment of Protestantism in 1560, Knox and his colleagues disputed with a Catholic, Alexander Anderson. The reformers argued that the Mass blasphemes the death of Christ, because in offering it, the priest usurps Christ's office as the only mediator between God and humankind.[72] Shortly thereafter, Knox praised God for purifying worship in Scotland. In his opinion "no realm this day upon the face of the earth" administered the sacraments in such purity. In this comparison, he criticized other Protestant churches—probably Lutheran, for maintaining impure liturgical practices—despite the overall correctness of their doctrine.[73] It must be remembered that the Lutheran practice eliminated what the Bible expressly condemned, while possibly retaining what Scripture did not forbid. On the other hand, the Reformed churches would not allow anything in worship not expressly commanded by the Bible.

Though the Reformation had been partially established and Catholicism abolished, Knox could not relax his crusade against the Mass. The arrival of Mary Queen of Scots in 1561, supported by the French and devotedly attached to the Catholic faith, proved a misfortune to the reformers. The revival of Romanism was no idle threat to Knox. Mary Queen of Scots apparently desired to restore Catholicism, to say nothing about the threat of French intervention on behalf of the Roman faith.

Accordingly, Knox objected to Queen Mary's private Mass. In so doing, the Scots reformer not only demonstrated a fear of the Catholic Mass, but also an understanding of its potential danger. Queen Mary's private Mass posed a threat to the Reformation—because in the sixteenth century a people usually adopted their sovereign's religion—and Catholicism still lingered among the Scottish people. Thus Knox concluded, "That one Mass . . . was more fearful to him than if ten thousand armed enemies were landed in any part of the Realm, of purpose to suppress the whole religion."[74]

Shortly after Queen Mary's arrival, Knox debated with several Catholic priests over the Mass and other related matters. Quintin Kennedy, the Abbot of Crossraguel, published a tract against the Scottish reformers. He rejected Knox's definition of idolatry as set forth in *A Vindication*. In

71. *Works*, 5:503–22.
72. *Works*, 2:139.
73. *Works*, 2: 263–65.
74. *Works*, 2:276.

PART ONE: Historical and Theological Foundations

turn he designated Melchizedek—who supplied bread and wine for Abraham's retainers—as a type of Christ, who had by this act made an oblation of bread and wine to God. Hence Christ had to make an offering of his body and blood in the Last Supper, or else he was not a priest according to the order of Melchizedek. Although Knox found this line of argument somewhat difficult to understand, he nevertheless defended his Reformed position by arguing that Melchizedek brought bread and wine to Abraham as a refreshment and not to make an oblation or sacrifice.[75]

Indeed, Knox's celebrated debate with Maitland of Lethington in 1564 demonstrated how the reformer's theory of resistance depended on his concepts of God and idolatry. Maitland said the commandment to slay an idolatrous monarch was no longer in effect. Knox countered by insisting that the commandment for putting an idolater to death is perpetual and still in force because, as he said, God is immutable and his commands remain constant. Therefore, Christian nations are still bound by the judicial laws of Israel and must enact the same penalties against all breach of moral law.[76]

John Knox equated Catholicism with idolatry. To be a Catholic was to be an idolater. The fight against the idolatrous Mass so dominated his thinking that virtually no major area of his thought was free from it. The anti-idolatry theme stemmed from his Old Testament hermeneutic and permeated his political thought, his doctrine of salvation, his sacramental and ecclesiastical thought, his view of church discipline, and even his perception of Christ's office as high priest.

---

75. *Works*, 6:159–86, 200–201. Kennedy's *Ane Compendious Ressonying* is reprinted in *Works*, 6:157–65. See also Laing, ed., "Ane Compendius Tractice," vol 1. It should be noted that the Abbot's position on the sacrificial nature of the Mass resembled the Tridentine teaching despite preceding the council by a year. At the same time, a priest named Winzet challenged Knox to prove that he was validly ordained and entitled to act as a minister. Though centered on other matters, the conversation touched on the Mass. Winzet denied that the celebrant in the Mass sought to intrude between God and human beings. Rather he sought only to act as the high priest of Christ. McRoberts, ed., *Essays on the Scottish Reformation*, 264. See also Ridley, *John Knox*, 408–12; Winzet, *Certain Tractates Together with the Book of Four Score Three Questions*.

76. *Works*, 2:447.

Part Two

Vocational Considerations

7

Thunder from the Pulpit

"I LOVE TO BLOW my Master's Trumpet," proclaimed John Knox. This little phrase is pregnant with meaning; it succinctly captures the very essence of his ministry. Historians have focused on Knox as the leader of a reformation, the instigator of a rebellion, and an opponent of female rule. While these impressions may be valid, they do not reflect Knox's self-perception and the way his contemporaries viewed him. He saw himself as a simple preacher proclaiming God's Word, a watchman warning the people to obey God. His contemporaries—both his supporters and opponents—also regarded him as a preacher.[1]

As a minister, Knox performed many tasks—preaching, administering the sacraments, counseling his parishioners, organizing churches, writing confessional statements, and more. But preaching was his priority. God called him to preach and Knox had no doubt about his vocation. In his aptly titled biography, *Trumpeter of God*, W. Stanford Reid has captured this theme. Believing himself to be called as were the Hebrew prophets, Knox's chief purpose in life was to summon people to repentance and faith in Jesus Christ as Lord and Savior. Like John the Baptist, he saw himself as a "voice crying in the wilderness," an instrument trumpeting the divine message. This "trumpeter theme thus became central to his thinking."[2] Or as Douglas MacMillan puts it: this "total commitment to preaching

---

1. *Works* 4:367–71; 6:229–31; MacMillan, "John Knox—Preacher of the Word"; Kirk, "John Knox and the Historians," 20.

2. *Works*, 6:229–31; Reid, *Trumpeter of God*, xiv.

and to what preaching alone can achieve provides the real key to understanding Knox as a man, a Christian, and a reformer."[3]

The First Blast of the Trumpet (1558) alerted people to the notion of Knox "blowing his master's trumpet." But he began to trumpet God's message much earlier than this. In 1547 at St. Andrews, Knox received a dramatic call to proclaim God's Word. And it did not take him long to obey this summons: the next week he was in the pulpit preaching his first sermon. Knox did not embark upon his preaching career until age 32. Except for the occasions when he had no access to a pulpit, he preached for more than twenty-five years, until a few days before his death in 1572.[4] Knox apparently had skills as a leader, politician, church organizer, pastoral counselor, and perhaps even as a writer. But preaching was his greatest strength. He could skillfully interpret Scripture. And according to contemporary accounts, he was a forceful compelling preacher with considerable charisma who could motivate people to action.[5]

The task of preaching was central to Knox's life and career. Why have most modern historians not picked up on this theme? In part, examples of Knox's preaching are scant; he only wrote down a few sermons.[6] But we are not totally without evidence. We have some tracts that were versions of earlier sermons. In fact, many of Knox's writings, even his *History*, have a sermonic cast to them. Knox was so focused on preaching that "he only took to his pen when his voice was silent," said Maurice Lee. Knox's *History* was a sermon without an audience, a preaching book, "one long inflammatory speech in behalf of God's truth," as the reformer saw it.[7] Another window to Knox's sermons are the impressions of his contemporaries. Both his followers and opponents voiced their reactions to the reformer's sermons—some singing his praises, others expressing their outrage.[8]

---

3. MacMillan, "John Knox—Preacher of the Word," 6.

4. *Works*, 1:187–93; 6:xxii–xxv, i–ii, 634; 4:373–420; Edington, "John Knox and the Castilians," 30.

5. *Works* 1:192–93; 6:643–44; Melville, *The Diary of Mr. James Melville*, 21, 26; Bishop, "John Knox: Thundering Scot," 73–74.

6. *Works*, 4:87–114; 6:221–71. These represent Knox's only fully intact sermons. Aspects of others can be found in his *History* and in his tracts. See *Works*, 1:189–92; 4:87–114.

7. Lee, "John Knox and his History," 80, 87–88.

8. *Works* 1:192–93; 2:372, 379, 384, 388, 497–98; 6:230–32, 633, 643–44; Melville, *Diary of Melville*, 73–74.

Knox's preaching has been neglected for other reasons. Earlier biographers such as Thomas M'Crie have accorded great importance to Knox's preaching.[9] But in the modern era, few historians have emphasized this subject. Why? For one reason, in the early twenty-first century, the sermon does not play the central role that it has in the past. In an age of television, the Internet, and cheap paperbacks, sermons are no longer the primary shaper of ideas. Another factor is the transitory nature of a sermon. The impact of a sermon largely depends on chemistry, charisma, and emotions—subjects that are not easily measured by biographers. Thus historians have turned to more accessible themes.[10]

PREACHING BEFORE KNOX

The Reformation did not invent preaching. Christian preaching has as ancient lineage, being rooted in the Old Testament prophets and the message of the apostles. The patristic era also produced many remarkable preachers. Some examples include Origen, Basil of Caesarea, John Chrysostom, Gregory of Nazianzus, Ambrose, and Augustine. The early Middle Ages saw the art of preaching fall into a long night of obscurity until the high Middle Ages experienced a revival of preaching. The preaching of the crusades and the rise scholasticism prodded such a surge. But another decline set in. The church of the late medieval world focused on the sacraments, prompting the parish clergy to adopt a fundamentally sacramental role. Thus preaching was neglected and what existed became frivolous and decorated with illustrations. Yet some outstanding preachers still could be found, including John Wycliffe, the Lollards, John Hus, Nicholas of Cusa, Jean de Gerson, John of Capistrano, and Savonarola.[11]

Still the Reformation did return the Bible to the people, and in the process it ushered in a new era of biblical preaching, in both quality and quantity. Most of the reformers, including Knox, preached several times a week. Bullinger preached through the Bible in about fifteen years. Luther's sermons filled twenty volumes, Calvin's forty. In fact, except for Philip Melanchthon, all of the major reformers were preachers.[12]

9. M'Crie, *The Life of John Knox*.
10. MacMillan, "John Knox—Preacher of the Word," 7–9.
11. See Baird, "Preaching," 868–69; Old, "History of Preaching," 286–87; Dargan, *A History of Preaching*; Brilioth, *A Brief History of Preaching*.
12. See Parker, *Calvin's Preaching*; Stephens, *The Theology of Huldrych Zwingli*; Althaus, *The Theology of Martin Luther*; Buttrick, "Theology of Preaching," 289–90.

Part Two: Vocational Considerations

Differences between medieval and Reformation preaching go beyond quantity; they also concern quality. The churchmen of the Middle Ages adopted a fourfold method of biblical interpretation: literal, moral, allegorical, and anagogic. But in general, the medieval preachers regarded the Bible in a figurative sense, thus reducing the authority of Scripture. The reformers reversed this trend. In various degrees, they opted for a literal interpretation of Scripture. And this change fostered the recovery of expository preaching; that is, the reformers worked their way through the Bible passage by passage. Their sermons were biblical, emphasizing the Gospel, and the reformers never doubted that they were preaching the "Word of God." Luther, Zwingli, Calvin, Bullinger, Oecolampodius, Knox, and nearly all the major reformers were faithful biblical preachers. Of the leading reformers, Calvin had the greatest impact on Knox's preaching—second only to those he encountered in Scotland.[13]

However, before having any direct contact with the Continental reformers, Knox began to thunder from the pulpit. Who taught him how to preach? Knox had a number of homegrown models, some who had come under the influence of the Continental preachers. As on the Continent, preaching in the Scottish Catholic Church had sunk to low levels. The content of their sermons and homilies revolved around devotion to Mary, the Mass, the sacraments, and good works. Still, a few priests must have preached God's Word, for Knox acknowledged that some "would occupy the pulpit and truly preach Jesus Christ." But most did not.[14]

Undoubtedly, the early Scottish Protestants had the greatest impact on Knox's preaching. Patrick Hamilton was a preacher at St. Andrews from 1523 to1527. On the Continent, he came under the influence of Erasmus, Luther, and Tyndale. In Scotland, he eloquently preached justification by faith—so disturbing was his message that the church declared him a heretic and had him burnt at the stake. Yet he inspired other men who would have a direct impact on Knox.[15] More immediately, Knox came under the influence of several former Dominican friars—Thomas Guilliame and John Rough. These fiery preachers directly ministered to

---

13. See Smalley, *The Study of the Bible in the Middle Ages*; Parker, *The Oracles of God*; Old, "History of Preaching," 287; Buttrick, "Theology of Preaching," 289; Oberman, "Preaching and the Word in the Reformation," *Theology Today,* 16–29; Gerrish, "Biblical Authority and the Continental Reformation," 337–40.

14. *Works* 1:105; Bray et al., "Preaching: Themes and Styles," 668; McKay, "Parish Life in Scotland," 85–115; Cowan, *The Scottish Reformation*, 70–71.

15. *Works*, 1:13–19; McGoldrick, "Patrick Hamilton, Luther's Scottish Disciple," 81–88; McGoldrick, *Luther's Scottish Connection*, 46–54.

Knox, who recorded their impact in his *History*. He described Guilliame as a fluid speaker with solid judgment, wholesome doctrine, and adequate knowledge for that day. Nevertheless, Guilliame was too moderate in his opposition to Catholicism for Knox's liking. Knox characterized Rough as more simple and not that well learned, but more rigorous in combating the Catholic faith.[16]

Of these early Protestants, George Wishart had the most enduring influence upon Knox's preaching. Wishart had been exiled to the Continent where he came under the sway of the Swiss reformers. He returned in 1542, first to England and then to Scotland. During 1544–45, he popularized the doctrines of the Swiss reformers—including justification by faith, the Apostles' Creed, and a fierce condemnation of Catholic doctrines and practices. Wishart was a charismatic orator who preached with a fiery passion. His thundering denunciation of Catholicism attracted many who desired the purification of religion and society. In his *History*, Knox records his approval of Wishart's sermonizing; he glorified God by preaching his Word with vehemence. As a result many were converted to the Protestant faith.[17]

Scottish Protestant preaching took the teaching of Scripture as its only authority. In fact, according to the *Scots Confession*, the mark of the "true Kirk of God we believe, confess, and avow to be, first, the true preaching of the Word of God." Given this importance, Scotland needed many preachers. While Knox may have been renown for his preaching, there were other gifted Scottish preachers such as William Harlow (1500–75), John Willock (1512–85), John Craig (1512–1600), David Fergusson (1525–98), Andrew Melville (1545–1622), and Robert Bruce (1554–1631).[18]

PREPARATION AND CHARACTRISTICS

Knox did not blow his master's trumpet without considerable preparation, both spiritually and intellectually. The basis for his pulpit ministry lay in his conversion experience and dramatic call to the ministry. He had cast his anchor in Jesus Christ and received a call to preach, which he interpreted

---

16. *Works*, 1:95, 96; Gill, "John Knox, The Preacher," 104; Kyle, "Guilliame, Thomas," 380; Cowan, *Scottish Reformation*, 101; Reid, *Trumpeter of God*, 11, 24–25; Edington, "John Knox and the Castilians," 30, 39–40.

17. *Works*, 1:125–55, 534–37; Gill, "John Knox, The Preacher" 105; Kirk, "The Religion of Early Scottish Protestants," 382–83; Ridley, *John Knox*, 37–44; Edington, "John Knox and the Castilians," 39

18. *Works*, 2:110; Philip, "Preachers," 665–66.

PART TWO: Vocational Considerations

as coming directly from God. To be sure, Knox cannot be regarded as a sophisticated theologian. Still, he had a solid grasp of Reformed doctrine, even though he expressed it in a practical if not systematic manner. But more importantly, Knox was a man of the Word. He diligently studied Scripture, describing himself as "sitting at his books" and using the church fathers as a guide to the Bible. Consequently, he acquired a commanding knowledge of Scripture, which allowed him to have a thorough understanding of Christian doctrine and a detailed recollection of biblical events. And Knox used his knowledge to carefully prepare his sermons.[19]

From the pulpit, Knox could roar with the voice of authority. This great confidence came from his conviction that the Bible was God's Word and his only job was to proclaim it. Despite his occasional reliance on other sources, throughout his public ministry, he claimed Scripture as his sole authority in religious matters. In regard to religion—especially worship—human beings could not add to nor subtract anything from what God expressly commanded.[20] Undoubtedly, this reliance on Scripture had a twofold effect: Knox's sermons could be inflexible, but they also had great authority.

His approach to Scripture impacted his preaching in still other ways. Not only did he regard the Bible as the authoritative Word of God, but he upheld the perspicuity of Scripture—that it is clear and intelligible to the average person. Phrases such as "the plain Word of God," the "strict Word of God," "the plain Scripture," and the "express Word of God" frequently bombard even the casual reader of Knox's works.[21] As noted in chapter 2, in one of his encounters with Queen Mary of Scotland, Knox insisted that the Bible was intelligible to all people, and thus the native meaning of the Bible with the aid of the Holy Spirit sufficed. The Holy Ghost had inspired every verse and, as God, he can never be self-contradictory. Therefore, the meaning of vague texts must be in agreement with the interpretation of distinct passages: "The Word of God is plain in the self; and if there appear any obscurity in one place, the Holy Ghost which is never contrarious to

---

19. *Works*, 3:75, 351; 4:310, 314–15, 322, 383–86, 390, 392–93, 492–94, 511, 512, 519, 524; 5:32, 33, 39, 62, 75, 170, 171, 180, 326, 331, 332, 344, 419; 6:194, 202, 501, 505; MacMillan, "John Knox—Preacher of the Word," 16.

20. *Works*, 3:34, 166, 4:44, 80, 231, 446, 469, 470, 478; 5:59, 310, 421; 2:93, 96, 112, are but a few examples. See also Kyle, *Mind of Knox*, 30–36; Greaves, "The Nature of Authority in the Writings of John Knox," 30–51;

21. *Works*, 3:34, 35, 37, 38; 4:437; 5:516. These citations are only a few examples of these phrases.

himself, explains the same more clearly in other places: so that there can remain no doubt, but unto such as obstinately remain ignorant."[22]

How did this impact Knox's preaching? Because he believed that the plain Scripture—with the aid of the Holy Spirit—was understandable to most people, he primarily used the literal method for ascertaining the meaning of a particular passage.[23] Thus his sermons also proclaimed the literal meaning of Scripture. They were direct and clear, and left little doubt as to their meaning. Like Scripture itself, they didn't need any sophisticated explanation. Actually, Knox took a rather low view of his own preaching. He did not see himself as interpreting the Bible, but declaring what was self-evident. He was simply God's mouthpiece, his voice, proclaiming the truth entrusted to him. Like Joshua, he was but a rude trumpet for God.[24]

In yet another way, Knox was prepared for an international preaching ministry. He knew several languages. The reformer had an adequate knowledge of Greek and learned some Hebrew during his stay in Geneva; thus he could study Scripture in its original languages. Moreover, he preached in several languages. Knox's native tongue was Lowland Scots, but he chose to preach and write in English. For this, some have criticized him, but English allowed him to reach a wider audience with the Gospel of Christ. Knox spoke French—which he may have learned during his stay in a French galley—and he put it to good use in Dieppe. On his trips to and from the Continent, he stayed in Dieppe, sometimes for weeks. And he utilized his time well—preaching frequently, encouraging believers, and winning converts to the Protestant faith. And his command of French did not leave him during his years in Scotland. On his deathbed, he requested that Calvin's sermons in French be read to him.[25]

Knox left us with few examples of his preaching. Still, the general characteristics of his pulpit style can be ascertained. Like most of his Protestant counterparts, he preached long sermons several times a week. In Geneva, Knox preached three times a week and the sermons lasted between two and three hours. As the minister at St. Giles in Edinburgh from 1559 to 1572, he sermonized twice on Sundays and three times during the week. Indeed, Knox knew nothing of the once-a-week, twenty-minute sermon so common in the modern church. What's more, Knox suffered

---

22. *Works*, 2:284.

23. *Works*, 5:261–62. See Kyle, "The Hermeneutical Patterns in John Knox's Use of Scripture," 19–32; Kyle, *Mind of Knox*, 42–45.

24. Percy, *John Knox*, 53; MacGregor, *The Thundering Scot*, 44.

25. *Works*, 6:642–43; 4:257–60; MacMillan, "John Knox—Preacher of the Word," 16, 17; Ridley, *John Knox*, 241–64.

PART TWO: Vocational Considerations

from a minister's occupational hazard—he could not stop preaching. As noted previously, his writings had a sermonic quality. And "even in private conversations, he lectured as if he was in the pulpit."[26]

The word "extemporaneous" can mean several things: uttered on the spur of the moment, or carefully prepared but delivered without notes or text. The latter meaning can be applied to Knox's preaching style. He did not write his sermons down before delivering them. On two occasions, however, he had them published after the fact, and the substance of other sermons found their way into some of his writings. Rather, the reformer would speak from the notes made on the margins of his Bible. Still, he carefully prepared his sermons. He studied the passages, constructed an outline for the message, and even planned the exact words he would use to express his thoughts. Despite not using a written text, Knox could recall the substance of his sermons several days and even years after they had been delivered. This indicates that they had been well prepared.[27]

The medieval preachers employed an allegorical interpretation of Scripture, which had many hidden meanings. Like other reformers, Knox broke from this trend and preached expository sermons—messages setting forth the clear explanation of a passage. His general pattern was twofold. He would take a book in the Bible, such as the Gospel of John or Isaiah, and preach through it verse by verse. Or he might select a doctrinal or practical subject like prayer and build a sermon from a text related to that topic. Whether he selected a biblical book or subject, the method was the same. Knox would begin with an exposition of the passage, thus assuring his listeners that he was preaching God's Word. Next, he drew doctrinal or practical implications from the text, at times attacking Catholic teachings and leaders or addressing spiritual issues.[28]

In closing a sermon, Knox applied the text and doctrinal implications to contemporary topics and people—the state of society, political leaders, villains, heroes, and more. And in doing so, he often drew parallels that stretched to the limit his literal approach to Scripture. Such applications brought down the wrath of the political and ecclesiastical establishments upon Knox. Even by the standards of the day, he could be brutally pointed in his references to contemporary leaders

26. Gill, "John Knox, The Preacher," 107; MacGregor, *Thundering Scot*, 57, 89; MacMillan, "John Knox—Preacher of the Word," 16; Ridley, *John Knox*, 481.

27. *Works*, 3:263–65; 4:87–114; 6:223–73; MacMillan, "John Knox—Preacher of the Word," 16.

28. *Works*, 4:87–114; 6:223–73; Reid, *Trumpeter of God*, 76–77; Gill, "John Knox, The Preacher," 107.

and institutions. He went well beyond inferences, making many direct comparisons: Mary Tudor with "Jezebel, that cursed idolatrous woman," England with Israel or Judah; Catholicism with idolatry; the papacy as Antichrist; Queen Elizabeth with Deborah, and more.[29] Such parallels were hardly diplomatic; they came as a bludgeon. For example, in the reformer's later years, Maitland of Lethington, a supporter of Mary Stewart, complained that Knox "in his sermons . . . has slandered me as an atheist, and enemy to all religion. . . ."[30]

When Knox blew his master's trumpet, the sound could be harsh—and he knew it. He acknowledged that, in part, this could be his fault. But he attributed the strident blast of the trumpet largely to the mandate of his office as a preacher. In several of Knox's confrontations with Queen Mary, she noted the offensive manner in which he spoke, both from the pulpit and in private conversations: "Your words are sharp enough as you have spoken . . ." said the Queen. Or in another place: "I have . . . borne with you in all your rigorous manner of speaking . . ." To this, Knox insisted that he took no joy. Rather, it was a necessity of his function as a preacher. Regardless of the consequences, the trumpet must blow: "Without the preaching place, Madam, I think few have occasion to be offended at me; and there, Madam, I am not master of myself, but must obey Him who commands me to speak plain, and to flatter no flesh upon the face of the earth."[31]

Knox's pointed applications partly arose out of his method of interpreting Scripture. He often transferred people and events from the Old and New Testaments to his own time so literally that it seemed as though history had repeated itself.[32] Knox constantly compared Israel and Scotland, and Israel and England—comparisons that often went beyond analogies or lessons and seem to become historical equivalents. For example, in *A Faithful Admonition*, Knox recalled his last sermon preached before King Edward VI in 1553. This message, which condemned Edward VI's ungodly ministers, paralleled the wicked officials of David and Hezekiah with the hidden papists in Edward's ministry. Old Testament Israel became England; David became Edward VI; Ahithophel became Dudley,

---

29. *Works*, 3:286, 293-96, 298; Reid, *Trumpeter of God*, 77; Gill, "John Knox, The Preacher," 108.

30. *Works*, 6:635; Percy, *John Knox*, 48.

31. *Works*, 2:333-34, 387.

32. D'Assonville, *John Knox and the Institutes of Calvin*, 74-75: Kyle, "Hermeneutical Patterns in Knox's Use of Scripture," 31.

Part Two: Vocational Considerations

Edward's minister; and Shobna became the Marquess of Winchester, Edward's treasurer.[33]

Also in *A Faithful Admonition*, Knox paralleled the English Reformation with the story of the disciples at sea: the calm part of the voyage compared to the rule of Edward VI while the storm corresponded with Mary Tudor's rule and the return of Catholicism.[34] John Knox, indeed, saw the drama of biblical times—particularly that of corporate Israel—being re-enacted in sixteenth-century England and Scotland. No wonder he made pointed applications in his sermons—comparisons that often got him into trouble.

The content of Knox's sermons rested on his view of God and his Old Testament emphasis. Divine immutability—that perfection of God by which he is devoid of all change—significantly influenced nearly all areas of Knox's thought, including his preaching. Because God's nature has not changed, neither can his law. What was condemned in the Old Testament (idolatry, immorality, injustice, and more) cannot be overlooked in the sixteenth century. Thus from the pulpit, Knox would vehemently denounce such sins. He demanded that God's law and justice be upheld in Scotland and England as they had been in ancient Israel. Otherwise, the same divine punishments (plagues, natural disasters, and invasions) would befall the Scots or English.[35]

A key factor determining the content of Knox's sermons was his Old Testament emphasis. His literal Old Testament hermeneutic, drawn from Deuteronomy 12:32—provided the window from which he viewed Scripture and much of life. This verse demanded that all aspects of religion conform to God's commands. Nothing should be added or subtracted from God's express instructions. This line of thought provided the impetus for much of Knox's sermons and writings. In fact, this drive to purify religion drove him to denounce Catholicism from the pulpit.[36]

Knox upheld the unity of Scripture and regarded the entire Bible as important. Why then, did he preach more from the Old Testament than the new? Largely because the reformer was preoccupied with corporate issues that are more readily addressed by the Old Testament—namely, the purification of religion, the covenant, the reformation of religion on a

33. *Works*, 3:280ff.

34. *Works*, 3:288–90.

35. *Works*, 2:442–43, 445–47; 3:171, 191, 247; 4:399; 6:408; Kyle, "The Divine Attributes in John Knox's Concept of God," 165–67.

36. *Works*, 3:29–70; Kyle, "John Knox and the Purification of Religion," 265–66; Percy, *John Knox*, 116; Eire, *War Against the Idols*, 277–78.

national scale, the legal establishment of Protestantism, the overthrow of the Catholic Church, and resistance to ruling authorities who promoted idolatry (i.e., Catholicism). Such objectives could be achieved by means of corporate models, which could only be found in the Old Testament.[37]

Knox favored the Old Testament, but in his preaching he did not ignore the New Testament. Like an Old Testament prophet, the reformer could thunder from the pulpit. But Knox the prophet was also Knox the pastor and Knox the evangelist. While he intensely sought the corporate purification of religion, he also concerned himself with individuals. His preaching called people to repentance and faith in Christ. As a pastor, his sermons and letters addressed spiritual problems: he comforted believers in distress, encouraged them to live a godly life, and instructed them in Christian doctrine. In fact, after Queen Mary's rule had ended in Scotland and Protestantism was more secure, Knox's sermons evidenced a different tone.[38]

KNOX'S SERMONS: SOME SAMPLES

Knox's specific sermons bear witness to many of the characteristics already noted. Unfortunately, he left us with only two messages. Still, aspects of other sermons have been recorded in Knox's *History* and impressions of others can be found in the writings of contemporaries. I will note six sermons presented in several locations: St. Andrews, England, central Scotland, Stirling, and Edinburgh.

Knox received his call to the ministry in 1547, probably in late April. Shortly thereafter he began to blow the trumpet in the parish church of St. Andrews. For his first sermon, he chose Daniel 7:24 and 25 as his text. This passage concerned the rise and fall of four empires, depicted as beasts: the Babylonian, Persian, Greek and Roman. Knox equated the last beast with the Catholic Church, arguing that the Roman Church had arisen out of the ruins of the Roman Empire. In this first sermon, Knox shot a volley at the Catholic Church; its doctrines and practices conflicted with those of Scripture. This church did not teach the doctrine of justification by faith.

---

37. Kyle, "John Knox: A Man of the Old Testament,"65; Kyle, The Christian Commonwealth: John Knox's Vision for Scotland," 248.

38. Reid, *Trumpeter of God*, 209, 249; Gill, "John Knox, the Preacher," 109–10: Kyle, "Hermeneutical Patterns," 24.

And worse yet, he spoke of the Roman Church as "the Man of Sin," "the Antichrist," and "the Whore of Babylon."[39]

This first blast of the trumpet set the tone for the rest of Knox's ministry. He anchored his sermons in Scripture, preaching with great conviction because he believed the Bible to be God's Word. He emphasized the doctrine of justification by faith, uplifting Christ as Lord and Savior, and shepherd of the church. On the negative side, he vehemently lashed out at the Catholic Church. So strong was his denunciation of the Roman Church that his listeners could be heard saying, "Others hewed (cut) the branches of the Papistry, but he strikes at the root, to destroy the whole."[40]

So successful was Knox's first sermon that it confirmed his call to blow his master's trumpet. He never seemed to doubt this call again, even during stressful times. For example, when chained to the oar of a French galley near St. Andrews, he pointed up to the church and noted that this is "where God first opened my mouth to his glory. . . ."[41] Two factors related to Knox's first sermon confirmed his call to preach: he firmly believed that he had preached God's Word and his listeners reacted quite positively. They confirmed his call to a pulpit ministry.[42]

Knox's sermon in Amersham, England, offers another perspective of his preaching. In attacking Catholicism, he did so with considerable political skill. Edward VI died on July 6, 1553, and for nearly two weeks the issue of succession hung in balance. Who would be the next monarch: Jane Grey or Mary Tudor? During this time, Knox preached a sermon in the Protestant stronghold of Amersham. In 1554, he penned *A Faithful Admonition to the Professors of God's Truth in England*, and he included portions of the sermon preached earlier in Amersham.[43]

Written in exile, *A Faithful Admonition* sharply attacks Mary Tudor, England, and Catholicism. But what we have of the sermon is more moderate. He warns England against papistry and against a marriage alliance with Catholic Spain: "But 'O England, England' if you obstinately will return into Egypt: that is, if you contract marriage, confederacy, or league, with such princes as maintain and advance idolatry . . . you shall be plagued and brought to desolation. . . ." As harsh as this may sound,

---

39. *Works*, 1:189–91. See Kyle, "John Knox and Apocalyptic Thought," 449–69.

40. *Works*, 1:189–92.

41. *Works*, 1:228; 3:3.

42. Reid, *Trumpeter of God*, 48–49; MacMillan, "John Knox—Preacher of the Word," 12.

43. *Works*, 3:307–9.

he spoke largely in generalizations and did not even mention Mary. He only attacked Charles V, the Holy Roman Emperor, whom he compared to Nero.[44]

Knox's *Exposition upon Matthew IV* provides an excellent window to his preaching: it represents one of his two published sermons. In 1555–56, Knox visited Scotland from Geneva. He embarked upon a preaching mission throughout Scotland, ministering to the privy kirks. From what we can tell, most of Knox's messages during this trip had a pastoral and evangelical tone; they aimed at instruction in biblical doctrines and for an informed decision to the claims of Christ. One of these sermons was on Matthew 4, which he subsequently wrote down for circulation among his friends. Years after his death, it was published in England.[45]

This sermon focused on verses one to four of this chapter, which dealt with Christ's temptation in the wilderness. Knox used this passage to attack the Catholic practice of Lent, arguing that it had no scriptural basis. But more important, the reformer began the sermon with an outline, providing us with an example of his style of biblical exposition. He began by defining temptation and shows how it is used in Scripture. Second, he tells us who is tempted and when this temptation occurred. Next, Knox describes how Christ was tempted. Last, he answers why Christ suffered these temptations and the benefit received from them. Then Knox ends the sermon with an application: "The very life and felicity of man consists not in abundance of corporal things. . . ."[46]

Knox's 1559 sermon at Stirling took a different tack: for victory to come to the Protestants, they must turn to God. While spiritual, his message also had political overtones and some have regarded it as the turning point of the Scotland Reformation. Knox returned to Scotland in May 1559. But by November 1559 when Knox preached his sermon at Stirling, the Protestants were a dejected and depressed group. They needed inspiration, and Knox gave it to them. He rallied the congregation, and some observers have regarded this message as Knox's best. The essence of this sermon is recorded in his *History*.[47]

Knox's message at Stirling is another example of his verse by verse expository preaching. At St. Giles, his sermons had been on Psalms 80:1–4.

44. *Works*, 3:308–9; Ridley, *John Knox*, 146–48; Kyle, *Mind of Knox*, 258–60.
45. *Works*, 4:87–88; Ridley, *John Knox*, 229; MacMillan, "John Knox—Preacher of the Word," 12–13; Bardgett, *Scotland Reformed*, 46–49.
46. *Works*, 4:95–96, 100–101, 105, 111; Reid, *Trumpeter of God*, 159.
47. *Works*, 1:465–73; MacMillan, "John Knox—Preacher of the Word," 13–14; Lamont, *The Swordbearer*, 112.

Part Two: Vocational Considerations

In Stirling, he continued the exposition, basing his message on verses four to eight. Instead of trusting in God for victory over the Catholic forces, apparently the congregation had turned to the Protestant nobility—especially the Hamiltons. For this, Knox condemned them. But armed with many Old Testament examples, he said that if they would repent and turn to God, victory would come. Knox's sermon electrified the congregation. They met for prayers and then took some more mundane steps to secure victory—namely negotiations with the English for military assistance. Years later, sources independent of Knox's *History* recalled how he had raised the flagging morale of the Protestant cause.[48]

On August 19, 1565, Knox preached from Isaiah 26:13-21. This sermon reveals much about Knox's sermonizing; it has been published in full, and to the message Knox attached a preface giving the rationale for his preaching style. July 1565 saw the marriage of Queen Mary and Lord Darnley, who was also proclaimed king. Darnley wavered between Catholicism and Protestantism, sometimes visiting the services of both faiths. On August 19, he attended St. Giles church listening to Knox's sermon while on a throne erected especially for him.[49]

In this sermon, Knox utilized his usual preaching style, a verse by verse exposition and a substantial application of the passage to contemporary life. The reformer told his listeners that kings do not have absolute power; it is limited by God's Word. Thus they cannot do whatever pleases them but must obey God's commands. Knox warned his audience against those who would persecute God's faithful followers. He also made passing references to idolatry and papal abomination, linking them to Old Testament figures. God gave Ahab victory over Benhadad. Did he then correct his idolatrous wife Jezebel? No! Knox closed by contending that God would punish those who fought for or supported idolatry.[50]

This sermon was milder than most Knox preached. He made only one direct reference to Scotland and did not mention Queen Mary or Darnley. The sermon still angered King Darnley. Why? The message was longer than usual. Undoubtedly, Darnley personalized Knox's comments regarding female rule, idolatry, and Ahab and Jezebel. Darnley complained to the Privy Council, who ordered Knox not to preach when the King and

---

48. *Works*, 1:465-73; "A Historie of the Estate of Scotland," 72; Buchanan, *The History of Scotland*; Reid, *Trumpeter of God*, 183-84; MacMillan, "John Knox—Preacher of the Word," 13-14; Ridley, *John Knox*, 358-59.

49. *Works*, 6:223-86.

50. *Works*, 6:229-33; Reid, *Trumpeter of God*, 239; Ridley, *John Knox*, 439-42.

Queen were in Edinburgh. However, the Edinburgh city council objected, declaring that Knox was free to preach when he wished.[51]

In response to the Privy Council's order, Knox published his sermon as proof that he had not attacked the King and Queen. To this sermon he affixed a preface, describing his philosophy and style of preaching. He did not write his sermon down because God had called him to preach, not to write books for future generations. Rather, he diligently studied a particular passage beforehand and then trusted the guidance of the Holy Spirit and his feelings for the mood of expression. What about the sharpness of Knox's tongue? To this he declared that he desired to offend no one, but in respect to preaching: "I consult not with flesh and blood what I shall propose to the people, but as the Spirit of my God who has sent me, and unto whom I must answer . . . so I speak. . . ."[52]

Knox returned to St. Andrews in May 1571 and spent over a year there. Now in his fifty-ninth year, he was an old man in poor health. But to the very end of his life, he could still be a pulpit thumper, preaching with great vigor and vehemence. During his stay at St. Andrews, he continued his usual expository style followed by an application of the passage. For most of the time, Knox based his messages on the book of Daniel.[53]

Knox's sermons at St. Andrews have not been recorded. Some contemporaries, however, did register their reactions to the reformer's preaching. Though old and ill, he preached each day. Walking with a cane, he had to be helped into the pulpit. Once there, he became energized. For about a half an hour he spoke quietly while explaining the passage, but when he began to apply the text to contemporary events, his oratory heated up. Knox openly attacked a number of political leaders by name—Grange, the Hamiltons, the Castilians, and even Queen Mary. On one occasion, a witch was brought to church and fastened to a pillar while Knox denounced her in a sermon. After the service, she was executed. Young James Melville, who took notes of Knox's sermons, said the reformer's preaching electrified him, so much so that "he could not hold a pen to write."[54]

---

51. *Works*, 2:497–500; 6:223–25; Ridley, *John Knox*, 440–41; Reid, "The Coming of the Reformation to Edinburgh," 34.

52. *Works*, 6:223–31.

53. Ridley, *John Knox*, 502–3; Reid, *Trumpeter of God*, 270–71; Bray, "Preaching: Themes and Styles," 668; MacGregor, *Thundering Scot*, 218–19.

54. Melville, *Diary of Melville*, 26, 33, 58; Ridley, *John Knox*, 502–3; Reid, *Trumpeter of God*, 270; MacGregor, *Thundering Scot*, 220–21; M'Crie, *The Life of John Knox*, 2:192–93.

Part Two: Vocational Considerations

THE IMPACT OF KNOX'S PREACHING

What were the results of Knox's preaching? Did his sermons further the Protestant cause in England and Scotland? Or did he pound the pulpit in vain? These are difficult questions. But any evaluation of Knox's preaching must take into consideration the immediate reaction of his contemporaries and long-term factors.

The Scottish Reformation established Protestantism in Scotland. To a considerable extent, the Reformed faith prevailed. What role did Knox play in these events? Recent scholarship has viewed the Scottish Reformation from several vantage points. Some see it as a social movement; others focus on the Reformation in the various cities or areas of the countryside. Still, some see the revival in sixteenth-century Scotland more as a revolution than a reformation of religion. And other scholars minimize Knox's role in these developments. They point to the work of others and say that the Reformation was well underway before Knox returned to Scotland in 1559.[55]

There are certainly elements of truth in these arguments. While the importance of other individuals and factors should not be minimized, Knox must be seen as the leading figure of the Scottish Reformation. He gave the movement direction and helped to change the future of Scotland. How did he do this? By his writings or diplomacy? No! He wrote much, and at times exhibited some political skill. However, Knox was first and foremost a preacher, and his impact came through his sermons, which were many. The sixteenth century differed from our day. Preaching counted. Before the age of nearly universal literacy and mass communications, preaching was a primary means of conveying ideas and motivating people. And Knox excelled at this means of communication.

The long-term impact of Knox's preaching can be measured in other ways. He influenced preaching in Scotland by institutional developments and by example. The *First Book of Discipline*, which Knox coauthored, endeavored to provide Scotland with a sufficient number of qualified preachers. Good preaching was central to the long-term success of the Reformation, a fact that Knox and his colleagues well knew. To legalize Protestantism was not enough. The people of Scotland had to sincerely embrace the Reformed faith and this could come primarily through

---

55. A few examples of these trends are as follows: Lynch, *Edinburgh and the Reformation*; Bardgett, *Scotland Reformed*; Cowan, *The Scottish Reformation*; Donaldson, *The Scottish Reformation*; Verschuur, "The Outbreak of the Scottish Reformation of Perth 11 May 1559," 41–53.

preaching. On a personal level, Knox set a standard for preaching in Scotland. His careful preparation, solid exposition, sound evangelical doctrine, and forceful presentations were imitated throughout Scotland.[56]

Knox's contemporaries certainly recognized him as a great preacher. His supporters praised his oratorical skills while his opponents cursed his sharp tongue. To fear a speaker, as his opponents did, is to acknowledge his ability. Undoubtedly, Knox was a fervent and compelling speaker. After his first sermon, his listeners said that "Master George Wishart spoke never so plainly. . . ." James Melville said that in the pulpit, Knox was "so active and vigorous that he was like to beat the pulpit into pieces. . . ." And at his graveside, the regent Morton declared, "Here lies one who neither flattered or feared any flesh." But apparently Knox did more than pound the pulpit. Contemporary historian George Buchanan also praised his eloquence.[57] Still, in assessing the impact of Knox's preaching, a problem arises. Much of the praise heaped upon Knox was either recorded in his *History* or came from his supporters. And such sources had an obvious bias, presenting Knox's own version of the events.

---

56. Healey, "The Preaching Ministry in Scotland's First Book of Discipline," 343-45; Gill, "John Knox, The Preacher," 110; Taylor, *The Scottish Pulpit from the Reformation to the Present Day*, 62; Kirk, *Patterns of Reform*, 95-153.

57. *Works*, 1:192; Melville, *Diary of Melville*, 26, 33; Bishop, "John Knox: Thundering Scot," 74; MacMillan, "John Knox—Preacher of the Word," 14-15; Calderwood, *The History of the Kirk of Scotland,*, 3:242.

8

Son of the Prophets

JOHN KNOX THUNDERED DIRE warnings from the pulpit and penned some radical pamphlets that sent tremors through Europe. He denounced the Roman Church and Catholic rulers in the harshest of terms. What instilled Knox with such boldness? What prompted such courage? His firm conviction of biblical authority, to be sure. His powerful sense of personal vocation, undoubtedly. But more specifically, the reformer saw himself as a preacher—a watchman—cast in the mold of the Hebrew prophets.[1] More than any of the major reformers, Knox most strongly identified himself with the prophetic tradition. "In his own eyes, he was essentially a propagandist, God's mouthpiece, a trumpet, as he repeatedly called himself." Knox saw the "drama of the Old Testament re-enacted in Scotland, with himself as Moses, Joshua, Isaiah, Jeremiah, Ezekiel, and Daniel rolled into one."[2]

Knox's identification with the Hebrew prophets opens another window to his ministry. The reformer had his greatest impact as a preacher and a prophet—two related but not identical vocations. He was both a preaching and writing prophet, proclaiming God's will and denouncing sin by both tongue and pen. In his prophetic role, the dominant image of Knox emerges—harsh, tactless, and castigating. But it must be remembered, prophets make terrible diplomats. They do not negotiate or debate; they proclaim.

---

1. *Works*, 6:229; Reid, *Trumpeter*, xiv, xv.

2. *Works*, 3:173; 4:102, 366; 2:268; Greaves, *Theology and Revolution*, 56; Murison, "Knox the Writer," 33, 43 (quote); Mason, "Knox, Resistance and the Moral Imperative," 411–12.

Son of the Prophets

The Book of Ezekiel tells of God's pronouncements upon the watchman who saw judgment coming and failed to warn the people to repent. Knox took these verses with deadly seriousness.[3] He saw himself performing this role. His vocation was not primarily to remind individuals of their personal sins. Rather, he must be a watchman warning both church and nation of corporate sin and God's approaching judgment. This conviction motivated Knox because he believed failure to admonish would bring divine punishment upon him.[4]

KNOX AND THE PROPHETIC TRADITION

The word prophet as used in the Old Testament refers to one who speaks as God's mouthpiece. He is under divine restraint and his proclamations are the work of the Lord of history. The prophet's message takes two forms: forthtelling and foretelling. Most often, it was one of reproof and admonition of the wicked, or one of comfort and consolation for the righteous. God knows the end from the beginning and his word will always stand. This conviction enabled the prophets to make predictions regarding future events. How the word of the Lord came to these prophets is uncertain. Yet one thing is definite. The prophets were personally aware of the divine influence which came over them and that their message came from God.[5]

As in the Old Testament, prophecy in the New Testament involved forthtelling and foretelling. However, the words of consolidation, admonition, and prediction now related to Christ, his kingdom, and his victory over the forces of evil. In the New Testament church, the prophet was an authoritative office, second only to the apostles. The prophet uttered words for the general benefit of the Christian community—improvement, encouragement, instruction, and consolation. But there was another dimension. He often came under the direct inspiration of the Holy Spirit and the words spoken in this capacity became the command of the Lord. Such inspired utterances usually occurred in the context of a worshipping congregation. In contrast with teaching, which was bound to traditional

---

3. *Works*, 4:370–71, 503, 529; Rupp, "The Europe of John Knox," 9; Hazlett "'Jihad' against Female Infidels and Satan," 284.

4. *Works*, 2:334, 338, 340.

5. Rad, *The Message of the Prophets*, 30–49, 50–76, 100–101; Limburg, *The Prophets and the Powerless*, 1–12; Jewett, "Prophecy," 806; Lamorte and Hawthorne, "Prophecy, Prophet," 886–87.

knowledge, prophecy had the quality of direct revelation.[6] But the office of the prophet passed away. The early church rested on the triad of apostles, prophets, and teachers. By the third century, there remained only the teachers. Increasingly, the word prophecy became limited to the prophetic portions of Scripture. And gradually, the prophet gave way to the teacher who expounded true doctrine by reference to the authoritative text of Scripture.[7]

Given the decline of the prophetic office, how can we speak of a sixteenth century prophet? By this time, the prophetic tradition had taken a different shape but was not completely dead. Nearly all of the Protestant reformers agreed that the miraculous gifts of the Spirit had ceased with the early church. The canon had been completed and no need existed for extra biblical inspired utterances. More specifically, Calvin insisted that prophecy had ended with Christ.[8] Yet Calvin and Zwingli viewed themselves as a type of prophet. And many of their contemporaries agreed. How could this be? Calvin and Zwingli regarded their prophetic ministry largely as an extension of their pastoral and teaching duties. To such a ministry, they had received an extraordinary call.[9]

Actually, preaching and teaching had become synonymous with prophecy. For Zwingli the term prophet was somewhat of an inclusive term, touching on many aspects of the ministry. As time went on, however, he came to regard prophecy as the explanation of Scripture.[10] Clearly, Calvin adapted the Erasmian approach to the subject: prophecy is not the gift of foretelling future events. Rather, for Calvin, prophecy was correctly expounding Scripture in its natural sense. He clearly regarded his preaching as a prophetic act.[11] But for Zwingli and Calvin, prophetic preaching was more than just proclaiming God's Word. They brought Scripture to

---

6. Aune, *Prophecy in Early Christianity and the Ancient Mediterranean World*, 248–70; Jewett, "Prophecy," 806, 887; Lamorte and Hawthorne, "Prophecy, Prophet," 887.

7. Jewett, "Prophecy," 887.

8. Calvin, *Institutes*, 2:15.2; Reid, "John Calvin, Pastoral Theologian," 66.

9. Engammare, "Calvin: A Prophet without a Prophecy," 644–52; Stephens, *The Theology of Huldrych Zwingli*, 279–80; Petersen, *Preaching in the Last Days*, 151–59.

10. Stephens, *Theology of Zwingli*, 279–81; Courvoisier, *Zwingli*, 21; Locher, *Zwingli's Thought*, 8–12, 15–17.

11. Calvin, *Calvin's New Testament Commentaries*, 271; Engammare, "Calvin: Prophet Without a Prophecy," 648–51; Johnson, "Prophecy, Rhetoric and Diplomacy," 66–67.

bear on contemporary issues, and in doing so, they spared no feelings. In their denunciations, they named names and were very specific.[12]

In yet another sense, Calvin functioned as a prophet. He admonished the civil government in respect to right and wrong and the truth of God's Word. Given the assumption that he could correctly interpret Scripture, Calvin did not hesitate to warn and even harangue monarchs. He believed that an earthly kingdom must be governed by Holy Scripture and he reminded sovereigns of this, sometimes doing this politely but at other times in violent terms.[13] Still, Calvin did not completely rule out the possibility of miraculous gifts functioning in the post apostolic era. He believed that God could raise up men for extraordinary tasks. And by the sixteenth century, the Catholic Antichrist had led the church astray, so Calvin believed. Thus he concluded that God raised up Martin Luther to combat the Antichrist. But such a calling had no regular place in the constituted church; it was extraordinary.[14]

How did John Knox connect with this prophetic tradition? He saw himself in a long line of prophets. In past times when God's people became corrupt and turned from him, Knox said God stepped outside the formal priestly or clerical line and directly raised up "simple and obscure men" to rebuke sin and idolatry. For examples, he pointed to Isaiah, Jeremiah, and Amos and in his day to the "Zwinglians, Lutherans, Oecolampadians, and Calvinists." And Knox unequivocally identified himself with such men. He believed that he wore the mantle of a prophet in order to reform religion in England and Scotland along Protestant lines.[15]

The Old Testament prophet, as God's mouthpiece, could bring a word of commandment, judgment, or admonition for their contemporaries (forthtelling) or a word of promise and prediction for the future (foretelling). Knox believed that God had endowed him with the ability for both types of prophecies. In his prophetic ministry, the two models often overlapped, but on the whole, admonition clearly took precedence over prediction. In both interest and commitment, John Knox was a man of the present. He largely concerned himself with the immediate job of

---

12. Rupp, "The Europe of John Knox," 13.

13. Engammare, "Calvin: Prophet Without a Prophecy," 654–57; Calvin, *Institutes* 4:20.3–6.

14. Calvin, *Institutes* 4:3.4. McNeill says Calvin was referring to Luther. See footnote 4 on page 1057 of volume 2. Johnson, "Prophecy, Rhetoric, and Diplomacy," 67.

15. *Works*, 6:191–92 (quote); Greaves, *Theology and Revolution*, 74; Johnson, "Prophecy, Rhetoric, and Diplomacy," vii. 55.

combating idolatry (Catholicism) and securely establishing Protestantism in Scotland. And admonition and exhortation best served this purpose.[16]

Yet some of Knox's prophecies concerned future events, and they came in two forms, general forewarnings and specific predictions. Most common were his general admonishments regarding sin coupled with a prediction of judgment if such warnings were not heeded. Such prophecies rested on Scripture and Knox's concept of God—not on some extra biblical revelation. This approach is evident in *A Godly Letter*, written to the Protestants in England. Knox urges them to uphold the faith and flee from apostasy. Failing this, divine judgment would befall them. Knox claimed no supernatural insight. Rather, this prediction grew out of his confidence in Scripture. "My assurances are not the marvels of Merlin, not yet the dark sentences of profane prophecies, but . . . the plain truth of God's Word. . . ."[17]

Still, Knox's prophecies could have a mystical cast to them, based not on Scripture but on direct revelations. In making such predictions, Knox ran counter to the general approach of the Protestant prophetic tradition. In the preface to his sermon on Isaiah, he defended his call to preach. In doing so, he revealed the source of some of his prophecies: "I dare not deny . . . that God hath revealed unto me secrets unknown to the world; and also . . . to forewarn realms and nations. . . ."[18] Such predictions tended to be specific, perhaps pointing to the death of an individual. And they did not rest on Scripture but on information Knox believed God had revealed to him personally.[19]

Knox's message also evoked the memory of the Old Testament prophets. These men largely proclaimed a denunciatory message. So did Knox. The prophets of old confronted the sins of idolatry and social injustice. The crusade against idolatry (Catholicism) and the creeping apostasy—which often led to it—dominated Knox's ministry. Therefore, his prophetic pronouncements largely condemned the Roman Antichrist and its supportive agencies, both religious and political. Like the Hebrew prophets, Knox also called for social justice and warned of judgment if it did not come. But on this subject, he was not so radical as to provoke a revolution or to alienate the nobility, whose support he needed for a

16. *Works*, 1:3, 190, 405; 2:543; 4:446, 470, 511, 513; 6:400–402; Kyle, *Mind of Knox*, 221; Greaves, *Theology and Revolution*, 1.

17. *Works*, 3:168.

18. *Works*, 6:229.

19. Johnson and McGoldrick, "Prophet in Scotland," 4–7; Johnson, "Prophecy, Rhetoric, and Diplomacy," 69.

successful reformation. Old Testament prophets desired an Israel free of idolatry and social injustice. Knox embraced a similar vision for Scotland and England. In the quest of such an ideal, he behaved like the prophets of old. He did not hesitate to confront even monarchs.[20]

Knox certainly regarded himself as a prophet with the powers to both proclaim God's Word and to predict the future. Did his contemporaries share this opinion? His closest followers did. But some of his opponents regarded him as a false prophet. Within a few years of Knox's death, James Smeton attested to Knox's prophetic powers by circulating stories demonstrating how his prophecies came true. James Melville and other Scottish writers picked up on these stories and even elaborated upon them. In his 1812 biography, *The Life of John Knox*, Thomas M'Crie also said that Knox's contemporaries credited him with the power to predict the future. M'Crie himself was more cautious. He believed that God had occasionally given virtuous men the gift of foretelling the future, and that Knox may have been one of these men.[21]

THE BASIS FOR KNOX'S PROPHETIC CONSCIOUSNESS

Knox saw "himself as a prophet who went up to Sinai to receive the commandment of God, and [then] descended to give it to the people."[22] What prompted such a self-image? Several events and ideas drove his prophetic consciousness. High on the list was his apocalyptic worldview. A sense of the apocalyptic undergirded Knox's perception of his vocation—that is, his call to be a prophet and proclaim God's Word. The word apocalypse means revelation, the uncovering or unveiling of a divine secret. Apocalyptic thinking has several characteristics. It is dualistic, viewing human history as a cosmic struggle between absolute good and evil. The apocalyptic outlook is also catastrophic; it holds that this historical conflict will be settled by battles and disasters in which evil will be defeated. Although the word apocalypse is usually used as a synonym for disaster, this is only a

---

20. See Kyle, "John Knox and the Purification of Religion," 265–80; Kyle, "The Christian Commonwealth," 247–59; Kyle, "John Knox: A Man of the Old Testament," 65–78; Greaves, *Theology and Revolution*, 111–12.

21. *Works*, 6:657; Melville, *The Autobiography and Diary of Mr. James Melville*, 33–36; Spottiswoode, *History of the Church of Scotland*, 1:373; M'Crie, *The Life of John Knox*, 2:264–67; Ridley, *John Knox*, 626; Reid, *Trumpeter of God*, 270–71.

22. MacGregor, *The Thundering Scot*, 44.

half-truth. "Apocalypse" concerns both cataclysm and victory, tribulation and triumph. Finally, apocalyptic thinking is deterministic, assuming that the sequence of events in the final conflict is "preset in a heavenly clock."[23]

Prophets often embrace a polarized worldview, viewing events in black and white terms. They seldom see any grey. Such a dualism can prompt prophets to denounce evil in no uncertain terms. Along with a rigid view of divine providence, apocalyptic considerations powerfully influenced Knox's concept of history—polarizing his worldview and instilling his thought with a sense of conflict, collision, and militancy. Knox's intense convictions, and even his intolerance, originated in part from his belief that he was in God's army and engaged in a great cosmic struggle, which was to take place at the end of the world. The great enemy in this conflict, of course, was the Catholic Church, whom the reformer constantly denounced as the "Antichrist"—an entity that Knox not only regarded as the Roman Church but also as the fulfillment of the prophecies of Daniel and Revelation.[24]

As noted in chapter 3, Knox related his prophetic pronouncements to his apocalyptic view of history. In his *History of the Reformation in Scotland*, Knox's apocalyptic worldview shaped his description of detailed events, personal affairs, political developments, and military conflicts. He did not depict the various struggles (Protestantism against Catholicism, church against the state, monarchy against the people, revolution against reaction, future against the past) in a political sense. Rather, his *History* portrayed a cosmic war between the forces of God and the supporters of Satan, namely, the Catholic clergy.[25] Knox regarded every issue as secondary to the conflict between the Roman Church and the gospel of Christ. This struggle became a ruthless, unrelenting battle between the forces of light and the forces of darkness.

Personal experiences significantly forged Knox's apocalyptic worldview. His powerful sense of vocation helped to shape his outlook. Knox's initial call in 1547 left a lasting impression on him, directing his action and thinking for the remainder of his life.[26] The persecution of Protestants in Scotland (especially the death of Wishart), Knox's enslavement in a French galley, England's violation of the covenant and Mary Tudor's

---

23. Kyle, *The Last Days Are Here Again*, 19; Zamora, ed., *The Apocalyptic Vision in America*, 3, 14.

24. Kyle, "John Knox and Apocalyptic Thought," 449; Kyle, *Mind of Knox*, 215.

25. *Works*, 1:4; Dickinson, *The Scottish Reformation*, Murison, "Knox the Writer," 43 (quote).

26. *Works*, 6:229; Reid, *Trumpeter of God*, xiv, xv.

subsequent oppression of Protestants, and the trauma of being exiled first from Scotland and then from England—all intensified Knox's fear of Catholicism and prompted him to see all of history in terms of a life and death struggle. "Like the first Christians, Knox lived in a world where 'martyr' and 'apostates' were a grim polarity, even though it might be a gradual apostasy of little compromises...."[27]

During Knox's formative years the mood of Europe was certainly conducive to the growth of the apocalyptic. By 1545, papal reform was stirring, the military power of the Empire had experienced a resurgence, and Europe moved toward the terrible period of religious wars. Luther had been quoting more from Daniel and Revelation, and in Knox's writings, as well as in the *Scots Confession*, there appeared an "apocalyptic undertone, a new sense of collision between the true and false church and the appearance of the antichrist," something formerly reserved for the radical sects. "Apocalyptic thought seems to recur in those moments in history when things come to a boil...." Certainly, the volcanic mood of Europe in the 1550's crept into Knox's writings.[28]

Still, Knox's prophetic consciousness was driven by more than his apocalyptic worldview and personal experiences. Certain religious beliefs also powerfully influenced his thinking in this regard. Both aspects of Knox's prophetic message, the admonitory and predictive, heavily depended on his notions of God and authority and on his methods of interpreting Scripture. In *A Godly Letter*, Knox summarized the basis of his prophetic beliefs. He said that his prophetic message rested not on the popular secular predictions of his day, but on the truth of God's Word, the invincible justice of God, and the ordinary course of divine punishments from the beginning of time.[29]

In most cases, Knox made the text of Scripture his sole authority on questions pertaining to religious faith. In nearly all areas of religion Knox pushed biblical authority to the extreme, even in matters of indifference. To some women in Edinburgh, Knox wrote, "In the religion there is no middle: either it is the religion of God, and that in everything that it is done it must have the assurance of his Word . . . or else it is the religion

---

27. *Works*, 1:4-5, 119, 169, 170, 212, 271, 467; 2:59; 3:165, 167, 170-71, 187; 4:106, 403, 433, 479; 5:413; 6:12, 21, 192, 251; Reid, "John Knox and His Interpreters," 15-19; Firth, *The Apocalyptic Tradition*, 114-15, 130; Walzer, *The Revolution of the Saints*, 92-113; Rupp, "The Europe of John Knox," 8 (quote).

28. Rupp, "The Europe of John Knox," 3-4 (quote); Kyle, "Knox and Apocalyptic Thought," 455; Christianson, *Reformers and Babylon*, 36.

29. *Works*, 3:168-69.

of the Devil."³⁰ As a consequence, Knox opposed anyone who substituted an inner light or some subjective experience for the authority of written Scripture. This eliminated much of the speculative element from his prophecy. Knox largely based his prophetic message on the written Word. Not everyone shared his interpretations or applications of Scripture, particularly the analogies he drew from the Bible. Yet Knox's prophetic pronouncements usually had a biblical base.

Nevertheless, Knox could be inconsistent in many areas, including this one. On most occasions, he equated Scripture with the Word of God. At times, however, he linked it with the power of God, the person of Christ and the proclamation of the gospel. As noted earlier, Knox even claimed to experience some direct revelations from God. Such revelations, of course, were infrequent enough as not to negate the notion that Knox was "first and foremost a man of the Bible." Still, he based some of his predictions upon these direct revelations. And in doing so, he did not practice what he claimed, namely a subscription to *sola scriptura*.³¹

Knox's manner of interpreting Scripture affected both aspects of his prophetic message—admonition and prediction. His prophetic hermeneutic of applying the Old Testament burdens of Israel almost literally and unequivocally to the religious and political situation of his day powerfully influenced his prophetic pronouncements. He failed to see the differences between the testaments, and thus overidentified the Old with the New Testament, losing sight of the historic process in divine revelation. In addition, he interpreted Scripture so literally that the Bible often became a book of precedents, a handbook for the judgment of God upon nations and powers in the world.³²

Knox's literal Old Testament hermeneutic affected his prophetic thinking in several ways. First, Knox constantly paralleled the situations in England and Scotland with those in ancient Israel. Such parallels were more than lessons or analogies, and came close to being historical equations. When circumstances matched, similar conclusions followed. By using examples of Scripture, Knox called down or predicted the same

30. *Works*, 4:272. See also *Works*, 1:194, 196–97; 3:34.

31. *Works*, 6:229; Kyle, *Mind of Knox*, 307; Johnson, "Prophet in Scotland," 76, 82, 86.

32. Works, 2:185; 6:309, 246–47; 5:328–29, 331, 334; 1:197; 3:35–38; 165–216, 263–330; 4:377–403; 2:372, 432–33; 1:412; 2:438; 3:170, 234; 245; 4:232, 281, 472, 273; 5:261–62; 4:437, 468; 5:516; 2:446; 3:64, 154, 197; 4:519; 5:33. These are only a few random examples of Knox's literal Old Testament hermeneutic. See also Kyle, "The Hermeneutical patterns in John Knox's Use of Scripture," 19–32.

judgments upon his contemporaries that he found in Scripture.³³ This method of drawing analogies between biblical and contemporary events for the purpose of promoting one's policies was called "prophesying" by the Marian exiles and Puritans.³⁴ Second, Knox's insistence on applying the Old Testament instructions regarding worship so literally that they became legal precedents fostered a sense of the apocalyptic in this thinking. In all events, past or present, Knox saw no middle course. Everything was either the work of God or the work of the devil.

In yet another way, Knox's handling of Scripture impacted his role as a prophet. Despite demanding an explicit biblical warrant for all religious practices, he took considerable liberties with the Bible. His major concern was the contemporary application of Scripture, not a precise exegesis of it. Thus he moved "quickly from the exposition to the application; the text being only a point of departure for his own [opinion] . . . ," claims James Stalker. Knox's freewheeling application of Scripture often evolved into prophetic pronouncements.³⁵

Knox's concept of God, particularly his emphasis on divine immutability substantially determined his prophetic message. As Knox stated frequently, the character and law of God never changes. The justice of God is infinite and immutable, and what he damned in one place and in one time cannot be excused in another.³⁶ This belief directed Knox to demand that God's law be upheld in the commonwealths of England and Scotland as if these nations were Old Testament Israel. Otherwise, the same divine judgments, which the Hebrews had experienced, would befall them. When coupled with the reformer's method of interpreting Scripture, this emphasis on divine immutability inclined Knox to see the present as a re enactment of the past. Therefore, he based his admonitions and predictions on the conviction that the acts of God: past, present, and future, would not change.³⁷

---

33. *Works*, 3:280ff.; D'Assonville, *John Knox and the Institutes of Calvin*, 74–75. See Kyle, "John Knox's Concept of History," 4–19.

34. See Vander Molen, "Providence as Mystery, Providence as Revelation," 40; Collinson, *The Elizabethan Puritan Movement*, 168–76; Knappen, *Tudor Puritanism*, 253–56; New, *Anglican and Puritan*, 106–7; Lehmberg, "Archbishop Grindal and the Prophesyings," 76–145.

35. Stalker, *John Knox: His Ideas and Ideals*, 133; Johnson, "Prophet in Scotland," 77–78.

36. *Works*, 3:171, 191; 4:399; 6:408.

37. Kyle, "Knox and Apocalyptic Thought," 458–59; Kyle, *Mind of Knox*, 224.

Part Two: Vocational Considerations

THE PROPHET AT WORK

Knox's prophetic consciousness began early in his career and never left him. If his *History* can be believed, both the admonitory and predictive types of prophecy ran the course of his ministry. Still, the timing of some predictions raises questions. Several were recorded in his *History* a number of years after the fact, and thus may be *ex post facto*. The point is not whether Knox actually made these predictions, but he believed that he had such an ability—perhaps more so later in his career than at the beginning. According to Dickinson, "It is evident that a conviction of prophetic powers grew with the years."[38]

During his formative years in the 1540's, Knox came to admire Wishart for many reasons, including his powers as prophet, not only in admonishment but also in prescience. Wishart had both "godly knowledge" in order to instruct and the "spirit of prophecy" to foretell "things . . . afterward felt, which he forespoke not in secret, but in the audience of many. . . ."[39]

Accordingly, Knox's *History* records several of Wishart's predictions: the approach of his own death, and the plagues and bondage that would befall the town of Haddington. Later in his *History*, Knox noted the fulfillment of Wishart's prophecies: "and so did God perform the words and threatening of his servant, Master George Wishart. . . ."[40]

Knox preached his first sermon, drawing from the Book of Daniel, to condemn the Roman Church as Antichrist. Preaching to the killers of Cardinal Beaton, he made his first prediction. For protection, these men trusted in the castle's thick walls and help from England. Instead, Knox declared that the walls, "should be but egg-shells" and "you shall not see them [the English]; but you shall be delivered into your enemy's hands, and shall be carried to a strange country."[41] That year, the French captured St. Andrews Castle and forced the rebels to become galley slaves. In all of this, Knox may have been simply reading current political developments. Still, he saw these unfoldings as a fulfillment of his prophecy.[42]

---

38. Knox, *John Knox's History of the Reformation in Scotland*, 1:lxxi. Hereafter, this will be cited as Knox, *History*, followed by the volume and page number. See also *History*, 1:123, 265.

39. *Works*, 1:125.

40. Knox, *History*, 1:68, 113.

41. Ibid., 1:95-96.

42. Ibid., 1:95. See also Johnson, "Prophet in Scotland," 79; Reid, *Trumpeter of God*, 53.

Son of the Prophets

The French regarded Knox as one of the Castilians, and thus forced him to become a galley slave. During his stay on the galley ship, he made two prophecies. "Will we ever be delivered from this imprisonment?" asked a fellow prisoner. Knox predicted that "God would deliver them from that bondage...." and he went a step further. At that point, the galley ship rested off the Scottish coast near St. Andrews, where he received the call to preach. Here, the reformer predicted not only his release but that he would again preach at St. Andrews: "I am fully persuaded . . . that I shall not depart this life, till that my tongue shall glorify his godly name in the same place."[43] Both prophecies came true. All but one of the prisoners were freed, and Knox preached again at St. Andrews.

The positive responses to his preaching, plus his success at predicting both his release and that of the other prisoners on the French galley, helped to convince Knox that he had "the gift of special illumination—an ability not only to interpret the Word of God but to speak it."[44] So Knox's prophetic work continued. After his release, he went to England. While preaching in Newcastle and Berwick, he warned that the plague would be the result of divine judgment for their unrepentant sin. These congregations subsequently experienced the "sweating sickness," a fatal disease common in the England of Edward VI. In *A Godly Letter* (1552), written as a Marian exile, Knox reminded them of his prediction.[45]

Knox's writings as a Marian exile continued to reflect his prophetic consciousness. As noted earlier in *A Godly Letter*, he insisted that the basis of his prophetic message was nothing less than God's unchanging Word and character.[46] *A Faithful Admonition* (1554) contained examples of both his admonitions and predictions. In a general sense, Knox strongly warns his readers to avoid conforming to the Roman rites of worship. To resist Catholicism may bring persecution from human instruments. But if the faithful compromise with idolatry, they will experience the wrath of God. And this will result in grievous punishments now and through eternity.[47]

In *A Faithful Admonition*, Knox also reminds his readers of a more specific prediction made while still in England. He warned John Dudley (the English Regent and the Duke of Northumberland) that God would punish him for any harm done to Edward Seymore, the Lord of Somerset.

---

43. Knox, *History*, 1:108–9.
44. *Works*, 1:192, 229; Firth, *Apocalyptic Tradition*, 117 (quote).
45. *Works*, 3:167. See also Lorimer, *John Knox and the Church of England*, 82.
46. *Works*, 3:168–69.
47. *Works*, 3:263–330. See also Reed, ed., *Selected Writings of John Knox*, 220.

Seymore, the former Protector, had been forced from office by Dudley who ignored Knox's warning and proceeded to execute Seymore. But the next year, Dudley himself was beheaded for attempting to keep Mary Tudor from the throne. Knox regarded this as a fulfillment of his prediction: "Remember, that whatever was spoken by my mouth that day, is now complete and [has] come to pass."[48]

The exile years saw two related developments: the further unfolding of Knox's prophetic consciousness and a radicalization of his writings. In other letters to afflicted Protestants in England and Scotland, Knox continued to refer to the role of the prophets in pronouncing God's judgment on idolaters and tyrants with a particular emphasis on Jehu's denunciation of Jezebel.[49] *The First Blast* (1558) contained a full expression of Knox's prophetic denunciation. In this tract, he paralleled his pronouncements with those of Jeremiah, Jehu, and Daniel, and regarded himself as a "watchman" whose duty it was to blow his master's trumpet.[50] Knox's other political writings, penned in 1558, referred to Jeremiah, Elisha, Moses, and Ezekiel and continued to echo the prophetic theme—even asserting that God controlled the tongues of the prophets.[51]

Leaving the political arena, Knox's prophetic consciousness also emerged in his 1559 predestination treatise. The reformer saw no incompatibility between his role as prophet and divine predestination. In this treatise, the reformer indicated that God had given a true knowledge of himself to all of his elect. Nevertheless, the prophets incurred a special responsibility to pronounce God's judgment. They were a special divine vehicle to call the elect to faith and repentance, and to warn the reprobate that their action would result in damnation. Knox's prophetic consciousness and his firm belief in divine predestination were paradoxical convictions. But this did not seem to bother him.[52]

Knox's prophetic pronouncements did not end with his return to Scotland in 1559. They continued until his death in 1572. In 1560, the English and Scots attacked a French fortification in Leith, suffering heavy losses. Mary of Guise, the Queen Regent, rejoiced at their casualties. In a

---

48. *Works*, 3:277–78. See also Johnson, "Prophet in Scotland," 7–80: Reid, *Trumpeter of God*, 114–15.

49. *Works*, 3:166–68, 170, 175, 178, 184–88, 190–94, 239, 244–45, 247, 274, 282, 283, 286, 293–98, 308–9.

50. *Works*, 4:365–71.

51. *Works*, 4:456, 458, 499, 503.

52. *Works*, 5:388–89, 412, 312; Greaves, *Theology and Revolution*, 33. See also Kyle, "The Concept of Predestination in the Thought of John Knox," 33–43.

sermon at St. Giles, Knox predicted that God would punish not only those who had committed this deed but also those who had exulted in it. Mary soon contracted a fatal disease (probably dropsy) which Knox regarded as a divine judgment and the fulfillment of his prophecy. But the reformer recorded this prediction in his *History* at a later date and apparently Mary had fallen ill before his sermon.[53]

In 1560, Knox preached a series of sermons from the prophet Haggai, who urged the Israelites who had returned from exile to rebuild God's house. Likewise, Knox called for radical religious reform, including the reconstruction of the churches. William Maitland mocked Knox's call to action. Knox responded by predicting negative consequences for Maitland's own house. When Maitland's son died in exile and in poverty, many believed this to be a fulfillment of Knox's prophecy, thus contributing to his image as a prophet.[54]

The Old Testament prophets personally confronted monarchs over the issues of sin and idolatry. So did Knox. By pen, he had denounced Mary Tudor. But in Scotland, he clashed with Mary Queen of Scots in person. And in these confrontations, he wore the mantle of prophet. Mary regarded herself as at the summit of society and saw Knox as a peasant and "a renegade priest" with "no legal existence." Conversely, he considered himself to be the Moses or Amos of Scotland. He regarded Scotland as the new commonwealth of Israel, and being utterly "convinced of his divine prophetic ministry," he resisted Mary's attempt to undo the Reformation.[55]

In their first meeting, she accused him of inciting rebellion. Knox advised Mary of his vocation to be a watchman and to reform religion, and if teaching people the truth of God's Word caused them to rebel against the sovereign—then he accepted full responsibility: "If to teach the truth of God in sincerity, if to rebuke idolatry, and to will a people to worship God according to his Word, be to raise subjects against their Princes, then cannot I be excused."[56]

The subject of the Queen's marriage became the flashpoint for another clash between Knox and Mary. The reformer got wind of the negotiations for a marriage between Mary and Don Carlos of Spain. As usual, Knox

53. Knox, *History*, 1:319, 359; Ridley, *John Knox*, 373-74; Johnson, "Prophecy, Rhetoric, and Diplomacy," 25.

54. Knox, *History*, 1:335; Johnson, "Prophecy, Rhetoric, and Diplomacy," 26; Reid, *Trumpeter of God*, 189-90.

55. Shaw, "John Knox and Mary Queen of Scots," 51-63; Wormald, "Godly Reformer, Godless Monarch," 220-41.

56. *Works*, 2:278.

placed his finger on the central issue: the fate of Protestantism in Scotland, England, and possibly even the Continent, depended on whether Mary married a Protestant or a Catholic.[57] Therefore, Knox preached to prevent a Spanish marriage. He warned that divine wrath would result from an alliance with Catholic Spain: "Ye bring God's vengeance upon the country, and a plague upon yourself. . . ."[58] Needless to say, in preaching such a message, Knox alienated both friends and foes alike. But prophets of God do not aim to win popularity contests.

Yet in other ways, Knox's prophetic consciousness became evident after his return to Scotland. Knox debated a Catholic priest in 1562. Here he declared that God had raised up individuals in his day (of which he was one), who spoke judgment on the "Babylonian harlot" (the Roman Church) with the same promise of fulfillment that the Old Testament prophets had.[59] By 1565, Knox's prophetic consciousness had grown to where he could openly claim the mantle of prophet. In a 1565 sermon preached at St. Giles Church, the reformer declared his vocation to be that of a preaching rather than a writing prophet, proclaiming the gospel of God's grace in Jesus Christ. In the preface, he unequivocally laid claim to divine inspiration. Knox believed that God had given him secret knowledge for the purpose of forewarning nations and their rulers regarding future developments. And, in his mind, these predictions came true.[60] In fact, several months earlier in one of his prayers, he thanked God for giving him special illumination: "Thou has given to me knowledge above the common sort of my brethren."[61] From 1565 to 1566, Knox also helped write *The Order and Doctrine of the General Fast*. This work can be seen as a prophetic outburst. The Scottish Reformation had fallen on hard times. Knox, by means of general fast, called the faithful in Scotland to repentance in order to forestall God's judgment.[62]

An unnamed individual penned a narrative describing a prophecy made by Knox at the time of his death. If this account is accurate, Knox

---

57. The question of Mary's marriage also involved such considerations as the threat of English national security, Mary's succession to the English crown, the relations between Philip II and the emperor, and a possible alliance between the Guises and Bourbons in France. See Ridley, *John Knox*, 425; Mahoney, "The Scottish Hierarchy," 49.

58. Knox, *History*, 2:81.

59. *Works*, 6:192.

60. *Works*, 6:229.

61. *Works*, 6:483.

62. See *Works*, 6:383–428; Hazlett, "Playing God's Card," 176–98.

made an amazing prophecy regarding the death of William Kirkcaldy of Grange. Knox regarded Kirkcaldy as a turncoat because he abandoned the reform party of Queen Mary's faction now exiled in England. On his deathbed Knox sent a message to Kirkcaldy: "Unless he is yet brought to repentance he shall die miserably . . . he shall be disgracefully dragged from his nest to punishment, and hung on a gallows in the face of the sun. . . ."[63]

Kirkcaldy failed to repent and continued to support the Catholic cause. And as Knox prophesied, he was hanged in Edinburgh. Jasper Ridley describes the details of Kirkcaldy's death: "He was hanged facing towards the east, but before he died, his body swung round to face the west. . . ."[64] Right down to the very particulars, Kirkcaldy died as Knox prophesied. But some scholars have challenged this account. Jasper Ridley points out that the eyewitnesses to Kirkcaldy's hanging were Knox's ardent followers. He and W. Stanford Reid note that Richard Bannatyne's 1573 account does not mention Knox's prophecy about Kirkcaldy. James Melville records Knox's prediction, but he wrote in 1600. Reid regards such reports about this prophecy as "part of the tradition that grew up shortly after [Knox's] death."[65]

Was Knox really a prophet? In the sense of proclaiming the Word of God as he interpreted Scripture, he certainly was. He did more forthtelling than foretelling. Knox believed he was living at the end of the age and that the world around him was collapsing. Desperate conditions required a prophet in such a role. Thus prophetic denunciations poured from his mouth and pen. But Knox went beyond mere forthtelling. He believed that God had given him the ability to predict the future. Most of these predictions were based on Scripture and were very general: God blesses the righteous and punishes the wicked. But some of his predictions were specific, usually detailing judgments on individuals. Whether Knox actually made such prophecies is beside the point. He certainly believed that he did. And so did many of his followers.[66]

---

63. *Works*, 6:657.

64. Ridley, *John Knox*, 519.

65. Melville, *Autobiography of James Melville*, 33; Ridley, *John Knox*, 519–20; Reid, *Trumpeter of God*, 284. See Johnson, "Prophet in Scotland," 80.

66. For some of these general concepts, see Johnson, "Prophecy, Rhetoric and Diplomacy," vii, 63, 175.

9

The Care of Souls

JOHN KNOX SERVED AS God's mouthpiece—as both a preacher and a prophet. He desired to reform religion on a national level in both England and Scotland, but did he limit his ministry to these public tasks? Did he ignore individual spiritual needs? His biographer, Eustace Percy, thought so: Knox was not "much of a pastor; the personal care of souls meant little to him, either for himself or as an aim of church policy."[1] From this judgment, I must dissent. Many of Knox's letters reveal that he had a pastor's heart. He had great concern for the spiritual well-being of individuals.

The term *pastor* comes from the Latin word *passere* and means to pasture or feed. In a biblical sense, it commonly refers to a shepherd's caring for a flock. Thus, Christ is called the Good Shepherd. The pastor is a designated New Testament office. Ephesians 4:11 says that some are appointed "to be apostles, some to be evangelists, some to be pastors [shepherds] and teachers."[2] In the early church, the pastor and teacher were often one position, two sides of the same coin. The pastor-teacher was to feed (teach God's Word) and care for the flock.

In the modern world, the teaching or feeding function of the pastorate has been diminished. Instead, the contemporary church emphasizes the caring and therapeutic aspect of this office. Modern Christians forget that the shepherd should both feed and care for the flock, but this was not the case in the sixteenth century. The Reformed pastor had three basic duties: preach God's Word, administer the sacraments, and enforce church discipline. Given these tasks, how would a pastor care for the flock? This

---

1. Percy, *John Knox*, 52.
2. Armentrout, "Pastor," 871; Morris, "Minister," 720–21.

was seen as an aspect of teaching the Scriptures. The pastor must proclaim God's Word both publicly (preaching) and privately (counseling), and the Reformed pastor based his spiritual advice and encouragement squarely on Scripture tempered with common sense and understanding. The Reformed tradition knew nothing of counseling devoid of Scripture. Thus, spiritual nurturing must be seen as an extension of teaching God's Word.[3]

As a spiritual advisor, how did Knox relate to this tradition? As far as I can tell, he conformed to the pattern of the Reformed pastor. He was first and foremost a preacher. Whenever possible, he blew his master's trumpet. In fact, the very success of his preaching created a need for counseling. His powerful messages won converts to the Protestant faith, and these new converts had many questions: Were they reconciled to God through faith alone? Could they disregard the ceremonies and rituals of the Catholic Church? The new Protestants faced these and many other spiritual issues.[4]

John Knox confronted these problems head-on—often with great care and concern. To be sure, he made preaching his first priority, but he regarded spiritual counseling as very important. His mother-in-law, Mrs. Bowes, apologized for troubling him over a spiritual matter. Knox replied that comforting her was no trouble at all. In fact, only preaching would take precedence over giving her spiritual counsel, "and no other labors save only the blowing of my Master's trumpet shall impede me to do the uttermost of my power [to comfort you.]"[5]

KNOX'S COUNSELING: HIS APPROACH

Knox was confronted with a number of spiritual questions, but most concerned the issues of salvation and the Christian life. The recent converts sought the assurance of salvation. Were they justified by faith without works? Many new Protestants had trouble accepting this doctrine. Were they among the elect? How could they know? If they indeed were justified and among the elect, why did they still sin? If facing persecution, could they participate in the Catholic Mass? What about the liturgy of the

---

3. See McNeill, *The History and Character of Calvinism*, 161; Arnold. "Pastoral Care," 270–71; Stephens, *The Theology of Huldrych Zwingli*, 274–78; Wallace, *Calvin, Geneva, and the Reformation*, 168–79; Reid, "John Calvin, Pastoral Theologian," 68–70.

4. Reid, *Trumpeter of God*, 79; Newman, "The Reformation and Elizabeth Bowes," 325.

5. *Works*, 3:368.

Church of England? Could they take part in it? While not as idolatrous as the Catholic Mass, it still represented a compromise.[6]

How did Knox deal with such spiritual problems? His approach was largely spiritual but not completely so. While most problems were theological in nature, they also had personal and political overtones. Whenever possible, Knox gave biblical answers. Or, if the questions arose from a problem in the understanding of Scripture, he would attempt to interpret the passage or give a theological explanation. Knox certainly regarded spiritual counseling as an extension of his preaching, but at times the reformer modified his biblical literalism with common sense, even humor. What is more, Knox's spiritual advice ranged between two extremes: encouragement and admonition. He could cheer and embolden those in despair. Conversely, the reformer would warn others not to slide back into idolatry or apostasy.[7]

In his handling of spiritual problems, Knox also showed considerable understanding, even empathy. For the most part, his responses to questions came as advice, not commands. When individuals came to him for spiritual counsel, he did not lord it over them or show any sense of superiority. Rather, in interacting with them, he often revealed his own weaknesses and sinfulness. Knox assured them that he had traveled down the same path—experiencing doubts, sinful thoughts, spiritual pride, and more: "I have sometimes . . . felt not sorrow for sin, neither yet displeasure against myself for any iniquity in which I did offend; but rather in my vain heart did flatter myself."[8]

In fact, Knox did not regard spiritual advice as a one-way street: It often became a give-and-take affair. The questions directed toward him by Mrs. Bowes and Anne Locke forced him to delve into Scripture more deeply than he normally would have done. Moreover, their struggles prompted Knox to examine his personal life, often seeing their problems as a reflection of his own conflicts: "The exposition of your troubles, and acknowledging of your infirmity, was first unto me a very mirror and glass wherein I beheld myself."[9]

---

6. For examples, see *Works*, 3:337–402; 6:12–14; 22, 26, 83–85, 103, 130, 602; Reid, "John Knox, Pastor of Souls," 3–5; Frankforter, "The Chronology of the Knox-Bowes Letters," 30–31.

7. See *Works*, 3:337–402; 4:219; 6:12–14, 22, 26, 83–5, 103, 130, 602; Reid, "Knox, Pastor of Souls," 1; Frankforter, "Elizabeth Bowes and John Knox," 338.

8. *Works* 3:386–87; Reid, *Trumpeter of God*, 80; Frankforter, "Elizabeth Bowes and John Knox," 337; Felch, "'Deir Sister,'" 55.

9. *Works*, 3:337–38 (quote), 379–80, 386–87; Frankforter, "Elizabeth Bowes and

The Care of Souls

In his role as a spiritual advisor, we see a different John Knox. He emerges as a caring, religious leader who is concerned with individuals—their spiritual well-being and their personal struggles. He could, of course, be a pulpit thumper and a prophet denouncing individual and corporate sin, but any balanced picture of Knox must take into consideration his gentler and kinder side.[10]

SOURCES AND CONTEXT

Having said all of this, one might assume that an abundance of evidence exists regarding Knox's pastoral activities. This is not the case. He did not deliberately write instructions on the subject. While he pastored congregations in Scotland, England, and on the Continent, we have little information regarding his pastoral work. However, indirect evidence regarding Knox as a spiritual counselor does exist. He wrote letters to his former congregations and to Protestants who were experiencing persecution. Most informative are the extant letters that Knox wrote to women: thirty to Elizabeth Bowes, fourteen to Anne Locke, and five to his "Sisters in Edinburgh." Unfortunately, what the women wrote to Knox has not survived. Regarding Knox's pastoral activities, two other sources are relevant. Elsewhere, he makes passing comments that indicate the nature of his pastoral concern. Also, the sheep—those on the receiving end of his spiritual advice—testify as to his pastoral effectiveness. They recognized Knox as one who was willing to help them.[11]

Why did so many women turn to Knox for spiritual guidance? If Knox was indeed a misogynist, why did they seek help from him? Did he not write *The First Blast of the Trumpet Against the Monstrous Regiment of Women*—a pamphlet that earned him a reputation as a woman hater? Actually, Knox was not the antifeminist that he has been made out to be. Despite this popular image, he did not have a natural dislike for women. In fact, he demonstrated a remarkable tenderness for females. He wrote many letters to women; he married twice and apparently enjoyed the

---

John Knox," 337; Reid, *Trumpeter of God*, 80.

10. Ridley, *John Knox*, 135; Lorimer, *John Knox and the Church of England*, 41–43; Donaldson, "Knox the Man," 19, 38.

11. *Works*, 3:337–402; 4:217–53; 6:11–15, 21–27, 30, 77–79, 83–85, 100–101, 103–4, 107–9, 129–31, 140–41. Reid, "Knox, Pastor of Souls," 2; Felch, "'Deir Sister,'" 50; Frankforter, "Chronology of Knox-Bowes Letters," 28. Knox wrote twenty-nine letters to Mrs. Bowes and a preface to his *Exposition of the Sixth Psalm of David*, which should also be seen as part of their private correspondence. *Works*, 3:119–21.

company of women. Furthermore, Knox directed *The First Blast* at Mary Tudor, whom he hated intensely—not for her gender but for what he considered her idolatrous practices. She persecuted Protestants in England and forced him into exile on the Continent.[12]

Still, Knox was a man of his time. He accepted the prevailing opinion that women were inferior to men in all areas of society—the home, the church, and the government. In particular, he detested female rule, which he regarded not only as contrary to Scripture and nature but also as illogical. How could a woman be barred from all leadership positions except that of a monarch? On a more personal level, he had conflicts with three female sovereigns—Mary Tudor, Mary of Guise, and Mary Stewart.[13]

Women, however, turned to Knox for spiritual advice for a more important reason—the context of the Protestant Reformation. The Reformation opened the door to many changes, especially in respect to religion. It was an age of uncertainty for both men and women. An entire generation experienced very real confusion: Their spiritual certainties, reinforced by centuries of tradition, had been shattered in a few short years. While many regional differences existed, for about a millennium Europeans had shared a common faith—one that centered on the Catholic Mass. Now all of this was changing. Many people embraced a new religion, one that said individuals were justified by faith and not the Catholic sacramental system. As Protestants, they had given up the traditional religious supports of Catholicism—especially the Mass and priestly intercession.[14]

Such changes affected both men and women, but women experienced even more ambiguities. Gone were the Virgin Mary and the female saints who had been role models and who had provided sisterly patronage. With the end of the confessional, many women sought spiritual help, and they often turned to the Protestant Reformers. Knox was not unique in this regard—many pious women also consulted Bullinger, Luther, Calvin, and other English Reformers for advice. Moreover, women no longer had the option of becoming nuns in communities governed by females, and

---

12. *Works*, 3:155–58; 338–97; 5:227–34; 6:4–97; Ridley, *John Knox*, 267; Greaves, *Theology and Revolution*, 160; Donaldson, "Knox the Man," 28; Stevenson, "John Knox and his Relations to Women," 299; Collinson, "John Knox, the Church of England and the Women of England," 74–75; Shepherd, *Gender and Authority*, 116–18.

13. Ridley, *John Knox*, 266–67; Greaves, *Theology and Revolution*, 160; Shepherd, *Gender and Authority*, 116–19; Wormald, "Godly Reformer, Godless Monarch," 227–30.

14. Frankforter, "Correspondence with Women," 159; Reid, *Trumpeter of God*, 70; Newman, "The Reformation and Elizabeth Bowes," 325, 333.

virginity lost its esteemed status. All women were now expected to marry, and both the ecclesiastical and the civil authorities required them to submit to their husbands.[15]

Not all the changes brought on by the Reformation affected women adversely, however. The Reformers elevated marriage to a spiritual vocation. Sexuality gained greater respect: It was now viewed as a natural human behavior and not just a means of reproduction. The responsibility for the spiritual nurture of children largely fell to the mothers, and this task assumed a moderate level of schooling in religious matters. Whether Protestantism improved the level of female education is uncertain. Yet, some women—especially the noblewomen—did study Scripture and developed an interest in theological matters, and through their correspondence with women, the Protestant Reformers encouraged them to understand theological issues.[16]

THE PASTOR AT WORK

A number of people came to Knox for spiritual advice. Still, his regular correspondence with Elizabeth Bowes provides the best insight into Knox the pastor. The daughter and co-heiress of Roger Aske—a nobleman in North Yorkshire—she became the wife of Richard Bowes, the captain of Norham Castle. Married in 1521, Elizabeth and Richard subsequently produced fifteen children. The Bowes family had a long tradition in the north of England on the Scottish border. Here, Elizabeth Bowes met Knox. After a stint on a galley ship, he received an appointment as a preacher in Berwick.[17]

Just when Mrs. Bowes became a Protestant is unknown, but her conversion came at a time of great religious change in England. Born during the last years of Henry VII's reign, she was raised in a preeminent Catholic family. When Henry VIII repudiated Rome's authority, northern England

---

15. Frankforter, "Correspondence with Women," 159; Newman, "The Reformation and Elizabeth Bowes," 325, 329; Reid, "Knox, Pastor of Souls," 3; Collinson, "The Role of Women in the English Reformation," 261.

16. Frankforter, "Correspondence with Women," 159; Bainton, "The Role of Women in the Reformation," 141; Steinmetz, "Theological Reflections on the Reformation and Status of Women," 197–207; Chrisman, "Women and the Reformation in Strasbourg, " 143–44.

17. *Works*, 3:333, 334; Reid, *Trumpeter of God*, 79–80; Newman, "The Reformation and Elizabeth Bowes," 326; Ridley, *John Knox*, 132; Collinson, "Knox and the Women of England," 79.

PART TWO: Vocational Considerations

remained loyal to the Catholic faith. When the Protestant wind blew during the reign of Edward VI, her family became nominal Protestants without antagonizing the local Catholic gentry. Apparently, at some point and against the wishes of her husband and most of her family, she became an enthusiastic Protestant—a decision that made her life even more difficult when Mary restored the Catholic faith.[18]

Some scholars have viewed Elizabeth Bowes as unstable and spiritually disturbed. Others have described her as a strong woman.[19] Actually, there is some merit to both perspectives: She overcame tremendous obstacles but still doubted her salvation. Knox saw her as a strong person who heroically struggled for the faith against tremendous odds: "In Scotland, England, France, and Germany, I have heard the complaints of divers that feared God, but of the like conflict as she sustained . . . I have not known." For her faith, Mrs. Bowes ignored social conventions and endured exile and estrangement from her husband. Still, doubts regarding her salvation nagged her to the end. For comfort she often turned to Knox—so much so that he confessed that her troubles were a cross for him to bear.[20]

What was Knox's relationship with Mrs. Bowes? They met in the north of England where Knox had a pastorate, but the exact date is uncertain. The correspondence between Knox and Mrs. Bowes is difficult to date. It began as early as 1551 when Knox's pastorate shifted from Berwick to Newcastle. It continued as late as 1560 with the peak of the correspondence coming in 1552–53.[21] Though she became his mother-in-law, their relationship was primarily ideological, spiritual, and sometimes emotional—not sexual as some have contended. Mrs. Bowes encouraged Knox's marriage to her daughter Marjory, a relationship deemed socially inappropriate because of the reformer's social status and Scottish birth. After Knox's exile to the Continent, Elizabeth and Marjory fled to Scotland. On Knox's visit to his homeland, the wedding took place, probably in 1555.

---

18. Ridley, *John Knox*, 131–32; Newman, "The Reformation and Elizabeth Bowes," 326; Reid, "Knox, Pastor of Souls," 3; Frankforter, "Correspondence with Women," 161–62.

19. See Collinson, "The Role of Women in the English Reformation," 264; Frankforter, "Elizabeth Bowes and John Knox," 335; Ridley, *John Knox*, 131; Greaves, *Theology and Revolution*, 22; Newman, "The Reformation and Elizabeth Bowes," 326–29.

20. *Works*, 6:513 (quote); Reid, "Knox, Pastor of Souls," 7; Frankforter, "Elizabeth Bowes and John Knox," 335, 336; Newman, "The Reformation and Elizabeth Bowes," 326–29.

21. Frankforter, "Chronology of the Knox-Bowes Letters," 29–30; Newman, "The Reformation and Elizabeth Bowes," 326; Frankforter, "Correspondence with Women," 161; Ridley, *John Knox*, 538–47; Muir, *John Knox: Portrait of a Calvinist*, 32.

Knox then took his wife and mother-in-law back to Geneva with him. When the reformer returned to Scotland in 1559, they came with him. Marjory died in 1560, and Elizabeth took care of Knox's two sons until his second marriage in 1564. She continued to live in Scotland until returning to England shortly before her death.[22]

Knox's correspondence with Mrs. Bowes focused primarily on one problem—the assurance of salvation—and the questions that grew out of this issue. The church and sacraments could no longer guarantee anything. Salvation was by faith alone, but did Mrs. Bowes have faith? Was she really saved? Was she among the elect? If so, how could she be certain? Thousands of people all over Europe were asking similar questions. Closely related is the issue of temptation. If the miracle of justification had taken place, why was she still tempted to sin? Why did she fall back into sin? There was also the problem of the old religion. That which Mrs. Bowes had embraced all of her life was now being called idolatry, and the fear of falling back into this idolatry haunted her. To complicate all of this, Mrs. Bowes was not a passive disciple. She studied Scripture and challenged Knox regarding the issues of justification, election, and temptation.[23]

How did Knox handle these questions? He offered Mrs. Bowes theological answers—but to no avail. To her, they seemed like circular arguments. He stressed justification by faith, but she brought up biblical passages that seemed to run counter to that doctrine. Did not Jacob wrestle with the angel until he received God's blessing? Was this not a work for salvation? Knox countered by saying that this story was a metaphor for grace. He argued that Jacob prevailed because of divine power—not his own strength. The same is true for our lives: "Hereby is signified, that our victory proceeds not from our own strength, but from the goodness of Him, who by his Spirit, pours into us understanding, will, sufficiency and strength."[24]

In respect to justification, Knox tried to move Mrs. Bowes beyond her subjective doubts. He pointed her to the finished work of Christ and the promises of God: "Your sufficiency stands not within yourself, nor yet in your repentance, but in the sufficiency of Jesus Christ." With pastoral

---

22. Ridley, *John Knox*, 134–35; Frankforter, "Correspondence with Women," 161–62; Frankforter, "Elizabeth Bowes and John Knox," 335–36.

23. McEwen, *The Faith of Knox*, 72–73; Newman, "The Reformation and Elizabeth Bowes," 328–29; Percy, *John Knox*, 134; Greaves, *Theology and Revolution*, 68–69.

24. *Works*, 3:399.

concern, Knox accentuated Christ's victory over Satan. He presented justification not just as a theoretical doctrine, but as an accomplished fact.[25]

For Knox, however, the bedrock of salvation rested on nothing less than God's eternal election.[26] He numbered Mrs. Bowes among the elect: "I am equally certified of your election in Christ, as that I am that I myself preach Christ to be the only Savior."[27] Mrs. Bowes did not share his confidence. She constantly doubted her election, largely on two grounds. She had problems with certain biblical passages, but of greater significance, she deemed herself as too sinful to be elected to salvation.

As Mrs. Bowes read Scripture, she became concerned about her election. Christ said, "many are called but few are chosen." Knox contended that this passage referred to those attempting to enter the kingdom of God by means other than Christ. Moreover, it applied to the reprobate, not to Christians.[28] Another passage bothered Mrs. Bowes: First Samuel 15:35 speaks of God's repenting for making Saul a king. If God had abandoned Saul, could he not change his mind about her? Knox generally advocated a literal interpretation of Scripture, but in this case, he cautioned against such an approach. At times God accommodates our weaknesses and speaks in a language understandable to humans. Knox insisted that from the beginning God knew the mind of Saul and that he had always been a reprobate. Just because God had elevated him to a lofty worldly position did not mean that he was among the elect.[29]

That which nagged Elizabeth Bowes the most was the psychological and the personal dimension of election. If God had elected her to salvation, why did she have so many spiritual struggles? Where were the signs of grace in her life? Sin and temptation were especially troubling. Mrs. Bowes experienced temptations. Did this mean that she was not a Christian? Knox told her that temptations are the work of the devil. Satan tempts all Christians—some so subtly that his "temptations appear to be the cogitations [thoughts] of our own hearts." In other cases, "He is a roaring lion seeking whom he may devour." While Mrs. Bowes felt that she had not repented enough, Knox assured her "that your sufficiency stands not within yourself, nor yet in your repentance" but in Christ alone.[30]

---

25. *Works*, 3:363–64, 368, 395; Reed, *John Knox: The Forgotten Reformer*, 150–51.

26. See Kyle, "The Concept of Predestination in the Thought of John Knox," 53–77; Kyle, *The Mind of Knox*, 102–25.

27. *Works*, 3:369.

28. *Works*, 3:351.

29. *Works*, 3:362–63. Calvin also enunciated this principle of accommodation.

30. *Works*, 3:367–68.

This theme continued in many of Knox's letters to Mrs. Bowes. In one, he let her know that to be tempted to sin is not sin; and even if we sin, we can repent and be forgiven.[31] Elsewhere, Knox made it clear that election must produce certain fruits and signs or something is wrong. Absence of sin, however, is not such a sign because the elect could sin grievously and at times even resemble the reprobate. Yet, God does not abandon them to perdition but hears their petitions and enables them to resist sin. Therefore, Mrs. Bowes was not to despair of her election because of isolated lapses into sin. In fact, Knox pointed out that her worries concerning her sin indicated that she was of the elect. Though the elect need not lose hope if they fall into sin, they cannot be devoid of all positive signs. The elect cannot delight in persistent evildoing and have a deep aversion in godliness and still claim the assurance of salvation. Rather, they must evidence a positive righteousness and a genuine desire to live a pure, holy life.[32]

In dealing with the issues of sin, temptation, and doubts, Knox revealed several of his counseling methods. In what modern therapists would regard as negative, at times he became impatient and even lapsed into sarcasm. For example, Mrs. Bowes compared her sins to those of Sodom and Gomorrah. Knox took her to task for exaggerating her sins and let her know that she did not know what she was talking about: "Mother, the cause of your unthankfulness I take to be ignorance in you, that you know not what were the sins of Sodom and Gomorrah."[33]

In another place, Knox resorted to logic. At times, Mrs. Bowes had doubted that there was a God, and this terrified her. "If you really believe that God does not exist, why should such a thought frighten you?" asked Knox.[34] Elsewhere he even tried some psychology on Mrs. Bowes. He contended that an understanding of one's spiritual insufficiency is a prerequisite for divine grace and a sign of salvation: "The chief sign of God's favor is, that we know . . . ourselves . . . to be nothing without his support."[35]

Most revealing was Knox's use of empathy, or co-counseling. He did not assault Mrs. Bowes' spiritual fragility with "the force of his masculine and professional authority." As noted, spiritual advice flowed in two

---

31. *Works*, 3:381–82.

32. *Works*, 3:338–39, 341, 342–49, 350, 353, 358, 360, 362, 363, 371, 374, 384, 393.

33. *Works*, 3:382–83.

34. *Works*, 3:360; Frankforter, "Elizabeth Bowes and John Knox," 343.

35. *Works*, 3:374; Frankforter, "Elizabeth Bowes and John Knox," 343.

directions. While he counseled her, she also supported him in his spiritual battles. In what was probably a deliberate pastoral technique, Knox confessed that he had also experienced Mrs. Bowes' problems. Indeed, she had helped him perhaps as much as he had aided her.[36] In fact, he admitted to being afflicted with the suffering of Job, and though his theology said that God would aid him, Knox often felt that he would not. In making such a confession, Knox had laid his soul bare to Mrs. Bowes. He had gone beyond self-disclosure, speaking "more plain than ever I spoke," and acknowledged her to be "one fellow and companion in trouble."[37]

Still, when it came to slipping back into idolatry, Knox was not as empathetic. Mrs. Bowes faced constant pressure to return to the Roman faith. Her husband and family encouraged her to attend Mass, and the possibility of a Catholic resurgence under Queen Mary made matters even more difficult. Mrs. Bowes had no confidence that she could withstand the temptations of her old faith, and if she failed to do so, she would have committed the sin unto death. Knox combined sarcasm, humor, and direct admonitions in dealing with this problem. On one hand, he gave her words of encouragement: she was to rest in Christ for he has already defeated Satan.[38] On the other hand, he warned her of great dangers if she were to cooperate with Catholic idolatry. She could not be a closet Protestant—outwardly conforming to Catholicism while preserving the Protestant faith in her heart.[39] In another place, he openly chided her for being attracted to the Catholic Mass, declaring that in this regard, "Alas, Sister! Your imbecility troubles me."[40]

Letters to Mrs. Locke

John Knox's pastoral side also came out in his letters to Anne Locke. Mrs. Locke lived in London and came from a merchant background—the daughter of a merchant and the wife to another. She and another woman, Mrs. Hickman, had a close relationship with Knox, serving as his confidantes after the death of Edward VI. In London, Knox lodged with them and they treated him with great care. Mrs. Locke was about fifteen years younger than Knox and a very gifted woman—apparently

---

36. *Works*, 3:337–38, 350, 379, 380; Collinson, "Knox and the Women of England," 81 (quote); Frankforter, "Elizabeth Bowes and John Knox," 337.

37. *Works*, 3:352–53; Frankforter, "Elizabeth Bowes and John Knox, 340.

38. *Works*, 3:353, 355, 361.

39. *Works*, 3:344–48; Frankforter, "Chronology of the Knox-Bowes Letters," 39.

40. *Works*, 3:361.

more sophisticated than Mrs. Bowes. While in Geneva, she translated into English Calvin's sermons on Hezekiah and a book by John Toffin. Mrs. Locke was a staunch Protestant, and while her husband also embraced the new faith, he apparently lacked her enthusiasm.[41]

Knox's letters to Anne Locke differed from those to Mrs. Bowes. Several came before their stay in Geneva, but most came after. Fearing the Marian persecution, Knox wrote at least three letters before 1556 urging her to come to Geneva. She did so, apparently with her husband's permission—for after her return to London, she lived with her husband until his death. Knox wrote eight of his fourteen letters to Mrs. Locke during the year 1559—a time when he was actively promoting the Scottish Reformation. During this period, Knox wrote to Anne Locke for two purposes: as a means to communicate news from Scotland about the Reformation and as a way to raise funds for the Protestant cause. Apparently, this latter endeavor met with little success. As a result, when compared to the letters to Mrs. Bowes, much less space is given to private pastoral concerns. Some, however, do tell about Anne Locke's spiritual anxieties and Knox's response to them.[42]

The main thrust of Knox's early letters to Anne Locke concerned predictions of imminent persecution, warnings not to succumb to idolatry, and pleas for her to come to Geneva.[43] Couched in these letters are more pastoral concerns. Apparently, Mrs. Locke shared some of Elizabeth Bowes' spiritual anxieties. Nevertheless, he assured her that her eternal life had not been purchased by gold or silver, the blood of calves or goats, or even the Catholic Mass but by the death of Christ.[44] In another letter, Knox urged Anne Locke to confide in him concerning her spiritual problems: "Touching your troubles (spiritual I mean) fear not to be plain with me," and in turn he communicated to her what the Holy Spirit "teaches me within his most sacred Word." Knox also told her that it is easy "to think well of God" during times of prosperity. The spirit of God, however, would help her turn to God even in difficult times.[45]

---

41. See Collinson, "The Role of Women in the English Reformation," 258–72; Reid, *Trumpeter of God*, 140–41; Ridley, *John Knox*, 246–47; Danner, *Pilgrimage to Puritanism*, 91–92.

42. Collinson, "Knox, the Church of England," 83–84; Frankforter, "Correspondence with Women," 167; Reid, *Trumpeter of God*, 141; Ridley, *John Knox*, 247.

43. *Works*, 3:219–22; 237–41; Felch, "'Deir Sister,'" 50–54.

44. *Works*, 4:221–22.

45. *Works*, 4:237; Frankforter, "Correspondence with Women," 168.

Part Two: Vocational Considerations

Knox's later letters to Anne Locke contain at least one reference to the spiritual anxieties that plagued Mrs. Bowes. At midnight, Anne Locke wrote to Knox regarding a spiritual battle. He advised her to continue the struggle knowing that many others had faced the same problems: "Be of comfort, Sister, knowing that you fight not the battle alone." What is more, he suggested that pride might lie at the root of her problems but that this was a problem that everyone faced.[46]

Still, a different pastoral concern dominated Knox's later correspondence with Anne Locke—namely her participation in the services of the Church of England. Knox had always disliked aspects of the English liturgy, but because he generally approved of the religious policies of Edward VI's government, he muted his objections. The Catholic Mary Tudor was now the queen and Anne Locke resided in Geneva. So, in a 1556 letter, he warned her not to compromise with Mary's idolatry, even if this entailed forsaking friends and possessions.[47]

The religious situation in England changed with the ascension of Elizabeth. She restored Protestantism—but by the puritan standards embraced by the Marian exiles—it fell far short of their religious ideals. Anne Locke found herself in a quandary. With Elizabeth on the throne, she could now return to England, but could she participate in the liturgy of the Church of England? Or would this be a compromise with idolatry? So she wrote to Knox from Geneva. By his own admission, he took a hard line that many considered "extreme and rigorous." The *Book of Common Prayer* still contained "diabolical inventions," he contended. Thus, he could never counsel anyone to participate in the "dredges of Papistrie" still found in the English service.[48]

Yet, more than external rituals corrupted the English worship. The sacraments were administered "without the Word truly and openly preached." Because of this, the clergy of the Church of England were "none of Christ's ministers, but Mass-mumming priests." In Knox's opinion, the English service lacked what was central to the Reformed faith—the preaching of God's Word. He believed that it had been so distorted by human inventions that it ceased being a worship service at all. In fact, Knox now implied that it was sinful to even attend an English worship service.

---

46. *Works*, 6:79: Felch, "'Deir Sister,'" 57; Frankforter, "Correspondence with Women," 168.

47. *Works*, 4:220; Frankforter, "Correspondence with Women," 168.

48. *Works*, 6:12; Felch,"'Deir Sister,'" 54–55; Frankforter, "Correspondence with Women," 168; Ridley, *John Knox*, 309–10. See Sutherland, "The Marian Exiles and the Establishment of the Elizabethan Regime," 253–85.

Thus, in his mind, Mrs. Locke was confronted with a major decision: Was she going to obey God or men?[49]

Anne Locke, however, continued to push Knox in this regard—so much so that he became exasperated. Referring to his earlier letter he wrote, "your questions . . . I have (more) than once answered." She should not participate in a "bastard religion" such as the "mingle mangle" then practiced in the Church of England. Still, he seemed to understand her dilemma: to not attend the English services would seem like sinful negligence to some, but to do so might further an idolatrous cause. Thus, the decision was hers to make. Knox's spiritual advice did not come as a command. Rather, he prayed that the Holy Spirit would guide her into the right decision.[50]

Women in Edinburgh

Elizabeth Bowes and Anne Locke were not the only women to seek Knox's spiritual advice. Some women in Edinburgh wrote to him concerning two practical but loaded questions. The first addressed the subject of female wearing apparel. Knox acknowledged that this was a difficult question to answer with any certainty. Two extremes existed—one would "restrain Christian liberty" while the other would open the door to "foolish fantasy." Moreover, individuals differed widely in their dress. Thus, Knox refused to make any specific prescriptions. Women must not dress ostentatiously, and women should not wear the garments of men or carry their weapons. In his reasoning for this rule, one can see shades of *The First Blast*—women are inferior to men. "The garments of women do declare their weakness and inability to execute the office of men."[51]

The second question addressed the issue of eating meat offered to idols. Would eating in a Catholic friend's home be tantamount to the sin condemned in 1 Corinthians? The women thought so, but Knox distinguished between attending the Mass and eating in a Catholic friend's home. The Mass had to be avoided at all costs, yet he did not condemn social engagements with Roman Catholics. Even in social gatherings, however, Protestants had to be prepared to be a witness to their faith.[52]

---

49. *Works*, 6:13–14; Felch, "Deir Sister," 55; Frankforter, "Correspondence with Women," 168; Ridley, *John Knox*, 310.

50. *Works*, 6:83–84; Frankforter, "Correspondence with Women," 168; Flech, "'Deir Sister,'" 55, 58–59.

51. *Works*, 4:225–29; Reid, "Knox, Pastor of Souls," 7.

52. *Works*, 4:230–31; Reid, "Knox, Pastor of Souls," 8.

Part Two: Vocational Considerations

Care for the Sick and Bereaved

Pastors also visit the sick and comfort the bereaved. What did Knox say about such a ministry? His writings reveal little on these subjects, though some information can be gleaned from the collective works that he sanctioned. The *Form of Prayers* used in Geneva gave some instructions on visiting the sick while the *Book of Common Order* contains a lengthy prayer regarding this subject.[53] Life was difficult in the sixteenth century. Medical knowledge was primitive; public health and sanitation barely existed. Disease and death frequently stalked people in all ranks of society. While the Reformers regarded sickness and death as coming from the hand of God, they also saw healing as a gift from God to be appropriated by both spiritual and medical means.[54]

In this regard, Knox followed the thinking of the continental Reformers. He urged ministers to pray for and visit the sick. Such tasks were "things very necessary," but he refused to prescribe a set procedure. Rather, the minister, "like a skillful physician," should tailor his visit to the circumstances. Visiting the sick could be an occasion to lift up an individual to "the sweet promises of God's mercy through Christ," or, if the sick person had no sense of his or her sins, the minister could "beat him down with God's justice." Moreover, the minister should go beyond praying for the sick during his visit. He should also lift up the sick in a public prayer before the entire congregation.[55]

In this chapter, we have seen a different John Knox—not a pulpit pounder or a Hebrew prophet proclaiming God's wrath. To be sure, Knox's beliefs remained the same, but his style changed. As a pastor in the care of souls, he demonstrated compassion, care, and empathy. He went to great lengths to help individuals with their struggles of conscience. He readily acknowledged that their struggles and failures were similar to his. Their anxieties were those of first-generation Protestants attempting to understand their new faith, and Knox usually gave them balanced and reasonable answers.

---

53. *Works*, 4:202–3; 6:327–33; Maxwell, *John Knox's Genevan Service Book*, 160.

54. Winter, "Presbyterians and Prayers for the Sick," 142.

55. *Works*, 4:202; Winter, "Presbyterians and Prayers for the Sick," 142; Maxwell, *Knox's Genevan Service Book*, 160.

Part Three

Political Considerations

10

The Road to Resistance

PERHAPS THE TITLES OF this section and chapters are somewhat misleading because John Knox was not basically a political theorist any more than he was a speculative theologian. In fact, Knox would have denied having political thought as such. His one purpose in life was to perform God's work, which he believed to be the reformation of religion in Scotland. Actually his so-called political theory extended his religious thought, which in turn had as its aim the reformation of religion. Therefore to divide Knox's thought into rigid religious and political categories is rather artificial. In this orientation Knox was not unique because other sixteenth-century thinkers based their political ideology on religious grounds.

It would seem, however, that Knox's so-called political thought utilized constitutional and political arguments less than many other reformers did (e.g., Luther, Calvin, Viret, Beza, and the Huguenots). Rather, his political pamphlets resembled the pronouncements of a Hebrew prophet who had little regard for legal niceties. Of course, this contention that Knox was fundamentally concerned with the reformation of religion and that his political thought grew out of this concern does not go unchallenged. Some authorities argue that constitutional theory—i.e., active opposition by the lesser magistrates to tyrants—provided the basis for Knox's concept of political resistance. Actually, the two views are not entirely incompatible because Knox endowed constitutional theory with a religious purpose and couched his appeal to the nobility and common people in terms of their religious obligations.[1]

1. Those scholars who largely present a religious emphasis are Gray and Vesey and to a lesser extent, Walzer. While Greaves does not discount theology as a factor and frequently alludes to the covenant, he argues that there is nothing in Knox's theology

PART THREE: Political Considerations

TRENDS TOWARD ARMED RESISTANCE

The breakup of Western Europe's religious unity accompanying the Protestant Reformation meant that two, and sometimes more, expressions of the Christian faith appeared in many areas. In most places where the civil authorities remained Catholic, they believed loyalty to the medieval church was synonymous with loyalty to the state. A number of Protestant princes held to the same general principle, adhering to the opinion that unity of religion was indispensable for public order. This general feeling is well expressed in a statement often attributed to the French king, Francis I: "One king, one law, one faith."[2]

Despite the appearance of religious unity, the medieval world never enjoyed complete harmony in this regard. Nevertheless, as the image of the religious solidarity of medieval Christendom unraveled in the sixteenth century, Christians were faced with the basic question of what would happen when civil government and the church opposed each other. In most European countries, religious minorities had to decide on a course of action when they saw what they considered to be the "true religion" in conflict with the beliefs of the ruling authorities. A number of fundamental questions had to be answered. For example, how should "true Christians" respond if the civil authorities actively and openly persecuted them? If Christians had to choose between their religion and their political overlord, where should their loyalty lie? May "true Christians" ever justly resist established political authority? If so, when may they resist? Who shall take action? And to what extent could this resistance be carried by the adherents of the "true faith"? If this opposition succeeded, were the "true Christians" then free to reorganize society after a new image?

---

that made a theory of resistance inevitable. See Gray, "The Political Theory of John Knox," 132–44; Vesey, "The Sources of the Idea of Active Resistance in the Political Theory of John Knox," 92–113; Greaves, *Theology and Revolution*, 127; Greaves, "John Knox, The Reformed Tradition, and the Development of Resistance Theory," 2. Those scholars who emphasize Knox primarily as a political thinker isolated from his religious thought are Russell and Burns. See Russell, "John Knox as a Statesman," 1–28; Burns, "John Knox and Revolution," 565–73. To some extent Ridley, Little, and Skinner follow this latter position. See Ridley, *John Knox*; Percy, *John Knox*; Little, "John Knox and English Social Prophecy," 117–72; Skinner, *The Foundations of Modern Political Thought*, 2 vols., 2:211.

2. Linder, "Pierre Viret and the Sixteenth-Century Protestant Revolutionary Tradition," 125; Thompson, *The Wars of Religion in France*, 10–11.

Lutheran Contributions

The idea of passive resistance holds that God rather than human beings must be obeyed, and no sixteenth-century religious thinker so much as suggested anything else. Nevertheless, though individuals must refuse to obey commands contrary to God's law, forcible resistance is never justified. Traditionally, Luther is seen as representative of passive resistance, but such an image of Luther is true only from 1523 to 1530. During these years he staunchly opposed any kind of resistance to the emperor.³

Most English pamphleteers during the reigns of Henry VIII and Edward VI wrote much in the same strain. Tyndale's *The Obedience of a Christian Man* is perhaps the most important evidence for this attitude of passive resistance. Some historians say even Calvin took much the same line. In his ideal commonwealth—resistance to the powers would be manifestly wrong—but in the absence of the ideal, he only gave partial support to the right of resisting duly constituted rulers.⁴

Traditionally, the theory of armed resistance is seen to have originated with the Calvinist tradition, but scholarship has demonstrated the contribution of Lutheranism in this regard. Lutheranism helped to transmit medieval revolutionary theories to the Calvinists, and it can be argued that from 1530 to his death in 1546, Luther increasingly supported the notion of princely resistance to the emperor on grounds of constitutional and natural law.⁵ Still, Luther's notion of the "two kingdoms" took him away from politics, and he never attempted to transform the earthly kingdom as Calvin did. Actually, two other developments did more to further the notion of the inferior magistrates resisting imperial power. They are the formation of the Schmalkadic League, the armed defiance by the city of Magdeburg, and resulting *Bekenntnis* of 1550—which justified resistance by inferior magistrates.⁶

---

3. Shoenberger, "The Development of Lutheran Theory of Resistance, 1523–1530," 64. See also Olson, "Theology of Revolution" 59ff; Skinner, *Modern Political Thought*, 2: 191ff.

4. Allen, *A History of Political Thought in the Sixteenth Century*, 63–67; Burns, "The Political Ideas of the Scottish Reformation," 251–52.

5. Shoenberger, "Lutheran Resistance Theory," 61, 64–65; Olsen, "Theology of Revolution," 56; Skinner, *Modern Political Thought*, 2:206ff.

6. Linder, "Pierre Viret and the French Tradition," 126; Schoenberger, "Lutheran Resistance Theory," 61, 74–75; Olsen, "Theology of Revolution," 56–59; Skinner, *Modern Political Thought*, 2:206.

Part Three: Political Considerations

Reformed Contributions

While the Calvinists were at first content to reiterate the radical Lutheran arguments, they did make contributions of their own; and as a consequence, the fully developed theory of resistance must be identified with the Calvinist tradition. If a theocracy is defined as a government by priests, then it is inappropriate to call Calvin's system a theocracy, for Calvin separated the magistracy from the clergy. What Calvin had in mind was a holy commonwealth with the church and state in close interaction and partners in service to meet people's needs.[7]

Yet when such a Christian commonwealth could not be established and the civil authorities persecuted the "true believers," did Calvin advocate armed resistance? Scholars by no means agree on this question. But while he taught no full-blown theory of political resistance, his writings seem to contain the seeds for such a development. Although Calvin taught that no private citizen could revolt against a tyrannical king, he did indicate that resistance was permissible if the inferior magistrates led the uprising. Calvin's desire to establish God's kingdom pushed him into politics and made resistance certain under the proper circumstances. While such conditions did not arise in Geneva, they did in France, England, Scotland, and the Lowlands.[8]

The strand of resistance certainly did not cease after Calvin: if anything, it intensified. Calvin's successor in Geneva, Theodore Beza, set forth a theory of political resistance by the lesser magistrates with greater clarity than Calvin did. Another Reformed leader, Pierre Viret, authorized armed resistance by inferior magistrates when the civil authorities encroached upon spiritual matters. Yet as Robert Linder points out, Viret denounced tyrants more vociferously than did Calvin; and he not only allowed inferior magistrates the right of resistance—he made it their duty to do so when tyrants threatened to destroy the gospel by force.[9]

---

7. Hunt, ed., *Calvinism and the Political Order*, 35–41. However, if *theocracy* means government by God through a balance of spiritual and secular powers with the clergy and magistrates acting in harmony, then the term *theocracy* is more acceptable. See Monter, *Calvin's Geneva*, 144; Hunt, "Calvin's Theory of Church and State," 71. See also Hopfl, *The Christian Polity of John Calvin*.

8. Allen, *Political Thought*, 52–60; Burns, "The Political Ideas of the Scottish Reformation," 251–52; Linder, "Pierre Viret and the French Tradition," 127–28; McNeill, "The Democratic Element in Calvin's Thought," 155–71; Walzer, *The Revolution of the Saints*, 26–30, 51, 54, 62–63; Skinner, *Modern Political Thought*, 2:192.

9. Linder, "Pierre Viret and the French Tradition," 138–39; Linder, "Pierre Viret and the Sixteenth-Century English Protestants," 149–70; Kingdon, "The First Expression of Theodore Beza's Political Ideas," 88–100, esp. 92.

The Road to Resistance

Two frequent case studies for the Calvinist resistance theory are the Marian exiles and the Huguenots. Both groups advocated resistance to constituted authority and both worked with essentially the same intellectual stockpile: medieval commonplaces plus the impact of Calvin's ideology. Nevertheless, historical circumstances created major differences in their respective resistance theories. The Huguenots moved cautiously between the old and new, that is, between feudalism and Calvinism. Conversely, the Marian exiles, who were individuals driven by persecution, adopted a new ideology with astonishing recklessness.

Both produced political ideologies filled with a sense of confidence and duty. Both urged explicit programs of political action. Yet the Huguenots, though Protestant, were also nobles and wealthy burghers. Frightened by the growth of royal power, they sought not only religious reform but also a new constitutional order in which they might play a secure and significant part. On the other hand, the Marian exiles—exiled from their native land and with old ties broken—hoped to discover a new legitimacy and a new rectitude forged from God's Word, religious reform, and revolution if necessary. They were people whose political activity was shaped more to the necessities of revolutionary organization than to constitutional order.[10]

The Political Context of Knox's Resistance Theory

John Knox, a Marian exile himself, sought the reformation of religion rather than the adjustment of political grievances. Yet one may never separate religious development from the context of the age, and accordingly Knox's reform efforts cannot be divorced from the political milieu of Europe and Scotland. The political world—domestic and foreign, in which the Scottish Reformation took place—was governed by forces that had little to do with the theological issues of the day. In the sixteenth century, politics and religion interacted in a way that is difficult for the twenty-first century mind to fathom. Religion, however, never dominated politics to the exclusion or even subordination of ordinary political motives. Forces were at work in the world of politics by which the religious leaders might gain or lose, but which they could do little to control.

Knox desired the reformation of religion in Scotland, and in his mind this restoration meant returning the Christian religion to the ideal

---

10. Walzer, *Revolution of the Saints*, 67–113. See also Skinner, *Modern Political Thought*, 2:239ff.; Neale, *The Age of Catherine de Medici*.

of spiritual Israel. The great obstacle to such reform was the power of the Catholic Church, established by law and promoted by the civil power. For any reforming movement to succeed, it must somewhere find the power to effect the changes it desires; and the early Magisterial Reformers found that power in the temporal state.

Scotland, however, did not have any sovereigns favorable to Protestantism as did the principalities of Luther's Germany, or the England of Edward VI. Thus for a Scottish Reformation to triumph, its proponents must advocate the overthrow of established temporal authority, the seizure of political power, and the use of that power to bring down the Roman Church. Both Protestants and Catholics were aware of this reality. Consequently, the Scottish Reformation was a revolution, dependent for its success on the wielding of political power.[11]

The Religious and Secular Thrust of Knox's Resistance Theory

John Knox did not develop his theory of resistance in a vacuum, for both the sequence of events and the thought of his time influenced it. The Scottish Reformation, indeed, depended on resistance to Mary of Guise and Mary Stewart for its very success. Moreover, the intellectual milieu of the exile years and Knox's consultation with other Reformed ministers played no small part in this development. Nor is it entirely accurate to view Knox's notions of opposition to rulers as entirely religious and non-political.

Still, Knox was a religious reformer, and as such, his resistance theory was but a means to an end: the reformation of religion in Scotland. The Bible, especially the Old Testament, was the primary source for Knox's theory of resistance.[12] Events and ideology notwithstanding, Knox's resistance theory could have no rational basis without his concepts of God, sin, idolatry, and the covenant. Most directly, John Knox's notion of political resistance was related to his belief in active resistance to sin. As Knox stated in his debate with Maitland, the faithful when in a minority are required only to separate themselves from idolatry. When they hold a dominant position and are reasonably unified, they must not simply separate from idolatry; they must abolish it. And if exterminating idolatry means overthrowing a Catholic sovereign, then such action becomes necessary.

---

11. See Kyle, *The Mind of Knox*, 245–46.

12. Vesey, "The Sources of Knox's Political Theory," 47–227. The argument of Vesey's dissertation is that Knox derived his theory of resistance from the Old Testament.

The Road to Resistance

Though Knox's general resistance theory rested on his opposition to sin, his concept of the covenant enabled him to overcome the belief that only the lesser magistrates could revolt. God had established his covenant with all inhabitants of the realm; thus every individual must promote the rule of godliness in the commonwealth.[13] Certainly, for his active resistance to idolatry and its political consequences, Knox adduced considerable support from the Old Testament.

Indeed, as noted previously Knox adopted the role and rhetoric of an Old Testament prophet and may even have integrated his personality into that of a Hebrew prophet. His resistance theory rested predominantly on religious grounds but not exclusively. In fact, Knox did not assail Mary Tudor solely as an idolatress but also displayed concern for the entire fabric of English society. For example, in *A Faithful Admonition*, he attacked her on the grounds of endangering national independence: "And now, does she not manifestly show herself to be an open traitress to the Imperial Crown of England, contrary to the just laws of the Realm, to bring in a stranger, and to make a proud Spaniard king, . . . to the utter subversion of the whole public estate and commonwealth of England?" According to J. H. Burns, in *A Faithful Admonition* Knox for the first time, resorted to a purely political argument. Here his remarks took on a secular character. The English commonwealth and English laws and liberties assumed the character of entities in themselves unrelated to specific biblical categories.[14]

Knox, however, used secular arguments in other writings as well. For example, in *The First Blast*, he argued against female rule from the grounds of natural law and man's empirical assessment of woman's folly as well as from scriptural prohibitions. In responding to a letter he received at Dieppe in 1557, Knox wrote to the nobility setting forth a bold concept of their rule in society. Though he concentrated on religious problems, he did not fail to note public grievances more generally. Furthermore, Knox did not bypass the existing political structure (e.g., monarch, nobility, estates). Rather he sought to animate the structure with a religious purpose. When Knox found no monarch to reform religion, he turned to the nobility. In this decision he demonstrated continuity with medieval legal precedents by assigning to the nobles a vital role in correcting grievances. Only when the sovereign and nobility failed to purify religion

---

13. *Works*, 2:442–43; 3:196–97; 4:500–525.

14. *Works*, 2:442–443; 3:196–97; 4:500–505; Little, "Knox and English Social Prophecy," 122–25; Burns, "The Political Ideas of the Scottish Reformation," 255.

did Knox advocate going outside the structure. The Scottish Reformation intermingled religious and political motives and though religion did dominate Knox's thought, as a typical sixteenth-century man, he could not completely separate the two.[15]

ST. ANDREWS CASTLE AND THE FRENCH GALLEY

John Knox is well known for his theory of resistance against constituted authority. The exact date, however, when he developed this theory is debated by historians. The traditional view, best represented by J. H. Burns, says Knox adhered to passive resistance until about 1558, when he became the apostle of armed resistance. Conversely, this view has been questioned by Richard Greaves, who maintains Knox demonstrated a practical belief in the right to rebellion as early as 1547. Greaves declares that "Knox's views on disobedience per se to secular authority never changed," and therefore his adherence to passive resistance while in Edwardian England was but a lull to accommodate a Christian ruler. Knox always advocated disobedience when higher authorities commanded something contrary to God's law, and according to Greaves, this disobedience later developed into a doctrine of armed rebellion at the popular level.

Nevertheless, J. H. Burns states "that Knox cannot be regarded, on the evidence of his writings down to 1557, as the advocate or theorist of rebellion. . . ." The interpretation that one accepts in this regard depends on whether the interpreter emphasizes Knox's deeds and inferences or his direct statements, because his actions and verbal implications ran ahead of his express theory. He hinted at the right to rebellion well before he actually advocated it. Shades of Knox's resistance emerged perhaps as early as 1547, and probably the exile and contacts at Geneva only intensified a trend already in motion. Yet Knox's writings did not explicitly reveal a full-blown doctrine resistance until 1558.[16]

    15. *Works*, 3:295; 4:373–420; Little, "Knox and English Social Prophecy," 122–25; Burns, "The Political Ideas of the Scottish Reformation," 256, 259–61; Burns, "Knox and Revolution," 565, 567–68.

    16. Burns believes Knox held to passive obedience until 1558 when he advocated armed resistance. See Burns, "The Political Ideas of the Scottish Reformation," 251–69, esp. 258; Burns, "Knox and Revolution," 108–16. Vander Molen says that while Knox issued no clear call for rebellion in 1554, his writings by that time certainly implied such and were interpreted as seditious by Cox's Anglican group at Frankfurt. See Vander Molen, "Anglican Against Puritan," 54ff. Greaves contends that Knox demonstrated a practical belief in the right to rebellion as early as 1547. See Greaves, "John Knox and Resistance Theory," 1–31, esp. 1–3, 14. Little and Ridley also seem to favor

The Road to Resistance

Did Knox advocate rebellion prior to his stay in England (1549-54)? To answer this question, two pieces of evidence must be examined: Knox's involvement at St. Andrews Castle in 1547 and his summary of Balnaves's treatise in 1548. Both indicators are subject to several interpretations. During the years 1543-46, Cardinal Beaton persecuted Protestants to the point of rebellion. The Cardinal's murder in 1546 was more political than religious and incidental to an attempted *coup d'etat*. Actually Beaton's death was less important than the fact that the murderers seized the castle.[17] Knox subsequently associated himself with the assassins by preaching and teaching in the castle. Richard Greaves argues that Knox's involvement with the rebels at St. Andrews Castle indicated his affirmation of the practical right of rebellion.

Conversely, Stanford Reid and Pierre Janton see Knox more as a victim of circumstances than as a willing participant in the events. Knox, indeed, seemed to sympathize with the Castilians (which the rebels came to be called) and regarded Beaton's death as justice from God upon a persecutor rather than as an act of murder. Thus his mind appeared to be moving toward rebellion, but the evidence is too tenuous to affirm an embryonic theory of rebellion.[18]

Knox spent more than a year at St. Andrews before the castle's fall. From here he was sent to a French galley where he wrote a summary of Balnaves's book. In this work he defined political justice as "an obedience which the inferior estate give to their superior; which should be kept because it is the command of God that Princes be obeyed." Knox laid heavy responsibility upon the prince, but emphasized that the ruler "should be obeyed in all things not repugning to the command of God; because they are ordained and placed by God to punish vice and maintain virtue."[19] Though Knox exempted Christians from obeying commands contrary

---

a date earlier than 1558. See Little, "Knox and English Social Prophecy," 117; Ridley, *John Knox*, 171, 174.

17. Ridley, *John Knox*, 47-48. The political implications were multiple: (1) The castle held by the rebels was only four hours sail from an English port. (2) Shortly after Beaton's death, the French—after months of negotiations—abandoned the Scots to the mercy of Henry VIII and made a separate peace with England.

18. *Works*, 3:177; Greaves, "John Knox and Resistance Theory," 3; Reid, *Trumpeter of God*, 45; Janton, *John Knox, l' homme et oeuvre*, 66.

19. *Works*, 3:25-26. In their respective articles, Greaves and Burns emphasize different aspects of Knox's summary of Balnaves's work. Greaves cites the possibility of disobedience while Burns stresses the absence of any references to resistance. Greaves, "John Knox and Resistance Theory," 3; Burns, "The Political Ideas of the Scottish Reformation," 253.

to divine law, he gave no hint that such disobedience should be armed resistance.

THE ENGLISH YEARS

John Knox lived in England from March 1549 to January 1554. Traditionally these years have been viewed as a time when Knox continued to adhere to passive resistance. This view, however, does not go unchallenged. Richard Greaves contends that though Knox had already rebelled at St. Andrews, he ruled out such action in England on pragmatic grounds. There simply was nothing to be gained by it now. Paul Little, in his analysis of the social trends prevalent in Edwardian England, also argues that the seeds for Knox's resistance theory were already present in English society even before the Marian exile.[20]

By 1550 the Magdeburg *Bekenntnis* had been published. Although Knox cited this literature in his 1564 debate with Maitland, this material did not seem to have any immediate effect upon the reformer. Living in England during the reign of Edward VI, Knox criticized sharply the details of ecclesiastical policy. Essentially the government moved in the right direction, but at too slow a pace. In fact, Knox praised Edward VI in *A Godly Letter* (1553-54), and later his *History* described the ruler as "that most godly and most virtuous King that has been known to have reigned in England, or elsewhere, these many years past."[21] Kneeling at Communion became an issue but otherwise no fundamental conflict with the government arose; and Knox's writings during this period are virtually devoid of political references. Indeed, the English officials offered Knox a bishopric, which he declined, but the government of Edward VI was not likely to offer such to a man who advocated rebellion against constituted authority.

Actually Knox wrote one of his most specific declarations of passive resistance during his stay in Edwardian England. His 1552 *Epistle to the Congregation of Berwick* emphasized that rulers merited obedience in all matters not contrary to God's truth, and even when disobedience became necessary, it must not be violent. Rather than rebel, the Christians were to suffer patiently for their faith: "that due obedience be given to magistrates,

---

20. Burns, "The Political Ideas of the Scottish Reformation," 254; Greaves, "John Knox and Resistance Theory," 3; Little, "Knox and English Social Prophecy," 117–22.

21. Knox, "Epistle to the Congregation of Berwick, 1522," 259. The full title of the Magdeburg *Bekenntnis* was *The Confession and Apology of the Pastors and other Ministers of the Church at Magdeburg*.

rulers and princes, without tumult, grudge or sedition; for, how wicked yet ever themselves be in life, or how ungodly that ever their precepts . . . be." In the face of this "you must obey them . . . ; except in chief points of religion; and then ought you rather to obey God not man; not to pretend to defend God's truth or religion (you being subjects) by violence or the sword, but patiently suffering."[22]

THE EARLY EXILE YEARS

Tyndale's doctrine of obedience held sway in the England of Henry VIII and Edward VI. Living in Edwardian England, Knox found such a doctrine convenient. Still, this doctrine soon became inconvenient for Knox, as it had been for the Protestants at St. Andrews Castle and Magdeburg. The accession of a Catholic, Mary Tudor, to the throne of England brought a change of events. Within a few months, events drove Knox into exile (January 1554). From this time until the deposition of Mary Stewart in Scotland some thirteen years later, he was more or less preoccupied with the problems of the "faithful Christian" confronted by "idolatry" and above all else by an "idolatrous" sovereign. Nevertheless, he approached the problem cautiously.

A Godly Letter

Whether Knox began to sound his trumpet in Edwardian England is a matter of debate; but with a Catholic on the throne, the sounds became loud and distinct. The first admonitory epistle pertaining to the resistance theme was *A Godly Letter*, probably started in England in December 1553, but finished at Dieppe in January 1554. When Mary became queen of England, the Protestants were hamstrung by the doctrine of Christian obedience, and Knox in *A Godly Letter* and other writings sought to infuse them with a spirit of disobedience.

As in most of his writings, Knox based his statements on Scripture, using not only Psalm 6, but also Jeremiah among other passages. He developed the theme that England transgressed worse than Judah in the days of Jeremiah, for he, Knox, had warned the Protestants repeatedly of troubles to come—but they had continued in their sinful ways. He urged the "true Christians" to flee in body and spirit from all fellowship with idolaters in

---

22. Knox, "Epistle to the Congregation of Berwick," 259.

their worship. Mass must not be attended, even if commanded by Mary herself. The faithful were to denounce idolatry not secretly, but openly as Daniel had done. Normally such reforms would be regarded as treason, but Knox—citing Jeremiah 37 where the prophets predicted the capture of Jerusalem—said God's prophet could advocate treason against political authorities and yet not sin. And those obeying the prophets in rejecting the Mass would not be offending God.[23]

Knox's argument in *A Godly Letter* centered on two related theological concepts: the covenant obligation and corporate responsibility for sin. Implicit in these ideas was Knox's emphasis on divine immutability, his Old Testament hermeneutic, and his definition of idolatry. Knox used the covenant to remedy idolatry. The covenant with God required the Christian to separate from any form of worship not expressly warranted in Scripture, specifically the Roman Mass. At this point the covenant responsibility required only passive disobedience, for Knox expressly prohibited Christians from taking up arms.[24]

Of even more importance, Knox developed an idea that played such a major role in his later doctrine: a people or nation incurred corporate guilt for even tolerating evil, namely "idolatrous" Catholicism. Knox prophesied that if Catholicism were maintained in England because people permitted it, the nation would be subject to divine judgment—namely plagues. To support this prediction, Knox cited an example of God's punishing the entire tribe of Benjamin, not because all were adulterers, but because they tolerated them.[25] In later writings, especially *A Letter to the Commonalty* (1558), Knox applied this principle to idolatrous government. Here he said God punished people for not revolting against idolatrous rulers. By 1554 when *A Godly Letter* was completed, Knox's thought on resistance had progressed to include the following. One, Christians must separate from idolatry or suffer divine judgments; two, believers were to openly denounce idolatry, but they must not take up arms; and three, a nation incurred corporate guilt for even tolerating idolatry though Knox did not specify how they should resist.

---

23. *Works*, 3:166, 168, 170, 175, 178, 184–88, 190–94; Ridley, *John Knox*, 173–78; Reid, *Trumpeter of God*, 107–10; Greaves, "John Knox and Resistance Theory," 12–14; Burns, "The Political Ideas of the Scottish Reformation," 254. Knox had been studying Jeremiah with the help of Calvin's commentary. See *Works*, 3:201. See also Kyle and Johnson, *John Knox*, 69–71.

24. In *A Godly Letter*, Knox's references to the covenant are many: *Works*, 3:191–93, 195–97, 212, 214. For support of passive resistance see *Works*, 3:192, 194.

25. *Works*, 3:189–90.

The Road to Resistance

Did Knox call for open resistance against an idolatrous monarch by the civil magistrates? In *A Godly Letter*, he said that "every Civil Magistrate" in England had the duty to slay all idolaters. Unfortunately the term *Civil Magistrate* is ambiguous. J. H. Burns believes it meant the monarch who, if idolatrous, could not be punished by any other authority. Richard Greaves says the term meant the civil magistrate in a broad sense, allowing revolt by designated people but not the populace in general.

Knox's statement permits no dogmatism, but the latter interpretation is more feasible for several reasons. First, Knox's words *every* magistrate and *all* idolaters seem to indicate active resistance by the civil magistrates in a sense broader than the monarch. Second, if Knox did revolt at St. Andrews, the latter view would help justify such a deed. Third, in a prior letter to Mrs. Bowes, Knox implied that magistrates—and not private citizens—could slay idolaters; but the monarch was not mentioned as either slaying or being slain. Thus it would seem that by this time Knox had cautiously adopted the constitutional theory of lawful resistance already embraced by several continental Lutherans and Calvinists, which permitted revolt by only the lesser magistrates.[26]

Nevertheless, Knox would not explicitly spell out a definite course of action in the case of an idolatrous monarch until 1558. It is also important to note that Knox blamed the return to idolatry on the nobility and the leading bishops of the old regime. He did not attack Mary herself, but seemed to hope that she would turn toward Protestantism.[27] Furthermore, though *A Godly Letter* pointed to future resistance, divine retribution was the more imminent threat.

Questions for the Swiss Reformers

At this point Knox's mind was unsettled. He left Dieppe and first arrived in Geneva some time in March 1554 and immediately approached Calvin with certain questions regarding disobedience. Calvin received Knox cordially, answered his questions verbally, and sent him on to Viret in

---

26. *Works*, 3:194–93; Burns, "The Political Ideas of the Scottish Reformation," 254; Greaves, "John Knox and Resistance Theory," 13–14; Danner, "Christopher Goodman and the English Protestant Tradition of Civil Obedience," 67.

27. Such an argument is borne out by *A Confession and Declaration of Prayers*, probably written in England but published along with *A Godly Letter*. In a *Confession, or Prayer*, attached to it, Knox lamented Edward VI's death but prayed God would illuminate Mary's heart. *Works*, 3:107.

PART THREE: Political Considerations

Lausanne and finally to Bullinger in Zurich.[28] Knox submitted four specific questions to Calvin, Bullinger, and presumably Viret. One, was the son of a king who inherited the throne as a minor a lawful magistrate and thus deserving of obedience by divine right? Two, could a woman ruling by divine right transfer the same authority to her husband? Here Knox—in an obvious reference to Mary Tudor and her husband Philip II of Spain—did not question divine right as such, but only as it pertained to a woman ruler and her foreign husband. Three, must people obey a magistrate who sought to enforce idolatry, and may local authorities holding a town by force lawfully resist such orders? Knox now touched on critical points in the political theory of the Swiss reformers: the issues of the right of revolt allowed to lower magistrates and the propriety of passive disobedience. Four, may Christians lawfully support a nobility who are resisting an idolatrous ruler? These queries indicate the direction in which Knox's thought on rebellion was moving.[29]

Calvin gave a negative answer to the crucial third question. Under no circumstances whatever may subjects justifiably resist an idolatrous ruler by armed force.[30] When Knox reached Zurich, Bullinger responded in writing and his answers were more encouraging than Knox might have expected. To Knox's first question, Bullinger designated Edward VI as a true monarch who should be obeyed. He gave a more evasive answer to the second question. Divine law ordains that a woman be a subject, not a ruler; but if she succeeds to the throne—it would be dangerous for pious individuals to rebel. Yet Bullinger gave Knox some room to maneuver at this point; for as he noted, Scripture spoke of nations being ruled by Deborah and other women. If a ruler is impious and tyrannical, "the Lord will in his own time destroy unjust governments by his own people, to whom he will supply proper qualifications for this purpose, as he formerly did to Jerubbaal, and the Maccabees and Jehoiada." Bullinger answered the crucial third question with less equivocation. He stated that the Christian

---

28. Calvin's and Bullinger's answers were given to a certain Scotsman and Knox was not named specifically. This vagueness has given rise to the speculation that Goodman might have been the Scotsman mentioned. The evidence, however, overwhelmingly supports the view that Knox was the Scotsman designated. *Works*, 2:219; Burns, "Knox and Bullinger," 90–91.

29. *Works*, 3:221–26. Knox's questions to Bullinger are not extant, but Bullinger repeated the questions in a letter to Calvin. In May 1554 Knox mentioned his trip through Switzerland and that he reasoned with the leaders on religious questions.

30. Ridley, *John Knox*, 179.

must not obey a king or ruler who condemns the "true religion" and enforces idolatry.

The Zurich reformer's answer clearly stressed passive disobedience, but he did open the door to resistance. The godly, particularly the magistrate, ought to resist a king even at the risk of their lives: "For the Holy Scripture not only permits, but even enjoins upon the magistrate a just and necessary defense." Yet Bullinger added a note of caution: Resistance by hypocrites under godly pretexts must be avoided. This admonition demonstrates why Bullinger said that specific cases of rebellion must be determined by the circumstances. On the fourth point, Bullinger gave Knox little help at all. When ought "true Christians" support a godly nobility fighting an idolatrous king? This issue must be decided according to the particular circumstances of each case.[31] As for Viret, his answers are unknown.

Did the Swiss reformers encourage or discourage Knox from rebellion? Once again only conjecture can be made, but the Swiss trip did not discourage Knox measurably. Whether it delayed or advanced his resistance theory must remain a point of debate.[32] On one hand, *A Faithful Admonition*—written after his Swiss trip—contained no new resistance doctrine, but continued in the theme of *A Godly Letter.* On the other hand, its language and implications were more radical. Therefore, *A Faithful Admonition* seems to show that Knox's thought had already incorporated the basis for resistance. Nevertheless, events had to push him into a full-blown resistance theory.

WRITINGS BEFORE THE OUTBURST

Knox left Switzerland and probably arrived in Dieppe in early 1554. Here cheering news did not greet him. Not only had Mary ousted the Anglican bishops from office and jailed many; but numerous laity—particularly the nobility—were now returning to Romanism. In response to this

---

31. *Works*, 3:221–26.

32. Those contending that Calvin and Bullinger's answers delayed Knox's conversion to resistance are Burns, "John Knox and Revolution," 568; Burns, "Knox and Bullinger," 91; Vesey, "The Sources of Knox's Political Theory," 236 (cf. 145–51); Allen, *Political Thought*, 108. Those breaking from the traditional position and viewing Bullinger's answers as satisfactory to Knox include: Greaves, "John Knox and Resistance Theory," 5–6, 17; Ridley, *John Knox*, 180. Vander Molen sees Bullinger's answers as disappointing to Knox, but Knox still respected them. Vander Molen, "Anglican Against Puritan," 55.

PART THREE: Political Considerations

discouraging situation, Knox wrote *Two Comforting Epistles* in Dieppe on May 10 and 31. Their general theme said that both before and after Christ's resurrection, the church was in a state of great depression because of persecution. Yet God eventually gave victory. Likewise, the Protestants in England should look forward to ultimate triumph.

Knox's views on political matters continued to take shape. In the first epistle, he not only threatened divine vengeance against Catholics primarily by plagues but also by human instruments. Yet he did not specify "whom God shall use to execute his wrath." Undoubtedly, at this point he was thinking of the common people—i.e., those outside the noble class. Knox also reiterated advice given in *A Godly Letter*: Christians must suffer patiently and completely break fellowship with idolaters. Furthermore, Knox apparently tried to strengthen Protestants against the charge that they were traitors because they did not submit to the queen's religious policy. He pointed out: "that all is not lawful nor just that is statute by Civil laws, neither yet is (sic) everything sin before God, which ungodly persons allege to be treason."[33]

The second epistle repeated the same basic themes—judgment by plagues, patient suffering, separation from idolatry, and vengeance by a divinely called instrument. Still, Knox cautioned Protestants not to take the law into their own hands: "presume not to be revengers of your own cause." At this time he wanted no popular revolution. While Protestants were allowed no carnal hatred, they must exercise a spiritual hatred and pray, as Jeremiah prayed, for vengeance upon their enemies—the Catholics: "as God is immutable, so assuredly shall he stir up one Jehu or other to execute his vengeance upon blood-thirsty tyrants and obstinate idolaters." In this statement Knox made a distinction between private and public vengeance. The Christian must forgive injuries committed against himself, but not against the Protestant religion. He must love his personal enemies, but hate the enemies of the evangelical faith. The notes of the 1558 Geneva Bible would also place emphasis on such a distinction.[34]

Having written *Two Comfortable Epistles*, Knox stayed in Dieppe for several months. During this interval he wrote *A Faithful Admonition*, one of his longest publications up to this time. Persecution in England became more violent, and Knox realized that Mary would stop at nothing to blot out the Protestant heresy. Stanford Reid maintains that Knox's thought

---

33. *Works*, 3:231–32, 234, 236; Reid, *Trumpeter of God*, 112, 133; Greaves, "John Knox, and Resistance Theory," 14–15; Ridley, *John Knox*, 183.

34. *Works*, 3:239, 244–45, 247; Ridley, *John Knox*, 183.

underwent a radical change at this time, and perhaps this pamphlet represented a turning point in his religio-political views.³⁵ If *radical change* means a rash of threats, prayers for vengeance, a favorable attitude toward regicide, direct attacks on the monarch, and political appeals—then radicalization increased. Yet if advocating popular rebellion is connoted, this development had to wait.

A Faithful Admonition

In a *Faithful Admonition*, Knox used all the epithets that could possibly condemn the English monarchy in the eyes of the Protestants. He openly railed against the leading Catholic bishops—Edmund Bonner, Cuthbert Tunstall, and Stephen Gardiner. Such attacks on Catholic bishops were commonplace in the tracts of other Protestant pamphleteers; but none criticized Mary, for they recoiled from violating the doctrine of Christian obedience. Yet Knox attacked Mary and, in the process, shocked many of his Protestants as well as Catholics. He classified the monarchy and the supporting ecclesiastics as a tyranny rather than as a rightful government: "those bloody tyrants within the realm of England do kill, murder, destroy, and devour man and woman, as ravenous lions now loosed from bonds." Furthermore, Knox compared Mary with "Jezebel, that cursed idolatrous woman"; and accused the queen of hanging twice as many English subjects as Jezebel had among the Israelites. Knox's violent hatred for both Catholicism and Mary Tudor, which would explode several years later in *The First Blast*, becomes evident in *A Faithful Admonition*.³⁶

Moreover, in *A Faithful Admonition* Knox entered the political arena more directly—not as a political theorist or as a political reformer, but rather as a prophet speaking against the persecution of God's elect. By most criteria—religious, national, legal, military, economic, and social—Knox condemned Mary as a traitor.³⁷ Diplomatically, the accession of Mary Tudor in England meant much more than the replacement of a Protestant by a Catholic sovereign. It signified the accession of a queen who was half Spanish herself and who—less than three months after her

---

35. Reid, *Trumpeter of God*, 114.

36. *Works*, 3:286, 293–96, 298; Vander Molen, "Anglican Against Puritan," 55; Greaves, "John Knox and Resistance Theory," 15–16. See also Greaves, "John Knox and the Ladies," 9–10.

37. *Works*, 3:295–96; Reid, *Trumpeter of God*, 116; Burns, "John Knox and Revolution," 568; Burns, "The Political Ideas of the Scottish Reformation," 255.

succession to the throne—was promised in marriage to the emperor's son, Philip of Spain. The marriage took place in July 1554.[38]

Under such conditions Knox blatantly appealed to English nationalism to gain support for his accusations, charging that Mary and her bishops had betrayed England to Spain. Knox exhorted the people to view their government as a Spanish one rather than English. He referred to the queen as one who "bears a Spaniard's heart," and asked Bishop Gardner why they "would have a Spaniard to reign over England." Furthermore, Knox related nationalism to a type of the covenant. He implied the essence of the covenant (social compact) between monarch and people based on national law and custom. Knox saw Mary's marriage to a Spaniard as a violation of her covenant with the English people and for this union he castigated her.[39]

Nevertheless, Knox's broadest condemnation of the English government said that England was repeating the history of Israel. Throughout the pamphlet he continually applied Old Testament prophecies to contemporary English life and constantly referred to Jewish heroes who had risen up as rebels to overthrow evil, idolatrous rulers. Knox did not appeal for a popular insurrection, but he repeated the themes of previous letters, praying for God to "stir up some Phinehas, Elijah, or Jehu" to overthrow the Catholic regime.[40]

In the meantime, Knox warned the Protestants not to attend Mass, even if such refusal meant death or exile. Though at this point he did not call for a popular revolt, he did indicate a willingness to accept any method God provided: "By what means that he shall perform that his merciful work, it neither appertains to you to demand, nor to me to defend."[41] While Knox still taught that a private citizen had no right or duty to remove an unfaithful monarch, he had now moved beyond the Swiss reformers. In fact, it occurred to the reformer that if during the reign of Edward VI the Protestant government had put Mary to death, she would not now be in a position to persecute Protestants. Such a reference led Knox's critics to accuse him of demanding regicide.[42]

---

38. McRoberts, ed., *Essays on the Scottish Reformation*, 14.

39. *Works*, 3:295–97, 308–9; Vander Molen, "Anglican Against Puritan," 55; Greaves, "The Knoxian Paradox," 96.

40. *Works*, 3:274–75, 282–83, 293, 308–9.

41. *Works*, 3:325; Greaves, "John Knox and Resistance Theory," 15–16.

42. *Works*, 3:293–95; Ridley, *John Knox*, 186–87.

The Road to Resistance

After delivering his *Faithful Admonition* in July 1554, Knox left Dieppe for Geneva. Here he planned to spend his time studying Greek and Hebrew and acquiring a deeper knowledge of Calvin's theology. In the next year or so because Knox was occupied in studies, church quarrels, and missionary labors, he wrote little relevant to his political views. About the time he left for Geneva, the Marian government intensified its persecution of Protestants.

Consequently Knox, prior to settling in Geneva, found himself thrust into the quarrels of these exiles at Frankfurt. The city authorities at Frankfurt expelled Knox, and he became associated with English Puritanism and at odds with the exiled Anglican establishment. This division plus a more encouraging situation in Scotland seemed to turn the reformer's thoughts away from England and toward his homeland.[43]

Knox returned from Frankfurt to Geneva in April 1555, but he did not settle in Geneva for long. He had only been there four months when he returned to Scotland. A situation had developed in Scotland that afforded great opportunities for the spread of Protestant doctrines. Circumstances had also changed in Scotland. Mary of Guise, the Queen Dowager, was attempting to arrange a marriage agreement between her daughter Mary Queen of Scots and the French Dauphin Francis. For this she needed the consent of the Scottish Parliament. Mary of Guise, desiring the success of this project, sought the approval of the Scottish nobility. Such nobles had Protestant sympathies, thus Mary of Guise pursued a friendly policy toward them. Therefore, French and family considerations took precedent over the preservation of Catholicism.[44]

Under these conditions Knox went to Scotland and spent nearly a year there, establishing congregations and performing general pastoral duties. In this context he wrote little relating to his political views. He did, however, pen *A Letter to the Queen Dowager*. The author of *A Faithful Admonition* now changed his style and addressed Mary of Guise with the proper respect. Two years earlier he had shocked even his friends by his fearless attack on Mary Tudor and his denunciation of the doctrine of obedience to rulers. Still, the situation was different in Scotland and the ever pragmatic Knox urged Mary of Guise to use her royal authority to establish the Reformation.

Therefore, he again mentioned the principle that toleration of sin was actually sin itself. He also emphasized that honor and obedience be given

---

43. Vander Molen, "Anglican Against Puritan," 45–47, especially 55ff.
44. McRoberts, *Scottish Reformation*, 13–16; Ridley, *John Knox*, 220–23.

PART THREE: Political Considerations

to magistrates in all things lawful. Moreover, Knox insisted that the rulers' duties included those of supporting "true religion," protecting Reformed preachers, and correcting the "negligence of bishops," and that failure in these functions would mean external pain and punishment. Yet he gave no hint of temporal or political sanction. Mary of Guise, however, apparently failed to take Knox's letter seriously because she referred to it in a derisive manner.[45]

---

45. *Works*, 4:78–79. Mary of Guise, having read Knox's letter, gave it to James Beaton, the Archbishop of Glasgow, and said to him: "Please you my Lord, to read a pasquil"—a pasquil being the name given in Rome to lampoons and satires. Knox referred to the Queen's remarks in both his *History* and in a second letter that he wrote to Mary of Guise in 1558. See *Works*, 1:252; 4:457.

11

Shocking Politics and Idolatrous Rulers

AFTER SPENDING A YEAR in Scotland, Knox sailed for Dieppe in July 1556. He stayed for a few weeks and then with his family made his way to Geneva. Why he left for Geneva is not entirely clear. While he faced some danger in Scotland, the threat was no greater than before. In fact, affairs in Scotland were improved. The answer probably lies in the fact that his congregation of English refugees in Geneva called him. Still, that "little flock" did not lack preachers, and their needs did not compare to reforming the entire nation of Scotland. The call of this congregation, however, was important and Knox did enjoy the peaceful years in Geneva.

During the last leg of his exile years (1556–59), Knox produced some of his most contentious political writings plus a major attack on the Anabaptists in which he defended predestination. Some of these works were penned in Geneva and some in Dieppe. What prompted these writings? Knox's outburst against political rulers had been a long time coming, but the explosion came in the late 1550s. During these years, Mary Tudor's persecution of Protestants in England intensified. Elsewhere in Europe, the Catholic forces were on the march and the survival of Protestantism hung by a thread.[1]

The English refugees in Geneva, including Knox, were in close touch with these events. Such developments pushed Knox over the edge. He abandoned the time honored duty to obey the secular rulers and at worst to engage in passive resistance to idolatrous commands. Instead, Knox advocated rebellion against idolatrous (Catholic) rulers. What prompted

---

1. Much of this chapter had been drawn from two sources. See Kyle and Johnson, *John Knox*, 92–108; Kyle, *The Mind of Knox*, 263–76.

PART THREE: Political Considerations

his outburst against the Anabaptists is more debatable and not the subject of this study.[2]

WRITINGS FROM DIEPPE

Knox arrived in Geneva in September of 1556 and spent the winter there. In May 1557 he received letters from the Scottish lords urging him to return because the situation, as they described it, seemed conducive to Protestantism. Knox reluctantly left Geneva and reached Dieppe in October intending to take the first ship to Scotland. But here a letter informed him that the Protestant nobility had reconsidered their invitation, and urged him to wait in Dieppe for a final decision on the matter. The Queen Regent's negotiations for the marriage of Mary Queen of Scots to the Dauphin had reached a critical stage, and the nobility believed Knox's preaching would impair a successful bargain.

The sudden change in plans had a radical effect on Knox's thinking. He now had to face two questions. Could one depend on the Scottish nobility to reform religion? Were the common people responsible to bring about "true religion"? The nobles now attempted to bring about some kind of compromise with Mary of Guise because they felt they could not effect a reformation of religion by force. On the other hand, Knox believed no compromise was possible. Why? In his eyes, the Queen Regent was a Guise dedicated to the maintenance of French and Catholic power in Scotland.[3]

First Letter

While Knox indignantly waited in Dieppe during the closing months of 1557, he wrote three letters that revealed his state of mind just prior to his vigorous pamphleteering of 1558. In the first letter, dated October 27, Knox set forth a bold conception of the nobles' constitutional and religious functions in society. Previously, he said magistrates must establish "true religion." Apparently, he now considered the nobility as magistrates and included them in that task. The nobles were entitled to be called "princes

---

2. For more on Knox and the Anabaptists, see Kyle and Johnson, *John Knox*, 111–34; Kyle, "John Knox Confronts the Anabaptists," 493–515.

3. Reid, *Trumpeter of God*, 142–43; Ryrie, *The Origins of the Scottish Reformation*, 148–49.

of the people" by reason of their office and duties and not because of their bloodline.

The nobles' responsibilities were twofold: they must protect their citizens and establish true religion. And they must carry out these functions even in the face of royal opposition. Here Knox advocated a course of action that ran counter to the doctrine of Christian obedience. He stated that the nobility were duty bound to compel the kings to introduce a reformation. But he did not specify the means—whether physical or moral—by which this compulsion should be applied.[4]

While waiting in Dieppe, Knox's worse fears were confirmed. He received news that the lords were using the Protestant movement for purely a selfish end. The role of Chaterlherault especially aroused his mistrust. Knox feared Chaterlherault—"who in the beginning of his authority and government began to profess Christ's truth, but suddenly sliding back, became one cruel persecutor of Christ's members"—would use the Congregation to further the dynastic ambitions of the House of Hamilton.[5] Four years earlier, Bullinger had warned Knox the nobles might rebel against the monarch under the guise of religion, although their motives were worldly.

Third Letter

Knox's second letter (December 1) addressed *To the Professors of Truth in Scotland*, said little in regard to political theory. But in the third letter (December 17), he attempted to clarify his thinking on the subject of rebellion for righteousness sake. He cautioned the Protestants not to "disobey or displease the established authority in things lawful." Yet at the same time, they must openly confess their faith and seek government support in furthering Protestantism or, at least, its toleration.

If the government, however, failed to reform religion, Protestants should take several steps. They must make a public declaration of their obedience to the crown "in all things not plainly repugning to God." Following that, they must demand the free preaching of the gospel and the proper administration of the sacraments. Knox also instructed the nobles—even in the face of royal opposition—to defend their Protestant

---

4. *Works*, 1:272. The first of the three letters to the nobility is found in Knox's *History* while the last two are found in *Works*, 4:262–86. See footnote 28 of this chapter, which cites a quotation in the body.

5. *Works*, 4:285.

subjects from persecution at all costs. He concluded by warning the Protestants against cooperating with those seeking their own profit.[6]

In these letters to the Protestants, Knox specifically appealed to the nobility and not to the magistrates. Why? Knox probably considered the nobility to be magistrates with the authority to suppress an idolatrous monarch. These letters show Knox continuing down the road to rebellion but with reservations. Even in late 1557, he had emphasized obedience at least as much as resistance, and he did not completely trust the aristocracy to bring about the Reformation.[7]

An Apology

The tensions in Knox's mind were evident even in his additions and preface to *An Apology* for Protestants imprisoned in Paris (December 1557). In the preface he referred to the problem dominating his thought—the duty of obedience and resistance to rulers. Knox denied that Protestantism was seditious. Rather Protestants, as he claimed, had always upheld the honor of rulers. Indeed they affirmed that every individual, "be he Pope or cardinal," must obey emperors, kings, and rulers.

In *An Apology*, Knox was more reticent about the rights of subjects to resist rulers than he had been in *A Faithful Admonition* (1554), probably because the circumstances had changed. Knox now desired to impress the authorities that Protestants were not traitors. He had no interest, nevertheless, in merely replacing a corrupt pope with an equally corrupt prince. Rather, Knox desired a religious reformation and he would not approve of any prince or king who failed to further this cause. He urged "that either Princes be reformed, and be compelled also to reform their wicked laws, or else that good men depart from their service." By this statement he meant that Protestants should resign from the service of Catholic kings.[8]

It is understandable that Knox had doubts as he formulated his religious doctrine to justify revolution. Though precedents to armed resistance existed both in fact and theory, Tyndale's doctrine still held sway. Knox must have been under great pressure from not only the leaders of

---

6. *Works*, 4:284–85.

7. Burns, "The Political Ideas of the Scottish Reformation," 258; Greaves, "John Knox, The Reformed Tradition, and Resistance Theory," 19; Reid, *Trumpeter of God*, 143, 145. In a letter to Cecil, Knox also seemed to consider the nobility as magistrates with the authority to suppress idolatry. *Works*, 6:32.

8. *Works*, 4:297–309, 324–25, 327.

the Church of England in exile but also from Calvin, whom he greatly admired.

Such caution also had a complex political background in the negotiations between the Lords of the Congregation and the Queen Regent. It is just possible, however, that the magnitude of what Knox contemplated caused him to hesitate. He wrote four revolutionary, political pamphlets in 1558, and one of them created a greater uproar than anything that had been published in Europe since Luther's three great treatises.[9]

Circumstances, however, propelled Knox past any hesitancy he might have had. Politically, the rapid progress of the negotiations for the French marriage of Mary Queen of Scots alarmed Knox. In religion, the continuing persecution in England right up until Mary Tudor's death added fuel to the flames. Personally, there was the rudeness with which Mary of Guise received his courteous letter of 1556, and of his being burnt in effigy by the clerical authorities after his departure from Scotland. Moreover, he had experienced four years of exilic turmoil. Besides, at this time chances for a successful revolution in Scotland were improving.

THE FIRST BLAST OF THE TRUMPET

Yet Knox's hesitation was more apparent than real. By December of 1557 he had already begun work in Dieppe on *The First Blast of the Trumpet Against the Monstrous Regiment of Women*, published secretly in Geneva in the spring of 1558. As Knox looked at the situation in Scotland and England, he saw the malevolent work of the female sex. Women had usurped the natural authority of men and were now causing problems for "true believers." This situation particularly applied to England. Here Mary Tudor had actually handed the kingdom over to her husband Philip of Spain, thus placing it in bondage to the most militantly Catholic power in Europe.[10]

Central Thesis

The central thesis of *The First Blast* said that it violated the law of God, as well as of nature, for a woman to rule a kingdom. Moreover, a female

---

9. Ridley, *John Knox*, 225, 264; Burns, "John Knox and Revolution," 569–70.

10. Knox's *History* provided a background for that period of time. *Works*, 1:248–312; Burns, "John Knox and Revolution," 571; McRoberts, ed., *Essays on the Scottish Reformation* 15–16.

ruler could not even turn over the power of government to her husband, particularly if he were a foreign monarch: "To promote a Woman to bear rule, superiority, dominion, or empire above any Realm, Nation, or city, is repugnant to Nature; contumely to God, a thing contrary to his revealed will and approved ordinance; and finally, it is the subversion of good order, of all equity and justice."[11]

The First Blast gained for Knox a reputation among his contemporaries of being a revolutionary, and among later generations of being a woman hater. Knox's misogynist image, however, is not accurate because—outside of *The First Blast*—his writings contained few denunciations of the female sex. On the contrary, out of Knox's surviving letters, more than half were written to women and many of them showed a high regard for the female gender.[12]

In fact, Knox's attack on female sovereigns was by no means original. Similar views were expressed for antagonism to a woman ruler ran high in the sixteenth century. Despite the fact that there had been several female sovereigns in Europe at that time, or perhaps because of it, many feared the consequences of a woman ruler.[13] The inferiority and subjection of women to men were both accepted in theory and in practice in all ranks of society. Paradoxically, society considered women ineligible for any public office except that of head of state. In *The First Blast*, Knox exposed the illogical nature of this system, which was to continue for another three hundred and fifty years. In doing so, he attacked the special position of the crown. Some theologians taught—though women must obey men in all areas of life—men must obey a queen as they would a male sovereign. In teaching this idea, they believed the divinely ordained power of the monarchy was strong enough to prevail over the divinely ordained power

---

11. *Works*, 4:373, 413.

12. It would seem that Knox preferred the company and friendship of women to that of men. He married twice and was on cordial terms with several others (e.g., Mrs. Bowes, Mrs. Locke, Mrs. Hickman, and Janet Adamson). On the other hand, Christopher Goodman appeared to be the only man for whom Knox felt a personal affection. *Works*, 3:155-58, 338-97; 5:227-34; 6:4-97; Ridley, *John Knox*, 267; Greaves, "John Knox and the Ladies, or the Controversy over Gynecocracy," 8-9.

13. The sixteenth century saw Mary Tudor as queen of England, Margaret of Austria and Mary of Hungary as regents in the Netherlands, Mary of Guise as regent in Scotland, and Catherine de' Medici as regent in France. Elizabeth Tudor and Mary Stewart became queens in England and Scotland respectively after Knox wrote *The First Blast*. See Greaves, "Controversy over Gynecocracy," 8-9.

of men over women. Because *The First Blast* directly challenged this notion, many considered it to be seditious.[14]

Intellectual Sources

In the preface of *The First Blast,* Knox criticized the "Watchmen of England" for their negligence in not warning the people about the sin of establishing a woman ruler.[15] Then he assumed the role of a watchman, believing himself to be called of God to this function. In supporting the proposition that a woman is not fit to rule, Knox used three sources: the Word of God, the ancient writers, and the ordinance of nature.

Though Knox used Scripture at large, he especially employed Pauline passages to support his contention "that woman in her greatest perfection was made to serve and obey man, not to rule and command him." Understandably, he stressed the doctrine of original sin in asserting that woman's subordinate position came by the sentence of God: "Thy will shall be subject to thy husband and he shall bear dominion over thee."[16] If, as Knox wondered, Scripture forbade female rule in home and the church, how could women have authority over an entire nation? Knox, along with many medieval thinkers, resorted to the writings of such church fathers as Tertullian, Augustine, Ambrose, and Chrysostom in order to place the female sex in a subordinate position.[17]

In addition, Knox made much more in *The First Blast* than in any of his earlier works concerning the concepts of nature and natural law. Female government, he alleged, is "repugnant to Nature" and an absurdity. If man were to submit to the rule of a woman, then he would do what no other species had done, for no male was prepared to be governed by his female: "For nature has in all beasts printed a certain mark of dominion in the male, and a certain subjection in the female, which they keep inviolate. For no man ever saw the lion make obedience, and stoop before the lioness...." Conversely, man—"who has been appointed by God to have dominion over women—has to his own shame and in violation of God's appointed order" stoop[ed] under obedience of woman...."[18]

14. Ridley, *John Knox*, 269–70.
15. *Works*, 4:365–71.
16. *Works*, 4:377–78. Some Pauline passages employed by Knox were 1 Corinthians 11 and 14; 1 Timothy 2.
17. *Works*, 4:381–86.
18. *Works*, 4:393.

Knox's premise, that female rule had subverted both the divine and natural order, did not seem so startling. What alarmed Europe was his conclusion: "The faithful, if afflicted by a female sovereign, "ought to remove from honor and authority that monster in nature," and if any support her they ought to "execute against them the sentence of death."[19] Using Old Testament prototypes, Knox cited the case of Athaliah to spur the nobility into action. Jehoiada, the high priest (Knox) had called upon the captain and chief rulers of the people to depose Athaliah (Mary Tudor) and place Joash on the throne. Knox pointed out to the nobility that the faithful Jews had executed both Athaliah and the high priest of Baal (Stephen Gardner).

Implications

At this point Knox introduced a major departure in his teaching. The duty of removing a female sovereign falls not only upon the nobility as estates, but also upon the people—especially the lairds and burgesses who favor Protestantism. His general argument said that "God by his own word has appointed an order" in the body politic. And if female rule perverts that order, the community acting either for themselves or through their authorized leaders must restore it. Moreover, not only must Mary be removed, but all those supporting her must be executed.

In this idea, a principle emerged that Knox would make more of in *The Appellation*—he no longer considered tyrannicide as the exclusive mission of divinely inspired individuals, but the vocation of every saint who would assume it. Previously, Knox had established the principle that it was sin to even tolerate sin. He now applied this precept to a female ruler. *Not* to revolt against an idolatrous ruler was "plain rebellion against God."[20]

To incite the nobility and common people to revolt against and even execute an idolatrous female sovereign was a revolutionary idea. Even more radical were the implications of such a principle if it were more broadly applied. In *The First Blast*, however, Knox tempered these principles by allowing for exceptions. He advocated no rebellion against either a male sovereign or even a Protestant queen. He brushed the counterexample of the biblical Deborah aside with the argument that an exceptional case did

---

19. *Works*, 4:415–16.

20. *Works*, 4:415–16. See also Greaves, "John Knox and Resistance Theory," 19–20; Burns, "The Political Ideas of the Scottish Reformation," 260; Walzer, *The Revolution of the Saints*, 108.

Shocking Politics and Idolatrous Rulers

not establish a general rule. Still, he acknowledged that God, at times, exempted women from their subordinate status. Knox wrote *The First Blast* before Elizabeth's accession, and Deborah was not then the favorite figure of Protestant writers. In any case, Knox minimized her importance at this time.[21] In subsequent writings, however, he amplified his view of Deborah as an exception, even as he extended the principle of active resistance to male sovereigns.

Reaction

Christendom was appalled at *The First Blast*. Though some of Knox's contemporaries agreed with his attack on female rule, many disagreed with his radical solutions.[22] Catholics, of course, very much opposed the views expressed, for they struck at both Mary Tudor and Mary Stewart. Yet this resistance surprised no one. More important to Knox was the criticism raised by Protestants of all shades. The remnants of the English congregation in Frankfurt were quite upset and attempted to excuse Knox. Calvin refused to take any responsibility for the Scottish reformer's views. As he explained to Cecil in 1559, he had not read the book until over a year after its publication and earlier had cautioned Knox against taking too radical a position in regard to female rule.

The stir caused from *The First Blast* came as much from its timing as from the argument itself. Knox directed *The First Blast* against Mary Tudor—despite the generality of the title—and she died a few months after its publication. Elizabeth was naturally indignant at *The First Blast*. In view of the weakness of her position, Knox embarrassed her by calling into question the basis of her rule. Despite some tactless efforts by Knox to make amends for his blunder, Elizabeth never forgave him.[23]

---

21. *Works*, 4:403-4, 406-8. Knox contended that Deborah did not usurp the magistrate's authority, but rather she judged Israel and rebuked idolatry by the Word of God and not by temporal authority.

22. *Works*, 4:351-62; Burns, "John Knox and Revolution," 571. On this subject, Knox's colleagues Goodman, Whittingham, and Gilby were certainly in accord with him. Furthermore, Bishop Ponet insisted that women should not rule.

23. *Works*, 6:15-21. Quite appropriate was the comment by John Aylmer, one of the Anglican exiles. He insisted that *The First Blast* would have been acceptable if limited to the person of Mary Tudor, but since it was not, "The Blast was blown out of season." *Works*, 4:355-56. In a letter to Cecil, Knox acknowledged that he had become odious to Elizabeth. *Works*, 6:31; 4:357ff.; Ridley, *John Knox*, 381; Reid, *Trumpeter of God*, 148. Normally Calvin rejected female rule, but he was more flexible than Knox in regard to exceptions to this situation. See Holwerda, ed. *Exploring the Heritage of Calvin*, 236 ff.

PART THREE: Political Considerations

From 1559 to his death in 1572, Knox seldom mentioned the subject. Knox retained his views on gynecocracy, however, until the end of his life—even defending the thesis of *The First Blast* in 1568 and 1571. In 1571, he responded to those in the general Assembly who had accused him of contradicting the views he had enunciated in *The First Blast*. That treatise, he said, was "grounded upon good reason upon God's plain truth and upon most plain and just laws. . . ."

Though Knox defended his views on female rule to the end, the real object of his dislike was not merely female sovereigns per se—nor women in general—but Catholic monarchs, especially female Catholics. In the context of his time, and in the first of several outbursts in 1558 that would gradually refine his views, Knox understandably failed to make clear the ultimate object of his dislike. After all, the female rulers with whom he had experience were all Catholics—namely, Mary Tudor, Mary of Guise, Mary Stewart, and Catherine de' Medici. He had not yet encountered any sixteenth-century Deborahs.[24]

LETTER TO THE REGENT OF SCOTLAND

Knox did not feel the repercussions of *The First Blast* for several months because it took time for the book to circulate and for readers to discover the anonymous author. Meanwhile Knox's pen was busy. By the summer of 1558, he had published three tracts in Geneva that put forward his views on revolution even more clearly. He wrote one to Mary of Guise, one to the nobility, and the third to the common people of Scotland. Moreover, he appended the abortive *Second Blast* to his last tract.

In these works, Knox condemned Tyndale's doctrine of Christian obedience to rulers as sinful. Most sixteenth-century theologians urged the people to obey the monarch—not from fear of earthly punishment—but from fear of God. Knox now instructed the opposite. If the people obeyed the unjust commandments of evil rulers, they would receive a far more terrible punishment from God than any sovereign could inflict upon them. In earlier works, Knox implied the right of resistance. He now imposed upon the nobility, estates, and common people the duty of armed resistance to a Catholic sovereign.

---

24. *Works*, 6:594, 558-59. This citation is also for the quote in the preceding paragraph. Greaves, "Controversy over Gynecocracy," 15-16; Greaves, *Theology and Revolution*, 167-68; Healey, "John Knox's History: Complete Sermon on Christian Piety," 319-33.

While in Scotland in 1556, Knox had originally written a letter to the Queen Regent. But she ridiculed it. He now broadcast it again with additions that drove home his point more forcefully. The nature of the two letters was entirely different because of the harsh additions in the second. Knox's theme stated that the Queen Regent should cooperate in reforming the Scottish church because Romanism had corrupted it. If, however, she failed to perform this duty, God's judgment would befall her.

In this letter, Knox once again asserted the concept of corporate responsibility for consenting to sin. Divine judgment would fall on those maintaining tyranny "or that do consent to their beastly cruelty." Then he attacked what he considered to be a Satanic lie: The civil magistrate cannot reform religion because such matters are referred to the church. To support this position, Knox maintained that God has established the secular power to reform religion and check the transgressions of the church. Yet what if the state merely supports the idolatrous practices of the church? Then the people must resist. Even lowly individuals—if they speak as God's ambassadors—have the authority to rebuke princes for their transgressions. The vocation of the prophet (which Knox believed himself to be) is to condemn idolatrous rulers. This second letter to the regent, because of its personal nature, did not intend to incite rebellion. But it did, for the first time, present revolt as a general religious proposition. *The First Blast* had been more specific in its objective. Knox now repeated his assertion that the real treason was not to oppose an idolatrous monarch to the death.[25]

THE APPELLATION

Having little hope of receiving a favorable hearing from Mary of Guise, Knox next turned his attention to the nobles. What he had said to the Queen Regent, he now put more clearly in *The Appellation*. *The Appellation* hammered at two points. One, the nobility were obligated to actively oppose and punish idolatrous rulers. Two, all subjects were duty bound to actively resist and punish idolatrous rulers. This pamphlet took the form of an appeal from the sentence of Scottish bishops—who had tried Knox in *absentia* and burned him in effigy—to the nobles and Estates of Scotland. In theory, at least, Knox did not appeal to the nobility as a class to take arbitrary action, but to an established constitutional body.[26]

---

25. *Works*, 4:435–36, 441, 445, 452, 458–59.
26. *Works*, 4:469–70.

Part Three: Political Considerations

Civil Authority

Knox went to considerable lengths to sustain his charge that the establishment of "true religion" pertained not only to the ecclesiastical estate, but to the civil authority as well. In this context, he referred to the nobility as the civil power. In the "Commonwealth of Israel," the magistrate was superior to the priest. In all matters, Moses the magistrate prevailed over Aaron the priest. Knox went on to cite many godly kings of Judah and Israel as illustrations of temporal authorities interpreting God's law and reforming religion.[27]

With these numerous Old Testament precedents, Knox found it inconceivable for anyone to question the right of the magistrate—or more specifically of the nobility—to reform religion. And Knox was greatly concerned that the nobility fulfill these duties. He told the nobles to prevent bishops from persecuting Protestants, to ensure the "right" instruction in religion, and to depose and execute those defrauding the people of God's Word.[28] God honored the nobles by placing them above other people for the purpose of promoting his religion and not just to honor them. As Knox put it: "God . . . has appointed you to be his lieutenants, and by his own seal has marked you to be Magistrates, and to rule above your brethren, to whom nature . . . has made you like in all points." Thus it would be horrible ingratitude if "you should be found unfaithful to him [who] has honored you."[29]

If Knox had found a monarch to reform religion, he would not have turned to the nobility. But he found no such sovereign. He therefore emphasized that when a ruler fails to maintain true religion, the task falls to the nobility. The nobles are duty bound to perform this charge even if it means rebellion against their sovereign. In this notion Knox espoused a doctrine similar to what Beza and Viret had previously embraced. To the nobles Knox said, "Now if your King be a man ignorant of God, enemy to his true religion, . . . and a persecutor of Christ's members; shall you be excused, if with silence you pass over his iniquity?" Certainly not, retorted Knox. God did not place the nobility in authority to "flatter your king in his folly or blind rage." Rather they must assist the sovereign in

---

27. *Works*, 4:485–87.
28. *Works*, 4:481–82.
29. *Works*, 4:481.

areas honoring God but "correct and repress" him in matters "repugning God's Word."[30]

In *The Appellation*, Knox denounced the orthodox doctrine of Christian obedience as sinful. He declared blind compliance to a wicked command to be sin. God has not required obedience to rulers when they decree impiety. To say that God does is no less blasphemy than to make God the author of sin. Moreover, if nobles and people comply with their sovereign in manifest wickedness, they will be punished along with him.[31]

In *The Appellation*, Knox also laid the foundation for the theme of his *Letter to the Commonalty*, which declared, "None provoking the people to idolatry ought to be exempted from the punishment of death." The personal status of such an individual was of no consequence, be they monarch or commoner. Moreover, the punishment of idolatry and blasphemy does not pertain only to kings and rulers. Rather, it relates to all persons according to their Christian vocation and the opportunity afforded to them by God to administer vengeance. Citing Deuteronomy 13, Knox issued the call for revolution—he directed Moses' commandment to slay idolaters to all people, not just to the nobles.[32]

Yet Knox never called for indiscriminate slaughter. He distinguished between the treatment to be accorded idolaters, who had never known "true religion," and those who had known it but had forsaken it. The apostles did not put non-Christians to death because they had never known God's Word. It was different, nevertheless, for England. This nation had established Protestantism under Edward VI and then had backslidden into idolatry. All English subjects—nobility and commoners alike—should have revolted against Mary and executed her along with her priests and assistants. Knox did not advocate the slaying of all Catholics in Catholic states, but for an application of the death penalty by a Protestant government against Catholic counterrevolutionaries.[33]

Covenant Obligations

Knox's concept of disobedience—particularly his extension of active resistance to the people—occurred in a covenant context. In his *Godly Letter*,

---

30. *Works*, 4:495. Knox also opened the door to revolt in the case of a tyrant's oppressing the people.
31. *Works*, 4:495, 497–98.
32. *Works*, 4:499–501.
33. *Works*, 4:500, 507; Ridley, *John Knox*, 276.

Knox spoke of a covenant between God and the elect. The *Faithful Admonition* implied the existence of a league between the king and the people. In *The Appellation*, Knox now gave the covenant new political implications. Previously, the covenant obligation only demanded separation from idolatry. But now the godly (nobles and people) must punish idolatry.

The covenant provided an important theological argument for Knox. It enabled him to overcome the idea that only the lesser magistrates can revolt, thus leading him to advocate popular rebellion as a means for removing idolatry and tyranny. Knox insisted that not only the magistrates but the people are bound by the covenant to uphold the rule of godliness and to revenge any injustices done to God's majesty or laws. The covenant binds not only the chief rulers but the whole people to punish idolatry and tyranny.

The Appellation witnessed three types of the covenant, all designed to promote true worship. A covenant existed between the sovereign and the people of Scotland, and Knox included the nobility in this covenant. Along with the monarch, they have obligations to the people to support "true religion." Furthermore, Knox saw a covenant between God and the nobles and magistrates to reform religion. Lastly, he still maintained the notion of a covenant between God and the people. This covenant provided the basis for his *Letter to the Commonality*[34]

LETTER TO THE COMMONALTY

Did Knox depend solely on the nobility? No! Because he felt the nobility had let him down before, he refused to leave the reformation of religion solely in their hands. He therefore penned *A Letter to the Commonalty*. He did not address this pamphlet to the lower classes—whom he designated elsewhere as a "rascal multitude"—but more to the middle class, that is the lairds and burgesses. Though the nobility were powerful, the middle class played a major role in bringing about the Reformation.[35]

The Letter to the Commonalty accompanied *The Appellation* and contained a similar theme: "What I have required of the Queen Regent, Estates, and Nobility, I cannot cease to require of you . . . which be the Commonalty of the same."[36] Knox began by establishing the spiritual

---

34. *Works*, 4:488–89, 500–506; Greaves, "John Knox and Resistance Theory," 16, 18, 22; Greaves, "John Knox and the Covenant Tradition," 27–28.

35. Reid, "The Middle Class Factor in the Scottish Reformation," 150.

36. *Works*, 4:523.

Shocking Politics and Idolatrous Rulers

equality of the commonalty. When he mentioned equality in his writings, he did so in a spiritual, not political context. Knox acknowledged a divinely ordained distinction between rulers and common people in civil policies. In regard to salvation, however, all are equal and share equal responsibility for promoting the faith.[37]

Knox then proceeded to lay down the duties of the commonalty in matters of religion. Subjects may legally require from their civil rulers the provision of "true" preachers and expel false prophets (i.e., Catholics). If the temporal powers refuse, then the people may provide for their own ministers and defend them against persecution. Moreover, the Protestants could withhold their tithes from the Catholic Church. Knox informed the people that they could not use their lowly status as an excuse for not establishing "true religion." Failure to reform religion would bring divine vengeance. God indeed punishes not only the chief offenders, but all who consent to iniquity.

Knox based his arguments here—as he did elsewhere—on the thesis that people who yield to the rule of idolaters commit idolatry themselves.[38] He required the commonalty to work with Parliament and the nobles in repressing tyranny, rather than against them. Yet, Knox did not desire anarchy or democracy, but rather reform in accord with God's law and the covenant obligation. Anarchy is obviously contrary to divine law and not conducive to the reform Knox had in mind. Moreover, in the social and political context of sixteenth-century Scotland, no one even considered social or political democracy as options.[39]

THE SECOND BLAST

Knox attached the abortive *Second Blast*, which he never completed, to his letters to the nobility and commonalty. Apparently, *The Second Blast* would have been more radical than *The First Blast*. Why? Here he applied revolutionary principles to cases other than female rule. *The Second Blast* acknowledged Knox's authorship to *The First Blast*, and then proceeded to set forth further propositions.

First, a king does not rule over a Christian people by birth only "but in his election must the ordinance of which God has established in

---

37. *Works*, 4:527–28. See also Greaves, "Calvinism, Democracy, and the Political Thought of John Knox," 86–87.

38. *Works*, 4:533–35.

39. Greaves, "John Knox and Resistance Theory," 22–23; Greaves, "Democracy and John Knox," 83.

PART THREE: Political Considerations

the election of inferior judges be observed." Next, no manifest idolater should be given public office in a kingdom that has once acknowledged Jesus Christ and the gospel. Third, no oath can bind people to obey and maintain tyrants against God and his known truth. Finally, if people have elected a ruler who then turns out to be an idolater, the people may depose and punish such a sovereign.[40]

The first proposition of *The Second Blast* declared that the basis of political authority depends on the ordinance of God. This statement may contain the climax of Knox's political thought. Still, *The Second Blast* also implied the covenant idea or social compact between the people and their rulers. Though Knox acknowledged that rulers receive their authority from God, he seemed to say that God bestows this authority through the people and estates.

Actually, at this point Knox attempted to answer a question that perplexed many sixteenth-century religious leaders: How are evil or tyrannical magistrates sometimes set in authority over people? Martin Bucer and Peter Martyr still insisted—as a just punishment for sins—that such a situation must be due to the ordinance of God. Knox gave a different answer. He did not mention how rulers are chosen. He indicated, however, that if a people discover they have an idolatrous or tyrannical ruler, this situation can only mean that they have made a mistake in selecting such a person. They failed to read the signs God had provided in order for a people to recognize a godly ruler.[41]

Four pamphlets published prior to August 1558 spelled out Knox's ideas regarding government and religion—namely, the rights of subjects against idolatrous and oppressive rulers. He introduced his ideas in *The First Blast*, but detailed his position in three subsequent pamphlets. Knox first asked the Queen Regent, Mary of Guise, to reform the church. She ignored him. So he then requested the nobles to force such reforms and called upon the lairds and burgesses to pressure the rulers toward the same objective. The Scottish reformer made his position unambiguously clear: Nobles have the right to depose an unrepentant monarch and, if the rulers fail to act, the common people can set up their own "reformed church." After the radical ideas of these four pamphlets, Knox more or less amplified or modified similar themes for the remainder of his career.

---

40. *Works*, 4:539-40.

41. *Works*, 4:539-40; Burns, "The Political Ideas of the Scottish Reformation," 260; Greaves, "John Knox and Resistance Theory," 23; Skinner, *The Foundations of Modern Political Thought*, 2: 229-30.

12

Church-State Patterns

KNOX IS WELL KNOWN for his theory of resistance to idolatrous (i.e., Catholic) and tyrannical rulers. But his political thinking went beyond resistance to constituted authority. He had more to say about political subjects. Two church-state patterns emerge from his writings. First and foremost is the Christian commonwealth, that is, a Christian society in which both civil and ecclesiastical powers cooperate in the cultivation of "true religion" and in promoting the common welfare of the body politic. Unfortunately, Knox's dream remained a vision. Scotland never implemented a Christian commonwealth. But his ideas on this subject reveal that he desired Scotland to walk uprightly and to embrace God's laws.[1] Second, Knox held to a version of the disestablished church based on both the godly remnant in Old Testament Israel and the model of the first-century church. Of these two church-state patterns, Knox clearly preferred the Christian commonwealth and only grudgingly acknowledged the disestablished church when Protestantism could not be established.[2]

Knox's church-state views related to his concept of the church. As noted in chapter five of this work, the church of John Knox displayed many faces.[3] Still, only two are relevant for an examination of Knox's church-state patterns and they are the small flock and the national kirk. Knox spoke of the small flock in many contexts, and in most cases this model

---

[1]. See Kyle, "The Christian Commonwealth, 247–59; Kyle, *The Ministry of Knox*, 149–64.

[2]. See Kyle, "The Church-State Patterns in the Thought of John Knox," 71–87; Kyle, *The Mind of Knox*, 280–90.

[3]. See Kyle, "The Nature of the Church in the Thought of John Knox," 485–501; Janton, *Concept et Sentiment*, 47, 157.

was disestablished. Nevertheless, the reformer did relate the small flock to the national church on a few occasions, usually as a small remnant within the larger body. The small flock was a godly remnant, usually containing the elect and maintaining the integrity of its faith and worship. The small flock has existed in a suffering condition in the commonwealth of Israel, as the primitive church, and in Knox's day where Protestantism was not established.[4]

The reformer mentioned the national kirk as early as 1552, but he spoke most often of this church in his post 1560 writings. Knox conceived of a national kirk as one established by law, supported by the state, encompassing all of society and containing both the godly and ungodly. He regarded the national church as a vital aspect of the Christian commonwealth, working closely with the civil government to enact God's will within a nation.[5]

THE CHRISTIAN COMMONWEALTH

Knox desired the reformation of religion in Scotland. And, in his mind this meant returning the Christian religion to the ideal of spiritual Israel. Every reformation needs a means to implement its objectives. While the adherents of the Radical Reformation largely eschewed any use of the secular state as an instrument of reform, the Magisterial Reformers did just the opposite.[6] They believed that the civil government must be a partner along with the church in establishing and maintaining the "true" faith. However, if the civil rulers presented an obstacle to the establishment of Protestantism, the Magisterial Reformers in various degrees—advocated resistance to any idolatrous and tyrannical commands. As we have seen, Knox went beyond most of his counterparts in this regard and advocated popular resistance to idolatrous rulers—that is, Catholics.

Still, Knox's resistance theory was but a means to an end—the end being the reformation of religion. The great obstacle to such reform was the power of the Catholic Church, established by law and promoted by the civil power. Therefore, Knox advocated the overthrow of established

---

4. Knox, *Works*, 3:5, 178, 241, 245, 264, 266, 273–80, 351, 388–90; 4:263, 459; 6:272, 507, 569, 591, are but a few citations.

5. Knox, "Epistle to the Congregation of Berwick, 1552," 225; *Works*, 2:118–19.

6. Williams, *The Radical Reformation*, xxiii–xxxi. "Radical Reformers" would include primarily the Anabaptists and Spiritualists. See also Verduin, *The Reformers and Their Stepchildren*, 11–20; Burns, "The Political Ideas of the Scottish Reformation," 251.

temporal authority, the seizure of political power, and the use of that power to bring down the Roman Church. These revolutionary ideas, nevertheless, were formed against a background of moral principle—the Christian commonwealth.[7] With Catholicism overthrown and Protestantism at least partially established in Scotland, Knox planned to use the Christian commonwealth as the primary instrument for purifying Scottish religion and society.

Knox's drive to establish Protestantism obviously had an Old Testament basis. His thought did not ignore the many themes associated with New Testament. Yet he largely concerned himself with Old Testament issues, namely, his crusade to purify religion—including resistance to idolatrous rulers (Catholics)—the covenant obligations, and the corporate return of Scottish religion to the ideal of spiritual Israel.[8] As his concept of reform and theory of resistance reflected his Old Testament orientation, so did his vehicle of reform—the Christian commonwealth.

Shades of the Commonwealth

Knox's most detailed comments regarding the Christian commonwealth came in *A Brief Exhortation to England* (1559) and the *Book of Discipline*. As he developed his theory of resistance in the 1550s, however, the ideological framework emerged. In *A Godly Letter* (1553–54), Knox praised the rule of Edward VI, implying the existence of a Christian commonwealth under his administration.[9] While Knox's ideal was the Christian commonwealth, in at least one place, he spoke of such an entity largely divorced from religion. In *A Faithful Admonition* (1554), the reformer did not attack Mary Tudor solely as an idolater, but also displayed concern for the entire fabric of English society. Here his remarks had a largely secular tone. The English commonwealth, its laws and liberties, assumed the character of entities in themselves unrelated to specific biblical categories.[10]

Knox's perception of the Christian commonwealth rested on his conviction that the state had a responsibility to establish and promote "true"

---

7. *Works*, 3:295–97; Little, "John Knox and English Social Prophecy," 123–24; Mason, "Knox, Resistance and Moral Imperative."

8. See chapter 2 of this study. Kyle, "John Knox, A Man of the Old Testament," 65–78; Kyle, "John Knox and the Purification of Religion," 265–80.

9. *Works*, 3:178.

10. *Works*, 3:294ff.; Little, "Knox and English Social Prophecy," 122–25; Burns, "Political Ideas of the Scottish Reformation," 255.

PART THREE: Political Considerations

religion. Such a belief emerged clearly in several of his 1558 writings addressed to the Protestants in England and Scotland. While the focus of *The First Blast* and *The Appellation* was the removal of idolatrous rulers, he went to great lengths to support his contention that the establishment of "true" religion pertained not only to the church, but also to the political authorities. Knox based this opinion on the fact that in the "commonwealth of Israel," the magistrate was superior to the priest. Knox then went on to list many godly kings of Judah and Israel as examples of civil authorities interpreting divine law and reforming religion.[11] In *A Letter to the Commonalty* (1558), he further widened the responsibility for establishing "true" religion and now included the middle class—that is, the lairds and burgesses. Subjects, Knox insisted may legally require civil rulers to provide "true" preachers and expel false prophets (that is, Catholics).[12]

Knox next moved beyond destroying Catholicism and establishing Protestantism. In *A Brief Exhortation to England*, shades of the Christian commonwealth envisioned in the *Book of Discipline* could be seen.[13] In fact, most of the key components of the Christian commonwealth—as set forth by the co-authors of the *Book of Discipline*—could be found in this earlier work. Because the *Book of Discipline* was a collective work, it cannot be certain if all of the details found therein were representative of Knox's thought. But the major outline for the Christian commonwealth can be found in *A Brief Exhortation to England*. Thus Knox's principal ideas on this subject can be known with a higher degree of certainty.

In *A Brief Exhortation to England*, Knox insisted that not only must the civil government install Protestantism, but the ruling authorities must also take definite steps to preserve such a religion. All papists must be removed from civil offices, for no Catholic can rule over a Protestant country. Next, ministers must be maintained in most cities and towns. Moreover, the church and state must work closely in discipline, with the state bringing its laws into harmony with Scripture. Lastly, schools ought to be set up in each parish and run by Protestant magistrates and educators. In this exhortation, Knox saw the state supporting the church in maintaining the Christian commonwealth. But at the same time he exhorted ministers not to become entangled in civil affairs. In his later writings, Knox, of course,

11. *Works*, 4:415–16, 485–87.

12. *Works*, 4:523, 527–28, 533–35; Reid, "The Middle-class Factor in the Scottish Reformation," 150; Greaves, "Calvinism, Democracy and the Political Thought of John Knox," 86–87.

13. Kyle, *Mind of Knox*, 277; Kyle, "Church-State Patterns," 76; Kyle, "Christian Commonwealth," 250.

would insist that the Reformed clergy could critically evaluate the practices of government in the light of Scripture.[14]

Visions of the Commonwealth

In the spring of 1560—as events were pushing Scotland in the direction of Protestantism—Knox turned his mind to the preparation of the two major documents of the Scottish Reformation, the *Scots Confession* and *Book of Discipline*.[15] The effect of these works, from the limited discussion on the Christian commonwealth, was twofold. First, the religious duties of the government were made much more specific. Second, Knox and his colleagues made it clear that if the church respected the ruler in his sphere, the ruler must submit to the moral discipline of the church: "To Discipline must all Estates within this Realm be subject, if they offend, as well as the Rulers as they that are ruled."[16]

According to Knox and his colleagues, a Protestant country was one that agreed "to live in conformity with the Gospel," one that consented "to organize both its civil and religious life in accordance with the same beliefs." Parliament's approval of the *Scots Confession* in 1560 implied both the acceptance of such an understanding of a Protestant country and an agreement to govern the country in conformity with the exposition of the Christian faith contained in that document.[17]

The *Scots Confession* not only confirmed the duty of obedience to rulers, but also expressed the civil government's responsibility toward the church: "Moreover, to Kings, Princes, Rulers, and Magistrates, we affirm that chiefly and most principally the reformation and purgation of the Religion appertains, so that not only they are appointed for civil policy, but also for the maintenance of true Religion, and for suppression of idolatry and superstition whatsoever."[18]

---

14. *Works*, 5:515–16.

15. See Shaw,"John Willock," 59–60; Cameron, ed. *The First Book of Discipline*, 2–4, 8–100.

16. *Works*, 2: 233.

17. *Works*, 2:95–96; Cameron, *First Book of Discipline*, 62 (quote). See also Mason, "Knox and Moral Imperative," 427.

18. *Works*, 2:118–19. On the other hand, in its final form, the *Scots Confession* contained a section on obedience to the civil magistrate, in which the duty of obedience to rulers was stated without qualification. On the basis of a letter from Randolph to Cecil—which implied that a section qualifying obedience had been omitted—Ridley conjectures that Knox laid down not only the duty of obedience to rulers, but also the

PART THREE: Political Considerations

In such a light, the authors of the *Book of Discipline* sought to fulfill their commission. The co-authored *Book of Discipline* defined a Christian commonwealth as a country in which both the civil and ecclesiastical powers cooperated in the cultivation of what they perceived to be the "true" religion. As James Cameron notes, Knox and his colleagues accepted the notion "that government has a responsibility for the establishment of true religion" and for abolishing all "held contrary to it." In effecting such a religious reformation, however, the civil power was strictly limited. The rulers had no power to admit anything not approved by Scripture.[19]

In the eyes of these reformers, such a submission to the Word of God would act as a guiding force upon the exercise of civil power and require cooperation between the secular government and ministers as the interpreters of Scripture. What's more, the reformers believed that the secular powers' acceptance of the authority of Scripture would require the government to support several religious functions—Jesus Christ had to be truly preached and his sacraments properly administered throughout the country, and idolatry had to be suppressed and civil laws and penalties must be brought into conformity with the requirements of Scripture.[20]

In adopting such an understanding toward the civil government and its responsibility to the church, the authors of the *Book of Discipline* showed agreement with many of their Reformed counterparts on the Continent. They desired the establishment of a Christian commonwealth in which both the civil and ecclesiastical powers cooperated in the cultivation of "true" religion. Given this understanding between the two powers, Knox and his colleagues "repeatedly requested the acceptance of the *Book of Discipline* by the estates." By the same token, Knox could not accept a Catholic queen as sovereign and at the same time maintain the Reformed church. His struggle with Queen Mary must be seen in this light.[21]

The ideal Christian society presented in the *Book of Discipline*—a people committed to the fulfillment of God's laws—presupposed two conditions, neither of which was realized. The first was "a single-minded devotion" to the Reformed cause on the part of those who had brought about the Reformation. For this condition, there were "too many who proved

---

circumstances in which they could be obeyed. *Works*, 6:120; Ridley, *John Knox*, 377.

19. *Works*, 2:183–86; Cameron, *Book of Discipline*, 62 (quotes); Reid, "The Book of Discipline," 36–37.

20. *Works*, 2:183–86; Cameron, *Book of Discipline*, 63; Reid, "Book of Discipline," 36–37; Reid, "John Knox's Theology of Political Government," 537.

21. Cameron, *Book of Discipline*, 67 (quote).

to be devoted" to "their own particular cause and worldly promotion."[22] Knox had believed that church and state should be "twin pillars of God's house on earth, twin aspects of the government of God's people," but the worldly-wise passed by the *Book of Discipline* and thus rejected his policy as "devout imagination."[23]

The second condition—something often overlooked in an assessment of Knox's political views—was "the rule of a sovereign devoted to the service of Christ's truth," the godly magistrate. "To such a sovereign the duty of Christian obedience would be simple and absolute."[24] The Reformation, however, brought no such ruler to Scotland. The personal reign of Mary Stewart (1561–67) presented some obvious problems for Knox's concept of the Christian commonwealth. How could a Catholic queen fill the role of the "godly magistrate" in an active partnership between church and state in the promotion of the "true" faith? Mary's deposition in 1567 brought a change in the relations between the Reformed Church and the crown—which was now "godly" in the person of the infant James VI and his Protestant regents. Protestantism was now firmly established. But Knox never felt quite sure that Mary would not return and undo the good work that had been accomplished. He therefore threw his whole weight behind the Protestant party.[25]

The close working relationship between church and state envisioned in the *Book of Discipline* was left somewhat vague, so on occasions the government interfered in ecclesiastical affairs. The church leaders, however, were committed to maintaining the independence of the church from the crown. Thus the second *Book of Discipline*—written after Knox's time—made quite clear the proper relationship of church and state. The godly magistrate was important. Not only did such a ruler possess important authority in civil affairs, but he or she also had the responsibility to uphold and defend the church. Still, the godly ruler was not the intermediary through whom Christ ruled the church—for even such an individual

---

22. *Works*, 2:310–11 (quote); Burns, "Knox and Revolution," 573 (quote).

23. *Works*, 2:310–11; Dickinson, *The Scottish Reformation*, 8 (quote).

24. Burns, "Knox and Revolution," 573. See Healey, "Waiting for Deborah," 371–86.

25. Donaldson, *The Scottish Reformation*, 144–45; Kyle, *Mind of Knox*, 290; Ridley, *John Knox*, 482; Brown, "In Search of the Godly Magistrate in Reformation Scotland," 556; Lynch, "Calvinism in Scotland, " 234–35; Mason, "Knox and Royal Supremacy," 156.

was subject to it in spiritual and moral matters. Instead, the church was directly responsible to Christ as its royal head.[26]

CHURCH-STATE COOPERATION

The *Book of Discipline* envisioned several areas of cooperation between the church and state in the Christian commonwealth. The magistrate had the responsibility for seeing that no one outside the church would determine its doctrine and polity. Beyond these obvious spiritual concerns, perhaps the closest areas of overlapping responsibilities—support for the clergy, education, and the poor—had economic implications or were related to the administration of discipline.[27]

In its final form, the *Book of Discipline* contained nine heads, or sections. The first three heads related to the most basic issues: the preaching of the Gospel, the right administration of the sacraments, and the suppression of idolatry and false teaching in the realm of Scotland. The remainder of the *Book of Discipline* is largely concerned with the steps necessary to implement the first three heads, which contained the essence of the reformation of religion. Without the actualization of the provisions, the reformers seriously doubted whether the reformation would become permanent.[28]

The authors of the *Book of Discipline* proposed a program of ecclesiastical, social, and national reform. The critical aspect of this program was the preaching of the gospel and the proper administration of the sacraments. These provisions, of course, could not be a reality without an adequate ministry. Broadly interpreted, the ministry included the ministers of congregations, readers, teachers, elders, deacons, and superintendents. Though the church selected these officers and examined them in respect to their qualifications, the state also had its hand in the process. The civil authorities could compel qualified men—that is, those individuals who did not respond to the church's call—to enter the ministry. Moreover, in the beginning, "the government was to appoint the superintendents," though the "usual procedure would be election for a term of three years."

---

26. Reid, "Book of Discipline," 40–41; Kirk, ed., *The Second Book of Discipline*, 11–13.

27. *Works*, 2:181–89; Cameron, *Book of Discipline*, 14–15; Reid, "Book of Discipline," 41.

28. *Works*, 2:189–258; Reid, "Book of Discipline, 41; Cameron, *Book of Discipline*, 14–15.

Church-State Patterns

In addition, financial support for the ministry was to come from both the local parish and the collection of ecclesiastical revenues from the lands held by the Catholic Church. To a considerable extent, these revenues would have gone to the aristocracy instead of the Reformed Church.[29]

Discipline

In regard to discipline, Knox probably envisioned the closest working relationship between church and state. In his *Brief Exhortation to England*, he tells us that once "true" religion becomes established in a realm, discipline prevents its decline and both minister and magistrate must cooperate in this process.[30] It is therefore no surprise to find in the *Book of Discipline* an entire section devoted to discipline. This head begins by defining the need for discipline in any organized community or commonwealth—and by analogy the church—which was to be administered similar to a city. This section states that all sins are transgressions against God and thus punishable by either the church or secular government, acting as God's instrument.[31]

Ecclesiastical discipline should reprove and correct those faults the civil government either neglects to punish or may not punish because of their nature. Capital crimes such as blasphemy, adultery, murder, and perjury ought to be punished by the civil sword. But offenses such as drunkenness, fornication, excesses, slander, and oppression of the poor ought to be punished by the church as God's Word commands—that is, in accordance with Matthew 18:15-18. However, Catholicism brought such confusion to the matter of ecclesiastical discipline that the church was often compelled to punish both classes of offenders with excommunication until they repented.[32]

Education

In *A Brief Exhortation to England*, Knox demonstrated a vision for broad, popular education in advocating "that Schools be universally erected in all

---

29. *Works*, 2:189-208, 221-26; Reid, "Book of Discipline," 41; Healey, "The Preaching Ministry in Scotland's First Book of Discipline," Reid, *Trumpeter of God*, 198 (quote).
30. *Works*, 5:81ff.
31. *Works*, 2:227-31.
32. *Works*, 2:22-33.

cities and towns." Still, the oversight of these schools must be committed to magistrates and godly, learned individuals. Knox understood the power of education to shape religion and saw the danger of non-Protestant teachers. A similar religious philosophy pervades the educational program set up in the *Book of Discipline*.[33]

The educational scheme of the *Book of Discipline* readily demonstrates the cooperation between church and state. The responsibility to provide for the continuance of the church in purity and liberty rests with the godly magistrate, so states the section on schools. Of course, education was a primary vehicle for perpetuating the Reformed Church. The *Book of Discipline* declared education to be for the individual and that for each person it had a twofold purpose: to implant in individuals the principles of morality and religion, and to develop their intellectual gifts so that they might serve both church and commonwealth.[34]

The schools existed not only to produce an educated ministry, but also to train young people to be godly in whatever occupation they served. The universities did not accept students who also failed to demonstrate a godly character. Besides being godly, the authors of the *Book of Discipline* wanted the students to be docile—that is, capable of being instructed from the Protestant viewpoint. In this religious emphasis, Knox and his colleagues were quite in harmony with both the medieval and sixteenth-century practice. Purely secular education did not exist, and the *Book of Discipline* certainly did not introduce it.[35]

This religious emphasis can be seen in the control of the Scottish educational system. The responsibility for supervising the system and for providing schools and schoolmasters resided with the church. Knox and his associates desired ecclesiastical control over the university because they recognized its potential to dominate the church. Conversely, they failed to see any danger in the church's control of the university. As Knox did not champion religious freedom, neither did he conceive of free intellectual inquiry. But few people did at this time. In the sixteenth century, ecclesiastical control over education was normative for Protestants and Catholics alike.[36]

33. *Works*, 5:520; Craigie, "Knox's Book of Discipline," 721.

34. *Works*, 2:209–13; Greaves, "The Social Awareness of John Knox," 43–44; Greaves, *Theology and Revolution*, 197–98.

35. *Works*, 2:209–13; Greaves, "Social Awareness of Knox," 43–44; Greaves, *Theology and Revolution*, 197–99.

36. Greaves, "Social Awareness of Knox," 43–44; Greaves, *Theology and Revolution*, 197–98.

Closely related to Knox's purpose in the *Book of Discipline*—of implanting religious values and developing intellectual ability to serve both church and commonwealth—was the concept of universal compulsory education. The authors made basic education compulsory for all (including girls). They felt that everyone needs religion and that natural talent exists in all social classes. Thus the opportunity to receive an education would depend on ability, not on wealth or social background. With this belief in mind, the kirks made some provision for needy scholars—a democratizing principle remarkable for that time. This concept of a universal and compulsory educational program distinguished the *Book of Discipline* from all other sixteenth-century writings on education.[37] The *Book of Discipline* advanced the idea of a graduated system of elementary and secondary schools and universities. On such an arrangement, which the authors of the *Book of Discipline* regarded as indispensable for the well-being of church and state, the schools were proposed.[38]

Social and Financial Issues

In his ideal Christian commonwealth, Knox did not envision an egalitarian society. He openly supported the stratification of society into princes, nobility, and commoners.[39] Moreover he advocated no equal distribution of goods. But he did have a concern for the poor. He did not regard poverty as solely the just punishment of God, or the result of laziness. In several earlier writings, Knox urged Protestants to care for the poor—the orphans, widows, and those unable to work—but not for those willfully unemployed regardless of their poverty. For these good deeds, Knox promised that God would bestow rich spiritual blessings.[40] The *Book of Discipline* also addressed the problems of poverty. Each kirk must provide for its own poor—orphans, widows and other unfortunates—but not for sturdy beggars. People unable to work must be returned to their place of birth or lengthy residence. The *Book of Discipline* intended that all able-bodied people work while the church cared for the needy.[41]

---

37. *Works*, 2:209–21; Craigie, "Book of Discipline," 722; Greaves, "Social Awareness of Knox," 42; Greaves, "Democracy and John Knox," 88–89.

38. *Works*, 2:209–21; Brown, *John Knox*, 1:135–37.

39. *Works*, 1:272; 4:481; Greaves, "Democracy and John Knox," 83.

40. Knox, "Epistle to the Congregation of Berwick, 1552," 264.

41. *Works*, 2:199–201. Historians have used modern phrases such as "Christian Socialism" and "Welfare State" to describe the *Book of Discipline*'s proposed ideal. See Brown, *John Knox*, 2:149; Mackie, *John Knox*, 23–24.

Part Three: Political Considerations

If the provisions of the *Book of Discipline*—regarding support for the godly clergy, education, and care for the poor—had been enacted, a virtual social revolution would have come about. For this basic reason, Parliament rejected the *Book of Discipline*. First, in the individual congregations, both ministers and elders—usually chosen from the burgesses and lairds—would gain new power and influence which would ultimately lead to the serious limitation of the nobles' authority and prestige. Of more importance, the financial provisions for these programs—support for the Reformed clergy, an ambitious educational system and care for the poor—were in part to be drawn from revenues from the lands of the Catholic Church. To a large extent, these monies went to the nobility. Thus the rise in power of the middle groups, plus the loss of revenues from the church lands, made the *Book of Discipline* completely unacceptable to the aristocracy and their supporters, such as Maitland of Lethington.[42] In addition, if the *Book of Discipline* were to be adopted, Catholicism would never return. And this aroused the opposition of the adherents of the old system, who still controlled much of the nation's wealth.[43]

THE DISESTABLISHED CHURCH

Knox clearly preferred that a Christian commonwealth be established in both England and Scotland. If such a vision failed, however, he reluctantly acknowledged another model—a version of the disestablished church. The Scots reformer mentioned this alternative church-state relationship because he regarded it as an option to be utilized only if the faithful were few in number and Protestantism could not be established. In fact, the support in his writings for such a model is indirect, emerging from his discussions on the small flock church and his theory of resistance. For Knox the disestablished church was a temporary expedient when circumstances did not permit the existence of the Christian commonwealth.

Can such a model then be regarded as an alternative to the Christian commonwealth in Knox's thought? The answer would seem to be yes. Despite his efforts to establish Protestantism on a legal basis in Scotland, he recognized the existence of a disestablished church-state pattern in several

---

42. Reid, *Trumpeter of God*, 206–7; Reid, "Book of Discipline," 38; Reid," Knox's Theology of Political Government," 536–37; Brown, "In Search of the Godly Magistrate," 571–73.

43. Reid, *Trumpeter of God*, 199. For more on the wealth of the revenues of the former Catholic Church lands, see Donaldson, *Scottish Reformation*, 71–89.

historical contexts: the godly remnant in the Old Testament, the early church, and the Protestant church in some countries during the sixteenth century.[44]

Quite often Knox spoke of the disestablished church in the context of the small flock, which has been noted in chapter five of this study.[45] This small flock was the "true" church persecuted throughout history—the spiritual remnant in Israel, the early church, the faithful in Marian England, and the Protestant community in Scotland.[46] This church in Scotland became known as the "privy kirks."[47] In the late 1550s the "privy kirks," though not established, did grow in numbers and in political strength, and unofficially Scotland had two churches—the new Reformed Churches and the old Catholic Church. The privy kirks alone, however, could not hope to change society or bring about a widespread revolution. Therefore, the phenomenon of the privy kirk represents an intermediate stage between an earlier phase of inchoate, unorganized Protestantism and the reformers' bid for power in the revolution of 1559-60, which brought them victory.[48]

On two occasions in the 1560s, after the establishment of Protestantism, Knox provided more information about the non-established church. The first instance was the reformer's initial encounter with Mary Stewart in 1561. Among other questions, Mary touched upon a fundamental issue: You have taught the people to receive another religion than the princes allow. And how can that doctrine be of God, seeing that God commands subjects to obey their princes?"[49] Mary believed that subjects must have the same religion as their subjects, but she failed to realize that such an idea no longer held universal acceptance. The peace treaty of Magdeburg had become a precedent for breaking this pattern.[50]

After the establishment of Protestantism, in practice two churches existed in Scotland. Officially a Protestant church operated everywhere and supposedly controlled the lives of the people, but in actuality it had little property or income. At the same time the Catholic Church, though forbidden to celebrate the Mass, still retained much of its property and

---

44. See Kyle, "Church-State Patterns in Knox's Thought, 81–82.
45. See also Kyle, "The Nature of the Church in the Thought of Knox," 485–501.
46. *Works*, 3:5, 231,239, 266; 4:309, 311, 315, 481, 487, 513; Janton, *Concept et Sentiment*, 47, 123, 139, 160.
47. *Works*, 4:129–40, 263.
48. Kirk, "The 'Privy Kirks' and Their Antecedents," 156–57, 168.
49. *Works*, 2:281.
50. Shaw, "John Knox and Mary, Queen of Scots," 64.

loyalty.[51] Neither Mary nor Knox looked with favor on such a situation. In his conversations with Mary, the reformer believed Protestantism to be properly established as the religion of Scotland and he was determined to see the law enforced, by the queen if necessary. Nevertheless, in the mind of Knox, the unity of the crown and people in matters of religion was not the only possible pattern of political and social structure.

Rather than comply with a Catholic monarch in respect to religion or accept Mary as the "godly magistrate" in a Christian commonwealth, Knox acknowledged another church-state pattern—the position the church held prior to the official recognition of Christianity. Citing many examples from the Old and New Testaments, Knox declared "that subjects are not bound to the Religion of their Princes, albeit they are commanded to give them obedience."[52] The Israelites did not accept the religion of the pharaoh, though they were his subjects. The apostles rejected the religion of the Roman emperors. Daniel and his colleagues were subjects of Nebuchadnezzar and Darius, but they did not worship their gods.[53] To Knox, these people represented a disestablished church, a small flock running counter to the prevailing religion. Even in this context, Knox indicated that if God had provided the means, these people would have resisted their ungodly rulers by force.[54]

The second occasion when Knox spoke about the disestablished church was in his 1564 disputation with Maitland of Lethington in the general assembly. Though this debate focused largely on the duty of citizens to obey or resist a wicked prince, two contrasting church-state patterns emerge, each with different responsibilities in regard to religion. In the Christian commonwealth, where the faithful are assembled in sufficient force, they must resist idolatrous rulers and keep their land free from idolatry. Conversely, when the church is disestablished—or to use Knox's terminology—when Christian subjects are dispersed or in a foreign land, they are required only to abstain from idolatry.

Knox found both church-state patterns in the Old Testament. For example, the Israelites, when a minority in Egypt represented the

51. Ridley, *John Knox*, 400; Kyle, *Mind of Knox*, 283.

52. *Works*, 2:281.

53. *Works*, 2:281. In the same conversation, after rambling about other subjects, Knox declared that he was prepared to live under Mary as Paul lived under Nero. This conversation is subject to several interpretations. One is that Knox was referring to a disestablished church. See *Works*, 2:279; Shaw, "John Knox and Mary Queen of Scots," 64.

54. *Works*, 2:282.

disestablished church, and thus must only separate from idolatry. When these Israelites came into Palestine, Knox saw them assembled in a commonwealth, and demanded that they enforce their religious values throughout the land. Without indicating specific localities, Knox also acknowledged the existence of both models during the sixteenth century, assigning them similar religious responsibilities.[55]

What sixteenth-century church-state pattern bears resemblance to Knox's disestablished church? Because the reformer spoke of such a church only in broadest terms, this question is difficult. Knox's version of a non-established church certainly did not resemble the Anabaptist model, that is, a committed group of believers remaining separate from society and the state. Rather, he considered the church as a mixed body containing the godly and the ungodly. The reformer did not declare that the small flock was pure—that is, it comprises only the elect and the godly. Instead, Knox regarded the persecuted small flock as the visible church most likely to contain the elect and maintain a standard of holiness.[56]

In fact, he castigated the radical sects of the Reformation, and like the other leading reformers, he formed the opinion that the Anabaptists must be suppressed if Christian society were to remain Christian or a society. Furthermore, Knox repudiated the Anabaptist assertion that the Christian is not a citizen in an earthly state and has nothing to do with civil government. He never hinted that members of the small flock were to refrain from political activity, implying instead that the faithful in the early church utilized the political means at their disposal.[57]

Perhaps the closest resemblance to Knox's disestablished church—and this comparison stands only in a broad sense—can be found in the congregations established by the Marian exiles, the Huguenot churches in France before the late 1550s, and the early separatist movement in Elizabethan England. In regard to internal administration and practices, these groups were not entirely uniform. Nevertheless, circumstances dictated a church pattern resembling the example of the early church. They were forced to establish congregations independent of state support, resembling Knox's small flock, particularly as it related to the privy kirks. The Marians, the Huguenots, and the Elizabethan separatists regarded these churches as a temporary expedient—a means to an end—the ultimate

---

55. *Works*, 2:442–43.
56. Kyle, "The Nature of the Church in the Thought of Knox," 493.
57. *Works*, 2:442, 444. See also Kyle, "John Knox Confronts the Anabaptists," 493–515; Kyle and Johnson, *John Knox*, 111–34.

objective being the establishment of a Christian commonwealth, which in most cases would embrace the Reformed faith.[58]

58. Knappen, *Tudor Puritanism*, 151–52; Donaldson, *The Scottish Reformation*, 50; Reid, *Trumpeter of God*, 10; Rothrock, *The Huguenots*, 60–62; Courthial, "The Golden Age of Calvinism in France, 77–78; Collinson, *The Elizabethan Puritan Movement*, 25–26, 87–91; Reid, "French Influence on the First Scots Confession and Book of Discipline," 14; Lake, *Moderate Puritans and the Elizabethan Church in the English Separatist Tradition*, 31; Kirk, "Privy Kirks," 168; Reid, "Book of Discipline," 35.

13

A Few Afterthoughts

WE ARE APPROACHING JOHN Knox's 500th birthday and he still remains a controversial, even paradoxical figure. In part, this situation has developed because he wore so many hats—pastor, preacher, prophet, reformer, and revolutionary. As a pastor he dealt with the personal needs of his parishioners. As a preacher he could roar like a lion from the pulpit. As a prophet he could call down God's judgment on nations and rulers. As a reformer he attempted to reform both church and society. And as a revolutionary he attacked the very basis of sixteenth-century society, especially its religious and political assumptions. By their very nature, such roles had a paradoxical impact. On one hand, Knox had his admirers both in his time and down to the present. Conversely, the reformer has aroused intense opposition through the centuries.

Knox was also a paradoxical figure because of his contradictory behavior. On one hand, he uttered chilling threats and condemned his opponents in the harshest language; on the other, he demonstrated understanding and compassion to those in need. The same man who was an irascible opponent to three Catholic queens—attacking them in somewhat crude language—evidenced a patient, gentle spirit to other women.

Historian W. Croft Dickinson puts it differently. Throughout Knox's public ministry the "spirit of Christ is absent." We do not find an appreciation for Paul's message, "Though I speak with the tongues of men and angels, and have not charity, I am become as sounding brass. . . ."[1] Only in his private and pastoral life did such a spirit emerge. The famous Protestant preacher C. H. Spurgeon echoed a similar indictment: "John Knox

---

1. Dickinson, Introduction to *History of the Reformation in Scotland*, 1:xxxv.

PART THREE: Political Considerations

undoubtedly preached the gospel of love—it is a pity he did not preach it more lovingly."[2]

Who was the real John Knox: a loud-mouthed bigot or a compassionate pastor? In part, this question can be addressed by focusing on Knox's vocation—the driving motive of his life. He believed that God had called him to restore the church of Jesus Christ in Scotland. Because of Catholicism's corruptions, this church had fallen into disrepute and near ruin. In being faithful to this calling or vocation, Knox often embraced many public roles—several of which could be quite confrontational. Moreover, Knox had a private and pastoral life, and in these positions he seemed to be a more amiable man than his public image would indicate. To some extent, Knox's paradoxical behavior can be explained by the expectations of these different roles.[3]

Knox was a builder. Nevertheless, before he could build up the Reformed Church in Scotland, he had to tear down the old Catholic Church. In doing so, he often acquired a negative image, especially to people in our day. But remember! Religious toleration and pluralism did not exist in the sixteenth century. For Protestantism to succeed, Catholicism had to go, and Knox saw himself as a preacher and a prophet engaged in a great cosmic struggle with Satan and the Antichrist. In such a conflict he became a pit bull, giving no quarter to God's enemies as he saw them.

Still, Knox did not assume the assault posture in all of his sermons and writings. When the situation warranted, his messages and letters could build up and comfort the faithful. And to even a greater degree in his pastoral role, he demonstrated great care and affection for his parishioners. As a national reformer, Knox also displayed concern for the entire fabric of Scottish society. He had religious motives, of course, but he endeavored to improve education and the lot of the poor.

As for the tone of Knox's tirades, several explanations can be given. He used blunt and forceful language, a reason why he is one of the more criticized figures of the Reformation. Without apologizing for Knox, it must be noted that strong language in a sermon was not unusual for that time. While Knox may have carried it further than most, the sermons of other preachers also included shocking and specific accusations. (For example, Luther used very strong language and attacked his opponents in ways that would disturb modern day Christians.) In the sixteenth century,

---

2. Quoted in Lamont, *The Swordbearer*, 176.
3. McCord, "The Faith of John Knox," 239, 243.

"people expected their preachers to be outspoken."[4] Second, Knox's personal experiences—his stay on a galley ship, the exile years, and harassment by Catholic rulers—fostered a deep hatred in his heart toward the Catholic faith. Last and most important was Knox's great conviction regarding both his call and the authority of Scripture. He never doubted that God had called him to be a watchman, warning people and nations of judgment to come. And he based his admonitions on Scripture—especially the Old Testament—which he interpreted literally and transferred almost verbatim to his day.

A FEW CONNECTIONS

In attempting to catch the spirit of John Knox, including his controversial behavior, this study has focused on three areas of the reformer's life—his theological foundations, his vocation, and his political thought. And they are closely intertwined. As noted, his thinking rested on a literal interpretation of the Old Testament, especially of passages condemning idolatry which he equated with the Catholic faith. He viewed God as immutable and sovereign. Thus, what God commanded in ancient times was applicable in a very literal way in the sixteenth century. Consequently, religion must be rigidly purified, including the termination of the Catholic Mass. Salvation came by faith, but in Knox's mind a sovereign God directed the path to salvation.

These theological foundations directed Knox's vocation—namely, a preacher, prophet, and pastor. Convinced that he was called by God to reform religion and end idolatry in Scotland, the Scots reformer utilized the vehicle of preaching to further this objective. Knox regarded himself as a simple preacher, a watchman warning people to obey God. He could roar like a lion from the pulpit—a characteristic confirmed by both his supporters and opponents. Not only did the reformer see himself as a preacher-watchman, but one cast in the mold of the Hebrew prophets. Thus prophetic denunciations poured from his mouth and pen. Coming from this prophetic role is the dominant image of Knox—tactless, harsh, castigating, and demeaning of women. But the Scots reformer also had another side, that of a pastor. His ministry was not limited to his public roles of a preacher and prophet. He pastored congregations and in this

---

4. Lamont, *The Swordbearer*, 34 (quote). See Reed, *John Knox: The Forgotten Reformer*, 184–216.

PART THREE: Political Considerations

capacity evidenced great concern for the spiritual well-being of individuals, especially women.

Knox jolted Europe with his theory of resistance to idolatrous or Catholic rulers, especially female sovereigns. In doing so, he has gone down in history as a firebrand, a prophet, and God's mouthpiece. But a theory of revolution is not the totality of Knox's political thought. His notion of resistance did not develop overnight. Like other Protestants, he insisted that Christians obey God and not the idolatrous commands of the ruling authorities; but he maintained that this disobedience must be peaceful. Circumstances, however, changed his thinking and by the late 1550s he advocated armed resistance. This notion of rebellion developed in the context of a moral background, namely, the notion of a Christian commonwealth. Knox desired that the law of God be upheld in England and Scotland in both the church and society. The church and state led by the "godly magistrate" had the obligation to enforce God's law throughout the country.

THE QUESTION OF INFLUENCE

As a reformer of religion, was John Knox successful? Did he have a significant impact in his day? Did he have any influence on future generations? The answers to these questions must be a qualified yes. But as Dale Johnson notes, Knox's stature throughout history has waxed and waned. While he has had his critics throughout history, on the whole he has been viewed in a positive light. In the last half of the twentieth century, however, revisionist historians have detracted from Knox's leadership and given him an "extreme makeover." Some have gone so far as to ignore him. Nevertheless, Knox has still maintained a moderate stature, especially on the American side of the Atlantic.[5]

Chronologically, Knox first influenced the course of English religion. During the reign of Edward VI, certain aspects of the English liturgy displeased the Scots reformer. But Edward's Protestant policy generally satisfied him so he muted his dissent. In Frankfurt, however, he clearly aligned himself with the non-conformist strand of English Protestantism. This trend continued in Geneva, where he pastored what became the first Puritan congregation. Knox's intense belief that worship must entail only what God has commanded in Scripture echoed throughout the Puritan

---

5. See Kyle and Johnson, *John Knox*, 182–97; Kellar, *Scotland, England, and the Reformation*; Wormald, *Court, Kirk and Community, Scotland*, 109–21, 200–201.

tradition. Yet Knox never sided with the extremes of separatist Puritanism. When Elizabeth became Queen in 1559—despite some appearances to the contrary—he did not encourage them to separate from the Church of England.[6]

Still, Knox had his greatest influence in Scotland. No, the Scottish Reformation did not originate with him. Its roots go back before his conversion to Protestantism, and the final struggle had begun before his 1559 arrival in Scotland. Yes, there would have been a reformation without Knox. In fact, Elizabeth and William Cecil—her principal secretary—did more to overthrow Catholicism in Scotland than Knox did. But Knox landed in Scotland as the Reformation lagged and its prospects for success seemed dim. At this juncture, he emerged as a revolutionary leader whose preaching and example inspired others to a greater effort.[7]

Knox's maneuvers to establish Protestantism were mostly successful. During the 1560s, however, his program for the Christian commonwealth met with considerably less success. Yet he gave the Reformation its shape. Without his efforts, Anglicanism—not the Reformed faith—may have replaced Catholicism in Scotland. Moreover, Knox was a major author of the *Scots Confession* and *Book of Discipline*—two documents which stand as a legacy to his work. The *Scots Confession* defined the faith of the Scottish Reformed Church, and while the *Book of Discipline* was never implemented, it established the church's ideals regarding education and care for the poor. In respect to the Presbyterian system of church government, this had to wait for Andrew Melville. But it can be argued that Knox pointed the way.[8]

The part which Knox "played between 1559 and 1561 in the making of the Reformation and thereafter in shaping the central character of the Reformed Church more than justify his position amidst the great reformers of the sixteenth century," notes historian Ian Cowan.[9] Many of Knox's contemporaries would have agreed. Certain sections of the Church of Scotland recognized his influence and position of leadership. While

6. Reid, *Trumpeter of God*, 286-87. See Cameron, "Frankfurt and Geneva, 50-73; Vander Molen, "Anglican Against Puritan," 45-57. Collinson notes that Knox may have had some discussions with the Puritans during the Vestiarian Controversy. See Collinson, "John Knox, the Church of England and the Women of England," 92-93.

7. Cowan, "John Knox and the Making of the Scottish Reformation," 25-26; Ridley, *John Knox*, 528.

8. Cowan, "Knox and the Scottish Reformation," 26; Ridley, *John Knox*, 128. See Cheyne, "The Scots Confession of 1560," 333.

9. Cowan, "Knox and the Scottish Reformation," 28.

PART THREE: Political Considerations

some Protestants hated him, many loved and revered him. As the 1560s progressed, Knox counted for little in politics, but he still exercised considerable influence over the Protestant movement that he helped to build up. Even the Earl of Morton—who had disagreements with Knox—would at his funeral pay tribute to the reformer's leadership and courage and declare that "here lies a man who in his life, never feared the face of man. . . ."[10] Knox's contemporaries on the Continent also recognized his prominent role in the Reformation movement. Writing shortly before Knox's death, Beza spoke of Knox as being at the helm of the Scottish Reformation. Even his Roman Catholic opponents regarded Knox as the primary leader behind the Protestant movement in Scotland.[11]

Vigorous preaching and uncompromising single-mindedness were the sources of both Knox's successes and failures. In part, the Protestant victory in 1560 must be attributed to Knox's pulpit pounding. According to Lord Eustace Percy, Knox was "a born preacher in the days when the pulpit was the main instrument of political as well as religious propaganda." In the modern world, people get information from many sources, especially television and the Internet. But in Knox's day, for news and views on a variety of subjects, people often gathered at church. In this method of communication, Knox had few equals. He knew the people and how to speak to them. And he could arouse a nation to action. Indeed, preaching was his most "obvious qualification for popular leadership."[12]

But this is why the Protestant political leaders dropped Knox before the job was done. Catholicism had been overthrown but the Reformation was not secure. Knox's skills—dynamic preaching, outspokenness, and unwavering determination—served the revolution well. When it came time to consolidate the Protestant gains, however, these skills embarrassed the political establishment. Giving offense to many—the Scottish government, Queen Mary, and then to the Elizabethan political leaders on whom the Scottish reformers were dependent—was unacceptable. At

---

10. Calderwood, *The History of the Kirk of Scotland*, 3:242; Ridley, *John Knox*, 518, 523; Reid, *Trumpeter of God*, 290.

11. *Works*, 6:613; Reid, *Trumpeter of God*, 290.

12. Percy, *John Knox,* 40 (quotes); Halliday, "Will the Real John Knox Please Stand?," 170; Lamont, *The Swordbearer*, 170; Dickinson, *The Scottish Reformation and its Influence upon Scottish Life and Character,* 7; Gill, "He made my tongue a trumpet. . . . John Knox, the Preacher," 110; MacMillan, "John Knox—Preacher of the Word," 14–15; Kyle, "The Thundering Scot," 135–49.

this juncture, the Scots needed a diplomat, not a prophet. So the Scottish political leadership put Knox on the shelf.[13]

Knox's influence in Scotland and elsewhere did not end with his death. His religious efforts have largely stood the test of time. Thanks to the groundwork laid by Knox and others, Presbyterianism became a reality under the leadership of Andrew Melville. Where Scots migrated throughout the world—especially North America—they have erected many Presbyterian churches bearing the name of Knox. Back home in most of its essentials, the Church of Scotland still worships as it did in Knox's day. Its "service is based on the Order of Geneva, and the Communion is received sitting." Moreover, Knox's belief that the church has a responsibility to care for the poor continued into the nineteenth century. Also, the *Book of Discipline*'s emphasis on the importance of education has become ingrained in the Scottish tradition at home and where the Scots have migrated in the world.[14]

Knox's greatest impact came through his ideas, especially his theory of resistance to rulers. Knox was a successful revolutionary. But his bark was worse than his bite; his ideas were more violent than his deeds. In theory, he was one of the most ruthless revolutionaries in history. Only Knox, some of his colleagues, and a few radical Puritans have ever proclaimed it to be sinful not to kill their enemies. Subjects were entitled to resist tyrants and idolatrous rulers by armed force, even slaying them if necessary.[15] Such ideas had a twofold effect. They horrified political leaders in both Knox's day and years after his death. But they also contributed to the struggle for human freedom. Despite his refusal to tolerate the Catholic faith, Knox taught the people that they had the right to fight tyranny—whether it be from religious or secular sources.

To denounce a man is to fear him—and Knox received many denunciations. In his day, both Catholics and Protestants alike attacked *The First Blast* and his subsequent political writings. Their response was twofold: political theorists criticized his ideas, and at times the rulers suppressed his writings. Years later, governments still regarded Knox as a danger to

---

13. Knox, *John Knox's History of the Reformation in Scotland*, 1:282–87; Dickinson, "Introduction," xlv–lvii; Halliday, "Will the Real John Knox Please Stand?" 170; Alford, "Knox, Cecil and the British Dimension of the Scottish Reformation," 205–10.

14. Kirk, "Introduction," *Second Book of Discipline*, 151; Reid, *Trumpeter of God*, 290; Ridley, *John Knox*, 528 (quote).

15. *Works*, 4:415–16. See Greaves, "John Knox, The Reformed Tradition, and the Development of Resistance Theory," 10, 19; Burns, "The Political Ideas of the Scottish Reformation," 260; Walzer, *The Revolution of the Saints*, 108.

established order. When James VI was 13 months old, Knox preached at his coronation. As a man, however, the king expressed great hatred toward Knox's political views. In the seventeenth century, the authorities at Oxford University publicly burnt Knox's writings.[16]

But Knox's doctrine—that subjects could forcefully resist their rulers—received a better reception in some quarters. The seventeenth-century Puritans derived much of their revolutionary political theory from Knox, and they put it into practice in England during the Civil War. Through the Puritan poet John Milton and others, Knox's ideas were passed on down to the American and French Revolutions. Indeed, the Scots reformer nearly cracked the ingrained belief in the duty of obedience to rulers. And in doing so, in spite of his intolerance, he contributed to the struggle for human freedom.[17]

Knox first came storming onto the stage of history brandishing a two-edged sword. In his last days on earth, however, he tells us how he first cast anchor in John 17. His soul seems serene as his wife read to him his favorite passages from Scripture. These two instances illustrate the Knoxian paradox: the warrior for God and a man secure in the evangel of Jesus Christ. Which was the real John Knox? Both. Yet it is the combative John Knox who emerged most often during his public ministry. We see Knox as a prophet calling down the judgment of God on the supporters of idolatry—that is, Catholicism. But this was not the only John Knox. He also emerges as a pastor of souls, a man with a close relationship with Jesus Christ. And in looking back at John Knox, this comprehensive and balanced perspective should not be forgotten.

---

16. Danner, "Resistance and the Ungodly Magistrate in the Sixteenth Century," 478; Ridley, *John Knox*, 523–25; Cassidy, "The Quest for Godly Rule," 8, Ann Lee, "A Bodye Politique to Governe: Aylmer, Knox and the Debate on Queenship," 242–61.

17. Greaves, *Theology and Revolution*, 223–24; Danner "Resistance and the Ungodly Magistrate," 479–30; Ridley, *John Knox*, 529–30; Cassidy, "The Quest for Godly Rule," 8.

Bibliography

Alford, Stephen. "Knox, Cecil and the British Dimension of the Scottish Reformation." In *John Knox and the British Reformations*, ed. Roger A. Mason, 205-10. Aldersgate, UK: Ashgate, 1998.
Allen, J. W. *A History of Political Thought in the Sixteenth Century*. London: Methuen, 1928.
Althaus, Paul. *The Theology of Martin Luther*. Philadelphia: Fortress, 1966.
Ann Lee, Patricia. "A Bodye Politique to Governe: Aylmer, Knox and the Debate on Queenship." *The Historian* 52 (1990) 242-61.
Armentrout, Donald S. "Pastor." In *Dictionary of Christianity in America*, ed. Daniel G. Reid et al., 871. Downers Grove, IL: InterVarsity, 1990.
Arnold, William V. "Pastoral Care." In *Encyclopedia of the Reformed Faith*, ed. Donald K. Kim, 270-71. Louisville: Westminster John Knox, 1992.
Aune, David E. *Prophecy in Early Christianity and the Ancient Mediterranean World*. Grand Rapids: Eerdmans, 1983.
Bainton, Roland H. "The Role of Women in the Reformation." *Archiv fur Reformationsgeschicte* 63 (1972) 141-226.
Baird, John S. "Preaching." In *Evangelical Dictionary of Theology*, ed. Walter A. Elwell, 868-69. Grand Rapids: Baker, 1984.
Baker, Wayne. *Heinrich Bullinger and the Covenant: The Other Reformed Tradition*. Athens: Ohio University Press, 1980.
Bale, John. "The Image of Both Churches." Preface to *English Experience*. Amsterdam: Theatrum Orbes Terratam, 1973.
Ball, Bryan W. *A Great Expectation: Eschatological Thought in English Protestantism to 1660*. Leiden: Brill, 1975.
Bannatyne, Richard. *A Journal of Transactions in Scotland*. Edinburgh: Bannatyne Club, 1836.
Bardgett, Frank D. *Scotland Reformed: The Reformation in Angus and the Mearns*. Edinburgh: Donald, 1989.
Barkley, John M. *The Worship of the Reformed Church*. Richmond, VA: John Knox, 1967.
Beard, Thomas. *The Theatre of God's Judgments: Or, a Collection of Histories out of Ecclesiastical, and Profane Authors concerning the admirable Judgments of God upon transgressors of his commands*. London: 1597.
Berkhof, Louis. *The History of Christian Doctrines*. Carlisle: Banner of Truth Trust, 1937.
Bishop, John. "John Knox: Thundering Scot." *Preaching* 8 (1992) 73-74.
Blake, William E., Jr. "Knox and Lethington: A Lesson in Religious and Political Alienation." *Scotia: American Canadian Journal of Scottish Studies* 5 (1981) 9-20.

Bibliography

Bonney, Richard. *The European Dynastic States, 1494–1660.* New York: Oxford University Press, 1991.

Bornkamm, Heinrich. *Luther's World of Thought.* St. Louis: Concordia, 1958.

Bray, D. A., et al. "Preaching: Themes and Styles." In *Dictionary of Scottish Church History and Theology,* ed. Nigel M. de S. Cameron, 668. Edinburgh: T. & T. Clark, 1993.

Breslow, Marvin A., ed. *The Political Writings of John Knox.* Cranbury, NJ: Associated University Press, 1985.

A Brief Discourse of the Troubles Begun at Frankfurt in Germany Anno Domini. England, n. c. p. 1575.

Brilioth, Yngve. *A Brief History of Preaching.* Philadelphia: Fortress, 1965.

Bromiley, G. W., ed. *Zwingli and Bullinger.* London: New York: SCM, 1953.

Brown, K. M. "In Search of the Godly Magistrate in Reformation Scotland." *Journal of Ecclesiastical History* 40, no. 4 (1989) 553–81.

Brown, P. Hume. *John Knox.* 2 vols. London: A. & C. Black, 1894.

Buchanan, George. *The History of Scotland.* 6 vols. Glasgow: Blackie and Son, 1845.

Buckle. Thomas. *On Scotland and the Scotch Intellect.* Chicago: University of Chicago Press, 1970.

Burkill, T. A. *The Evolution of Christian Thought.* Ithaca, NY: Cornell University Press, 1971.

Burleigh, J. H. S. *A Church History of Scotland.* London: Oxford University Press, 1960.

Burns, J. H. "John Knox and Revolution." *History Today* 8 (1958) 565–73.

———. "Knox and Bullinger." *Scottish Historical Review* 34 (1955) 90–91.

———. "The Political Background of the Reformation, 1513–1625." In *Essays on the Scottish Reformation,* ed. David McRoberts, 1–38. Glasgow: Burns and Sons, 1962.

———. "The Political Ideas of the Scottish Reformation." *Aberdeen University Review* 36 (1955) 251–68.

Buttrick, David G. "Theology of Preaching." In *Encyclopedia of the Reformed Faith,* ed. Donald K. McKim, 289–90. Louisville: Westminster John Knox, 1992.

Calderwood, David. *The History of the Kirk of Scotland.* 1650. Vols. 1–3. Edinburgh: Wodrow Society, 1842.

Calvin, John. *Calvin's New Testament Commentaries: The First Epistle of Paul to the Corinthians.* Ed. David W. Torrance and Thomas F. Torrance. Grand Rapids: Eerdmans, 1960.

———. *The Institutes of the Christian Religion.* Ed. John T. McNeill. Trans. Ford Lewis Battles. 2 vols. LCL 20–21. Philadelphia: Westminster, 1960.

Cameron, Euan. "Frankfurt and Geneva: The European Context of John Knox's Reformation." In *John Knox and the British Reformations,* ed. Roger A. Mason, 51–73. Aldershot, UK: Ashgate, 1998.

Cameron, James K. "Aspects of the Lutheran Contribution to the Scottish Reformation, 1528–1552." *Lutheran Theological Journal* 19 (1985) 12–20.

———. "The Historical Background." In *The First Book of Discipline,* ed. James K. Cameron, 3–13. Edinburgh: St. Andrew, 1972.

Cameron, James K., ed. *The First Book of Discipline.* Edinburgh: St. Andrew, 1972.

Carlyle, Thomas. *On Heroes, Hero Worship and the Heroic in History.* London: Chapman and Hall, 1897.

Cassidy, John. "The Quest for Godly Rule: The Development of Resistance Theory in Reformation Scotland." *Scottish Tradition* 14 (1988) 1–10.

Bibliography

Cheyne, Alax C. "The Scots Confession of 1560." *Theology Today* 17, no. 3 (1960) 323–38.

Chrisman V. Miriam. "Women and the Reformation in Strasbourg, 1490–1530." *Archiv fur Reformationgeschichte* 63 (1972) 143–44.

Christianson, Paul. *Reformers and Babylon: apocalyptic visions from the reformation to the eve of the civil war.* Toronto: University of Toronto Press, 1978.

Collinson, Patrick. *The Elizabethan Puritan Movement.* Berkeley: University of California Press, 1967.

———. "John Knox, the Church of England and the Women of England." In *John Knox and the British Reformations,* ed. Roger A. Mason, 73–96. Aldershot, UK: Ashgate, 1998.

———. "The Role of Women in the English Reformation Illustrated by the Life and Friendships of Mrs. Anne Locke." *Studies in Church History* 2 (1956) 258–72.

Courthial, Pierre. "The Golden Age of Calvinism in France, 1533–1633." In *John Calvin: His Influence in the Western World,* ed. W. Stanford Reid, 77–78. Grand Rapids: Zondervan, 1982.

Courvoisier, Jaques. *Zwingli: Reformed Theologian.* Richmond, VA: John Knox, 1963.

Cowan, Henry. *John Knox: The Hero of the Scottish Reformation.* New York: Knickerbocker, 1905.

Cowan, Ian B. "John Knox and the Making of the Scottish Reformation." *Proceedings of the Conference on Scottish Studies* 1 (1979) 22–30.

———. *The Scottish Reformation: Church and Society in Sixteenth-Century Scotland.* New York: St. Martin's, 1982.

Cowie, L. W. *Sixteenth-Century Europe.* Edinburgh: Oliver and Boyd, 1977.

Craigie, James. "Knox's First Book of Discipline." *The Scottish Educational Journal* 14 (1960) 720–22.

D'Assonville, V. E. *John Knox and the Institutes of Calvin: A Few Points of Contact in Their Theology.* Durban: Drakensberg, 1968.

Danner, Dan G. "Anthony Gilby: Puritan in Exile: A Biographic Approach." *Church History* 40 (1971) 415–16.

———. "Christopher Goodman and the English Protestant Tradition of Civil Obedience." *Sixteenth-Century Journal* 8 (1977) 67.

———. *Pilgrimage to Puritanism: History and Theology of the Marian Exiles at Geneva, 1555–1560.* New York: Lang, 1999.

———. "Resistance and the Ungodly Magistrate in the Sixteenth Century: The Marian Exiles." *The Journal of the American Academy of Religion* 46 (1981) 471–81.

———. "The Theology of the Geneva Bible: A Study in English Protestantism." PhD diss., University of Iowa, 1967.

Dargan, E. C. *A History of Preaching: From the Apostolic Fathers to the Great Reformers, AD 70–1572.* London: Hodder and Stoughton, 1905.

Davies, Rupert E. *The Problem of Authority in the Continental Reformers.* London: Epworth, 1946.

Davis, Kenneth R. "No Discipline, No Church: An Anabaptist Contribution to the Reformed Tradition." *Sixteenth-Century Journal* 13, no. 4 (1982) 43–58.

Dawson, Jane E. "The Two John Knoxes: England, Scotland and the 1558 Tracts." *Journal of Ecclesiastical History* 42, no. 4 (1991) 555–76.

Denney, James. "John Knox: His Religious Life and Theological Position." *The Hartford Seminary Record* 1905 (1905) 282–96.

Bibliography

Dickinson, W. C. Introduction to *History of the Reformation in Scotland*, 2 vols., by John Knox. Edinburgh: Nelson and Sons, 1949, xlv–lxxxv.

———. *The Scottish Reformation and Its Influence Upon Scottish Life and Character.* Edinburgh: St. Andrew, 1960.

Donaldson, Gordon. "Knox the Man." In *John Knox: A Quatercentary Reappraisal*, ed. Duncan Shaw, 18–32. Edinburgh: St. Andrew, 1992.

———. *Scotland: James V to James VII.* Edinburgh: Oliver and Boyd, 1965.

———. "The Scottish Episcopate at the Reformation." *English Historical Review* 60 (1945) 349–64.

———. *The Scottish Reformation.* London: Cambridge University Press, 1960.

Donaldson, Gordon, ed. *Accounts of the Collectors of the Thirds of Benefices 1561–1572.* Edinburgh: Scottish History Society, 1949.

Dunlop, Ian. "Baptism in Scotland After the Reformation." In *Reformation and Revolution.* Edinburgh: St. Andrew, 1967.

Durkan, John. "Scottish Reformers: The Less Than Golden Legend." *The Innes Review* 45, no. 1 (1994) 1–28.

Edington, Carol. "John Knox and the Castilians: A Crucible of Reforming Opinion?" In *John Knox and the British Reformations*, ed. Robert Mason, 29–50. Aldershot, UK: Ashgate, 1998.

Eire, Carlos M. *War Against the Idols.* Cambridge: Cambridge University Press, 1986.

Ellis, Hastings. "The Genesis of Martin Bucer's Doctrine of the Lord's Supper." *Princeton Theological Review* 24 (1926) 225–51.

Engammare, Max. "Calvin: A Prophet Without a Prophecy." *Church History* 67, no. 4 (1988) 644–52.

Estep, William. *The Anabaptist Story.* Grand Rapids: Eerdmans, 1975.

Felch, Susan M. "'Deir Sister:' The Letters of John Knox to Anne Vaughan Locke." *Renaissance and Reformation* 19, no. 4 (1995) 47–69.

Firth, Katherine R. *The Apocalyptic Tradition in Reformation Britain, 1530–1645.* London: Oxford University Press, 1979.

Forstman, H. Jackson. *Word and Spirit.* Stanford: Stanford University Press, 1962.

Frankforter, Daniel A. "The Chronology of the Knox–Bowes Letters." *Manuscripa* 31 (1987) 28–41.

———. "Correspondence with Women." *Journal of Rocky Mountain Medieval and Renaissance Association* 6 (1985) 159–72.

———. "Elizabeth Bowes and John Knox: A Woman and Reformation Theology." *Church History* 56, no. 3 (1987) 337–60.

Fraser, Antonia. *Mary Queen of Scots.* New York: Delacorte, 1969.

Froom, LeRoy. *The Prophetic Faith of Our Fathers.* 4 vols. Washington, DC: Review and Herald, 1948.

Froude, J. A. *The Reign of Edward VI.* London: Dent, 1909.

Gau, John. *The Richt Vay to the Kingdom of Heuine.* Ed. A. F. Mitchell. Edinburgh: Blackwood and Sons, 1897.

Gerrish, B. A. "Biblical Authority and the Continental Reformation." *Scottish Journal of Theology* 10 (1957) 337–60.

———. "John Calvin and the Reformed Doctrine of the Lord's Supper." *McCormick Quarterly* 22 (1969) 85–98.

———. "The Lord's Supper in Reformed Confessions." *Theology Today* 23 (1966) 224–43.

Gilick, Calvin C. "Non-Calvinist Influences on the Scottish Reformation." ThD diss., Knox College, University of Toronto, 1970.

Gill, Stewart D. "He made my tongue a trumpet . . . John Knox, The Preacher." *The Reformed Theological Review* 51 (1992) 102-10.

Goldingay, James. "Luther and the Bible." *Scottish Journal of Theology* 35, no. 1 (1882) 35-40.

Gonzalez, Justo L. *A History of Christian Thought*. 3 vols. Nashville: Abingdon, 1971.

Gray, John R., "The Political Theory of John Knox." *Church History* 8 (1939) 132-47.

Greaves, Richard L. "Calvinism, Democracy and the Political Thought of John Knox." *Occasional Papers of the American Society of Reformation Research* 1 (1978) 81-92.

———. "John Knox and the Covenant Tradition." *Journal of Ecclesiastical History* 24 (1973) 23-32.

———. "John Knox and the Ladies, or the Controversy over Gynecocracy." *Red River Valley Historical Journal* 2 (1977) 6-16.

———. "John Knox, the Reformed Tradition, the Development of Resistance Theory." *The Journal of Modern History* 58 (1976) 1-31.

———. "The Knoxian Paradox: Ecumenism and Nationalism in the Scottish Reformation." *Records of the Scottish Church History Society* (1973) 85-98.

———. "The Nature of Authority in the Writings of John Knox." *Fides et Historia* 10, no. 2 (1978) 30-51.

———. *Theology and Revolution in the Scottish Reformation*. Grand Rapids: Christian University Press, 1980.

Grislis, Egil. "Calvin's Doctrine of Baptism." *Church History* 31, no. 1 (1962) 46-64.

Gritsch, Eric W. *Martin Luther—God's Court Jester*. Philadelphia: Fortress, 1983.

Halliday, R. T. "Will the Real John Knox Please Stand?" *Expository Times* 106 (1995) 170.

Harbinson, E. Harris. *Christianity and History*. Princeton: Princeton University Press, 1964.

———. "History and Destiny." *Theology* 21, no. 4 (1965) 395-409.

Hargrave, O. T. "The Predestination Offensive of the Marian Exiles at Geneva." *Historical Magazine of the Episcopal Church* 42 (1973) 111-23.

Hastie, William. *The Theology of the Reformed Church in Its Fundamental Principles*. Edinburgh: T. & T. Clark, 1904.

Hazlett, Ian S. "Playing God's Card: Knox and Fasting." In *John Knox and the British Reformations*, ed. Roger A. Mason, 176-98. Aldershot, UK: Ashgate, 1998.

Hazlett, W. Ian P. "Jihad Against Female Infidels and Satan: The First Blast of the Trumpet." In *Calvin: Erbe und Auftrag*, ed. Von Willem van't Spijker, 285-90. Kampen, Netherlands: Kok Pharos, 1991.

———. "The Scots Confession 1560: Context, Complexion and Critique." *Archiv fur Reformationsgeschichte* 78 (1987) 287-320.

Healey, Robert M. "John Knox"s History: Complete Sermon on Christian Piety." *Church History* 61, no. 3 (1992) 319-33.

———. "The Preaching Ministry in Scotland's First Book of Discipline." *Church History* 58, no. 3 (1989) 339-53.

———. "Waiting for Deborah: John Knox and Four Ruling Queens." *Sixteenth-Century Journal* 25, no. 2 (1994) 371-86.

Henderson, G. D. "John Knox and the Bible." *Records of the Scottish Church History Society* 9 (1946) 97-109.

Bibliography

"A Historie of the Estate of Scotland, From the Year 1559 to the Year 1566." In vol. 1 of *The Miscellany of the Wodrow Society*, ed. D. Laing, 89–168. Edinburgh: Wodrow Society, 1847.

Holwerda, David, ed. *Exploring the Heritage of John Calvin*. Grand Rapids: Baker, 1976.

Hopfl, Harro. *The Christian Polity of John Calvin*. Cambridge: Cambridge University Press, 1982.

Hunt, George, ed. *Calvinism and the Political Order*. Philadelphia: Westminster, 1965.

Hunt, R. N. "Calvin's Theory of Church and State." *Church Quarterly Review* 8 (1929) 56–71.

Hunter, Mitchell A. *The Teaching of Calvin*, 2nd. London: Revell, 1950.

Janton, Pierre. *Concept et Sentiment De L'Eglise Chez John Knox: le reformateur ecossais*. Paris: Universitarieres De France, 1972.

———. *John Knox: L' homme et l' oeuvre*. Paris: Didier, 1967.

Jewett, Paul King. "Prophecy." In the *New International Dictionary of the Christian Church*, ed. J. D. Douglas, 806. Grand Rapids: Zondervan, 1974.

Johnson, Dale W. "Marginal at Best: John Knox's Contribution to the Geneva Bible." In *Adaptions of Calvinism in Reformation Europe*, ed. Mack P. Holt, 241–48. Aldershot, UK: Ashgate, 2007.

———. "Prophecy, Rhetoric and Diplomacy: John Knox and the Struggle for the Soul of Scotland." PhD diss., Georgia State University, 1985.

———. "Serving Two Masters: John Knox, Scripture and Prophecy." In *Religion and Superstition in Reformation Europe*, ed. Helen Parish and William G. Naphy, 133–53. New York: Manchester University Press, 2002.

Johnson, George. "Scripture in the Scottish Reformation. 1 Historical Statement." *Canadian Journal of Theology* 8 (1962) 249–57.

Johnston, Dale W., and James Edward McGoldrick. "Prophet in Scotland: The Self Image of John Knox." *Calvin Theological Journal* 33, no. 1 (1998) 76–86.

Kellar, Clare. *Scotland, England, and the Scottish Reformation 1534–1561*. Oxford University Press, 2003.

Kibble, David G. "The Reformation and the Eucharist." *Churchman* 94, no. 1 (1980) 43–56.

Kingdon, Robert. "The First Expression of Theodore Beza's Political Ideas." *Archiv fur Reformationgeschichte*, 46, no. 1 (1955) 88–100.

Kirk, James. "The Influence of Calvinism on the Scottish Reformation." *Records of the Scottish Church History Society* 8 (1972) 159–79.

———. "John Knox and the Historians." In *John Knox and the British Reformations*, ed. Roger A. Mason, 7–26. Aldershot, UK: Ashgate, 1998.

———. *Patterns of Reform*. Edinburgh: T. & T. Clark, 1989.

———. "The Privy Kirks and Their Antecedents: The Hidden Face of Scottish Protestantism." In *Voluntary Religion*, ed. W. J. Shields and Diana Wood, 156–68. Blackwell, 1986.

———. "The Religion of Early Scottish Protestants." In *Humanism and Reform: The Church in Europe, England, and Scotland, 1400–1643*, ed. James Kirk, 361–411. Oxford: Blackwell, 1991.

Kirk, James, ed. *The Second Book of Discipline*. Edinburgh: St. Andrew, 1980.

Knappen, M. M. *Tudor Puritanism*. Chicago: University of Chicago Press, 1939.

Knox, John. "Epistle to the Congregation of Berwick, 1552." In *John Knox and the Church of England*, by Peter Lorimer, 251–67. London: King, 1875.

———. *John Knox's History of the Reformation in Scotland*. Ed. William Croft Dickinson. 2 vols. Edinburgh: Nelson and Sons, 1949.

———. "Memorial or Confession to the Privy Council of Edward VI, 1552." In *John Knox and the Church of England*, ed. Peter Lorimer, 267–74. London: King, 1875.

———. "The Practice of the Lord's Supper Used in Berwick by John Knox, 1550." In *John Knox and the Church of England*, ed. Peter Lorimer, 290–92. London: King, 1875.

———. *The Works of John Knox*. Ed. David Laing. 6 vols. Edinburgh: Bannatyne Club, 1846–1864.

Koenigsberger, H. G., George L. Mosse, and G. Q. Bowler. *Europe in the Sixteenth Century*. 2nd ed. New York: Longman, 1989.

Kyle, Richard G., and Dale W. Johnson, *John Knox: An Introduction to His Life and Works*. Eugene, OR: Wipf and Stock, 2009.

Kyle, Richard. "The Christian Commonwealth: John Knox's Vision for Scotland." *The Journal of Religious History* 16, no. 3 (1991) 247–59.

———. "Church–State Patterns in the Thought of John Knox, The." *Journal of Church and State* 30, no. 1 (1988) 72–81.

———. "The Concept of Predestination in the Thought of John Knox." *Westminster Theological Journal* 46, no. 1 (1984) 53–77.

———. "The Divine Attributes in John Knox's Concept of God." *Westminster Theological Journal* 48, no. 1 (1986) 161–72.

———. "The Hermeneutical Patterns in John Knox's Use of Scripture." *Pacific Theological Review* 17, no. 3 (1984) 19–32.

———. "John Knox." In *Encyclopedia of the Reformed Faith*, ed. Donald K. McKim, 208–9. Louisville: Westminster John Knox, 1992.

———. "John Knox." In *Dictionary of Scottish Church History and Theology*, ed. Nigel M. de S. Cameron, 465–66. Edinburgh: T. & T. Clark, 1993.

———. "John Knox: A Man of the Old Testament." *Westminster Theological Journal* 54, no. 2 (1992) 65–78.

———. "John Knox and Apocalyptic Thought." *Sixteenth-Century Journal* 15, no. 4 (1984) 449–69.

———. "John Knox and the Care of Souls." *Calvin Theological Journal* 38, no. 1 (2003) 133–44.

———. "John Knox and the Purification of Religion: The Intellectual Aspects of His Crusade Against Idolatry." *Archiv fur Reformationgeschicte* 77 (1986) 265–80.

———. "John Knox Confronts the Anabaptists: The Intellectual Aspects of His Encounter." *Mennonite Quarterly Review* 75 (2001) 493–515.

———. "John Knox's Concept of History: A Focus on the Providential and Apocalyptic Aspects of His Religious Faith." *Fides et Historia* 18, no. 2 (1986) 5–19.

———. "John Knox's Concept of Providence and Its Influence on His Thought." *Albion* 18, no. 3 (1986) 395–410.

———. "John Knox's Methods of Biblical Interpretation: An Important Source of His Intellectual Radicalness." *Journal of Religious Studies* 12, no. 2 (1985) 57–70.

———. "John Knox: The Main Themes of His Thought." *Princeton Seminary Bulletin* 4, no. 2 (1983) 101–12.

———. *The Last Days Are Here Again*. Grand Rapids: Baker Books, 1998.

———. *The Mind of John Knox*. Lawrence, KS: Coronado, 1984.

Bibliography

———. *The Ministry of John Knox: Pastor, Preacher, and Prophet.* Lewiston, NY: Mellen, 2002.

———. "The Nature of the Church in the Thought of John Knox." *Scottish Journal of Theology* 37, no. 4 (1984) 485–501.

———. "Prophet of God: John Knox's Self-Awareness." *The Reformed Theological Review* 61, no. 2 (2002) 85–101.

———. "Thomas Guilliame." In *Dictionary of Scottish Church History and Theology*, ed. Nigel M. de S. Cameron, 380. Edinburgh: T. & T. Clark, 1993.

———. "The Thundering Scot: John Knox the Preacher." *Westminster Theological Journal* 64, no. 1 (2002) 135–49.

Laing, David, ed. "Ane Compendius Tractice." In *Miscellany of the Wodrow Society*, 1:175–259. Edinburgh: Wodrow Society, 1847.

———. "The Confession of Faith of the Churches of Switzerland." In *Miscellany of the Wodrow Society*, 1:1–24. Edinburgh: Woodrow Society, 1847.

———. *The Miscellany of the Wodrow Society.* Vol. 1. Edinburgh: Printed for the Wodrow Society, 1847.

Lake, Peter. *Moderate Puritans and the Elizabethan Church in the English Separatist Tradition.* Macon, GA: Mercer University Press, 1982.

Lamont, Stewart. *The Swordbearer: John Knox and the European Reformation.* London: Hodder and Stoughton, 1991.

Lamorte, Andre, and Gerald F. Hawthorne, "Prophecy, Prophet." In *Evangelical Dictionary of Theology*, ed. Walter A. Elwell, 886–87. Grand Rapids: Baker, 1984.

Lang, Andrew. *History of Scotland.* 4 vols. New York: AMS, 1970.

———. *John Knox and the Reformation.* London: Longmans, Green, 1905.

Law, Thomas Greaves, ed. *The New Testament in Scots.* Vol. 1. Edinburgh: Blackwood and Sons, 1901.

Lee, Maurice. "John Knox and His History." *Scottish Historical Review* 14 (1966) 79–88.

Lehmberg, Stanford E. "Archbishop Grindal and the Prophesyings." *Historical Magazine of the Protestant Episcopal Church* 34 (1965) 87–145.

Leslie, John. *The History of Scotland.* Ed. E. G. Cody. 2 vols. Edinburgh: Blackwood and Sons, 1887.

Limburg, James. *The Prophets and the Powerless.* Atlanta: John Knox, 1971.

Linder, Robert D. "Pierre Viret and Sixteenth-Century Protestant Revolutionary Tradition." *The Journal of Modern History* 38 (1966) 149–70.

———. "Pierre Viret and the Sixteenth-Century Protestants." *Archiv fur Reformationgeschicte* 58 (1967) 149–70.

Lindsay, Robert. *The Historic and Chronicles of Scotland.* Ed. A. J. G. Mackay. Vols. 1–3. Edinburgh: Blackwood and Sons, 1899.

Little, Paul M. "John Knox and English Social Prophecy." *Presbyterian Historical Society of England* 14 (1968–1972) 117–27.

Locher, Gottfried W. *Zwingli's Thought: New Perspectives.* Leiden: Brill, 1981.

Lorimer, Peter. *John Knox and the Church of England.* London: King, 1875.

———. *Patrick Hamilton, the First Preacher of the Scottish Reformation.* Edinburgh: Constable, 1857.

Lotz, David W. "The Sacrament of Salvation: The Inclusive Nature of Baptism in Luther's Writings." *Concordia Theological Monthly* 33 (1962) 645–57.

Lynch, Michael. "Calvinism in Scotland, 1559–1638." In *International Calvinism 1541–1715*, ed. Menna Prestwich, 234–35. Oxford: Claredon, 1985.

———. *Edinburgh and the Reformation*. Edinburgh: Donald, 1981.
Maccuum, Florence A. *John Knox*. London: Methuen, 1895.
MacGregor, Geddes. *The Thundering Scot: A Portrait of John Knox*. Philadelphia: Westminster, 1975.
Mackie, J. D. *John Knox*. London: Cox and Syman, 1951.
MacIver, Martha Abele. "Ian Paisley and the Reformed Tradition." *Political Studies* 35 (1987) 360–61.
Macmillan, D. *John Knox*. London: Melrose, 1905.
Macmillan, J. Douglas. "John Knox—Preacher of the Word," *Reformed Theological Journal* (1987) 5–19.
MacRae, John. "The Scottish Reformers and Their Order of Public Worship." *Records of the Scottish Church History Society* 5 (1929) 22–30.
Macy, Gary. "The Dogma of Transubstantiation in the Middle Ages." *Journal of Ecclesiastical History* 45, no. 1 (1994) 11–41.
Mahoney, Matthew. "The Scottish Hierarchy, 1513–1565." In *Essays on the Scottish Reformation, 1513–1625*, ed. David McRoberts, 39–84. Glasgow: Burns, 1962.
Manschreck, Clyde L. *Melanchthon: The Quiet Reformer*. Nashville: Abingdon, 1958.
Marshall, Rosalind K. *John Knox*. Edinburgh: Birlinn, 2000.
Mason, Roger A. ed. *John Knox: On Rebellion*. Cambridge: Cambridge University Press, 1994.
———. "Knox, Resistance and the Moral Imperative." *History of Political Thought* 1 (1980–1981) 411–36.
Maxwell, William D. *John Knox's Genevan Service Book, 1556*. Edinburgh: Oliver and Boyd, 1931.
McCord, James I. "The Faith of John Knox." *Theology Today* 29, no. 3 (1972) 239–45.
M'Crie, Thomas. *The Life of John Knox*. 2 vols. Edinburgh: Blackwood, 1818.
McCue, James F. "The Doctrine of Transubstantiation from Berengar through the Council of Trent." *Harvard Theological Review* 61 (1968) 385–430.
McDonald, Suzanne. *John Knox for Armchair Theologians*. Louisville: Westminster John Knox, 2013.
McDonell, Kilian. *John Calvin, the Church, and the Eucharist*. Princeton: Princeton University Press, 1967.
McEwen, James S. *The Faith of John Knox*. Richmond, VA: John Knox, 1961.
McGiffert, A. C. *A History of Christian Thought*. 2 vols. New York: Scribner's, 1932.
———. *Protestant Thought Before Kant*. Gloucester: Smith, 1971.
McGoldrick, James E. *Luther's Scottish Connection*. Cranbury, NJ: Associated University Presses, 1989.
———. "Patrick Hamilton, Luther's Disciple." *Sixteenth-Century Journal* 17 (1987) 81–88.
McKay, Denis. "Parish Life in Scotland." In *Essays on the Scottish Reformation*, ed. David McRoberts, 85–115. Glasgow: Burns.
McMillan, William. *The Worship of the Scottish Reformed Church, 1550–1638*. London: Clarke, 1931.
McNeill, John T. "The Church in Sixteenth-Century Reformed Theology." *The Journal of Religion* 22 (1942) 251–69.
———. "The Democratic Element in Calvin's Thought." *Church History* 18 (1949) 155–71.

Bibliography

———. *The History and Character of Calvinism*. New York: Oxford University Press, 1962.
McRoberts, David, ed. *Essays on the Scottish Reformation, 1513–1625*. Glasgow: Burns and Sons, 1962.
Melville, James. *The Autobiography and Diary of Mr. James Melville*. Ed. R. Pitcairn. Edinburgh: Wodrow Society, 1842–1836.
———. *The Diary of Mr. James Melville, 1556–1601*. Edinburgh: Bannatyne Club, 1829.
Mezger, Adrien. *John Knox et ses rapports avec Calvin*. Montauban: Imprimerie Cooperative, 1905.
Mitchell, A. F., ed. *A Compendious Book of Godly and Spiritual* Songs commonly known as *The Gude and Godlie Ballatis*. Edinburgh: Printed for the Wodrow Society, 1847.
Monter, William. *Calvin's Geneva*. Huntington: Krieger, 1975.
Morris, Leon. "Minister." In *Evangelical Dictionary of Theology*, ed. Walter A. Elwell, 720–21. Grand Rapids: Baker, 1984.
Muir, Edwin. *John Knox: Portrait of a Calvinist*. London: Cape, 1929.
Murison, David., "Knox the Writer." In *John Knox: A Quatercentenary Reappraisal*, ed. Duncan Shaw, 33–50. Edinburgh: St. Andrew, 1975.
Neale, J. E. *The Age of Catherine de Medici*. New York: Harper & Row, 1943.
Neuman, Gerhard J. "The Anabaptist Position on Baptism and the Lord's Supper." *Mennonite Quarterly Review* 35, no. 2 (1961) 140–48.
New, John. *Anglican and Puritan*. Stanford: University Press, 1965.
Newman, Christine M. "The Reformation and Elizabeth Bowes: A Study of a Sixteenth-Century Northern Gentlewoman." *Studies in Church History* 27 (1990) 325–33.
Niesel, Wilhelm. *The Theology of Calvin*. Philadelphia: Westminster, 1956.
Oberman, H. A. "Preaching and the Word in the Reformation." *Theology Today* 18 (1961) 16–29.
Old, Oliphant Hughes. "History of Preaching." In *Encyclopedia of the Reformed Faith* ed. Donald K. McKim, 286–87. Louisville: Westminster John Knox, 1992.
Olson, Oliver K. "Theology of Revolution: Magdeburg, 1550–1551." *The-Sixteenth Century Journal* 3 (1972), 56–79.
Ozment, Steven. *The Reformation in the Cities*. New Haven: Yale University Press, 1975.
Parker, T. H. L. *Calvin's Preaching*. London: Westminster John Knox, 1992.
———. *The Oracles of God: An Introduction to the Preaching of John Calvin*. London: Lutterworth, 1947.
Patrick, David. Introduction to *Statues of the Scottish Church 1225–1559*. Edinburgh: Printed at the University Press for the Scottish History Society, 1907.
Pelikan, Jaroslav. *The Christian Tradition*. Vol. 4, *Reformation of Church and Dogma (1300–1700)*. Chicago: Chicago University Press, 1984.
Percy, Lord Eustace. *John Knox*. Richmond, VA: John Knox, 1966.
Petersen, Rodney L. *Preaching in the Last Days*. New York: Oxford University, 1993.
Philip, James. "Preachers." In *Dictionary of Scottish Church History and Theology*, ed. David Wright et al., 665–66. Edinburgh: T. & T. Clark, 1993.
Potter, G. R. *Zwingli*. London: Cambridge University Press, 1976.
Quistorp, H. *Calvin's Doctrine of the Last Things*. Trans. Harold Knight. Richmond, VA: John Knox, 1955.
Rad, Gerhard von. *The Message of the Prophets*. New York: Harper & Row, 1962.
Raitt, Jill. "Three Interrelated Principles in Calvin's Unique Doctrine of Infant Baptism." *Sixteenth-Century Journal* 11, no. 1 (1980) 51–61.

Reed, Kevin. *John Knox: The Forgotten Reformer:* Dallas: Presbyterian Heritage, 1997.
Reed, Kevin, ed. *Selected Writings of John Knox.* Dallas: Presbyterian Heritage, 1995.
Reeves, Marjorie. *Joachim of Fiore and the Prophetic Future.* New York: Harper & Row.
Reid, W. Stanford, ed. *John Calvin and His Influence in the Western World.* Grand Rapids: Zondervan, 1982.
———. "John Calvin, Pastoral Theologian." *The Reformed Theological Review* 42, no. 3 (1982) 68–70.
———. "John Knox and His Interpreters." *Renaissance and Reformation* 10, no. 1 (1974) 14–24.
———. "John Knox, Pastor of Souls." *Westminster Theological Journal* 40, no 1. (1977) 1–21.
———. "John Knox's Theology of Political Government." *Sixteenth-Century Journal* 19, no. 4 (1988) 529–40.
———. "Knox's Attitude to the English Reformation." *Westminster Theological Journal* 21 (1963) 269–83.
———. "The Lollards in Pre-Reformation Scotland." *Westminster Theological Journal* 11 (1942) 269–83.
———. "Lutheranism in the Scottish Reformation." *Westminster Theological Journal* 6 (1944–1945) 91–111.
———. "The Middle Class Factor in the Scottish Reformation." *Church History* 16, no. 3 (1947) 137–53.
———. "The Reformation in France and Scotland: A Case Study in Sixteenth-Century Communication." In *Later Calvinism* ed. W. Fred Graham, 197. Kirksville, MO: Sixteenth-Century Essays and Studies, 1994.
———. *Trumpeter of God.* New York: Scribner's, 1974.
Richardson, C. C. *Zwingli and Cranmer on the Eucharist.* Evanston: Seabury-Western Theological Seminary, 1949.
Ridley, Jasper. *John Knox.* New York: Oxford University Press, 1968.
———. *Thomas Cranmer.* London: Oxford University Press, 1962.
Ross, Anthony. "Some Notes on the Religious Orders in Pre-Reformation Scotland." In *Essays on the Scottish Reformation 1513–1625,* ed. David McRoberts, 185–244. Glasgow: Burns, 1962.
Rothrock, G. A. *The Huguenots.* Chicago: Nelson Hall, 1979.
Rupp, E. G. "The Europe of John Knox." In *John Knox: A Quatercentenary Reappraisal,* ed. Duncan Shaw, 1–17. Edinburgh: St. Andrew, 1975.
Russell, E. "John Knox as a Statesman." *The Princeton Theological Review* 6 (1908) 1–29.
Ryrie, Alex. *The Origins of the Scottish Reformation.* Manchester: Manchester University Press, 2006.
Shaw, Duncan. "Forward, Zwingli Research—the Chasm in British Reformation Studies." In *Zwingli's Thought: New Perspectives,* ed. Gottried W. Locher, ix–xvii. Leiden: Brill, 1981.
———. "John Knox and Mary Queen of Scots." In *John Knox: A Quatercentenary Reappraisal,* ed. Duncan Shaw, 51–72. Edinburgh: St. Andrew, 1975.
———. "John Willock." In *Reformation and Revolution,* ed. Duncan Shaw, 42–69. Edinburgh: St. Andrew, 1967.
———. *Reformation and Revolution.* Edinburgh: St. Andrew, 1967.
———. "Zwinglian Influences on the Scottish Reformation." *Records of the Scottish Society* 22, no. 2 (1985) 119–39.

Bibliography

Shaw, Duncan, ed. *John Knox: A Quatercentary Reappraisal.* Edinburgh: St. Andrew, 1975.

Shepherd, Amanda. *Gender and Authority in Sixteenth-Century England.* Keele, UK: Keele University Press, 1994.

Shoenberger, Cynthia G. "The Development of Lutheran Theory of Resistance, 1523–1530." *Sixteenth-Century Journal* 8 (1977) 61–76.

Skinner, Quentin. *The Foundations of Modern Political Thought.* 2 vols. Cambridge: Cambridge University Press, 1978.

Sleidan, John. *A Famous Chronicle of oure time, called Sleidanes Commentaries.* Trans. John Daus. London: n.p., 1560.

Smalley, Beryl. *The Study of the Bible in the Middle Ages.* Oxford: Blackwell, 1952.

Smout, T. C. *A History of the Scottish People 1560-1830.* New York: Scribner's Sons, 1969.

Spitz, Lewis W. "Luther's Sola Scriptura." *Concordia Theological Monthly* 31 (1960) 740–45.

———. *The Protestant Reformation 1517-1559.* New York: Harper & Row, 1985.

Spotiswoode, Joannes. *The History of the Church and State of Scotland.* London: Royston, 1677.

Spottiswoode, James. *History of the Church of Scotland.* 2 vols. Edinburgh: Spottiswoode Society, 1851.

Stalker, James. *John Knox: His Ideas and Ideals.* London: Hodder and Stoughton, 1904.

Steinmetz, David C. "Theological Reflections on the Reformation and Status of Women." *Duke Divinity School Review* 41 (1976) 197–207.

Stephens, W. P. *The Holy Spirit in the Theology of Martin Bucer.* Cambridge: Cambridge University Press, 1970.

———. *The Theology of Huldrych Zwingli.* Oxford University Press, 1986.

———. *Zwingli: an Introduction to His Thought.* Oxford University Press, 1992.

Stevenson, Robert L. "John Knox and his Relations to Women." In *Familiar Studies of Men and Books,* ed. Robert L. Stevenson, 328–93. London: Collins, 1936.

Sutherland, N. M. "The Marian Exiles and the Establishment of the Elizabethan Regime." *Archiv fur Reformationsgeschichte* 78 (1987) 253–85.

Tawney, R. H. *Religion and the Rise of Capitalism.* New York: Scribner's, 1958.

Taylor, Maurice. "The Conflicting Doctrines of the Scottish Reformation." In *Essays on the Scottish Reformation 1513-1565,* ed. David McRoberts, 245–73. Glasgow: Burns, 1962.

Taylor, W. *The Scottish Pulpit from the Reformation to the Present Day.* London: Burnet, 1887.

Thompson, James Westfall. *The Wars of Religion in France, 1559-1576.* Chicago: University of Chicago Press, 1909.

Tillich, Paul. *A History of Christian Thought.* New York: Simon & Schuster, 1967.

Torrance, Iain R. "Patrick Hamilton and John Knox: A Study in the Doctrine of Justification by Faith." *Archiv fur Reformationgeschicte* 65 (1974) 171–84.

Trevor-Roper, H. "John Knox." *The Listener* 80 (1968).

Vander Molen, Ronald J. "Anglican Against Puritan: Ideological Origins During the Marian Exile." *Church History* 42 (1973) 45–57.

———. "Providence as Mystery, Providence as Revelation: Puritan and Anglican Modifications of John Calvin's Doctrine of Providence." *Church History* 47, no. 1 (1978) 27–47.

Verduin, Leonard. *The Reformers and Their Stepchildren.* Grand Rapids: Eerdmans, 1980.
Verschuur, Mary B. "The Outbreak of the Scottish Reformation of Perth 11 May 1559: Knox's History Re-Examined." *Scotia: American-Canadian Journal of Scottish Studies* (1987) 41–53.
Vesey, W. J. "The Sources of Active Resistance in the Political Theory of John Knox." PhD diss., Boston University, 1961.
Walker, Williston. *John Calvin.* New York: Schocken, 1906.
Wallace, Ronald S. *Calvin, Geneva, and the Reformation.* Grand Rapids: Baker, 1988.
———. *Calvin's Doctrine of the Word and Sacraments.* Grand Rapids: Eerdmans, 1957.
Walton, Robert C. *Zwingli's Theocracy.* Toronto: University of Toronto Press, 1967.
Walzer, Michael. *The Revolution of the Saints: A Study in the Origins of Radical Politics.* New York: Atheneum, 1973.
Warfield, Ethelbert D. "John Knox, Reformer of a Kingdom." *The Princeton Theological Review* 3 (1905) 376–98.
Watson, Philip S. *Let God Be God.* Philadelphia: Fortress, 1970.
Watt, Hugh. *John Knox in Controversy.* New York: Philosophical Library, 1950.
Weber, Max. *The Protestant Ethic and the Spirit of Capitalism.* New York: Scribner's, 1958.
Wendel, Francois. *Calvin: The Origins and Development of His Religious Thought.* New York: Harper & Row, 1963.
Whitley, Elizabeth. *Plain Mr. Knox.* Richmond, VA: John Knox, 1960.
Wilkinson, J. "The Medical History of John Knox." *Proceedings of the Royal College of Edinburgh* 28 (1998) 81–101.
Williams, George H. *The Radical Reformation.* Philadelphia: Westminster, 1962.
Winter, R. Milton. "Presbyterians and Prayers for the Sick: Changing Patterns of Pastoral Ministry." *American Presbyterians: Journal of Presbyterian History* 64 no. 3 (1986) 142.
Winzet, Ninian. *Certain Tractates Together with the Book of Four Score Three Questions and a Translation of Vincentius Lirinensis.* Edinburgh: Blackwood and Sons, 1888.
Wormald, Jenny. *Court, Kirk and Community: Scotland 1470–1625.* Toronto: University of Toronto Press, 1981.
———. "Godly Reformer, Godless Monarch: John Knox and Mary Queen of Scots." In *John Knox and the British Reformations*, ed. Roger A. Mason, 220–41. Aldershot, UK: Ashgate, 1998.
Yule, George. "Continental Patterns and the Reformation in England and Scotland." *Scottish Journal of Theology* 22 (1969) 305–23.
Zamora, Lois Parkinson, ed. *The Apocalyptic Vision in America.* Bowling Green, OH: Bowling Green University Popular Press, 1982.

Index

A' Lasco, John, 49, 112
Abraham, 60, 63–64, 118, 154
Additional Prayer, 91
Ahab, 47, 73, 170
Ambrose, 159, 233
Amersham, 168
Amos, 19, 37, 41, 177, 187
An Answer, 18, 24, 26–27, 30,
    59–61, 64, 78, 94–96, 99,
    102–3, 106, 108, 112
An Apology, 32, 37, 73, 102, 230–31
Anabaptists, 18, 23–24, 46,
    48–49, 60–61, 68, 87, 95–96,
    106–11, 131–32, 134, 136,
    138–41, 143, 227–28, 256
Answer to Tyrie, An, 34–35, 77,
    113, 116–18, 120, 127, 139
Answers to Some Questions
    Concerning Baptism, 101
Antichrist, 69, 71, 74, 77, 88, 165,
    168, 177–78, 180, 184, 260
Appellation, 18, 24, 27, 30, 32–33,
    56, 61, 73, 102, 121, 152,
    234, 237–40, 246
Arias (Arianism), 56, 102
Aske, Roger, 195
Assured Lords, 8
Athaliah, 234
Athanasius, 31
Augustine, 27, 31–32, 43, 52,
    63–64, 74, 77, 86, 159, 233

Bale, John, 75, 117
Balnaves, Henry, 14, 17, 40, 88–93
Basil of Caesarea, 159
Basil the Great, 31
Beard, Thomas, 67–68
Beaton, Archbishop, 8, 14–15, 184,
    215
Berwick, 17, 27, 122, 126, 185, 195
Beza, Theodore, 98, 207, 210, 238,
    264
Bibliander, Theodore, 98
Black Rubric, 17
Bonner, Edmund, 223
Book of Common Order, 26, 56, 84,
    204
Book of Common Prayer, 17–19, 29,
    51, 202
Book of Discipline (First), 9, 26, 31,
    42, 49, 124–27, 129–30, 137,
    172, 245–54, 263, 265
Bowes, Elizabeth, 25, 27, 32, 43,
    81–82, 94–95, 99–100,
    109, 113, 117, 152, 191–93,
    195–202, 219
Bowes, Marjory, 117, 197
Bowes, Richard, 195
Brief Exhortation to England, A, 30,
    98, 126, 152, 245–46, 251
Bruce, Robert, 161
Bucer, Martin, 47, 61, 121–22, 135,
    139, 144–48, 242
Bullinger, Heinrich, 15, 18, 53,
    94–95, 99, 111, 143, 160,
    195, 220–21, 229
Burns, J. H., 213–14, 219

Index

Calvin, John, 18, 21, 23, 28, 31, 33, 37, 39–42, 45–47, 52–54, 57, 61–62, 65–68, 80–83, 87, 93–104, 110–14, 119, 121, 125, 127, 134–41, 143–44, 146–48, 151, 160, 163, 176–77, 195, 201, 207, 209–10, 219–20, 231, 235
Calvinism, 14–15, 18, 84, 177, 219
Calvinist reformation, 61, 87–88, 134, 210
Calvinist theology, 94–113, 145, 209–10, 225
Cameron, James, 248
Castilians, 76–77, 171, 185, 215
Catechism of Archbishop Hamilton, 15
Catherine de' Medici, 236
Catherine of Aragon, 7
Cecil, William, 235, 263
Charles I of Spain, 7, 263
Chaterlherault, Duke of (also James Hamilton and Earl of Arran), 229
Chrysostom, John, 32, 159, 233
Church of England, 192, 202–3, 231
City of God, 7
Consensus Tigurinus, 144
Council of the North, 29
Counter Reformation, 104
Cox, Richard, 29
Cranmer, Thomas, 16–17
Crespin, Jean, 75
Cupar Muir, Battle of, 76
Cyrus, 62

D' Assonville, V. E., 93
Daniel, book of, 69, 167, 171, 174, 180–81, 184, 186, 256
Darnley, Lord, 19, 113, 120, 170–71
David, 51, 84, 109, 165
Deborah, 41, 48, 165, 220, 234–36

Declaration of the True Nature and Object of Prayer, 82–83
Deuteronomy, 40–41, 70, 148, 166, 239
Dieppe, France, 17, 217, 219, 221, 225, 227–30
Dominicans, 13, 160
Donaldson, Gordon, 122, 128
Dudley, John, 185–86

Edinburgh, 19, 29, 46, 167, 170, 181, 189, 193, 203–4
Edward VI, 17, 51, 71–72, 129, 152, 165–66, 168, 185, 201, 209, 212, 214, 216–17, 220, 224, 239, 245
Edwardian England, 216–17
Egyptians, 71
Elijah, 41, 73, 224
Elisha, 41, 186
Emperor Charles V, 7, 209
England, 6–8, 15, 18, 29, 51, 64, 66, 72–73, 95, 100, 119, 125, 128, 131, 145, 152, 165–69, 179–81, 183–85, 188, 193, 196, 210, 212–13, 215–17, 224, 233, 266
Ephesians, Epistle of, 190
Epistle to Newcastle and Berwick, 26, 216
Epistle to the Congregation of Berwick, 90, 98
Epistles to Mrs. Bowes, 99–100, 118, 152
Erasmus, 160, 176
Erskine of Dun, 14
Estates of Scotland, 237
Eutyches, 56
Exposition Upon Matthew IV, 25, 73, 81, 169
Exposition Upon Psalm VI, 27, 100, 118, 152
Ezekiel, book of 174–75

Index

Faithful Admonition, A, 18, 24, 51, 72, 75, 94–95, 100–101, 118, 124, 165–66, 168, 185, 213, 221, 223–25, 230, 240, 245
Familiar Epistles, 73, 91, 102
Federal Theology, 90
First Blast of the Trumpet, 18, 24, 32, 36–37, 41, 48, 58, 73, 96, 102–3, 152, 158, 186, 193–94, 204, 213, 223, 231–37, 241–42, 246, 265
Form of Prayers, The, 35, 49, 101, 137, 139–41, 146, 204
Fourth General Assembly of Scotland, 137
Fourth Lateran Counsel, 133
Foxe, John, 75
France, 6–9, 11, 16–17, 21, 66, 146, 153, 168, 184–86, 196, 210, 266
Francis I, 7, 125, 208, 225
Frankfurt, 67, 129

Gardiner, Stephen, 223–24, 234
Gau, John, 92
Genesis, 41, 118
Geneva, 18, 21, 37, 49, 53–54, 83, 93, 98, 101, 114, 116, 145, 163, 169, 197, 201–2, 210, 214, 225, 227, 231, 236, 265
Geneva Bible, 98
Geneva Confession, 122
Geneva Consistory, 122
Germany, 37, 196, 212
Gilby, Anthony, 98
Godly Letter, A, 23, 41, 60, 71, 100, 152, 178, 181, 185, 211, 217–19, 221, 239, 245
Grange, the, 171
Great Papal Schism, 12–13
Greaves, Richard, 96, 103, 130, 214–16, 219
Greek language, 85, 163, 225
Gregory I, 71

Gregory of Nazianzus, 159
Guilliame, Thomas, 17, 160

Haddington, 16, 76, 184
Hamilton, Archbishop, 15
Hamilton, Patrick, 14, 91–92, 160
Hamiltonians, 169, 171
Harlow, William, 161
Hebrew language, 85
Henry VIII, 7–8, 16, 209, 217
Hezekiah, 41, 51, 165
Hickman, Mrs., 200
History of the Reformation in Scotland, 13, 57, 61–78, 112, 125, 148–49, 158, 161, 167–70, 173, 180, 184, 216
Holy Ghost, 24–25, 27, 30, 40, 44, 46–48, 55, 83–85, 91, 100, 109, 114, 138–39, 141, 147, 162, 171, 175, 203
Holy Roman Empire, 6, 7
Hooper, John, 53, 94
House of Hamilton, 229
Huguenots, 207, 210, 257
Huldah, 41
Hus, John, 159

Institutes of Christian Religion, 52–54, 83, 93–94, 104, 110–11, 113
Irenaeus, 52
Isaiah, 164, 174, 177
Israel, 18, 51, 58, 70–71, 73, 118–119, 121, 126, 135, 149, 154, 165–66, 179, 182, 187, 224, 238, 244, 246, 255

James I (of England), 266
James IV, 13–14
James V of Scotland, 7–8, 15
James VI, 9, 19, 120, 266
James, Epistle of, 25
Janton, Pierre, 23–26, 54, 93, 215
Jehoiada, 220, 234

283

Index

Jehu, 41, 46, 48, 57, 186, 224
Jeremiah, 41, 152, 174, 177, 186, 218
Jerome, 31
Jezebel, 41, 165, 170, 223
Joachim, 77
Job, 63
Johnson, Dale, 262
Joseph, 59
Joshua, 41, 163, 174
Josiah, 71
Julian, 63

Kennedy Quintin (Abbot of Crossraguel), 11, 19, 26, 31–32, 34, 112–13, 153
Kirk, James, 129
Kirkcaldy, William, 189

Lausanne, 220
Lee, Maurice, 158
Lent, 169
Leslie, John, 11
Letter of Wholesome Counsel, 49, 100–101, 118, 131
Letter to the Commonalty, 102, 152, 218, 239–41, 246
Letter to the Queen Regent, 73, 152, 236–37
Letters to His Brethren, 95, 102, 124
Linder, Robert, 210
Locke, Anne, 192–93, 200–203
Lollards, 13, 159
London, 9, 17, 27, 49, 201
Lord's Supper, 135, 137–39, 141–48, 151
Lowland Scots, 163
Luther, Martin, 13–14, 17, 23, 25–26, 28, 39, 42, 44–46, 52, 57, 61, 65–66, 81–83, 89, 93, 119, 121, 138, 140, 159–60, 177, 195, 207, 209, 212
Lutheranism, 14–15, 87–93, 131–32, 134, 144, 148, 153, 177, 209, 219

Madrid, 9
Magdeburg *Bekenntnis*, 36, 209, 216–17, 255
Magisterial Reformers, 37–38, 44, 84, 86, 94, 96, 116, 121, 212, 244
Maitland, William, 36, 46–48, 123–25, 154, 165, 187, 212, 216, 256
Major, John, 16
Marcion, 56
Marian exiles, 29, 67, 96–97, 183, 185, 202, 210–11, 216, 227, 257
Marquess of Winchester, 51
Martyr, Peter, 98, 122, 242
Mary of Guise (Queen Regent), 7, 18–19, 30, 33, 76–77, 84, 152, 186–87, 194, 212, 225–26, 231, 236–37, 242
Mass (Eucharist), 17, 19, 28, 86, 133–34, 136, 142, 144, 148–51, 153, 160, 192, 194, 201, 204, 218, 224, 255, 261
McEwen, James, 46, 103, 136, 145–46
M'Crie, Thomas, 159, 179
Melanchthon, Philip, 61, 159
Melchizedek, 154
Melville, Andrew, 128, 161, 263, 265
Melville, James, 171, 179, 189
Mendicant Orders, 13
Middle Ages, 12, 28, 72, 132–33, 159–60
Moses, 41, 174, 186–87, 239
Murison, David, 65

Nestorius, 56
New Testament, 23, 39–44, 50, 58, 60, 85, 135, 150, 165, 182, 256
Newcastle, 17, 27, 29, 185
Nicholas of Cusa, 159
Nominalism, 59

Index

Observant Movement, 13–14
Oecolampodius, 160, 177
Old Testament, 5–6, 18, 23–27, 37, 39–44, 50–51, 55, 58–60, 67, 72, 78, 80, 89, 121, 135, 145, 148, 150, 154, 159, 165–67, 169, 175, 177, 179, 182–83, 187–88, 212–13, 224, 238, 243, 245, 255–56, 261
Order and Doctrine of the General Fast, 188
Origin, 31, 52, 159
Ozment, Steven, 12

Paris, 9
Passiley, Ian, 5
Paul, Apostle, 43, 49, 233
Pedersen, Christiern, 92
Pelagianism, 100, 102
Percy, Lord Eustace, 83, 190, 264
Philip II (of Spain), 220, 231
Phinehas, 224
Presbyterianism, 128–29, 265
Puritans, 20, 50, 66–67, 71, 183, 225, 263, 265–66

Reformed Church, 11, 15, 35, 116–31, 135, 138, 146, 153
Reformed Church of Scotland, 64, 67, 125–28, 137, 144, 263
Reformed faith, 9, 35, 78, 92–93, 99, 115, 126, 131, 148, 162, 172, 257
Reformed tradition, 44, 48, 61, 94, 98, 119, 135–36, 144, 191
Reid, W. Stanford, 4, 136, 157, 189, 215, 222
Revelation, book of, 27, 69, 77, 97, 117, 180–81
Ricco, David, 120
Ridley, Bishop, 141
Ridley, Jasper, 16, 41, 189
Right Vay to the Kingdom of Heuine, 92
Rough, John, 17, 160

Rupp, E. G., 20

Satan (Devil), 6, 24, 59, 63, 73–74, 76, 113, 118, 182, 260
Saul, 150
Savonarola, 159
Scots Confession, 9, 19, 30, 34, 40, 56, 64, 84, 112–13, 119, 122, 125–27, 137, 147, 161, 181, 247, 263
Scottish Catholic Church, 7–8, 15
Scottish Parliament, 8–9
Second Blast, 236, 241–42
Second Book of Common Prayer, 29
Semi-Augustinianism, 86
Semi-Pelagianism, 86
Sermon on Isaiah XXVI, 37, 113, 120
Seymore, Edward (Lord of Somerset), 185
Shaw, Duncan, 112, 147
Sleidan, John, 74–75
Sodom and Gomorrah, 57, 199
Solway Moss (Battle of), 76
Spain, 6–9, 220, 224
Spurgeon, C. H., 259–60
St. Andrews, 16–17, 23, 28, 40, 53, 144–45, 158, 160, 167, 171, 185
St. Andrews Castle, 184, 214–15, 217, 219
St. Giles, 163, 169–70, 186–88
Stewart, James (Earl of Moray), 19, 120, 124
Stewart, Mary (Queen of Scots), 4, 5, 7, 9, 16–17, 19, 31, 35, 47, 59, 120, 124–25, 131, 153, 162, 165, 167, 170–71, 187–89, 194, 212, 217, 225, 231, 235–36, 248–49, 255, 264
Summary of Balnaves on Justification by Faith, 82, 88
Switzerland, 18, 52

Index

Tertullian, 52, 233
Theatre of God's Judgments, 67
Trinity, doctrine of, 56–57
Tudor, Elizabeth (Queen Elizabeth), 9, 18, 76, 165, 235, 257, 263–64
Tudor, Mary, 17–18, 71–72, 95, 100, 117, 152, 166, 168–69, 180, 194, 196, 200, 202, 217–21, 223–24, 227, 231, 235–36, 239, 245
Tunstall, Cuthbert, 223
Two Comfortable Epistles, 72, 100, 222
Tyndale, William, 14, 160, 209, 217, 230, 236
Tyrie, James, 33, 121–23

Vindication, A, 23, 27, 41, 43, 71, 90, 145, 149–51, 153
Viret, Pierre, 207, 210, 219–21, 238

Weber-Tawney thesis, 68
Whittingham, William, 98
Willock, John, 112, 161
Winram, John, 28
Winzet, Ninian, 11, 19, 33–34
Wishart, George, 15, 17, 52–53, 93–94, 161, 173, 180, 184
Wycliffe, John, 15, 159

Zurich, 15, 98, 144, 220
Zwingli, Huldrych, 33, 36–37, 39, 41, 45–46, 49, 51–52, 57, 61, 66, 80, 83, 87, 94–95, 99, 104, 111, 121, 134, 138, 143, 148, 160, 176, 221
Zwinglian reformation, 15, 53, 132, 134, 177
Zwinglianism, 15, 53, 132, 134, 177

www.ingramcontent.com/pod-product-compliance
Lightning Source LLC
Chambersburg PA
CBHW071237230426
43668CB00011B/1481